ROBERT H. M...

in collaboration with KIM S. CAMERON

COFFIN NAILS AND CORPORATE STRATEGIES

PRENTICE-HALL, INC., Englewood Cliffs, New Jersey 07632

Library of Congress Cataloging in Publication Data

MILES, ROBERT H.
    Coffin nails and corporate strategies.

    Bibliography: p.
    includes index.
    1.—Cigarette industry—United States. 2.—Tobacco
industry—United States. 3.—Corporate planning—United
States. I.—Cameron, Kim S. II.—Title.
HD9149.C43U66   679′.7′068   81-17955
ISBN 0-13-139816-4   AACR2
ISBN 0-13-139808-3 (pbk.)

To my Mother
MILDRED CUTHRELL MILES

Editorial/production supervision and interior design by Pamela Wilder
Cover design by Zimmerman and Foyster
Manufacturing buyer: Ed O'Dougherty

Printed in the United States of America

10 9 8 7 6 5 4 3 2 1

ISBN 0-13-139816-4
ISBN 0-13-139808-3 {pbk.}

Prentice-Hall International, Inc., *London*
Prentice-Hall of Australia Pty. Limited, *Sydney*
Prentice-Hall of Canada, Ltd., *Toronto*
Prentice-Hall of India Private Limited, *New Delhi*
Prentice-Hall of Japan, Inc., *Tokyo*
Prentice-Hall of Southeast Asia Pte. Ltd., *Singapore*
Whitehall Books Limited, *Wellington, New Zealand*

Contents

I

SETTING AND CONTEXT 1

1

Strategic Organizational Adaptation: An Introduction 3

THEMES THAT BOUNDED THE SCOPE OF THE INQUIRY.   Understanding Organizational Adaptation: Competing Views.   The Natural-Selection Perspective.   *Organizational Inertia and Captivity.   Environmental Choice and Immutability.*   The Strategic-Choice Perspective.   *Contributions of an Amateur Scholar.   Emergence of the Field of Business Policy.   Studies of the Large Corporation.   Role of Strategic Management.   Management Options.*   The "Invisible" vs. the "Visible" Hand.   Critical vs. Routine Decisions.   Organizational Efficiency vs. Legitimacy.   *Organization and Society.   Organizational Legitimacy: A Question of Values.*   The General Framework.

2

The U.S. Tobacco Industry: Environmental Threats and Strategic Responses 29

THE MARKET ENVIRONMENT: EARLY DEVELOPMENT AND PRESENT STRUCTURE.   *The "Trust Bust."   The Structure of Competition.*   THE INSTITUTIONAL ENVIRONMENT AND THE LEGITIMACY THREAT.   Institutional Environment Trends.   *Domestic*

II

THE STORY: ADAPTATION AMONG THE BIG SIX 55

3

Domain Defense 57

4

Domain Offense 91

Records of the Big Six: Sprints, Hurdles, and Marathon. *Domain-Offense Strategies and Financial Performance. Domain-Offense Strategies and Market Performance. A Second Look at the Defender.* SUMMARY

5

Domain Creation   116

DOMAIN CREATION: LEARNING FROM ENACTING.   OVERSEAS EXPANSION: PATTERNS AND CHOICES.   Difficulties Posed by a Global Strategy.   Big Six Overseas Strategies. *Philip Morris's Overseas Strategy. Reynolds's Overseas Strategy. American Brands' Overseas Strategy. Liggett's Overseas Strategy.* Overseas Summary. DIVERSIFICATION: PATTERNS AND CHOICES.   U.S. Merger Activity: Three Major Waves.   Diversification: A Framework from Hindsight. *Diversification Motives. Related vs. Unrelated Diversification. The Concept of "Relatedness."* DIVERSIFICATION AMONG THE BIG SIX.   Diversification at R.J. Reynolds.   Diversification Elsewhere in the Tobacco Industry. *Domain Dependence and Diversification.* SUMMARY

6

Learning from Diversifying   154

ORGANIZATIONAL LEARNING: AN INTRODUCTORY FRAMEWORK.   Conditions for Organizational Learning.   Decomposing the Process of Organizational Learning. HISTORICAL ANALYSIS OF STRATEGY FORMATION: AN AGENDA. *"Learning from Diversifying."* The Interview Study.   The Birth of a Strategy. *Overdependence on a Single Domain. Condition of Extreme Liquidity.* THE DEVELOPMENT AND INSTITUTIONALIZATION OF THE DIVERSIFICATION STRATEGY. *PHILIP MORRIS. The Legacy of Company Leaders. Points of View and Acquisition Choices. Early Acquisitions: the Financial Orientation. Turnaround at Miller Brewing: the Marketing Orientation. Learning from Diversifying. Integrating the Diversified Portfolio. Diversification Outcomes. THE LIGGETT GROUP. On Management and Motive. An Informal Beginning. Early Acquisitions: 1964 – 1970. Early Divestitures. Acquisition Criteria Distilled from Experience. Evolution of Management and Structure. Diversification Outcomes. The Fate of the Declining Tobacco Business. On Being Acquired. R.J. REYNOLDS. Some Early Experiments. Creation of the Diversification Committee. Initiation of Purposive Diversification. Early Lessons. Diversification into Unrelated Areas. Learning from Diversifying. Managing the Diversified Portfolio. Diversification Outcomes.* Developmental Patterns among the Diversification Strategies. ORGANIZATIONAL LEARNING AND STRATEGY FORMATION.

III

ASSESSMENTS, ISSUES, AND IMPLICATIONS   197

7

Patterns of Strategic Organizational Adaptation:
An Assessment   199

STRATEGIC ORGANIZATIONAL ADAPTATION: AN ECONOMIC ASSESSMENT.   Domain
Defense, Offense, and Creation.   *The Early Defense of Domain.   Maintaining
Position in a Stagnating Domain.   Domestic vs. Overseas Tobacco
Businesses.   Tobacco vs. Nontobacco Businesses.   Domain Creation and
Dependence.*   Economic-Goal Attainment: Individual Firms.   *Growth.
Profitability.   Financial Slack.   Investment Risk.*   Overall Economic Assessment:
Industry Level.   THE QUESTION OF LEGITIMACY: A SOCIOPOLITICAL ASSESSMENT.
Cigarette-Consumption Trends.   *"Gradual Chinese Water Torture."   Shift toward
"Safer" Cigarettes.*   Public-Opinion Trends.   *The Roper Report.   Smokers and
Health.   Rights of Nonsmokers: the "Passive"-Smoking Issue.   Industry
Consultant's Suggested Tactics.   "Roper Report: Implications and
Recommendations."   Industry Image.   Public Attitudes vs. Government Actions.
Conflicting Values and Dependences.*   CONCLUSION.

8

Implications for Strategic Management   228

MODES OF STRATEGIC ORGANIZATIONAL ADAPTATION: A FUNDAMENTAL
TYPOLOGY.   MANAGERIAL CHOICE VS. ENVIRONMENTAL DETERMINISM.   Natural
Selection vs. Strategic Choice.   Organizational Captivity and Environmental
Immutability.   Organizational Inertia and Character.   *Strategic Predisposition.
Dominant Values and Executive Succession.   Distinctive Competence.
The Character-Defining Properties of Complex Organizations.*
Organizational Slack.   *Economic Slack.   Political Slack.   Managerial Slack.*
TOWARD A DEVELOPMENTAL THEORY OF ORGANIZATIONAL BEHAVIOR AND
ADAPTATION.   The Boundary Conditions.   Character-Formation and
Strategy-Formation Processes.   The Quality of Executive Leadership.   FUTURE
PROSPECTS AND DIRECTIONS.

9

Implications for Public Policy Makers   261

GOVERNMENT REGULATION: "ALL THUMBS, NO FINGERS."   *The Health-Warning
Paradox.   The Broadcast-Ban Paradox.   The "Overseas Oversight"?   "Filter*

Preface

This is the story of how complex organizations adapt under conditions of externally imposed stress and crisis. It focuses on the choices made by strategic managers of traditionally competitive corporations in a major U.S. industry to cope with a fundamental threat to the legitimacy of their right to do business. It chronicles the quarter-century development of a complex web of relationships among these organizations and elements of the markets and the societies they served. This saga about the behaviors of the "Big Six" corporations in the U.S. tobacco industry and of the agents of the smoking-and-health controversy in their institutional environment provides insight into the range of strategies available for organizational adaptation and into some important linkages between corporate and public policies and values. Thus, our concern will not be confined to just the role of corporations in society, but will extend necessarily to the role of society in corporations.

THE STRUCTURE OF THIS BOOK

Setting and Context. This book is organized into three parts. Part I describes the setting and context of the investigation. First, a review is conducted of the major developments in the market and institutional environments of the U.S. tobacco industry over the past quarter century. Particular attention is paid to the major environmental events and trends that characterized the external political economy of the Big Six and that constituted a fundamental threat to the legitimacy of the tobacco business. Next, we examine the knowledge regarding the process of organizational adaptation that helped us frame the investigation. Finally, we provide an introduction to the three modes of strategic adaptation— domain defense, domain offense, and domain creation—developed by the tobacco Big Six corporations to cope with an increasingly unreceptive and hostile environment.

The Story. In Part II we tell the story of the Big Six as they struggled to adapt to the economic and political implications of the smoking-and-health threat. This part begins with a chapter on the political strategies of *domain defense* employed by the Big Six to restore the legitimacy of their traditional business. Particular attention is given to their creation of joint political ventures and their tactics for reversing the momentum achieved by the antismoking forces. The next chapter focuses on the *domain offense* strategies developed by members of the tobacco industry to maintain or enhance their share of the stagnating domestic market for cigarette products. It is in this chapter that we first discover the relatively enduring strategic predispositions of the companies, which are shown later to possess important implications not only for how well their domain offense strategies fared, but also for the ways these firms went about creating new domains of opportunity for profitability, growth, and security.

Next we take up the strategies of *domain creation*, which include both domestic diversification and overseas expansion. The Big Six were not content to leave their fates in the clutches of an increasingly uncertain tobacco business. Shortly after the emergence of the smoking-and-health controversy, some of these firms began to experiment with the creation of new operating domains; the others followed suit shortly thereafter. Thus, by the end of our quarter-century study period, all six firms had been transformed from single-business tobacco companies to global, multibusiness megacorporations.

But their early experiments were not always successful. Sometimes they overstretched the competencies of their creators, and at other times they violated the internal pecking orders and strategic predispositions that had been each firm's historical mainstays. Therefore, we felt that it would be appropriate to close our story of strategic adaptation among the Big Six by exploring what senior managers in the corporations have learned from their attempts to create new opportunities for their beleaguered enterprises. The final chapter in Part II, ''Learning from Diversifying,'' explores how and what these senior executives have learned from their attempts to spread the economic and political risks associated with their traditional business.

Assessments and Implications.   Part III contains both an overall assessment of strategic organizational adaptation among the Big Six and a distillation of the implications of our findings for both senior executives and public policy makers.

The chapter on assessment illustrates the political economy in which modern corporations operate. It contains an evaluation of the overall pattern of industry adaptation, as well as the specific strategic choices made by member firms, on both economic and political grounds. The next chapter distills the typology of strategic adaptive modes discovered in the story and examines the competing models of organizational behavior in light of the evidence about the tobacco Big Six. The construction of a new developmental model, which attempts to reconcile the assumptions and implications of earlier models serves as the chapter conclusion. This new perspective focuses on the critical role played by executive leaders in managing the processes of character formation and strategy formation in complex organizations exposed to external threat.

The subject of the final chapter then turns to a discussion of the paradoxes we discovered in almost every well-intentioned initiative taken by public policy makers during the smoking-and-health controversy. This discussion, we believe, has important implications for the development of both future public policies and future public policy makers. The book concludes with the identification of some potentially important side effects for society of the major strategies used by the Big Six to cope with their increasingly inhospitable environment.

Coffin Nails and Corporate Strategies represents an attempt to tell a complex story—one laden with important subtleties, paradoxes, and surprises, which reveal much new and useful information about the dynamic relationships between business and society, between economics and politics, and between strategic managers and public policy makers in the United States. The telling of a story such as this requires a broad scope, spanning a number of practical perspectives and traditional academic disciplines. It is little wonder, then, that publication of this investigation of twenty-five years in the lives of six corporations took five years of analysis and writing.

Although we are certain that we have not captured all there is to know about our protagonists and antagonists, or all the refinements that a variety of knowledge domains (e.g., organization and management theory, business policy, political science, public policy and administration, industrial economics, business and society, and organizational sociology) have to offer, we believe this investigation has been more sensitive than most to the diversity of perspectives and levels of analysis, and that the mosaic we have assembled constitutes at least a minimal basis for understanding the process of strategic organizational adaptation.

Our immediate objective, therefore, will be achieved if this book helps citizens, executives, regulators, and students of organization, management, and public policy develop a richer appreciation of the political economy of the complex organization in American society and of the role of executive leadership in complex organizations. Our broader objective is to convince those who are in the business of creating and disseminating this knowledge that it is necessary to embrace a more holistic view than their specialized disciplinary perspectives have allowed in the past if they are to make real progress in understanding, managing, and assessing the strategic behaviors of complex organizations in society. If this study helps to identify an area of overlap among the currently competing specialized disciplines, it will have made progress toward the realization of its longer-lerm objective.

Acknowledgments

Any attempt to build a cross-disciplinary framework for understanding the behavior of complex organizations presents to a professional operating primarily in one field a number of formidable challenges, not the least of which is the possibility of misunderstanding and perhaps oversimplifying other points of view. An important part of this work, therefore, has been the sharing of various stages of the preliminary results with professionals representing other frames of reference. I want to take this opportunity to express my appreciation to those who took time away from other pressing commitments to review the preliminary work and to give me suggestions that have led to improvements in the quality of both my thinking and the investigation.

Among the organizational behaviorists that played an important part in this process are Marianne Jelinek, McGill University; Michael Tushman, Columbia University; Robert Duncan, Northwestern University; Ray Zammuto, National Council on Higher Education Management Systems; Michael Evanisko, Bain and Company; Andrew Van de Ven, University of Minnesota; and Michael Beer, John Kotter, Paul Lawrence, and Jeffrey Sonnenfeld, my colleagues in the informal "organizational adaptation" discussion group at Harvard Business School. Stacy Adams, University of North Carolina, and Richard Hackman and Victor Vroom, Yale University, represented the social psychologists who influenced my thinking; Andrew Pettigrew, University of Warwick, John Kimberly, Yale University, and Jay Barney, UCLA, effectively represented the political and sociological perspectives on organizations. Richard Nelson, Yale University, was an especially helpful early critic from the world of industrial economics. Finally, the realities of the business policy and strategy perspectives were argued forcefully by Joseph Bower and Jay Lorsch, Harvard University; Raymond Miles, University of California at Berkeley; Charles Snow, Pennsylvania State University; and Henry Mintzberg, McGill University. The work of political scientist Lee Fritschler was a particularly helpful resource in developing Chapter 3. Finally, Arvind Bhambri and Carolee Weber served as capable research assistants on various aspects of the overall investigation.

Kim Cameron, my former student at Yale University and collaborating author, has been an invaluable resource throughout the project. His commitment to helping me get the project off the ground and in responding critically to numerous drafts of the manuscript has been indispensible. Without his sustained intellectual and emotional support, it is very likely that this book would still be a shamble of papers in the bottom drawer of my filing cabinet.

Sincere thanks also go to Ted Jursek, my editor at Prentice-Hall for his continued encouragement, and to Pamela Wilder, my very patient production supervisor who graciously suffered through the many final-hour adjustments I made to the manuscript.

In all cases, I have been encouraged in this attempt to build a broad framework for understanding and managing the process of organizational adaptation; but it is fair to say that I could not give equal weight to all suggestions and criticisms. Instead, I want to thank these individuals for their participation in this endeavor, which certainly benefited from their efforts. Any errors of omission, oversimplification, or excess are appropriately mine, and mine alone.

In addition, a project of this scope and duration requires the support of institutions as well as individuals. In this regard, I wish to recognize the Yale School of Organization and Management for providing the stimulus for initiating a project focusing on the interface between business and society, and the Division of Research at the Harvard Business School for providing both the release from teaching and the financial resources to enable me to pursue the investigation with vigor, as well as the rich intellectual climate necessary for nurturing a multidisciplinary study. The breadth of intellectual activity at this institution, with its more than 150 faculty members, provides a rare opportunity for a struggling scholar; and this quality, I would add, is exceeded only by the patience and willingness of these faculty members to help each other as they struggle with their own agendas for personal and intellectual development.

Finally, I wish to express my appreciation to Margaret Filipowich, Kate Fitzgerald, and Gloria Buffonge, who typed repeated revisions of the manuscript and who in so many thoughtful ways helped me to cope with what was until now an uncertain enterprise spanning half a decade.

R.H.M.
Boston, Massachusetts

Prologue

A FUNDAMENTAL CRISIS OF LEGITIMACY

The smoking-and-health controversy posed one of the most significant threats in the U.S. business history to the well-being of an established industry. It exposed members of the domestic tobacco industry not only to an unprecedented wave of unwanted scrutiny and publicity, but to a long and cumulative series of government regulations restricting their ability to do business. It threatened their historical growth patterns. It hurt their pocketbooks. It took away their access to the public broadcast media. It put warning labels on their products. It forced them into unfamiliar domains. And it threatened the careers of their senior managers. Just as important, it tarnished their image and wounded their pride.

To make matters worse, the threat came not from the familiar marketplace, but from the more remote and less understood institutional environment surrounding the tobacco business. Because of the timing of the crisis, the tobacco industry became one of the first major U.S. industries in modern times to have to confront head-on the now-widespread issue of corporate social responsibility. In short, the smoking-and-health controversy amounted to a legitimacy crisis of fundamental proportions for the tobacco Big Six—a crisis that served as the harbinger of both political and economic implications for an entire industry population and that called for both political and economic response from its member firms.

The controversy centered around the unanticipated consequences of the consumption of the industry's most profitable product—cigarettes, or what smokers and nonsmokers alike have come to refer to only half-jokingly as "coffin nails." It arose from the efforts of those who believed that the smoking habit contributes to the ill health of the ultimate consumer far more than is contributed by the immediate satisfaction he or she obtains from "lighting up," including longer-term health disorders of heart disease and lung cancer. Moreover, as the evidence linking smoking to health cumulated, it became apparent that these adverse effects might extend beyond the person choosing to smoke to those who share the same physical space as the smoker. This immediate health issue began to snowball as it took on moral and ethical connotations, as the evidence from health research on cigarette consumption continued to unfold, and as antismoking forces within and outside the government began to coalesce around the issue.

The controversy also fell into a domain economists refer to euphemistically as "external diseconomies," or simply, "externalities." These are the costs created by a productive function in society that are not covered within the operation of the function itself. Robert Miller, an economist with the U.S. Department of Agriculture, a federal agency usually aligned with the tobacco interests, spoke of some of the uncovered costs—those passed on to society—of cigarette smoking in a speech he delivered at the 1978 annual meeting of the American Agricultural Economics Association:

> *Recent studies estimate direct health care costs of smoking at $8.2 billion (1976 prices). The cost of each disease related to smoking was multiplied by the incidence related to smoking. Indirect cost (loss of earnings attributable to such sickness or death) is estimated higher than $19.1 billion. Cost of property fires estimated to have been caused by smoking were $176 million.* The total direct and indirect cost of these diseases and fires was $27.5 billion. . . . *These figures will undoubtedly be refined with further analysis, but it appears that the direct health care costs approach the annual tax revenues from cigarettes and foreign exchange earnings from tobacco and tobacco products.**

These huge estimates raised the inevitable question of who should pay for the uncovered costs of smoking tobacco products. They also raised the issue of whether the benefits derived from this business function in society are great enough to justify the enormous social costs they incur, regardless of who pays. These issues were the seeds, then, from which the crisis of legitimacy grew within the U.S. tobacco industry over the past quarter century.

As events—moves and countermoves—unfolded, a full-blown confrontation emerged between corporate policy and public policy that not only captured the attention of the executives and bureaucrats directly involved, but set off powerful reverberations in the Congress of the United States, across the variegated landscape of institutional and autonomous agencies of society, among important elements of the prevailing corporate order, and throughout the general public they all serve. Our story, if properly told, therefore, could not help but

*The original source quoted by Miller was Bryan R. Luce and Stuart O. Schweitzer, "Smoking and Alcohol Abuse: A Comparison of Their Economic Consequences," *The New England Journal of Medicine,* Vol. 298 (10) (1978), 569–71.

surface a number of important issues about the workings of this context in which the tobacco corporations were embedded.

NATURE OF THIS INQUIRY:
ON SETTING AND METHOD

These broad objectives, however, took us outside the mainstream of organizational research and called for atypical methods that required experimentation, learning, and elaboration on our part, over a period of five years, before the story could be told. This mix of methods can best be described as systematic, longitudinal, comparative, investigative reporting. We were not seeking to test specific hypotheses, but to describe events, their causes, and their consequences as accurately as possible; and from that process to raise issues and implications about the process of strategic organizational adaptation and the role of the corporation in society.

PROFILE OF AN IDEAL SETTING

We began by agreeing on some minimal characteristics of what we believed would be an ideal setting for examining the process of strategic organizational adaptation. First, the setting should include a number of organizations facing a similar external environment—organizations that possessed similar resources and repertoires for coping with shared contextual developments. Such a setting would permit us to examine in detail the variability and relative effectiveness of the organizational choices of adaptive strategies.

Second, the setting should involve an external environment sufficiently threatening to the focal organizations to necessitate strategic adaptive behaviors. The strategy of doing nothing would not be a viable one over the long haul. Third, the environmental threat should be unequivocal in its importance for the long-term survival of members of the organizational population. Preferably, it would be possible to identify objectively the nature and timing of the initiation of the threat and the major events upon which it was borne and to conceptualize them as marked discontinuities in the context of our organizational population. Being able to operationalize the external environment as consisting of a demonstrable trend with relatively discrete events would help us rule out rival hypotheses about the underlying cause—effect chain consisting of environmental events and organizational choices and behaviors. Fourth, to help us control for possible spurious influences, the major discontinuities in the external environment should be unique to the organizational population under investigation.

Fifth, the ideal setting should also possess available, consistent, and objective data on organizational adaptive strategies over an extended period of time. In the initial phase of the study, we wanted to minimize our reliance on subjective data sources, which had been the mainstay of the research on organization–environment relations that had preceded our own. Recollections of past decisions and feelings would be used only to corroborate and help us understand the documentary evidence on organization and environment. Special attention was paid, however, to the interpretations and decisions made by key decision makers in the organizations and their environments that appeared in real time in the historical archives. In addition, the longitudinal focus of the study would enhance our assurance that organizational history was being taken into account and that observed discontinuities were not aberrations in the larger scheme of things.*

Finally, the ideal setting had to involve an engaging and important issue concerning the relationship between organization and environment; one that, regardless of how it was resolved, if at all, would make a difference in the larger milieu in which both the organization and its immediate context were embedded. We wanted to study critical decisions, and ones involving a major confrontation between organizational and societal values were particularly appealing.

Having agreed on these general characteristics, we had surprisingly little difficulty in identifying an ideal setting. Among those we rejected were the "electronics revolution" in the watch industry, in which the centuries-old mechanical timepiece had become obsolete with the development in the electronics industry of the digital watch; and the impact of U.S. and foreign government policy on the domestic automotive industry. But neither setting could compete with the plight of the "Big Six" corporations that cohabited the U.S. tobacco industry and their attempts to cope with the smoking-and-health controversy over the past quarter century.

METHOD OF INVESTIGATION: INITIAL CHOICES

With one important exception, the primary data are archival in nature. The information we relied on initially (excluding only the data in Chapter 6 on the process of learning that took place as our organizations created new domains of opportunity) was obtained primarily from published sources. These sources included press releases and publications from the corporations and their trade associations; special reports and public transcripts of hearings and debates of government agencies; reports and press releases of special interest groups,

---

*This decision alone was very much at variance with the mainstream of research in the United States on complex organizations. For example, a review of the journals likely to contain studies of organizational adaptation for the years 1965–74 revealed only two studies that employed a longitudinal research design (Darran, Miles and Snow, 1975:8).

nonprofit organizations, and investment analysts; and published research by fellow academics in related disciplines. Because of the issues they raised during our analysis, these archival sources were supplemented by interviews and lengthy correspondence with almost every important constituency of the U.S. tobacco industry. And because we believed that the documentation of such a study as ours was of critical importance, we have made extensive citations of our sources throughout the manuscript.

In the main, these data are factual matters of public record and, as such, overcome some of the criticisms levied at earlier studies of organization—environment relations that have relied almost exclusively on perceptual data from key individuals. The present data are largely expressed in objective and consistent units throughout the quarter-century study period, in contrast to the subjective and equivocal units of measure commonly employed in research of this kind. These data also reflect real-time uncertainties and reactions stimulated by events as they actually occurred, rather than retrospective reports of what is thought to have occurred. Therefore, by paying special attention to chronological development in our story, we could present events as they appeared in real time to our actors.

The three major environmental "inductions" that occurred naturally in our time-series design were derived by reviewing all these data sources. They were judged not only by the extent to which they dominated the written records (annual reports and media releases) of member firms of the tobacco industry, but also by the reports of "industry watchers" (e.g., key personnel in regulatory agencies, investment analysts, journalists, and other researchers) and by the reactions (e.g., stock-market performance, demand shifts, and so on) of investors and consumers. The 25-year data series revealed that (1) the 1953 Sloan-Kettering release, (2) the convening of the Surgeon General's Committee in 1962 and its subsequent Report in 1964, and (3) the series of events leading to the broadcast-media advertising ban of 1970 were three unequivocal environmental sources of threat and uncertainty to the tobacco industry, both collectively and on a firm-by-firm basis.

With the dominant sources of decision-making uncertainty emanating from the external environment of the Big Six identified, the next research task was to examine the reactions of these firms to each of the major environmental inductions. Because our primary objective was to understand organizational adaptation to environmental pressure and change, both industry-level and firm-level strategic responses to each of the three environmental inductions were examined using a naturally occurring time-series investigation.

The time-series design, according to Campbell and Stanley (1963:39—41), "is particularly appropriate to those institutional settings in which records are regularly kept and thus constitute a natural part of the environment." These theorists indicate that this design "may frequently be employed to measure effects of a major change in administrative policy," but they caution that the major threat to the validity of this experiment is that some more or less simultaneous external event, rather than the one identified by the researcher, may have produced the discontinuity in the time series under observation. "It is upon the plausibility of ruling out such extraneous stimuli that credence in the interpretation of this experiment in any given instance must rest." Fortunately, in our case the major external sources of stress derived from our environmental analysis are highly specific to the tobacco industry (i.e., the smoking-and-health campaign and the ensuing antismoking regulations).

Having satisfied ourselves on these grounds, we began to examine the extent to which the three events, as well as the overall trend they created, were associated with marked discontinuities in the time series of data representing major adaptive strategies at industry and firm levels. But, as the story will reveal, our initial choices of method provided only a way of beginning to understand this episode of interactions between complex organizations and their environment. Although we now believe more strongly than ever that our initial intuitions and choices were correct, the kinds of information we sought and the methods we employed to obtain them expanded as we learned from our early efforts.* Some insight into the context in which we were working at the time of initiation and the events that occurred in our lives as the project unfolded may help to place the focus and design of our investigation in a clearer perspective.

EVOLUTION OF THE STUDY: LEARNING FROM DOING

The initiation of this project was a direct outcome of Miles's first doctoral seminar on "Macro Organizational Behavior" at the new Yale School of Organization and Management, in which Cameron was a student. Both of us left this extensive review of the knowledge on complex organization with an uncomfortable feeling that there were important omissions and unfortunate biases in the literature.† At the same time, we were part of the birth of a new school of

---

*Our commitment to these choices was reinforced throughout the investigation period as leading scholars in different disciplines continued to conclude their literature reviews with a call for this kind of research (e.g., organizational sociology: Hirsch, 1975; business policy: Mintzberg, 1978; organizational theory: Meyer, 1978; organizational behavior: Pfeffer and Salancik, 1978). As examples, Hirsch urged future investigators to "explicitly take into account relations among organizations at the institutional level of organizations, and the reciprocal impact of organizational policies on individuals and groups in the general environment" (1975:10); and Pfeffer and Salancik concluded their review of the literature on the external control of organizations with the following observation and prescription for organizational analysis: ". . . speculations about the evolution of social systems require facts and knowledge that are not presently available. Because it has not been studied, there is little information about how organizational responses and environments evolve over time. The cycle of contextual effect, organizational response, and new contexts must be examined more fully in the future to describe adequately the external control of organizations" (1978:286).

†The reader is referred to a book published by the senior author which mirrors the literature in vogue at the time this investigation was begun: Robert H. Miles, *Macro Organizational Behavior* (Santa Monica, Calif.: Goodyear Publishing, 1980).

organization and management whose fundamental purpose was to engage the issues of critical importance that linked business and society. We soon agreed that a study linking the smoking-and-health controversy to the strategic adaptive behaviors of the tobacco Big Six would enable us to explore this underdeveloped domain and to generate issues and agenda for our own future research and, we hoped, that of our colleagues at other institutions. A small grant from the Research Program in Government-Business Relations, which was established in the Yale School in 1975, enabled us to begin our preliminary inquiry.

The first phase of our project began with a careful examination of the content of twenty-five years of annual reports published by member firms of the tobacco Big Six. At first, we were looking for major discontinuities and trends, for the content and timing of reactions by each company to events that they acknowledged were of strategic importance. Each of us worked independently on these materials before comparing notes. From this preliminary analysis, we generated a long agenda of activities that would have to be performed to fully document and verify the initial patterns and preliminary issues we had uncovered.

From that point, we broadened the scope of our investigation. We gathered and analyzed secondary data from a wide variety of sources, including the reports of Congress, government administrative agencies, special-interest groups and trade associations, and investment analysts. We also combed the quarter century of lore on our subject generated by journalists and researchers who had taken up special issues associated with the smoking-and-health controversy. Finally, to help explain or resolve some inconsistencies that were uncovered, we conducted interviews and engaged in lengthy correspondence with representatives of a variety of constituencies surrounding the tobacco industry.

Indeed, we wish to acknowledge where the responsiveness to our data needs by representatives of Congress, the Federal Trade Commission, the Federal Communications Commission, the U.S. Department of Justice, Action on Smoking and Health, the U.S. Department of Agriculture, the American Cancer Society, and the U.S. Department of Health, Education and Welfare, as well as those of a variety of trade associations and investment houses.

From this wealth of information, we were able to build and cross-validate objective inventories of critical environmental events and strategic organizational responses. The interaction of these events and responses formed a montage that addressed the first and most fundamental question posed by this investigation: *What is the range of strategic options available to complex organizations for adapting to extreme environmental stress?* But because it included the responses of each member of a whole population of organizations, all operating initially under the same stressful conditions, this data base also permitted us to examine over an extended period of time another important question: *What is the relative effectiveness of different patterns of strategic adaptation (of strategic variation) within an industry population?*

From this montage, we developed a working paper (Miles and Cameron,

1977) that summarized our preliminary findings and discussed a number of issues that they raised for theory building and research on complex organizations. In the fall of 1977, this paper was circulated widely to scholars representing a variety of disciplines. In the spring of 1978, Miles used the paper as the basis of colloquia he presented to the management faculties at several universities. The audiences were enthusiastic about the unusual method and scope of the preliminary investigation. Their excitement stemmed in part from its comprehensiveness, in part from its realism, in part from the issues it raised, and also from the fact that we had developed ways to illustrate objectively some rather elusive concepts such as organizational strategy and behavior and environmental change and turbulence. In short, we left these encounters with our colleagues with some assurance that we were on an important, unbeaten track. But what astonished us at the time was that they all wanted us to continue what had already become a two-year investigation!

On the main findings, they wanted to know more about *why* and *how* the corporations chose particular strategies and at different times. On specific issues, they simply wanted to know more. For instance, our working paper included only a one-page discussion of the political strategies employed by the tobacco Big Six to deal with an increasingly turbulent institutional environment. It made only occasional reference to some of the unanticipated consequences of certain governmental and corporate actions. Because of our decision to look at an industry population of firms, economists took an interest in our preliminary work and encouraged us to give more attention not to the overall adaptive patterns, but to the competitive strategies that distinguished one firm from another. Business-policy experts, especially, encouraged us to look more closely at some of the subtler but more important elements of our findings, particularly the role played by executive leaders. As a result of these suggestions and the overall positive response to what we were attempting to do, we committed ourselves to a continuation of the investigation. But events in both our careers caused the project to receive second priority for a time.

In 1978, Cameron was graduated from the doctoral program at Yale and moved on to the University of Wisconsin to take up his new career. That same year, Miles moved to the Harvard Business School, where he set himself to the task of understanding the unique practice focus that separates that institution from its discipline-focused peers. Because of Harvard's traditional emphasis on the problems of general managers, the move to Boston caused Miles to begin to broaden the issues that required attention in the tobacco-industry study. More detail on company differences in competitive behavior, strategy formation, and managerial cultures and beliefs crept unavoidably into the study—questions that had been scarcely touched on in the discipline-based literature to which the investigators had previously been exposed. The Harvard environment also stimulated Miles to read more broadly in the literatures of business policy, industrial economics, and political science than was normally encouraged in his native field of organizational behavior. As a result, certain questions not covered in the preliminary working paper could now be framed and sharpened. The formation of an informal organizational-adaptation study group at the Harvard Business School provided a vehicle for thinking seriously about whether and how to continue the project, possibly toward the objective of a book-length manuscript that might have broad appeal across academic disciplines and public and private sectors.*

Data collection and update continued; but so did developments within the field of organizational theory. As the time frame of our project expanded, so did the rate of accumulation of ideas and findings on our subject. Of particular help was the fact that a "warming" of the traditional boundaries separating the subfields of business policy and organizational behavior had begun, and with it had come some new perspectives on organization−environment relations. Happily, the occasion of our investigation was well timed to benefit from these developments as we continued to refine the questions we asked; and we have attempted throughout this book to give credit to the sources of these ideas as they emerged. Beyond our own field, some concurrent studies by political scientists and econometricians provided answers to some important questions that continued to elude us.

Finally, in the spring of 1980, Miles was awarded a grant by the Division of Research at the Harvard Business School to conduct a pilot study of what and how corporations have learned from an extended experience with a program of diversification. Because so much was already known about the specific choices made in developing this strategy among the tobacco Big Six, the pilot project for this new program of research focused on them.

By 1980, five years after both the end of our quarter-century study period and the initiation of our investigation, the tobacco independents had each logged fifteen to twenty years of experience with their own programs of diversification, a strategy that figured heavily in the way these companies had chosen to adapt to their changing environment. Therefore, in-depth interviews, conducted on site with the senior managers who had developed and nurtured these programs of domain creation, provided a unique window into the patterns of organizational choice and learning that each company had experienced, and into the important "hows" and "whys" of their processes of adaptation. This preliminary interview study also served to raise important issues and questions that would form a broader-based study on learning from diversifying that would follow. But more important for our present story, the interviews provided a look inside the Big Six—one taken long after much of the pain of the smoking-and-health controversy had subsided, but among managers for whom this experience would always be a memorable one. The research note summarizing what was

*Among the members of this group who gave especially valuable criticism and advice were Michael Beer, Paul Lawrence, and Jeffrey Sonnenfeld.

discovered in this retrospective study of learning from diversifying was cleared by the participating companies in the winter of 1980—81, and it is included in this book as a conclusion to our story of strategic organizational adaptation.

With most of the elements of this multifaceted investigation in place, a leave from teaching at the Harvard Business School during the 1980—81 year led Miles, in collaboration with Cameron, to the decision to attempt a book-length manuscript and to call a temporary end to this long but fascinating study of the behavior of complex organizations in society. But we wish to emphasize here that the study evolved over time as we learned from the process itself and from our interactions with both close and distant colleagues and the literatures they were creating along the way. In this sense, the study itself resembled in several respects the attempts by senior managers in the tobacco companies to create and develop viable models of organizational adaptation. Both they and we were experimenting with new strategies for coping with obstacles and creating opportunities that led us into unfamiliar and largely uncharted domains.

I

SETTING AND CONTEXT

1

Strategic Organizational Adaptation

an introduction

Before we begin our tale, we want to pause briefly in this introductory chapter to place our investigation in its own context—or rather, the context in which we were working when we decided to commit ourselves to this project and when we had to make some important choices that framed the scope and direction of our inquiry into the relationship between complex organization and complex society. In this chapter, we will discuss some major themes from the existing body of knowledge about complex organizations that helped us bound our investigation. In the next chapter, we will set the stage for the story, first, by describing developments within the institutional and market environments that were the sources of stress and crisis among and within the tobacco Big Six and, second, by summarizing the three basic modes by which these firms attempted to adapt to these developments. From that point on, we will chronicle the story of strategic organizational adaptation among the Big Six, together with our assessments of that quarter-century process—a process that the media still remind us has not reached its conclusion and that, from what we already know about organizations, is not likely to be resolved in the near future.

THEMES THAT BOUNDED THE SCOPE OF THE INQUIRY

We relied on three broad, historical themes from the existing body of knowledge on complex organizations to frame our investigation of strategic organizational adaptation. These themes represent ongoing dilemmas for those who dedicate their careers to the advancement of the state of knowledge and practice of organization and management. They also represent domains of intense dialectic among scholars who share our objective but who appear to be locked into narrow disciplinary points of view.

The first theme deals with the question of whether environmental determinism or organizational choice best explains the process of strategic organiza-

5

tional adaptation. This, of course, is not a dilemma invented at the level of analysis of complex organizations, but one that has been the subject of much debate concerning the behavior of individuals as well.[1] Regardless of the level to which it is addressed, in our opinion the question has to be reformulated from "whether?" to "how much?"; for in almost all conceivable instances, elements of both volition and determinism will be present.

Second, the literature on complex organizations divides along its focus on routine versus strategic or "critical" decisions, and the balance of existing knowledge has been tilted heavily toward the more mundane decisions because of the choices made by previous researchers. One factor that has reinforced this orientation is the relative ease of access into organizations afforded to those who want to understand "everyday" or "operational" decisions at the lower levels of organizations. These are the decisions that are made far away from the centers of organizational power, that commit relatively insignificant amounts of resources, and that are made within the existing framework of organizational purposes and structures that are created and reinforced from the top. Because the issue of purpose, and hence of legitimacy, is preempted at the lower reaches in organizations, operational-decision-making studies have avoided the "messiness" of organizational transformation that is the product of critical decisions.

The third theme concerns the concept of organizational effectiveness. Basically, it comes down to this: the extent to which an organization's effectiveness is judged in terms of doing "well" or doing "good." The emphasis on organizational efficiency versus legitimacy divides the major contributions to organizational theory. But we believe that both are important components of organizational effectiveness; therefore, we have chosen a research setting that highlights the issues of organizational legitimacy in order to counter the overemphasis on efficiency that characterizes the literature on complex organizations.

UNDERSTANDING ORGANIZATIONAL ADAPTATION: COMPETING VIEWS

As we began to design our investigation, we were aware that the vast majority of previous studies on the relations between organizations and environments had been characterized by two limiting features: first, a view of environments as being deterministic and immutable with respect to the organizations that were dependent upon them; and second, a static, cross-sectional, and ahistorical orientation toward organizational analysis.

As the primary contributors, economists had built a rather elegant, formal theory of the firm, in which the behavior and fate of populations of organizations were largely predictable, given certain specified characteristics of the market environment in which they existed. With variations in market environment (e.g., competitive, oligopolistic, or monopolistic markets), different classes of organizational behaviors and outcomes and different degrees of organizational choice could be predicted, at least theoretically.

A similar framework of organizational behavior emerged from the contingency school of organizational behavior (e.g., Dill, 1958; Burns and Stalker, 1961; Lawrence and Lorsch, 1969; Lorsch and Morse, 1974). According to these theorists, organizational effectiveness was a function of the correctness and tightness of "fit" between the structure and processes of an enterprise and of its environment; but the duty of engineering such alignments was presumed to be entirely the organization's. The market environment confronting the organizations was taken as an immutable given that imposed certain constraints and contingencies, or "dominant survival issues," for the population of organizations it contained. For example, complex and dynamic environments were believed to create information-processing problems that resulted in decision-making uncertainty within organizations. This uncertainty, in turn, could be managed effectively by the presence or adoption of organizational structures better able to facilitate the process of informational assimilation and integration.

Thus, the theories of organizational adaptation that prevailed as we began our study rested on the fundamental assumption of a given, deterministic, immutable market environment. Organizational adaptation was viewed as the process by which organizations *adjusted themselves*—their scale of operations or structure—to conform to the dictates of the immediate environment. Failure to engineer these internal adjustments was predicted to result in relative organizational inefficiency and ultimately in the inability to persist. Little was said about an organization's choice of strategy.

The research mounted in support of the contingency view virtually ignored the *processes* by which organizational adaptation occurred, focusing instead on verifying the relative effectiveness of different *alignments* between organizational and environmental states. Data on a variety of organizations and their environments were sampled, but at only one point in time. Comparisons were made between the adaptive and maladaptive alignments both among populations of organizations in the same environment and between different organizational populations and environments. But no attempt was made to understand the etiology of these organization—environment alignments or the processes by which adaptive processes were successfully or unsuccessfully engineered. The role of management was viewed as one of exercising *structural* choice. Little attention was given to the processes by which management chose a new design or implemented it. Other management options were virtually ignored.

It will become important later to recognize that the economic and contingency models of organizational adaptation shared one additional limiting assumption: Both confined their treatment of environment to the immediate market or industry surrounding an organizational population. Forces in the broader institutional environment surrounding an organizational population, as well as its market environment, were virtually disregarded. Explicitly or implicitly, both perspectives assumed that an organization operated and would continue to operate in a single market environment or domain. In short, they put the organization "between a rock and a hard place" and looked to the organization itself for any changes or adaptations that would be required to negotiate a successful passage.

This deterministic view of organizational behaviors and fates anchored one edge of the boundary around our study of organizational adaptation. At the opposing edge was the work of business-policy scholars and students of "institutional" analysis that emphasized the role of *strategic choice*. The latter took the position not only that organizations were capable of learning and adapting to a changing context, but that they often exercised a considerable measure of choice about the kinds of environments they would operate in and adapt to.

Before we got far with our investigation, however, an even more extreme view of environmental determinism emerged to capture the attention of students of organization. It rapidly became known as the "natural-selection" perspective. Because this perspective denied the role of organizational learning and adaptation, and thereby extended the full range of adaptive possibilities for organizations, we amended the constitution of our study to embrace it.

THE NATURAL-SELECTION PERSPECTIVE

The "natural-selection" perspective on organizational adaptation traces its roots to Darwinian theory and its subsequent refinements (e.g., Hawley, 1950, 1968). In the most general terms, this perspective argues that organizations cannot adapt, and that changes in the environment, not in the organization, determine organizational effectiveness and survival (Campbell, 1969; Hannan and Freeman, 1977; Aldrich, 1979; Brittain and Freeman, 1980). Several critical assumptions are obviously necessary to support this argument. First, organizations are characterized profoundly by inertia. Second, organizations are captives of their environments. Third, following from the first two assumptions, any variation that occurs within a population of organizations, such as among member firms of an industry, results not from changes made within organizations but from the entry into the existing population of new organizations with different forms. And fourth, the embedding environments of organizations are immutable. Thus, the natural-selection model focuses on the differential survival rate of alternative types or forms of organizations that are viewed as predominantly inert and effectively captured within their embedding environment.[2] From this perspective, the environment, and not the organization's management, does the selecting.

To understand this extreme view of organizational adaptation—which, indeed, denies the possibility that organizations can and do adapt—we must review briefly the arguments underlying its critical assumptions. These constraints on organizational choice have been summarized by Hannan and Freeman (1977) under the rubric of the "population ecology" of organizations.

Organizational Inertia and Captivity. First is the assumption of organizational inertia.[3] From the perspective of natural-system theorists, the range of adaptive capabilities of an organization is constrained by factors originating both within the organization itself and outside in its embedding environments. On the internal side, sunk costs, resource allocation and career politics, and historical precedents and norms serve to preserve the status quo of organizational strategy and structure. Heavy investments in existing technologies, structural arrangements, and human skills, these theorists argue, are costly to alter or replace. The career orientations of key decision makers, together with the resource-allocation charters that have served to differentially nurture and protect the subunits they represent, reinforce the status quo. And the individuals and subunits of greatest power tend to represent the maintenance of the existing organizational thrust and form. Finally, myths, cultures, and belief systems emerge within organizations about such things as its distinctive competences and its role vis-à-vis other organizations and within society at large. All these internal factors constrain the choice of alternative strategies and structures that might otherwise be managerial options in an organization attempting to cope with a changing environment.

According to this tradition, external pressures toward inertia seem to be at least as strong as the internal ones supporting the status quo. Legal and economic barriers to entry into and, occasionally, exit from an industry or operating domain constrain organizational choice. Insurance companies must obtain a license to operate in a given state. Public utilities cannot withdraw from a geographic area just because it is unprofitable or its citizens are negligent in their payments. Agencies of the federal and state governments must often operate under a mandated charter that specifies not only the population they must serve, but also the services they are to render and the technologies by which they must deliver them.

Information about the environment, needed to determine whether a change is required in strategy or structure, is costly. In addition, such information may be distorted by the nature of the sensory mechanisms already in place within organizations. Environmental scanning activities may be focused only on external sectors or trends that have been of strategic relevance historically. Thus, the environmental-appreciation set as well as the organizational-response set of an enterprise may not be broad enough to provide either useful intelligence about threatening or opportunistic developments in the environment or an adequate repertoire of strategic and structural alternatives for effective coping. These potential limits to choice are constrained further by the element of "bounded rationality" in complex organizations (March and Simon, 1958). The more complex and dynamic developments are in the environment, the greater will be the difficulty experienced by organizational decision makers, given the human limits on their ability to process new information.

Finally, organizations must operate under legitimacy constraints. Many structural and operational alternatives for adaptation (e.g., those prohibited by the Sherman Antitrust Act and the Occupational Safety and Health Act) may be viewed as illegitimate and, therefore, outside the feasible set of options otherwise available to the organization. These factors when taken together, according to natural-systems theorists, powerfully constrain the adaptive potential of complex organizations. "Failing churches do not become retail stores," assert Hannan and Freeman (1977:957), "nor do firms transform themselves into churches. . . . Until we see evidence to the contrary, we will continue to doubt that the major features of the world of organizations arise through learning and adaptation."

Natural-systems theorists also assume that the organizations of interest are "captured" by a particular environment. Because they minimize the role of organizational choice, emphasizing instead that organizational variation occurs only with the addition of new organizations and not within old, inert ones, they focus on the dynamics of populations of organizations—populations that, in turn, are defined in terms of the environment (e.g., industry or domain) that they cohabit. Thus, choice of domain is ruled out as an option to organizations seeking to escape or spread the risks posed by their current environment.

Aldrich (1979), for instance, relies on the "barriers to entry" into alternative industries often cited by economists (e.g., Caves, 1977; Porter, 1980) to raise the issue of captivity. He argues that economy-of-scale barriers may prevent the encroachment of new entrants into an established industry in which large firms enjoy low-unit-cost advantages from high production volume. Entry into a new environment may also be prohibited by the capital required to start a new firm or division. Finally, entry into an alternative domain may be prevented by the fact that established firms there have already achieved brand recognition and consumer loyalty.

Environmental Choice and Immutability. In summary, the natural-systems view of organization denies an important role of organizational choice and minimizes the possibility of adaptation by individual organizations. Instead, adaptation is viewed as a property of organizational populations that occurs as a consequence of three ongoing and interrelated processes. First, *variation* within a population is created largely from the entry of new organizations. Second, environmental *selection* separates the "fittest" organizational forms for survival while discarding the remaining members of the population. This does not imply that all surviving firms will be identical, for the theory permits variation among "generalist" and "specialist" organizations whose forms are suited for coping with the selective pressures of the general environment of the whole population and the "niches" that may exist within it, respectively. But, again, this kind of variation is attributed to differences between organizations in the population, not to any abilities of individual organizations to transform themselves from one type to another. The sequence ends with *retention* among the surviving population of organization forms that are aligned with the embedding environment and its niches.

Overarching this presumed sequence is the belief that from the point of view of members in an organizational population, the environment they share is immutable. Virtually no attention is paid by these theorists to the possibility that organizations, individually or collectively, may influence the environments upon which they depend for their effectiveness and persistence. In short, the role of strategic choice and organizational adaptation is minimized by those adhering strictly to the natural-systems perspective.

Taking a somewhat more moderate view, one of the current spokespersons for the natural-systems perspective stakes out his position on the issue of organizational adaptation as follows:

> *Whether strategic choice operates only at the margins of change (producing small effects of little consequence) or at the forefront of change (remaking environments in the organization's image) is ultimately an empirical question, open to resolution only through the cumulation of historical research.* [Aldrich, 1979:160]

THE STRATEGIC-CHOICE PERSPECTIVE

We have observed, so far, that the natural-selection perspective and its precursors from economic and organization theory have either denied or ignored, respectively, the *process* by which organizations adapt to their changing environments. At the opposite end of the spectrum on organizational adaptation is the strategic-choice perspective.[4] This view emphasizes the role of learning and choice in the process of organizational adaptation, and observes not only that complex organizations have the ability to alter themselves to conform to the contingencies—constraints and opportunities—posed by their environment, but that they may exercise considerable influence on the environments in which they operate. Indeed, these choices may range from the manipulation of environmental features to make them more accommodative of organizational goals, strategies, and structures to the actual choice of the environments in which an organization wishes to operate. From this perspective, it is more than anything else the fundamental *quality of executive leadership* that enables an organization to minimize the constraints on adaptation outlined by the natural-selection theorists and to maneuver their organization through or around environmental obstacles and into domains more abundant in resources and opportunities.

Contributions of an Amateur Scholar. The point of embarkation for the strategic-choice perspective was established not by a prominent organizational scholar but by a person who had served as president of New Jersey Bell Telephone and, after retirement, of a number of philanthropic organizations. With the publication in 1938 of his book, *The Functions of the Executive,* Chester I. Barnard set forth a view of formal organization as "that kind of cooperation among men that is *conscious, deliberate, purposeful"* (p. 4). He observed that "most formal organizations are partial systems included within larger organizational systems" (p. 79), and that "adjustment of cooperative systems to changing conditions or new purposes implies special management processes and, in complex cooperation, special organs known as executives or executive organizations" (p. 37).

Barnard's broad experience in a variety of institutions led him to conclude that adaptation is the rule, not the exception, underpinning organizational effectiveness and persistence: "Once established, organizations change their unifying purposes. They tend to perpetuate themselves; and in the effort to survive may change the reasons for existence . . . in this lies an important aspect of the executive function" (p. 87). Indeed, from Barnard's point of view, "The most strategic factor in human cooperation is executive capacity" (p. 282); a capacity that requires "the sensing of the organization as a whole and the total situation relevant to it" (p. 235). His contribution placed strategic management as the mediator between environment and organization and as the center of responsibility for organizational purpose and adaptation.

In summary, Barnard established the importance of the role of top management in creating and managing an organization's purpose. But he also warned, "A purpose does not incite cooperative effort unless it is accepted by those whose efforts will constitute the organization."[5] Commitment to an organizational purpose first has to be believed by the organizational membership. Thus, Barnard recognized a second important function of executive leadership: Executives not only have to create and steer organizational purpose under changing environmental conditions, they also have to create and administer a structural framework to channel and reinforce the contributions of organizational members and coalitions toward the direction and achievement of that purpose. Moreover, the executive function has to be capable of changing these purposes when necessary and of restructuring the organization and its operating systems in order to modify beliefs and behaviors to conform to new purposes.

Emergence of the Field of Business Policy.   The work of Barnard stimulated the development of the field of "business policy," which has been described as:

> . . . *the study of the* functions and responsibilities of the senior management *in a company, the* crucial problems *that affect the success of the total enterprise, and the decisions that determine its directions, shape its future, and produce the results desired. The policy problem of business, like those of policy in public affairs, have to do with the* choice of purposes, *the* molding

of organization identity and character, *the* unending definition *of what needs to be done, and the* mobilization of resources *for the attainment of goals in the face of aggressive competition or adverse circumstances.* [*Andrews, 1980:iv*]

From this perspective, "The highest function of the executive is still seen as leading the continuous process of determining the nature of the enterprise and setting, revising, and achieving its goals" (Andrews, 1980:iii). The subsequent works of Alfred P. Sloan, former president of General Motors, and Alfred D. Chandler, Jr., a Pulitzer-prize-winning business historian, are representative of the early stream of knowledge that began to emerge as a result of Barnard's stimulus.

Studies of the Large Corporation.   Both Chandler (1962) and Sloan (1972) chronicled the history during the first half of this century of the strategic and structural adaptation of major U.S. corporations in response to environmental changes.[6] In all cases, the firms embarked on significant evolutionary changes in their strategies in order to cope with the opportunities for growth created within their market environments. But most organizations at the time operated with a simple functional structure in which specialized units reported to a single general manager, usually the founder or a representative of the founding family. These highly centralized structures were not capable of responding to the strategies each firm had adopted to achieve its growth objectives. As Chandler observed:

> Growth through diversification into several lines increased the number and complexity of both operational and entrepreneurial activities even more than a world-wide expansion of one line. . . . By placing an increasing intolerable strain on existing administrative structures, territorial expansion and to a much greater extent product diversification were brought into the multidivisional form. [*1962:44*]

Thus, with strategic change came parallel though lagging realignment in organizational structure. Sparing details for the moment, these in-depth case histories of major enterprises indicated that at least some complex organizations can and do adapt to changes in their external environment, and that the forces of inertia and captivity can be overcome by skillful executive leadership. But Chandler also observed, "Relatively few other large industrial enterprises followed the example of these pioneers before the massive economic boom that followed World War II" (1962:44).

"The organization of these new domains was," in Chandler's view, "as difficult and as challenging as their creation" (1962:36). At the time, there existed few if any "useful precedents of organization building." Because of the absence of either systematic knowledge about the strategic management and design of complex organizations or educational programs for the development of professional managers, the leaders of the corporations Chandler studied had to *invent* administrative structures to cope with their new strategies.

Out of these pioneering studies came a firmer belief, first, that organizations can exercise considerable choice in adapting to their environments, and second, that organizational effectiveness is largely a function of top management's ability to create and maintain congruence among the factors of environment and of organizational strategy, structure, and competence.

Role of Strategic Management. The strategic-choice perspective emphasizes the existence of organizational volition. As Child (1972:10) has argued:

> . . . *environmental conditions cannot be regarded as a direct source of variation in organizational structure. . . . The critical link lies in the decision-maker's evaluation of the organization's position in the environment areas they regard as important, and in the action they may consequently take about its internal structure.*

Thus, strategic management is viewed as playing an important mediating role between environment and organization—a role that involves two primary areas of responsibility: First, it is the duty of strategic managers to understand and develop not only organizational but environmental resources, competences, and commitments. On the internal side, this involves identifying and developing the "distinctive competences" (Selznick, 1957) of the organization—its strengths and weaknesses relative both to those of its rivals for the same domain and to the constraints and opportunities inherent in the environment they share. On the external side, strategic managers must develop an appreciation of the constraints and opportunities posed by the larger environment in which their organizations operate. They must consider not only the resources and constraints associated with their traditional domain, but also the features of subsets or "niches" within that domain and other domains that might accommodate their organization's distinctive competencies. So part of the first duty of strategic management is to stay abreast of the organizational resources (potential as well as realized) and the opportunities and risks presented by organizational environments (potential as well as operational). From this ongoing process of assessment, strategic management is responsible for *identifying* feasible and satisfactory alignments of environmental opportunities and risks, on the one hand, and organizational capabilities and resources, on the other.

The second duty of strategic management is to *create and maintain effective alignments between the organization and its environment.*[7] To cope with this responsibility, top management has at its disposal three major classes of options: (1) strategic options, (2) structural options, and (3) performance options (Child, 1972).

Management Options. Included among the *strategic options* is the choice of which domains or segments of domains an organization will operate in. The degree of "domain-choice flexibility" available to strategic managers (Miles, 1980: 233−35) will, no doubt, vary from situation to situation. For instance, there appear to be fewer domain-choice constraints imposed upon private-sector corporations than upon public-sector agencies. The latter are often thought to be constrained by legislative charter in the kinds of populations they can serve, technologies they can employ, structures they can use, and outputs they can produce. But even under these circumstances, there is evidence that substantial domain maneuvering can and does occur within public organizations (e.g., Downs, 1967; Kaufman, 1975; Weihl, 1974). On the subject of private corporations, there is little doubt but that these complex organizations often wield considerable discretion in the choice of which domains they will and will not become a part of. As one strategic-choice theorist has observed:

> Some degree of environmental selection is open to most organizations, and some degree of environmental manipulation is open to most larger organizations. These considerations form an important qualification to suggestions of environmental determinism. [*Child, 1972:4*]

Indeed, some scholars believe not only that the distinction between environment and the large corporation is meaningless, but that the corporation is capable of actually remaking the marketplace and society at large in its image (Galbraith, 1979; Lindblom, 1977, Perrow, 1979; Reid, 1976). In summary, strategies may be developed to create new environments for the organization, or to dispose of old ones, or to segment the environment in order to tailor relevant portions of it to the organization's competences and resources. With strategy, the environment may be aligned in whole or in part to the organization.

The choice of *internal structures and processes* is a second option available to strategic management. This choice can serve two purposes related to the alignment problem. Rearrangement of the structural framework can be used to channel organization competences, resources, and commitments in support of a new strategy or an altered environment. But structural rearrangement also may be used in lieu of a change in either strategy or environment. On this option, Bower's (1972) study of the resource-allocation decisions in a complex organization is instructive.

By tracing the initiation of new project ideas up through the organizational hierarchy, Bower discovered that the executive committee at the top seldom turned down a project proposal that had reached its final review process. Instead, he found, the prevailing strategies and structures of the corporation, those established and managed by senior executives, had created a context that served to filter and reinforce the upward movement of capital-expenditure requests that were consistent with the corporation's prevailing goals and strategies. This context, consisting of structure, rewards, measurements, definitions of managerial jobs, and career precedents, according to Bower, established the "rules of the game" within the organization:

> . . . the role of structural context is that it shapes the purposive manager's definition of business problems by directing, delimiting, and coloring his focus and perception; it determines the priorities which the various demands on him are given. Structural context has this role because it is the principal way in which the purposive manager learns about the goals of the corporation. [Bower, 1972:73]

Moreover, Bower stressed the importance of these structural options for strategic managers:

> Structural context is particularly important because all of its elements are subject to control by top management. Thus, management has in its hands the levers that influence behavior of managers many levels below the top of the hierarchical organization. [1972:73]

In short, all that may be required to perform under certain environmental conditions is a structural adjustment that refocuses organizational capability or reinforces the mobilization and motivation or organizational resources. From the strategic-choice perspective, influence over the structural options rests largely with those who reside at the top of the organizational pyramid.

Finally, alignment between organization and environment may come about through a managerial option of changing the *performance standards* under which the organization operates. Almost any aspect of organizational adaptation will require the introduction of slack (Cyert and March, 1963) through at least a temporary reduction in performance. *Performance* is almost always a management option. Strategic and structural retooling requires a certain learning period before such changes can reach their potentials. Even in the case where neither strategy nor structure changes, attempts to alter the organization's environment will require the diversion of resources normally consumed in the ongoing operations of the enterprise to the process of adaptation. Finally, the organization may choose to ignore some misalignments with its environment, by remaining inert and by choosing to do so by simply reducing its performance standards.

Few if any organizations operate under conditions of performance maximization that leave no room for slack, although virtually all the deterministic theories of organizational adaptation (e.g., the economic theory of the firm and the natural-selection model) assume that profit-maximization expectations and low-slack conditions prevail in complex organizations. Instead, organizations "satisfice" (March and Simon, 1958); they seek to perform at a level that ensures that they minimally satisfy the expectations imposed upon them by their strategic constituencies, including their members, their owners or sponsors, and the society at large. Moreover, strategic managers may actually choose less than maximally efficient structures in order to satisfy their own needs or those of internal interest groups upon whose support their survival depends:

> If performance exceeds this "satisficing" level (and one is assuming that this represents a degree of return that is at least sufficient to secure resources required for the fulfillment of present and future plans), then the decision-making group may take the view that the margin of surplus permits them to adopt structural arrangements which accord better with their own preferences, even at some extra administrative cost to the organization. In such circumstances the dominant organizational power-holders may also permit other interest groups to make or retain their own preferred structural adaptations, a kind of organizational slack. . . . [Child, 1972:11]

Because of the rise of professional managers in corporations (Chandler, 1977) and of career bureaucrats in public institutions (Kaufman, 1975, 1976), the interests of owners and stockholders and government policy makers have become displaced, in part, by the interests of those who actually run the complex organizations. Under these circumstances, those who guide the behavior of organizations may be inclined to make choices that enhance organizational growth and perpetuation, and hence professional career progression, to the subordination of maximum return on the investments that outsiders have made in them (Penrose, 1952, 1980; Galbraith, 1979; Lindblom, 1977; Marris, 1964; Mueller, 1969). Thus, professional managers may be even more inclined than their entrepreneurial forefathers to introduce slack into the organization—environment equation.

THE "INVISIBLE" VS. THE "VISIBLE" HAND

In summary, the strategic-choice perspective provided us with a compelling counterpoint to the natural-selection view of organizational adaptation. The latter emphasized the constraints on organizational choice posed by external and internal factors. The role of managerial intention and learning plays no role in this model; instead, it is Adam Smith's (1776) "invisible hand" that spins the wheel of organizational fortune. In direct opposition is Alfred Chandler's (1977) notion of the "visible hand" of professional management that he believes has risen to create more consistency and order in the games that join complex organizations and their environments. It is this visible hand, or, more generally, the quality of executive leadership, according to the disciples of Barnard and Chandler, that separates the organizations that adapt and persist from those that disappear from the field:

> . . . *giant organizations are obviously not pushed and pulled and hauled by market forces which overwhelm them; rather, they demonstrably choose to follow a certain course of action which differs from other courses which they might have chosen and which, indeed, some of their number do elect to follow. Discretion is present. How important it is in the end result is still a moot point, but at least there is no basis for pretending that it has no effect.* [*Chamberlain, 1968:47*]

This quote, together with the one we used to close the discussion of the natural-systems perspective, sketches the broad outlines of our study of strategic organizational adaptation.

CRITICAL VS. ROUTINE DECISIONS

To narrow the scope, we chose to focus our study on "critical" as opposed to "routine" decisions in complex organizations. Organization theorists, from the time they appeared in the first decade of this century, have been preoccupied with the study of "routine" decisions, particularly decisions that pertain to the improvement of the ongoing operations of an enterprise. Moreover, the external environment has been treated in value-free terms by these decision theorists, who characterized organizational contexts simply in terms of the information-processing demands they placed on the structure of decision making within organizations. As Philip Selznick observed more than two decades ago, ". . . the choice of goals and of character-defining methods is banished from the science of administration . . . they say *given* your ends, whatever they may be, the study of administration will help you achieve them. We offer you tools [1957:80]. . . . The cult of efficiency in administrative theory and practice is a modern way of overstressing means and neglecting ends" (1957:135).

With this pronouncement, Selznick launched both an attack on the school of "administrative" decision making, pioneered by Herbert Simon (1945), and a new "institutional" school of organizational analysis. The focus of this new school was to be on "critical" decisions and the role of institutional leaders, as distinguished from the routine decisions of administrators and technicians. Questions of "What shall we do?" and "What shall be?" would form the grist of Selznick's institutional analysis. Its focus would be "marked by a concern for the evolution of the organization as a whole, including its changing aims and capabilities [1957:5]; [it promised to] . . . lead us to the knottiest and most significant problems of leadership in large organizations'' (1957:3).

The functions of institutional leaders, in Selznick's view, are ''to define the ends of group existence, to design an enterprise distinctively adapted to these ends, and to see that that design becomes a living reality. These tasks are not routine; they call for continuous self-appraisal on the part of the leaders; and they may require only a few critical decisions over a long period of time'' (1957:37). More specifically, an institutional leader must (1) define the organization's mission or role, (2) build commitment to the organization's purpose, (3) defend the organization's integrity, and (4) bring order to conflict within the organization. To ensure the survival of the organization, ''The leader's job is to test the environment to find out which demands can become truly effective threats, to change the environment by finding allies and other means of external support, and to gird his organization by creating the means and the will to withstand attacks'' (1957:145). So ended Selznick's evocative appeal.

But nothing much has changed in the field of organization theory to alter the state of affairs observed by Selznick. We still know far more about how to make an organization work than why to make an organization. Herbert Simon was awarded the Nobel Prize in 1978 for his contributions to the administrative theory of organizations (e.g., Simon, 1945; March and Simon, 1958). By that time, aside from Selznick's works on the Tennessee Valley Authority and the Soviet Communist Party and the few studies we cited in our discussion of the strategic-choice perspective, only a handful of other investigations based on the institutional perspective have been reported; moreover, most of them have neglected the large, complex corporation, focusing instead on public agencies and nonprofit organizations. Does this quiescence signal the lack of importance of institutional inquiry or of the role of institutional leadership? We think not. Instead, we believe it says more about the obstacles that must be negotiated by institutional researchers and the peculiar choices they have made in the design of their investigations.

Selznick was certain about one priority. He said that ''in appraising organizations we cannot draw conclusions regarding administrative practices unless we can place those practices in a *developmental* context [1957:118]. . . . The study of institutions is in some ways comparable to the clinical study of personality. It requires a genetic and developmental approach, an emphasis on historical origins and growth stages'' (1957:142). But as the senior author has observed:

> *It seems clear . . . that if we are to begin to understand important organizational processes, we must first develop ways for coping with the obstacles to longitudinal research. . . . Among the more important obstacles are organizational access and commitment to the longitudinal approach by the host organization, the time commitment imposed upon the researcher*

and its relation to career rewards, and the thorny methodological issues
surrounding longitudinal data collection and analysis. [*Miles and Randolph,*
1980:82][8]

Indeed, periods of critical decision making within complex organizations are
likely to be particularly inaccessible to outside observers. It is during these often
infrequent but momentous occasions that the fluff and fanfare normally associated with executive leadership are laid bare by the force of problems that
challenge fundamentally the persistence of an enterprise and the choices
managers make that shape its developmental course. Except under the most
unusual circumstances, executive leaders are loath to have exposed to the public
eye their assumptions and choice processes during these critical decision
situations.

In the face of obstacles such as these, institutional researchers have been
forced to make some critical choices of their own that, in turn, have shaped the
course of their own tradition. Because of the enormous commitment required by
historical analysis, one important choice has been to focus on single, "unique"
institutions—often, institutions in the public domain for which information and
access was believed to be more readily available.[9] The most serious limitation of
this resolution has been that the influences of rival or potential rival organizations
have been minimized. It is as though the definition of an "institution" has
preempted their consideration. Thus, if an institutional researcher were to study
the development and adaptation of, say, the National Aeronautics and Space
Administration, it is likely that one of the tradeoffs would be made in favor of
excluding potential rival organizations. It could be argued, for instance, that
NASA is an "institution," a unique enterprise operating alone in a domain of its
own creation (space technology). But this tradeoff would ignore the fact that
many of the critical decisions made within NASA during its heyday were
influenced by and responsive to those of other organizations—the Defense
Department and its military venture in Vietnam, the civil-rights movement, and
so forth—that competed vigorously, not in the same domain as NASA but for the
same pool of resources upon which all were dependent for their development and
persistence. Even when some attempt has been made to account for these indirect
influences, the subject organizations constituting this stream of research (e.g.,
the Tennessee Valley Authority, Selznick, 1949; the Bolshevik Party, Selznick,
1957; the March of Dimes, Sills, 1957; the Young Men's Christian Association,
Zald, 1970; and the Environmental Protection Agency, Weihl, 1974) have not
been confronted by the intense, direct competition from rivals operating in the
same immediate domain that is a feature of the world of business enterprise.

Thus, borrowing from the institutional school, we prepared to study critical
decisions taken over a quarter century of organizational history. But we were
resolved to study these decisions in their competitive context, and therefore we
selected an industry population of organizations instead of a single "institution"

for investigation. This choice led us down a different path from the one well worn by our predecessors; a path that forced us to consider both the relative efficiency of competitors for the same domain and their ability to maintain the legitimacy in society of their privilege to work in the domain they all shared.

ORGANIZATIONAL EFFICIENCY VS. LEGITIMACY

All complex organizations must contend with at least two fundamental aspects of organizational effectiveness: efficiency and legitimacy. Corporations in particular are both economic instruments that must bear the test of relative efficiency in some kind of market domain *and* social subsystems that perform roles for and within their embedding society. As sociologist Talcott Parsons has observed:

> *A formal organization . . . is a mechanism by which goals somehow important to society, or to various subsystems of it, are implemented and to some degree defined. But not only does such an organization have to operate in a social ennvironment which imposes the conditions governing the processes of disposal and procurement, it is also a part of a wider social system which is the source of the "meaning," legitimation, or higher-level support which makes the implementation of the organization's goals possible. [1960:63−64]*

Organization and Society. Organizations are never wholly independent from the society in which they are embedded and its systems of values. To varying degrees, all organizations are subject to institutional controls, whether they exist in the form of generalized norms and values in society, or in society's systems of laws, or in the organs of government to which society has entrusted the "public interest" and invested "political" authority. Therefore, organizations must develop the means to ensure their legitimacy and, hence, the privilege to continue to perform their chosen or assigned function within society.[10]

That complex organizations must to varying degrees understand and manage the expectations and contingencies posed by their institutional and market environments means that their effectiveness and ultimate survival depends on both doing "well" (that is, enhancing the efficiency by which they transform resources into products or services) and doing "good" (that is, maintaining the legitimacy of their purposes, their contributions, and their methods of operation in the context of societal values).[11] Of the two, organizational efficiency has been the easiest to define and measure and, consequently, has been the major focus of research on complex organizations. As the standard of what we have referred to as the "administrative" perspective, it has often been expressed in tangible quantitative terms such as input−output and cost−revenue ratios, relative market-share standings, or rates of growth in outputs, assets, or operating earnings.

Traditionally, in a free-enterprise system such as the one in the United States, the market environment is the primary mechanism for reconciling economic values. When markets fail to perform this function, the institutional environment representing society at large may step into the breach. The Securities and Exchange Commission and the Antitrust Division of the U.S. Department of Justice represent some of the economic regulatory institutions that operate just outside but upon our imperfect market system. Together with the market, these institutions help to safeguard the economic values prevailing in a society. But the market system is not obliged to safeguard noneconomic social values.

Organizational Legitimacy: A Question of Values. Social values are maintained and enforced to a greater or lesser degree by the existence of widely shared norms in society, by the prevailing system of laws, by specific institutions whose primary responsibility is to safeguard certain classes of social value (e.g., "social" regulatory agencies and the free press), and through the exercise of popular, and occasionally individual, protest.

In contrast to the standards of efficiency, measures of organizational legitimacy are characterized by their intangible and subjective qualities. Organizations are said to be "legitimate" to the extent that their activities are congruent with the values of the superordinate system. Therefore, the assessment of legitimacy must involve comparisons between organizational purposes, goals and means, and societal values. These values are the "modes of normative orientation of action in a social system which define the main *directions* of action without reference to specific goals or more detailed situations or structures" (Parsons, 1960:171). If such values can be defined only in the most general terms of "direction," the complexity associated with the measurement of and adjustment to social values by organizations is intensified, because:

> There is also a great deal of diversity in the values held by a society and its various subgroups at any one point in time, so that the possibility of an organization finding some subgroup espousing values consistent with its activities would be quite high. [Pfeffer and Salancik, 1978:194]

Thus, the multiplicity of values and the ambiguity of reality in society at any given moment may permit conflicting assessments of organizational actions. Indeed, it is conceivable that pockets of support may exist in society for almost any purposes, methods, or products that an organization may wish to take up. Therefore, the struggle for power in a society, according to Parsons, consists of the "competition for support and authorization among the many different organized interests of the society" (1960:91). Legitimacy, then, may be viewed as a political resource granted an organization by society, on a contingent basis, that is revocable or renegotiable when the organization fails to meet its social obligations.

For many value-purpose intersections, the rule of law and the role of governmental administrative authority diminish the intensity of the power struggle. It should not be surprising, then, to find that the struggle between representatives of different interests and values is perhaps most intense at times when the passage of new laws or the adoption of new regulatory proposals is imminent. Such is the case in the story that we are about to tell. But outside these discrete occasions, organizations and elements of society may be found constantly engaged in efforts to insert their interests into the mainstream of societal values and, hence, to create or safeguard the legitimacy of their definition of the "right" social order.

In this regard, complex organizations have several possible alternatives for managing their legitimacy (Perrow, 1979; Dowling and Pfeffer, 1975). Short of closing up shop when their legitimacy is in question, organizations may attempt (1) to modify their goals or methods to *conform* to societal values; (2) to *influence* societal values to conform to their purposes or methods; or (3) in some cases, to *avoid* the process of direct comparison by becoming identified with symbols, values, or institutions that have a stronger basis in social reality than either the source of the threat or the particular subset of values it champions. It is to these hypothetical options that we were sensitive as we traced the responses of the tobacco Big Six during the smoking-and-health legitimacy threat.

But it is important here to emphasize that the study of the relationship between the institutional environment and complex organization, and of the questions of legitimacy that link the two, were far from the mainstream of organizational research when we began our study (Perrow, 1979; Hirsch, 1975). We have already discussed some of the obstacles to the study of "critical" decision making in complex organizations, to which we can now add the intangibility and subjectivity usually associated with the assessment of organizational legitimacy. But it is quite possible that another factor, also rooted in the contemporary reality, has contributed to the relative neglect of the interactions among complex organizations and society, and of the question of legitimacy.

Until recently, the question has not been the most salient one for complex corporations in modern industrial society, particularly in the United States. Most industrialized nations have enjoyed a period of economic growth under conditions of resource abundance since the end of World War II. It was not until the mid-1960s in the United States that social concern about the value of such growth and of the by-products it had begun to stockpile (e.g., resource depletion, environmental degradation, human injustice) had coalesced and found vehicles for expression. It has been reported, for example, that in 1965, industries subject to pervasive federal regulation accounted for roughly 7 percent of the U.S. gross national product. By 1978, the growth of regulation was such that heavily regulated industries accounted for over 30 percent of GNP (Kasper, 1978:1).

Moreover, the rate of growth in "economic" regulation was overtaken in the United States during this time by an unprecedented surge in "social" regulation. Between 1970 and 1975, the growth in expenditures of U.S. federal agencies responsible for traditonal economic regulation increased 157 percent, from $166 to $428 *million*. During that same five-year period, expenditures of the new "social" regulatory agencies, including the Equal Employment Opportunity Commission, the Environmental Protection Agency, the Occupational Safety and Health Administration, and the Consumer Product Safety Commission, rose more than 200 percent, from $1.4 to $4.3 *billion* (Lilley and Miller, 1977).

These trends signal an increased concern about *what* is being produced by organizations and *how* their productive function is performed—questions of legitimacy, not of efficiency—as well as an increased influence of the institutional environment representing society on the affairs of complex organizations. In 1970, organizational sociologist Charles Perrow warned:

> *Most of our formal theories of organization take legitimacy for granted—as do most organizations themselves. But both theory and practice do so at their peril. In a time of rapid social change and rising social criticism, the legitimacy of organizations in every sector of our society has been questioned, and the questioning has begun to expose the elaborate methods used by some organizations to forestall inquiry, divert attention, or to create legitimacy for questionable operations. The social sciences have done little to investigate this area of interface between the organization and the public. [1970:112]*

By 1978, another organizational theorist read the situation as follows:

> *We see organizations more as competing politically for institutional legitimacy in contemporary environments and less as competing technically for market advantages. Organizational outputs are increasingly institutionally defined by the environment and are increasingly defined at highly aggregated and abstracted levels. [Meyer, 1978:365]*

We believe this is an overstatement of the case, because the concepts of organizational legitimacy and efficiency, and the political and economic activities of strategic managers, not only are difficult to separate but under many circumstances are mutually interdependent.

Under some conditions, for instance, organizational efficiency may serve as an indicator of legitimacy. The criterion of efficiency is usually paramount in the values and interests of only a few of the organization's constituencies—those directly dependent on the organization's performance. In this sense, a strategic constituency, such as a firm's work force or traditional customers, may signal its view of the organization as illegitimate by withdrawing its commitment.[12] The work force may perform in a manner that lowers the firm's productivity; customers may fail to continue their habituated purchase of its goods or services. In either case, the erosion of perceived legitimacy among these immediate constituencies may cause them to withhold resources needed by the organization or to curtail their consumption of its outputs. These decisions, in turn, would directly affect the status of the organization's efficiency.

But there are many cases in which organizational legitimacy and efficiency may be only loosely coupled. Among them are the situations that economists label euphemistically "negative externalities." Under this situation, a firm may be performing efficiently in the narrow sense and satisfying the expectations of its immediate constituencies; but the by-products or unanticipated consequences of its operations or outputs may negatively affect more remote constituencies. They include "clear-cutting" by wood-products companies, water pollution by chemical manufacturers, and atmospheric degradation by the use of aerosol sprays manufactured by cosmetic firms. The question of whether these externalities exist is no longer under contention; that of who should bear the costs of these "side effects," or whether they should be borne at all, is hotly debated.

Additionally, there are circumstances in which the two criteria of organizational effectiveness are in conflict. Organizational resources may have to be diverted from efficiency-enhancement strategies to those designed to restore or maintain the legitimacy of the enterprise. But it is almost always the case that these goals, the strategies pursued to achieve them, and the contexts that impose them upon an organization are mutually interdependent. Indeed, it will be shown in this book that institutional forces shape the character and intensity of market competition, and that competitive strategy, in turn, may become in part both a response to and a determinant of the legitimacy accorded to a particular product-market domain. Furthermore, the extent of this interdependence and of its implications for management is likely to vary in direct relation to the social and economic prominence of an organization. Thus, it is the large, complex organizations in society that must bear much of the burden of reconciling this duality. This category includes, certainly, the firms that control most of our concentration of economic resources and, consequently, most of the power to influence political events in a market-oriented society. Indeed, it is largely their decisions and behaviors that contribute most to the "direction" in which economic development proceeds within a society.

THE GENERAL FRAMEWORK

The purpose of the foregoing discussion has been to sketch the context in which we were working when we began the study of strategic organizational adaptation among the tobacco Big Six. By now it should be obvious that we wanted to tackle what we believed were some of the most significant but least understood issues concerning the behavior of complex organizations in society. The general framework we chose for this investigation established quite broad boundaries around the variety of organizational adaptations that we were willing to consider, but confined the analysis to only those "critical" events and decisions that establish or reshape the fundamental purposes of organizations and the persistence they enjoy. Moreover, it has not been our purpose to study either the economics or the politics of organizational behavior because, as we have already hinted, these sets of factors are often closely interrelated. Instead, we intended to provide a rich account of the political economy of the modern business corporation, which would in turn provide some insights into the ways in which politics and economics interact to influence large, complex organizations and their embedding society. Finally, ours was to be a study of "institutions" rather than proprietorships, because our intent was to understand organizations whose behaviors have significant social as well as economic moment.

For all these reasons, this investigation falls into the domain of exploratory research. Because so little systematic research had been done on this subject about corporations, there were no comprehensive theories to subject to rigorous testing. Instead, we decided to focus on the patterns of adaptation that emerged as a whole industry population of firms attempted to cope with a major external threat. From these overall patterns, together with the variations that occurred among member firms, we hoped to be able to identify factors that would generalize to other industries and adaptive situations and might be the building blocks for an eventual theory of strategic organizational adaptation.

To be able to make progress toward these objectives, we addressed our investigation to two initial questions. The first question was, *What is the range of strategic options available to complex organizations for coping with extreme environmental stress?* But because our investigation would also identify the responses of each member of a whole population of organizations, all operating under the same stressful conditions for an extended period of time, we were able to address a second important question: *What is the relative effectiveness of different patterns of strategic adaptation (of strategic variation among member firms) within an industry population?* In addition, as we worked with the accumulating data over five years, we were gradually able to develop insight into *how* executive leaders in these organizations implemented their adaptive strategies and *why* they chose to do so in different ways. Answers to these guiding research questions, we believe, have important implications not only for strategic managers and public-policy makers, but for informed citizens who wish to understand the potential scope of managerial discretion and corporate power and the limits of current public policy and government authority in the United States.

FOOTNOTES

[1]Opposing points of view at the individual level of analysis have been expressed forcefully by Skinner (1971) and Rogers (1961).

[2]The origin of the attempt to transfer strict evolutionary metaphors from biology to organization theory is somewhat obscure; but it appears that economists (e.g., Alchain, 1959; Boulding, 1950; Enke, 1951; Penrose, 1952; and Winter, 1964) anticipated the early attempts by organizational theorists by at least a decade and a half. In certain important respects, the perspective of economists—the theory of the firm—was well suited to the critical assumptions of the "natural-systems" model. The economic theory of the firm focuses on populations of organizations whose activities are contained within a single market or industry, and until recently has virtually ignored the dynamics of managerial behavior.

[3]Arthur Stinchcombe (1965) was one of the early organization theorists to develop the notion of organizational inertia. The influence of the environment, in his view, is greatest at the time of the founding of a new organization. Stinchcombe observed that "the organizational inventions that can be made at a particular time in history depend on the social technology available at the time." Moreover, he argued that organizations become "imprinted" at birth with a set of goals, structures, and beliefs that tend to persist even when conditions in the external environment have changed dramatically. Some support for these ideas was demonstrated by Kimberly (1975) in his historical study of government-sponsored sheltered workshops.

[4]This tradition has its origins in the literature on military campaigns (e.g., von Clauswitz, 1832), in the studies of major institutions (e.g., Barnard, 1938; Selznick, 1949, 1957; Chandler, 1962; and Sloan, 1972), and most recently in the emergence of the field of applied knowledge known as "business policy" (e.g., Andrews, 1971, 1980; Bower, 1972; Mintzberg, 1978).

[5]As later pointed out by Alfred P. Sloan (1972), former president of General Motors, this was a lesson he learned during the episode in which he attempted to reorient his automotive company and its managers away from the traditional water-cooled engine to a new copper-cooled prototype.

[6]The firms subjected to the in-depth historical analysis of Sloan and Chandler included Du Pont; General Motors; Sears, Roebuck; and Standard Oil of New Jersey.

[7]Thompson (1967:148) has described this basic function of strategic management as one that "involves shooting at a moving target of co-alignment."

[8]The reader is referred to Kimberly, Miles, and associates, *The Organizational Life Cycle* (1980), for an introduction to the developmental perspective on organizations and a discussion of some of the issues and approaches in historical and longitudinal research on organizations.

[9]To some extent, this choice has been reinforced by Selznick's insistence that only certain organizations qualify as "institutions." Institutions are, according to Selznick, "infused with value" beyond the technical requirements of the task at hand. "They are products of interaction and adaptation; they become receptacles of group idealism; they are less readily expendable" (1957:21−22).

[10]Parsons viewed the essential feature of organizations as their goals, and the value system of a business firm as a version of "economic rationality" in society that, he asserted, "legitimizes the goal of economic production. . . . Devotion of the organization (and hence the resources it controls) to production is legitimized as is the maintenance of the primacy of this goal over other functional interests which may arise within the organizations." But he also observed, "For the business firm, money return is a primary measure and symbol of success and is thus *part* of the goal-structure of the organization. *But it cannot be the primary organizational goal becuase profit-making is not by itself a function on behalf of the society as a system*" (1960:21).

[11]More formally, Parsons (1960:175) has defined the process of legitimation as "the appraisal of action in terms of shared or common values in the context of the involvement of the action in the social system."

[12]Miles has defined an organization's strategic constituencies as follows: ". . . those individuals, interest groups, coalitions, and organizations upon which the focal organization is

critically dependent. . . . Dependence, in turn, may be viewed as a function of three factors associated with an organization's relationship with a constituency: (1) the amount of uncertainty the constituency can create for or manages on behalf of the organization; (2) the extent to which an organization is unable to replace the relationship it has with the constituency or to avoid the relationship the constituency imposes upon it; and (3) the extent to which decisions or action of the constituency could directly disrupt the operations or plans of the organization'' (1980c:375). Relying on this concept, Miles has defined organizational effectiveness as ''. . . the ability of the organization to minimally satisfy the expectations of its strategic constituencies'' (1980c:375).

2

The U.S. Tobacco Industry

environmental threats and strategic responses

The behavior of complex organizations, like the behavior of individuals and groups, cannot be understood apart from its contexts. Just as individuals and groups must relate to their immediate performance situations as well as to broader societal norms and sanctions, so, too, complex organizations must respond to factors in their immediate market environments as well as in their broader institutional environments. Yet the field of organizational behavior, comprising the contributions of many loosely connected disciplines, has failed to deal comprehensively with the interdependence between organizations and these two overlapping contexts.

This separation of the study of organizational contexts—artificially imposed for the convenience of specialized fields of knowledge—has greatly impeded the development of an organic/holistic understanding of how and why complex organizations emerge, grow, stagnate, decline, disappear, and sometimes reappear. We are less aware of what behaviors they exhibit in their struggles for efficiency, legitimacy, and survival. But the fault does not lie entirely with theoreticians of complex organizations; it is also shared by practitioners and the general populace.

Judging from what little recorded history we have about the development of business enterprise in the United States, the relative emphasis placed on market performance and institutional legitimacy by practitioners as well as scholars has waxed and waned with the larger cycles of American economic and political life. At the turn of the century, it was Frederick Winslow Taylor (1911) who helped U.S. businesses improve their efficiency through "scientific management"; but after the "crash" in the late 1920s, Elton Mayo (1933) appeared with his *Human Problems of Industrial Civilization*. The Great Depression brought John Maynard Keynes (1936), with his theory of the role of big government in economic affairs, which had previously been the province of the microeconomic theory of the firm. The institutional school of organization theory (e.g., Selznick, 1949, 1957) also emerged from the Depression; this school focused on the legitimacy of organizations, their purposes and practices, within complex society. With World War II came Herbert Simon (1945), whose rational theory of decision making rekindled the emphasis on organizations as production systems.

By the mid-1960s, although several different perspectives on organizations attempted to justify their particular claims to organizational theory, Simon's efficiency school clearly proved to be the most efficient. As a result, the institutional analysis of organizations, with its focus on purposes, goals, and values, was upstaged—that is, until the emergence of the "Great Society" and a resurgence of interest in the proper role of complex organizations in society. During this latest era, business has been subjected once again to fundamental questions about the means it employs and the ends it seeks to achieve. Some have argued that the breadth and depth of this questioning about the proper role of business in society have been unprecedented. But modern business leaders have not had much experience with institutional issues, and the efficiency academics have been of little help.

This is the situation that the members of the tobacco Big Six found themselves in at the outbreak of the smoking-and-health controversy. Indeed, the legitimacy threat to the tobacco industry emerged a full decade and a half ahead of the eruption of public interest in corporations at the beginning of the Vietnam era of social ferment in the United States. It was tempting, therefore, to use the occasion of our investigation to reassert the institutional approach to understanding the behavior of organizations. But we have attempted to avoid confining our analysis to the relationships that developed over time between our sample population of firms and elements of the threatening institutional environment. Rather, we maintain that the study of market structure and dynamics is essential to understanding the behavior of organizations under conditions of institutional threat. Indeed, we maintain that these distinctions in organizational contexts have been largely artificial and that, for the most part, our quarter-century account of the tobacco industry reveals that they have been quite interdependent.

We take the position, therefore, that the fate of any business is inextricably tied to the context in which the firm operates. To function effectively, a business must not only be *efficient* in relation to its competitors in the market environment or to rivals for its operating domain; it must also be *legitimate*, in the sense that its products, services, and operations are valued by the broader institutional environment. No matter how efficiently a firm converts inputs into outputs, it is not likely to survive if either the means it employs or the ends it achieves are not valued by the society at large. By the same token, gross inefficiencies can threaten the existence of an organization whose purpose is viewed by society as highly legitimate.

To begin our investigation of strategic organizational adaptation, we will review the major developments that occurred within the market and the institutional environments surrounding the Big Six during our quarter-century (1950–1975) study period. Later in this chapter, we will provide a brief introductory sketch of the adaptive strategies employed by the Big Six to cope with the following environmental events and trends. Chapters 3−6 will chronicle the interactions of these organizational behaviors and environmental events as the process of mutual adaptation unfolded.

THE MARKET ENVIRONMENT:
EARLY DEVELOPMENT AND PRESENT STRUCTURE

Tobacco production in colonial American originated to satisfy foreign demand, but by the end of the nineteenth century, the United States's domestic market had become the largest consumer of its own tobacco products. Small, independent manufacturers served as the primary sources of tobacco products until James B. Duke assembled what became known as the "Tobacco Trust" during the last two decades of the nineteenth century. The Tobacco Trust was made possible when Duke secured the exclusive rights to a newly developed cigarette machine that halved production costs and permitted greatly expanded operations.[1]

The "Trust Bust." The Trust captured an estimated 85 to 95 percent share of the domestic market until it was "busted" in 1911 for being in violation of the Sherman Antitrust Act as a monopoly in restraint of trade. The breakup of the Trust resulted in the formation of sixteen small tobacco-producing firms. From these sixteen emerged most of the current Big Six, which dominated the domestic market during the quarter century from 1950 to 1975, the focus of this book. Each of the Six emerged on the strength of a single, dominant cigarette brand.

The Structure of Competition. In 1913, the R.J. Reynolds Tobacco Company introduced its first domestic cigarette, Camel, a non-filter-tip brand, which remains on the market today. It promptly captured 35 percent of the domestic market. Liggett & Myers and the American Tobacco Company quickly followed by introducing the Chesterfield and Lucky Strike cigarette brands, respectively. By 1925, these three brands accounted for 82 percent of the domestic market. Lorillard's Old Gold, the other major brand, never achieved the popularity of the other three.

During the Depression, two new competitors successfully entered the market. Although hundreds of companies were trying to break into the domestic cigarette market, only Brown & Williamson, a subsidiary of British-American Tobacco Company, and Philip Morris, a small independent producer, were successful. They completed what is now generally known as the Big Six in the U.S. tobacco industry. Brown & Williamson entered in 1929 with an innovative, redeemable-coupon marketing strategy. They followed this early success with the introduction of the first filter-tip brand, Viceroy, and one of the first mentholated cigarettes, Kool.

Philip Morris, the last of the Big Six to achieve market prominence, introduced its Philip Morris brand in 1932 at 15¢ per pack—3¢ above the popular price. One cent was earmarked for advertising and two cents were used to generate wholesaler and retailer interest.Since dealer profit margins had previously been maintained at rock-bottom levels, the added incentive provided by this innovative policy had a favorable effect on distribution and sales of Philip Morris cigarettes.

By 1975, these six companies—R.J. Reynolds, Liggett & Myers, American, Lorillard, Brown & Williamson, and Philip Morris—accounted for 99.8 percent of U.S. tobacco sales (Maxwell, 1975) and were unchallenged by other competitors in the domestic market.

Price competition among the six tobacco firms has not generally occurred (Nicholls, 1951; Telser, 1962); instead, intraindustry rivalry has centered around advertising and product innovation. After 1920, price competition gave way to a system of "price leadership" in the U.S. tobacco industry, with Reynolds and American generally considered the price leaders. Challenges in 1956 by Liggett & Myers and again in 1965 by Lorillard were unsuccessful. At the end of 1975, Reynolds led the industry with 32.1 percent of the domestic market, followed by Philip Morris with 23.6 percent, Brown and Williamson with 16.9 percent, and American Brands with 15.0 pecent. Lorillard, a wholly owned subsidiary of Loew's Theatres since November 1968, claimed 7.9 percent of the domestic market, and Liggett was last with 4.2 percent (Maxwell, 1975).

The domestic cigarette market has been characterized by relatively high barriers to both entry of new competitors and the exit of traditional industry rivals (Porter, 1980; Porter and Salter, 1979). In terms of entry barriers, competition with the Big Six would entail not only an enormous capital outlay for production capacity, but also a heavy commitment to advertising and other promotional activities in order to penetrate the market for branded cigarette products that are already established. Similarly, exit from the industry is not easily accomplished in the short term. Huge amounts of capital are tied up in cigarette-production facilities that cannot be adapted to other products or industries. Therefore, exit can be predicted to be slow, even for firms deciding to withdraw from the field. To compound the short-term exit barriers, U.S. antitrust law generally enjoins the sale of domestic production capacity from one domestic competitor to another because of the high degree of industry concentration.

For all the reasons above, the overall structure of the U.S. tobacco industry has remained a classical oligopoly. The Big Six link two competitive marketplaces: tobacco farmers and wholesalers on the one side, and retailers of finished tobacco products on the other. According to economic theory, an industry qualifies as an oligopoly if the share of market accounted for by the top four firms exceeds 80 percent of the total market (Adelman, 1951; Weiss, 1963).[2] This index, commonly referred to as the industry concentration ratio, has exceeded 80 percent throughout our 25-year (1950–1975) study period, starting from 87 percent in 1950, dropping to 81 percent during the turbulent interim years, and reaching 88 percent in 1975. The emergence of political forces in the institutional environment—*not* the articulation of economic forces in the market environment—has threatened the fundamental legitimacy of the tobacco industry. It has caused managerial uncertainty and strategic organizational adaptation among the Big Six.

Few other industries in American history have experienced the negative institutional environment that the tobacco industry has. Many federal agencies, health organizations, and lobbying groups have been organized expressly with the intent to diminish if not destroy the cigarette industry. Not only has this industry survived these grave environmental pressures, but it expanded at the rate of approximately 3 percent per year up until the mid-1970s (Howard Chase Enterprises, 1976).

A major purpose of this book is to record, interpret, and evaluate the strategic behaviors employed by the U.S. tobacco industry to cope with its unreceptive external environment. Consequently, we must identify the major contingencies in the institutional environment faced by the tobacco industry, their interactions with market forces, and the subsequent strategic responses of its member firms. But before we begin our story proper, we will describe the events and trends in the institutional environment surrounding the Big Six that precipitated strategic adaptation.

THE INSTITUTIONAL ENVIRONMENT AND THE LEGITIMACY THREAT

INSTITUTIONAL ENVIRONMENT TRENDS

The institutional environment of the Big Six can be described in terms of specific events and general trends with which member firms have had to cope. The major events associated with the legitimacy threat in the tobacco industry are depicted chronologically in Figure 2-1. The Sloan-Kettering release, the advent of the Surgeon General's Report, and the events leading to and concluding with the broadcast advertising ban are the most important. But in order to fully understand the impacts of these special events, it is necessary first to appreciate some of the more conventional trends also confronting planners.

Domestic Consumption. Certainly an important environmental trend has been the consumption behavior of tobacco users. Per capita and total consumption of cigarettes rose consistently in the United States from World War II until the "health-scare" publicity of the early 1950s. Beginning in 1953, the first two-year decline in cigarette consumption since the Great Depression occurred (see Figure 2-2).

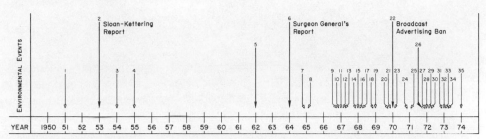

FIGURE 2-1 Key Events in the Institutional Environment of the U.S. Tobacco Industry, 1950–1974.

1. 1951 Excise tax increase (federal); excess profits tax levied.
2. 1953 Sloan-Kettering Report linking smoking to cancer.
3. 1954 *Reader's Digest* article relating smoking to cancer.
4. 1955 First FTC advertising guidelines imposed.
5. 1962 Surgeon General's committee formed to study smoking and health.
6. 1964 Surgeon General's Report.
7. 1965 FTC Advertising Code passed (required package warning label).
8. 1965 National Clearinghouse on Smoking and Health established.
9. 1967 FTC initiated tar and nicotine studies.
10. 1967 FTC began reporting (by law) to Congress on effectiveness of cigarette advertising.
11. 1967 Antismoking television ads began.
12. 1967 The equal-time ruling was made (equal antismoking advertising time required on broadcast media).
13. 1967 First World Conference on Smoking and Health held.
14. 1968 FTC first recommended ban of cigarette advertising on broadcast media.
15. 1968 A major antismoking-broadcast media campaign was launched.
16. 1968 ASH, the antismoking organization, was launched.
17. 1968 Extreme pressure was exerted on the broadcast media to air antismoking advertisements (WNBC was threatened with license revocation).
18. 1969 The "Fairness Doctrine" was upheld by the Supreme Court.
19. 1969 California banned television advertising of cigarettes.
20. 1970 Major airlines begin to institute no-smoking sections on planes.

21. 1970 Cigarette package warning labels were required to be stated more unequivocally.
22. 1970 Legislation passed banning cigarette advertising from all broadcast media (radio and television).
23. 1970 Fourteen states raised cigarette taxes.
24. 1971 A bill was proposed in Congress to eliminate all federal subsidies to tobacco growers.
25. 1971 The ICC banned smoking in all interstate buses except for the last five rows.
26. 1972 The constitutionality of the television and radio advertising ban was upheld by the Supreme Court.
27. 1972 The Second Surgeon General's Report established that low-tar cigarettes are not as dangerous to health and that breathing other people's smoke is dangerous to the nonsmoker's health.
28. 1972 Health warnings were made mandatory in all cigarette advertising.
29. 1972 A federal tax increase on tobacco was defeated.
30. 1972 All airlines volunteered to establish no-smoking sections.
31. 1973 The Little Cigar Act was passed.
32. 1973 Arizona became the first state to pass a law banning smoking in public buildings.
33. 1973 The CAB issued a regulation requiring separate smoking/nonsmoking sections on all commercial airlines.
34. 1973 A bill to ban all cigarettes over 21 mg tar was introduced into Congress.
35. 1974 Twenty-seven states had passed laws relating to nonsmoker's rights.

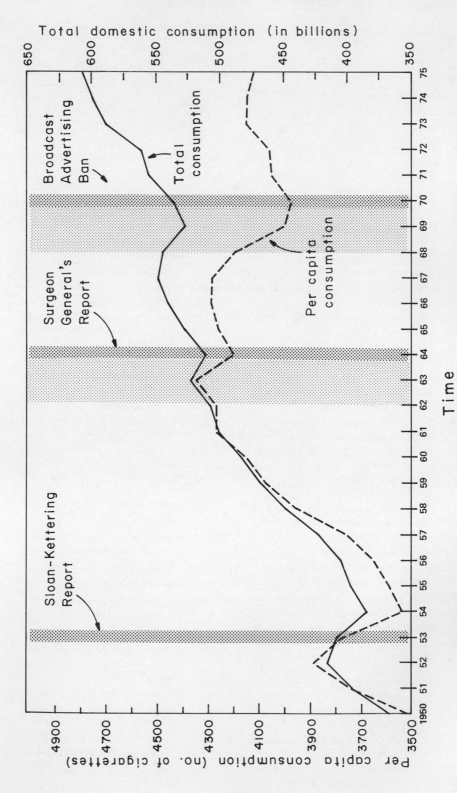

FIGURE 2-2 Domestic Cigarette-Consumption Patterns, 1950–1975. Source: Commodity Economics Division, Economic Research Service, U.S. Department of Agriculture

By 1955, however, consumption patterns had increased again and continued to grow until the release of the Surgeon General's Report in 1964. Thereafter, per capita cigarette consumption first declined, then leveled off for the remainder of the study period, while the increasing growth in the young-adult smoking population in the United States continued to push total domestic consumption upward. Although population growth has continually increased aggregate sales, the proportion of the population in each major age group who smoke has declined since 1964 (Miller, 1974a). U.S. cigarette consumption rates have been significantly lower than those forecasted by the industry in years when antismoking events were prevalent (Miller, 1979). Furthermore, Public Health Service and American Cancer Society surveys have indicated that almost nine out of ten smokers have made at least one serious attempt to give up the habit. Finally, the steadily decreasing birthrate in the United States has already had some effect in reducing the slope of the total consumption curve; this trend can be expected to continue. In short, cigarette consumers seem to have become more and more aware of and concerned about the health consequences of smoking; they are consistently becoming a smaller percentage of a general population that is growing at a slower rate.

Taxation. U.S. tobacco products are subject to taxation at the federal, state, and municipal/county levels. The persistent trend—which began long before the present study period—has been for higher and higher cigarette taxes.

The tobacco industry has been the subject of federal taxation since the Civil War. And whereas most consumer goods were relieved of the burdensome federal excise tax at the end of World War II, the federal tobacco tax has been maintained to the present. It has remained at 8¢ per pack over the past twenty-five years.

Iowa became the first state to levy a tax on cigarettes in 1921. Since then, all fifty states have levied cigarette taxes, which currently range from 2¢ to 21¢ per pack and are projected to increase in the near future. In addition, by 1975, over 365 municipalities had levied taxes on cigarettes, ranging from 1¢ to 10¢ per pack. So heavy has been taxation that most of the annual variation in deflated retail cigarette prices can be accounted for by tax increases (Miller, 1972).

Without taxes, a pack of cigarettes in 1975 would have retailed for approximately 21¢. With taxes, the price of a pack of cigarettes in 1975 ranged from 36.6¢ in North Carolina to 58.4¢ in Connecticut. In fact, tax revenues from cigarettes—which by 1975 accounted for approximately $5.7 billion annually—are *five times* the income from tobacco farm sales (Tobacco Tax Council, 1976). Because of widespread industry resentment toward this unusually high tax burden, various tobacco-related groups—from growers to vendors—have together mounted a counteroffensive.

Farm Production Allotments and Intraindustry Relationships. Tobacco growers have long been subjected to federally imposed production quotas: first, on the basis of farm acreage allotments; later, on the basis of tobacco leaf poundage. In any given year, only a certain number of specified acres can be under cultivation.

These federal allotments have placed an upper limit on tobacco output, thereby protecting growers from the price instability that is characteristic of unregulated farm products. Indeed, one of the important effects of governmentally imposed acreage and production quotas has been to make tobacco one of the highest-yield products in the U.S. economy in terms of dollar volume per acre (as shown in Figure 2-3).

From 1947 to 1972, the federal allotments were frequently cut, but since 1972, they have been increased substantially (Miller, 1973). Tobacco growers and manufacturers have always supported the acreage allotment system, and a relatively stable, reciprocal relationship has existed between the U.S. Department of Agriculture (USDA) and the tobacco industry. When Senator Brooke of Massachusetts introduced legislation to terminate federal subsidies to tobacco growers and thus disrupt the friendly relations among growers and between growers and the USDA, the measure was soundly defeated.

Relations between tobacco firms and their suppliers (growers and warehousers) and outlets (wholesalers and retailers) have likewise enjoyed a long history of relative stability, especially since World War II. Strikes and boycotts are virtually unheard of in this industry, and these groups have collaborated in responding to the larger institutional environment.

EMERGENCE AND EVOLUTION OF THE SMOKING-AND-HEALTH CONTROVERSY

By far the most important series of events in the modern life of the Big Six has been the emergence and evolution of the smoking-and-health controversy. This controversy has brought corporate policy and business policy into direct and intense conflict. Public objections to the smoking habit date back to the introduction of smoking materials in Europe during the sixteenth and seventeenth centuries; but it was not until the widespread publication of the results of scientific research in the early 1950s, linking smoking to health disorders in the United States and Great Britain, that pressure began to mount in the institutional environment. The threat to the legitimacy of the tobacco industry continually intensified over the next two decades. Eventually, the issue came to the attention of Congress and to the agendas of several important regulatory institutions. In the sections that follow, we chronicle the development of this threat to legitimacy through the succession of events that took place in the tobacco business's institutional environment.

Smoking-and-Health Publicity.   The first scientific article linking smoking to health dates back to 1906. And a small number of journal articles appeared almost annually for the 20-year period after 1930, as shown in Figure 2-4; but the public in general and the Big Six in particular seemed unconcerned about the issues raised in these scholarly publications.

FARM VALUE PER ACRE
FOR SELECTED CROPS, 1978

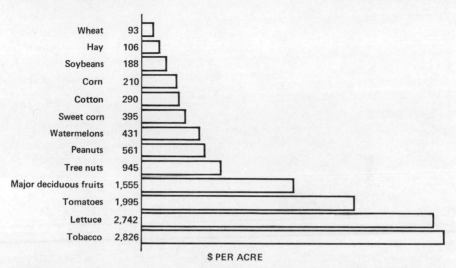

FIGURE 2-3 Farm Value per Acre for Selected Crops, 1978. Source: U.S. Department of Agriculture, *Tobacco Situation*, TS-169, September 1979, p. 54

The first time these issues were taken seriously was in 1950, when four retrospective studies were published on the smoking habits of lung-cancer patients. Medical authorities began to look more seriously at the possible dangers of smoking. Then in 1953, when investigators at what is now the Sloan-Kettering Institute announced that they had induced cancer in mice by painting their backs with "tars" from cigarette smoke, the tobacco industry acknowledged the smoking-and-health threat and launched a variety of adaptive strategies to counter it. By July 1954, when a lead article in *Reader's Digest* (Miller and Monahan, 1954) ensured general exposure to the smoking-and-health issue, well over one hundred scientific and popular magazine articles had been published (see Figure 2-4). The most immediate impact of the Sloan-Kettering release and related antismoking publicity was a sharp decline in both total and per capita cigarette consumption in the United States (see Figure 2-2). But, as we have already mentioned, the decline was short-lived; by 1955, cigarette consumption was again rising. This turnabout stimulated the first congressional hearings on smoking and health, in 1957. In 1962, the U.S. Surgeon General announced the creation of an Advisory Committee on Smoking and Health to review the evidence pertaining to the controversy.

Formation of the Surgeon General's Advisory Committee. The circumstances surrounding the formation of the Surgeon General's Advisory Committee on Smoking and Health warrant particular attention. During the late 1950s, the

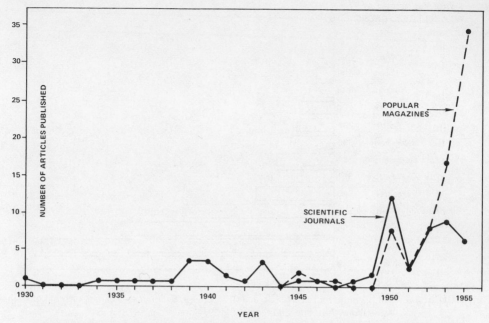

FIGURE 2-4 Number of Articles Published Connecting Smoking to Health Problems. Sources: *Reader's Guide,* 1945–55; U.S. Department of Health, Education and Welfare, *Report to the Surgeon General,* 1971

antismoking forces lacked money, a large, organized constituency, and momentum. Congress, which was heavily influenced by the tobacco lobby, had been sitting on a proposal to establish a presidential commission on tobacco and health. "Had it not been for the efforts of an enterprising reporter, it might have been interred forever in the legislative graveyard" (Fritschler, 1975:40).

That reporter, at one of President John F. Kennedy's major televised news conferences, asked Kennedy what he intended to do about the question of smoking and health. Although he had earned a reputation for skillfully handling press-conference questions, President Kennedy was caught off guard and embarrassed by this one. His response came awkwardly:

> *The—that matter is sensitive enough and the stock market is in sufficient difficulty without my giving you an answer which is not based on complete information, which I don't have, and therefore perhaps we could—I'd be glad to respond to that question in more detail next week. . . .*[3]

Immediately after the news conference, President Kennedy asked Surgeon General Luther Terry to report on what the U.S. Public Health Service had been doing in the field of smoking and health. Terry announced that he would establish a high-level advisory committee to study the evidence concerning the effect of smoking on health. Both the appointment of the committee and the unusual attempts Terry made to ensure that it would be an important one gave the health-warning issue the momentum it needed to receive serious consideration as national policy.

Terry began to create a "stage presence" for his commission by the method he chose to select its members. He stated publicly that the group was to include scientific, professional people concerned with all aspects of smoking and health. He eliminated from consideration all potential candidates who had made public statements on the smoking-and-health controversy. Indeed, the person selected to serve as the committee's executive director was sacked shortly after his appointment because he suggested publicly that tobacco was a health hazard (Neuberger, 1963). The committee was composed of the most distinguished members of their professions. There were three cigarette smokers in the group and two who smoked pipes and cigars on occasion. As Fritschler (1975:44) observed, "The selection process underscores the great pains to which the Surgeon General went to make certain that the report of the committee would not be attacked on the grounds that the membership was stacked against any particular interest."

Terry heightened the suspense created by the committee by taking extraordinary precautions against "leaks." Transcripts of committee meetings were not to be released to the public. The effects of this unusual degree of secrecy were, according to Fritschler, ". . . so out of character for the Public Health Service that tensions were exaggerated for those who already entertained substantial fears about the content of the committee's report. . . . the secrecy [also] . . . provided some suspense, and by the time the report was ready to be released, all the major news agencies of the nation focused their attention on the Advisory Committee. . . . Virtually none of the speculation gave any comfort to those whose fortunes were dependent upon the sale of tobacco and tobacco products" (1975:46–47).

The Surgeon General's Report. The report of the committee—known generally as "The Surgeon General's Report"—was released in January 1964. Its two most important conclusions were:

> *Cigarette smoking is a health hazard of sufficient importance in the United States to warrant immediate action.*

> *Cigarette smoking is causally related to lung cancer in men; the magnitude of the effects of cigarette smoking far outweighs other factors. The data for women, although less extensive, point in the same direction. [Public Health Service, 1976]*

"The report produced shock waves," according to the American Cancer Society (1976). "There was an immediate public reaction, and a sharp, albeit short-lived, drop in cigarette sales.'' In addition, the momentous formation of the Surgeon General's Advisory Committee and the negative findings of its final report created an unfavorable climate for investment in the threatened tobacco industry. The initial shock to the industry during this time resulted in sharp declines, relative to the general U.S. industry trends, in the stock prices of the four independent tobacco companies (see Figure 2-5). These declines reflected investor uncertainty about the future prospects for the beseiged industry.

The impact of this event on the Big Six is revealed in a statement that appeared in Lorillard's 1964 annual report:

The year 1964 was perhaps the most disconcerting in P. Lorillard Company's 205 year history. Starting with the Report of the Advisory Committee to the Surgeon General of the United States on Smoking and Health in January, it was a period marked by consumer confusion, Congressional and

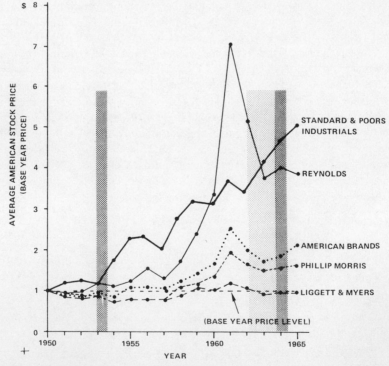

FIGURE 2-5   Average Common-Stock Prices for the Tobacco Independents, 1950–1965. *NOTE:* The actual average prices in 1950 were: RJR, $11.2; PM, $4.4; LM, $40.7; and AB, $17.4. The prices reported in this figure have been standardized using 1950 as the base year and dividing the prices for each year thereafter by the 1950 base-year price. Actual prices have been adjusted for stock splits. Source: *Moody's*.

Government hearings, industry-imposed cigarette advertising restrictions and anti-cigarette campaigns. Cigarette sales reacted sharply with the greatest impact coming within the first six months.

The report also served to stimulate a flurry of governmental regulatory actions, legislation, and research. Almost immediately, congressional legislation was introduced and more hearings were called. The Public Health Service, Veterans Administration, and Department of Defense discontinued free distribution of cigarettes in their hospitals. The Federal Trade Commission (FTC) and the Federal Communications Commission (FCC) began hearings prior to issuing trade regulations on the sale and advertising of cigarettes. The American Cancer Society, American Medical Association, several university medical centers, and other federal agencies initiated or intensified scientific research on the health implications of tobacco use. By June 1974, thirteen federal actions pertaining to smoking and health had been passed (Miller, 1974b). What had once been a fairly benign environment and an unquestionably lucrative domain had now become turbulent, interconnected, and complex. The net result was a fundamental threat to the legitimacy of a major U.S. business.

Federal Trade Commission (FTC) Regulations. The first FTC guidelines, proposed in 1955, prohibited representations in cigarette advertising or labeling that referred to the presence or absence of any positive physical effects from tobacco use. But through the late 1950s and early 1960s, little was done to police cigarette advertising.

Following the report of the Surgeon General's Committee in 1964, however, the FTC issued a press release saying that "smoking is a health hazard of sufficient importance in the United States to warrant remedial action" (FTC, news release, January 11, 1964). The remedial action took the form of new aggressive rulings.

In 1965, for example, the Trade Regulation Rules on Cigarette Labeling and Advertising became effective, requiring that a health warning be placed on all cigarette packages, that no cigarette advertisements be directed at youth (under 25), that no advertising be done in schools and colleges, that no prominent athletes or "stars" be used to endorse cigarette brands, that no strenuous activity be portrayed in ads, and that no filter or cigarette product claim any health benefits. By 1967, industrywide testing of tar and nicotine levels in cigarettes had begun, and antismoking annual reports and legislative recommendations were being routinely submitted to Congress by the FTC.

Application of the "Fairness Doctrine." By 1967, the Federal Communications Commission (FCC) had unexpectedly and provocatively entered the smoking-and-health controversy. It did so by the unprecedented application of the so-called "Fairness Doctrine" in broadcasting to the advertisement of cigarettes on television and radio.

Among other things, the Fairness Doctrine obliged broadcasters to give both notice and equal broadcasting time to those exposed to personal attack on the public airwaves. It was created during the time of the Hoover administration to ensure that broadcasters would not abuse their public trust by presenting only one viewpoint. The doctrine had traditionally been applied to protect the "honesty, character, integrity, or like personal qualities of a person or group" during the presentation over the broadcast media of views on a controversial issue of public importance. The FCC's application of the Fairness Doctrine to the radio and television advertising of cigarette products, however, was unprecedented in the history of consumer products in the United States. Although the doctrine had never been applied to a consumer product, it was upheld by the U.S. Supreme Court when its constitutionality was challenged in 1969 by the national broadcasters, who stood to lose valuable advertising time to free antismoking commercials.

Broadcasters were now required by law to allocate a "significant amount" of free time to antismoking messages. For the antismoking forces, who could now take their message to the public free, it was a great victory. In 1969, the FTC estimated that a viewer was exposed to one antismoking commercial for every 4.4 cigarette advertisements (FTC, *Report to Congress*, 1969). For the Big Six, the precipitous decline in per capita cigarette consumption (Figure 2-2) that began in 1967 with the initiation of the Fairness Doctrine meant that the FCC's entry into the controversy constituted a major and immediate threat to the legitimacy of their industry. The more the Big Six advertised their cigarette products to counter this trend, the more free time broadcasters allocated to the antismoking forces.

The Broadcast-Advertising Ban.   After pressing for two years to have all cigarette advertising banned from the broadcast media, the FTC finally persuaded Congress to pass the Public Health Cigarette Smoking Act in 1970. This act banned cigarette advertising from radio and television and required a more forceful and unequivocal warning label on cigarette packages. Challenged by the tobacco industry, the act was upheld by the Supreme Court in 1972. As a result of the 1970 legislation, the tobacco industry volunteered to disclose tar and nicotine levels in all advertisements and agreed to publish health warnings in all advertisements.

Other Legislative Activities.   The 1973 Little Cigar Act, proposed by the FTC after R.J. Reynolds began advertising Winchester Little Cigars on nationwide television in 1970, required that little cigars be subjected to the same advertising stipulations as cigarettes. Other federal bills pending in Congress at the end of our study period included such provisions as these:

1 Establishing a maximum acceptable level of tar, nicotine, and other incriminating agents in cigarette smoke;

2 Levying an additional tax on cigarettes ($2.50 per thousand) to support heart-and-lung disease research;

3 Levying a progressive tax on cigarettes based on their tar and nicotine content, with receipts earmarked for health research;

4 Strengthening the warning statement to include specific mention of coronary heart disease, chronic bronchitis, pulmonary emphysema, and other diseases as smoking health hazards;

5 Prohibiting smoking in any enclosed area in any federal facility and requiring separation of smokers from nonsmokers in other areas.

In addition to legislative activity, the FTC and other federal agencies have exerted direct regulatory influences in the environment of the tobacco industry. Annual reports concerning the status of research on smoking and health are required of the firms in the industry, for example, by the Secretary of Health, Education and Welfare. Likewise, the Big Six must file reports with the FTC regarding advertising practices and cigarette sales statistics. The FTC also monitors cigarette warning labeling, checks disclosure of tar and nicotine contents, and studies the effects of advertising themes, practices, and media on consumer behavior (e.g., Fishbein, 1977).

Ambient-Smoke Legislation. Although much research had been conducted on the effects of smoking on smokers' health, relatively little was known publicly about the effects on the health of the nonsmoker of breathing ambient cigarette smoke. However, in 1972 the Surgeon General issued a second report, which summarized studies since 1957 conducted on nonsmokers. The report concluded that atmosphere contaminated with tobacco smoke ". . . may, depending on the length of exposure, be sufficient to be harmful to the health of the exposed person" (Surgeon General's Report, 1972, p. 131).

Although this was not the first study to draw this conclusion, the 1972 report convinced forty-eight states to introduce 423 pieces of legislation regulating cigarette smoking and tobacco products in the first ten months of 1975 (FTC, 1976). Until 1970, legislation had dealt solely with product manufacture and sales; after that time, the legislative focus gradually shifted to consumer behavior.

The first federal regulations relating to ambient cigarette smoking were passed in March 1970. In response to a legal petition by Action on Smoking and Health, the Federal Aviation Administration took the first steps toward requiring separate smoking and nonsmoking sections on airplanes. In April 1971, United Airlines became the first to institute separate sections on its flights. Later that year, the Interstate Commerce Commission limited smoking to the last five rows on interstate buses. Smokers had been relegated to the back of the bus! In 1973, Arizona became the first state to pass a comprehensive law prohibiting smoking in elevators, theaters, libraries, museums, and art galleries, and on buses. By 1975, twenty-seven states had passed legislation designed to protect the rights of the nonsmoker (Action on Smoking and Health, 1976). Litigation by those forced to breathe ambient smoke in a work setting was becoming more common.

In 1980, Robert Miller, a leading tobacco economist at the U.S. Department of Agriculture, revealed the cumulative impact of the ambient smoking evidence in an address to tobacco producers and wholesalers:

> *Ten years ago you could smoke cigarettes, cigars, and pipes almost everywhere. But how times change! The 1972 issue of the U.S. Surgeon General's* Health Consequences of Smoking *reported a danger from passive smoking (involuntary smoking) which occurs from breathing in a smoke-filled room. The next year (1973) Arizona and Oregon enacted the first smoking prohibition laws. There are now 38 states that have laws prohibiting smoking in certain public places or segregating smokers from nonsmokers. Last year alone 8 bills were enacted in 7 states and the District of Columbia.*
>
> *. . . About 13 percent of the U.S. adult population resides in states classified with "heavy" restrictions and 44 percent in states with "less heavy" restrictions. Eighteen percent of the population resides in states with "more limited" restrictions and 25 percent in states with no restrictions. [1980; 4–5]*

SUMMARY

Three major events characterized the increasingly hostile institutional environment of the tobacco Big Six: the Sloan-Kettering release, the Surgeon General's first report, and the broadcast-media advertising controversy (beginning with the Fairness Doctrine and ending with the ban). These three major events were accompanied by a proliferation of other, minor environmental events that have been summarized in Figure 2-1.

It is important to appreciate the overall pattern of the occurrence of these events. They began in isolation. Not much followed the early Sloan-Kettering warning until the Surgeon General's Committee convened a decade later. The announcement of the formation of the Surgeon General's Committee alone, however, caused quite a stir in tobacco circles. Thereafter, significant events occurred in rapid succession, with government, nongovernment, and consumer-interest groups reinforcing one another in the antismoking campaign. All these events began to assume both a direction and a cumulative and reinforcing momentum.[4]

Four major epochs, as summarized in Figure 2-6, characterize the institutional environment's threat to the legitimacy of the tobacco industry. The pre-1950 epoch was of little or no threat. During the decades preceding the

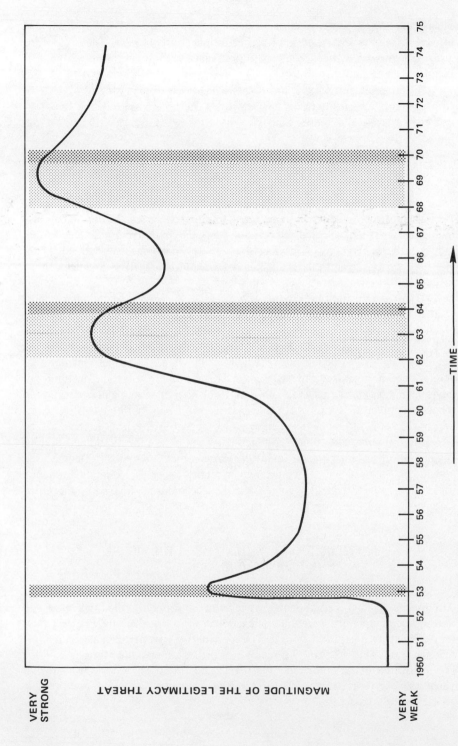

FIGURE 2-6 Magnitude of the Institutional Environment's Threat to the Legitimacy of the U.S. Tobacco Industry: A Quarter-Century Perspective.

Sloan-Kettering Report and related antismoking publicity, the industry enjoyed relative autonomy with respect to the institutional environment. The only major issue that brought tobacco companies in contact with government was that of taxation.

The period from 1953 to 1962 was characterized by early signals of "noises" from the institutional environment. During this period, the smoking-and-health issue was raised and the questioning of the legitimacy of the industry's basic business began.

The period from 1963 to 1968 was one of mounting threat, a trend that was crystalized by antismoking legislation and actual intervention by institutional forces into the internal affairs of the tobacco industry.

Finally, the time from 1968 to 1975 became the manifest period. Antismoking forces effectively coalesced to create very restrictive regulations, including two unprecedented interventions into the advertising practices of this industry: the application of the Fairness Doctrine, and the enforcement of an absolute ban on cigarette advertising in the public (i.e., radio and television) media.

Thus, the institutional environment after the Surgeon General's first report can be characterized as a "turbulent field" (Emery and Trist, 1965; Terreberry, 1968; Miles, 1980c). The Big Six had a very difficult time unilaterally dealing with the dynamic and interrelated elements in their institutional environment. In the early stages of the controversy, when events were isolated and institutional actors were unorganized, the Big Six were able to manage the institutional environment; but as these events and actors took on momentum and cohesion, the tobacco companies' attempts became inappropriate and ineffective. For example, having failed to repeal the Fairness Doctrine, tobacco firms were forced to retreat from the broadcast media altogether—even before the 1970 ban—simply because of the damage their industry sustained by compulsory, equal-time antismoking advertising. Having failed to immediately and directly influence initiatives of the antismoking forces, the tobacco industry devised a number of independent and joint adaptive strategies.

PATTERNS OF ADAPTATION AMONG THE BIG SIX:
AN INTRODUCTION

The forces in the institutional environment surrounding the U.S. tobacco industry created a very different context for the Big Six from the one to which they had been accustomed. In order to cope with the new performance situation, member firms had to shift the relative priorities among their goals, call for greater overall effort from their members, and invent or adopt new ways of behaving. The purpose of this section is to develop some important concepts for understanding the strategic behaviors of complex organizations and to provide an introduction to the patterns of adaptation that emerged as the Big Six attempted to cope with their changing environment.

OUR FOCUS: STRATEGIC ORGANIZATIONAL ADAPTATION

Organizational adaptation is defined as the process by which an organization manages itself or its environment in order to maintain or improve its performance, legitimacy, and, hence, its survival potential. This definition creates a necessarily broad net of possibilities that might be discovered in a comprehensive, long-term assessment of the process of organizational adaptation. The definition also places the emphasis on a focal organization or population of organizations, even though, as we shall see, organizational adaptation has two faces. It typically requires the mutual adaptation of two or more organizations—at the very least, a focal organization under investigation and another organization in its environment. We will not pass up the opportunity to look closely at the interactions linking both sides of the adaptation process; but our primary frame of reference will be the efforts of the Big Six to cope with an increasingly complex, turbulent, and unreceptive environment.

With this broad perspective, then, organizations may adapt by reacting to environmental changes or by complying with external mandates. They may adapt by forecasting or anticipating environmental events so as to either restructure to cope with them in advance or prevent or avoid their occurrence. Organizations may adapt by adding to, subtracting from, or even trading off threatening environments or environmental segments for ones more receptive to their needs, goals, strategies, resources, skills, competences, modes of operation, and outputs (including their by-products and wastes). Or organizations may attempt to adapt the environment to their goals and methods of operation or to restructure the patterns of interdependences that link them to elements of their environment.

Our investigation of strategic organizational adaptation among the tobacco Big Six was guided in particular by the following observation of William Starbuck:

> An adaptive system is both reactive and selectively active. It reacts to changes in and signals from its environment, and possesses a characteristic repertoire of response patterns. It also selects environmental settings to which it is capable of responding, and either learns new reaction patterns that match its environment's requirements, or undertakes to modify its environment's properties to bring them into line with its own capabilities. So to analyze such a system effectively, a researcher must strive to distinguish among and to comprehend individually the system's short-run, immediately programmed reactions, its flexibilities for learning new reaction patterns or

rigidities for preserving old ones, and its long-run strategies for selecting or
creating appropriate environmental settings. [1976:1102 –3]

By focusing on an industry population of firms under conditions of extreme
environmental press, we were able not only to understand the range of adaptive
strategies employed, but also to provide some insight into the relative effectiveness of both the choices and the timing of adaptive strategies among the Big Six.
By employing a variety of methodologies and data sources, we were able to
understand some important factors about why certain choices were made at
particular times by individual firms and about the process of organizational
learning that unfolded as each of them struggled to cope with an increasingly
uncertain and unreceptive environment.

But before we turn to our story, we must first provide an overview of the
general patterns of organizational adaptation selected by the tobacco Big Six.

PATTERNS OF STRATEGIC ADAPTATION: AN OVERVIEW

Three major patterns of strategic adaptation characterized the response of the Big
Six to the threat to their traditional business. These patterns consist of bundles of
related goals and strategies that were identified not only from the stated
intentions of senior executives and the observations of industry watchers at the
time of the smoking-and-health controversy, but also from the patterns that
emerged from that time forward in the strategic resource allocations, manifest
behaviors, and organizational states of the Big Six.[5] Each of these modes of
adaptation, in turn, could be characterized by its primary goal(s), its strategies,
its referent domain of organizational activity, its implications for relations among
rivals in the traditional industry, and its primary target. These patterns of
strategic response, along with their defining features, are summarized in Table
2-1.

Implicit in the purpose of most complex organizations are four ultimate
goals whose achievement is the primary responsibility of strategic managers.[6]
The first goal is the creation and preservation of organizational legitimacy: the
establishment and maintenance of the organization's right to perform a certain
function in society and of society's tolerance of the organization's discretion in
the choice of means for performing its function. The second goal involves the
maintenance and enhancement of organizational efficiency in the performance of
its function. Having chosen to operate in a particular domain, an organization
will do what it can to ensure its growth and prosperity relative to rivals who share
or seek to share the same domain. The final two goals, concern the creation of
new opportunities for organizational growth and security. Balancing the rates of
progress in achieving these three goals is perhaps the most basic responsibility of
executive leaders, for it is through this effort that they are able to achieve

TABLE 2-1 PATTERNS OF STRATEGIC ADAPTATION AMONG THE BIG SIX

Adaptive Modes	Goals	Strategies	Referent Domain	Primary Target	Relations Among Traditional Competitors
Domain Defense	Preservation of legitimacy and autonomy of traditional domain (LEGITIMACY)	Creation and control of vital information; Lobbying and coopting institutional gatekeepers	Traditional product/market	Agents in the institutional environment surrounding the traditional product/market	Cooperative
Domain Offense	Enhancement of economic performance in traditional domain (EFFICIENCY)	Product innovation; Market segmentation	Traditional product/market	Rivals for the traditional product/market	Competitive
Domain Creation	Creation of new performance opportunities; minimization of risk exposure (GROWTH & SECURITY)	Diversification; Overseas expansion	New product/markets	Rivals for the new product/markets	Independent

effective short-term performance, mobilize commitment from important external and internal constituencies, and enhance the survival potential of their enterprise.

Each domain in which an organization chooses or is obliged to perform may be conceptualized in terms of the services rendered, the population served, and the technology employed (Levine and White, 1961; Thompson, 1967). These domain choices or mandates, in turn, expose the organization to relevant market and institutional environments. The domains selected by the Big Six, and the balancing act imposed on their strategic managers, provide the basis for the mix of strategic behaviors that profile the responses of these companies to the legitimacy crisis.

Domain Defense. The most immediate response of the Big Six to the smoking-and-health controversy was one of domain defense. The primary goal of this response was to restore and preserve the legitimacy of the cigarette business in the traditional domain. The response to the threat was the formation of industrywide, joint political ventures, which employed two primary strategies: the creation and control of vital information about the health consequences of cigarette consumption, and the lobbying and cooptation of influential elements of the institutional environment. This response required a major departure from the traditional competitive relations among rivals in the tobacco domain, who began to coalesce around the issues posed by the legitimacy threat in an attempt to influence or overpower antismoking elements in the institutional environment.

Domain Offense. As a result of the impact of the smoking-and-health controversy on the contraction of product demand in the traditional domain, the Big Six also engaged in unprecedented competitive rivalry for market share. This response set off a new wave of performance efficiency, involving major redeployments of capital toward product innovation and market segmentation. Thus, the Big Six were able to partition their traditional domain into political and market arenas, and to simultaneously engage in collaborative domain-defense strategies and competitive domain-offense strategies. Moreover, the external threat to the traditional domain served as the primary stimulus to both responses. Finally, the two responses were mutually reinforcing. Successful domain defense created more opportunity for performance in the traditional marketplace, and the legitimacy threat spurred on competitive innovations that led to the development and market acceptance of cigarette products lower in allegedly harmful "tar" and nicotine content, thereby reducing some of the intensity of demands placed on the industry by antismoking forces.

But domain-defense and domain-offense strategies were not sufficient to permit the Big Six to continue to enjoy their traditional prosperity and growth. At best, the traditional industry was stagnating, and decline was a major prospect over the horizon. So the firms had to look elsewhere for places to employ excess cash, which could not be reinvested profitably in the domestic tobacco business, and to reduce their risk exposure to the threatened traditional domain.

Domain Creation. It was not long after the initial publicity of the smoking-and-health controversy, therefore, that the Big Six began casting about for opportunities to create new domains offering greater growth potential and less economic and political risk. Among the strategies all seized upon were overseas expansion of their tobacco business and domestic diversification into entirely new businesses. These strategies brought them into contact with new rivals and, barring the exception of certain international markets shared by domestic tobacco companies, were conducted relatively independently with respect to their historical competitors in the traditional domain. Moreover, it was their strategies of domain creation that most informed strategic managers in these tobacco companies about their strengths and weaknesses and those of the complex organizations for which they were responsible.

COMMENCEMENT

In summary, under "normal" circumstances, one might expect to find all four goals—legitimacy, efficiency, growth, and security—at least implicit within the purposes and orientations of complex organizations. But under those same conditions, it is most likely that the strategic emphasis on them will conform to a hierarchy, with greatest immediate emphasis on efficiency and least on legitimacy. The legitimacy threat to the tobacco industry upset this natural ordering of priorities. In so doing, it put the Big Six in a position of having to pursue *simultaneously* major strategies of domain defense, domain offense, and domain creation. Our quarter-century story will reveal not only these overall patterns of adaptation that characterized the domestic tobacco industry, but also differences in the nature and timing of strategic behaviors among the Big Six that have accounted for their relative successes and failures. It is to their story and our assessments of the patterns, the variations, and the interdependences among their strategies that we now turn.

FOOTNOTES

[1]For detailed accounts of the emergence of the Duke Trust, refer to Alfred D. Chandler, Jr., *The Visible Hand* (Cambridge, Mass.: Harvard University Press, 1977), Chap. 12, especially pp. 382–91; and Patrick G. Porter, "Origins of the American Tobacco Company," *Business History Review*, Spring 1969, pp. 59–76.

[2]Industry "concentration" is computed for a given year by dividing the total industry net revenues by the combined net revenues of the four largest member firms.

[3]*The New York Times*, May 24, 1962, p. 16.

[4]The specific nature of the legitimacy-threat curve in Figure 2-6 results from the interactions of the Big Six with elements and events in their institutional environment, a subject we will take up in Chapter 3 under the topic of "domain defense."

[5]To discipline our review of the patterns of strategic organizational adaptation, first, we attempted to distinguish between organizational goals and strategies. As Miles (1980c:366) has observed, organizational ineffectiveness may result from inappropriate goals as well as inappropriate strategies. Therefore, strategies were regarded as the means developed to achieve organizational goals or ends. Second, we tried where possible, to obtain evidence concerning three aspects of organizational strategy: (1) intended strategy, based on the stated intentions of senior executives and more importantly on the timing of major reallocations of organizational resources; (2) manifest strategy, based on observable changes in the actual behavior of an organization; and (3) realized strategy, based on the extent to which the organizational state (not the organizational goal) the strategy was designed to achieve is realized. Thus, in our efforts to understand the process of corporate diversification within members of the Big Six, we attempted to document answers to four basic questions. When (if at all) did the firm decide to diversify (intended or unintended strategy)? Is it diversifying (manifest strategic behavior)? And, is the firm diversified (realized or unrealized strategy)? After providing data to answer these questions about strategy, we attempted to answer the question: Did the realized strategy lead to the achievement of the goal(s) for which it was implemented? Generally, the first three questions are answered in the chapters devoted to each of the major strategies pursued by the Big Six (Chapters 3, 4, 5, and 6); the last question constitutes the central objective of Chapter 7.

[6]After Etzioni (1975:103), an organizational goal is ". . . a desired state of affairs which the organization attempts to realize."

II

THE STORY:
ADAPTATION
AMONG
THE BIG SIX

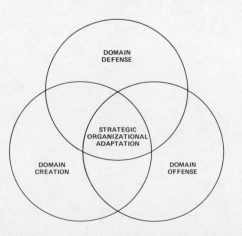

3

Domain Defense

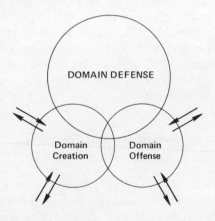

The smoking-and-health controversy threatened the legitimacy of one of the most profitable industries in U.S. economic history. It should not come as a surprise, therefore, that the most immediate response of the Big Six was one of *domain defense*. Tobacco manufacturers quickly partitioned their relations into competitive (market) and noncompetitive (political) spheres. The former were closely monitored by the Antitrust Division of the U.S. Justice Department, which prohibits collusion that might tend to reduce marketplace competition. But a number of other activities, particularly those involving relations among individual firms and elements of the institutional environment surrounding their industry, were organized into formal joint ventures that were cosponsored and financially underwritten by the Big Six.

FORMATION OF JOINT VENTURES

With the exception of the Tobacco Tax Council, which was set up in 1949 to lobby against increased taxes on tobacco products, collaborative ventures during the last quarter century in the tobacco industry emerged in direct response to specific smoking-and-health events. These ventures include the Council for Tobacco Research, which made huge grants to fund research on smoking and health; the Tobacco Institute, the primary lobbying arm of the Big Six; and the Cigarette Advertising Code, Inc., which tried to enforce the industry's attempt to police its own advertising practices during the years immediately preceding the broadcast-media ban on cigarette advertising.

Throughout the early 1950s, member firms initiated defensive strategies primarily on their own as each felt the need to do so. But by the mid-1950s, the smoking-and-health threat had become recognized as serious by all members of the Big Six. It was at that time that these corporations began to pool their resources and to carefully orchestrate their responses to this major event in their institutional environment.

One by one, strategies of individual firms that were oriented toward domain defense became institutionalized into formal, collaborative efforts as external events unfolded. Member firms began their own defense by shifting their in-house research efforts away from tobacco yield and manufacturing efficiency to the relation between smoking and health. In addition, they joined forces to award large grants to important gatekeepers in industry-relevant medical-research fields. Attempts by individual firms to rally their local constituencies to support the individual right to smoke gave way, as the Federal Trade Commission (FTC) entered the arena, to a concerted lobbying effort. This lobbying effort, which was orchestrated by the jointly sponsored Tobacco Institute, involved tobacco growers, warehousers, manufacturers, wholesalers, retailers, advertisers, and politicians from tobacco-growing states. Likewise, attempts by individual firms to restrain their advertising programs were superseded by a joint self-policing code desiged to preempt initiatives by the FTC, the Federal Communications Commission (FCC), and the Congress to restrict and ultimately ban cigarette advertising through the broadcast media.

Out of these individual and joint efforts emerged three primary strategies that were used by the Big Six to defend their threatened domain: (1) the creation and control of smoking-and-health information, (2) the lobbying and cooptation of gatekeepers in the institutional environment, and (3) the control and management of cigarette advertising. Although the creation of each joint venture was in direct response to or in anticipation of a particular issue or event in the smoking-and-health controversy, the Tobacco Institute emerged as the standard-bearer for all three strategies. These strategies of domain defense, and the tactics employed by the Big Six to implement them, are analyzed in the sections that follow. The chapter concludes with a discussion of the implications for other settings of what we have learned about the use by the Big Six of joint political ventures.

VITAL INFORMATION: CREATION AND CONTROL

The Big Six were not unaware of the scattered studies published between 1939 and 1950 linking cigarette smoking to health hazards. Consequently, to a limited extent prior to the 1953 Sloan-Kettering report, research was conducted within at least some of the companies on the physiology of smoking and the pharmacology of smoke, and their relationships to health (e.g., PM *Annual Report*, 1951; AB *Annual Report*, 1954). However, until the early 1950s, the great majority of expenditures on research by the Big Six had been devoted to developing new products, improving quality control of the cigarettes produced, and devising better methods of crop yield and cigarette manufacture. Health-related research was clearly of minor importance. Yet, whereas not one word was mentioned about the smoking-and-health controversy in the annual reports of the Big Six prior to the Sloan-Kettering release, full discussions, all designed to counter this external threat, appeared thereafter in these reports. But the industry's response involved far more than rhetoric. With the publicity devoted to the alleged association between cigarette smoking and health, particularly in regard to lung cancer and heart disease, the industry's traditional orientation toward research shifted dramatically. Focused efforts in the area of research on smoking and health were conducted at both firm and industry levels.

RESEARCH STRATEGIES OF INDIVIDUAL FIRMS

At the firm level, major capital expenditures for in-house research facilities were expanded and research sponsored by eminent scientists and medical-research institutions was funded. The traditional section featuring "tobacco yield and cigarette production research" in the Big Six annual reports was scrapped in 1953. In its place, beginning with 1954, all six firms published lengthy statements on the issue of smoking and health, and without exception, strong arguments were advanced to counter or minimize the conclusions of the antismoking forces. In fact, several of the firms attempted to use their annual reports to persuade their investors that the controversy was only temporary. In 1953, American Brands announced, for example:

> *Unwarranted attacks on tobacco products are as old as the industry itself. Today, after reviewing extensive research of many other professional groups, our Research Department, as it has consistently reported from the beginning, says that proof that cigarette smoking causes lung cancer is lacking. In fact the cause of this disease is still unknown. Accusations without proof in the past have not prevailed. Thus, it appears that this factor should be of diminishing significance.*

A year later, Philip Morris similarly sought to minimize investor concern about the smoking-and-health issue by releasing the following statement in its annual report:

> *At one time or another within the past 350 years practically every known disease of the human body has been ascribed to the use of tobacco. One by one these charges have been abandoned with the realization that they were not tenable.*

Despite this apparent nonchalance, strategic choices that altered the focus of tobacco research and the future of the industry were initiated. American Brands declared that the size of its research laboratory "devoted to the study of what makes up tobacco and tobacco smoke" would be doubled in 1954, and later that a research grant to the University of Virginia Medical College for studies on the physiological effects of smoking had been awarded in September 1954. By 1954, R.J. Reynolds was reporting a doubling of its research-laboratory capacity, adding new radioisotope equipment to make possible "tracer work" on cigarette smoke. In 1956, Philip Morris announced plans for the construction of a new research laboratory and disclosed an expansion of company grants to higher education to support research in "health, scientific, and agricultural fields." Moreover, these efforts by individual firms were being reinforced by similar, concerted research activities at the industry level.

CREATION OF THE TOBACCO RESEARCH COUNCIL

The Tobacco Industry Research Committee, later renamed the Council for Tobacco Research — USA, was created by a coalition of tobacco interests in January of the year following the Sloan-Kettering Report. The sponsorship and public goals of this joint venture were described in 1954 as follows:

> *The Tobacco Industry Research Committee, supported by your Company and representatives of leaf growers, warehousemen, cooperatives, dealers, and other manufacturers in the industry, is now a well-organized, functioning group with a Scientific Advisory Board of ten eminent scientists. These scientists are leaders in the fields of pharmacology, physiology, pathology, surgery, statistics, and related specialties. The Committee, on the recommendations of this Board, is already making grants for research projects as part of a broad, comprehensive plan of investigating tobacco, tobacco smoke, and the effects of smoking on health. The Committee has increased to $1,000,000 its fund for such independent scientific research. [American Brands, Inc., Annual Report, 1954]*

During the decade separating the Sloan-Kettering and Surgeon General's reports (1954 — 1964), the Tobacco Research Committee awarded grants in excess of $7 million to some 230 scientists in more than 100 hospitals, universities, and research institutions around the country—individuals and organizations that might otherwise have been seeking research funds or working on the payrolls of government regulators and nonprofit antismoking groups.

This first wave of reorientation in research strategy among the Big Six began precisely at the time of the Sloan-Kettering release in 1953. The dramatic turnaround in research orientation, the emergence of anti-antismoking rhetoric, the expansion of in-house research facilities and independently funded research on smoking and health, and the creation of the jointly sponsored Tobacco Research Council to pool, integrate, and expand these initiatives leave little doubt that the precipitating factor to this strategic reallocation of resources was the increase in smoking-and-health publicity. Traditional competitors in the tobacco industry had coalesced under a shared-fate condition created by forces outside their market domain. They were building a joint defense while developing valuable lead time on their adversaries by building both a substantial body of industry data on smoking and health and a network of interdependences with important gatekeepers in the scientific and medical communities. But this was only the first wave in the new research strategy of the Big Six, a wave that served as a precursor to a second, more intensified one that was initiated in 1964 with the release of the Surgeon General's Report on Smoking and Health.

The Surgeon General's Report marked what many industry observers would characterize as a primary, unequivocal, and direct threat to the legitimacy of the Big Six. The findings and implications it contained, identifying cigarette smoking as a major national health problem contributing to a host of preventable diseases, were decidely negative for the tobacco industry. The response of the Big Six was stepped-up sponsorship of the Tobacco Research Council and its research-grants activity, as well as separate joint funding by the Big Six of research studies of major gatekeepers and institutions in the medical and scientific communities.

As shown in Figure 3-1, financial support of the Tobacco Research Committee the year after the Surgeon General's Report almost doubled the total cumulative support that this joint venture had received during the previous ten years of its existence; by 1975, its cumulative funding had reached almost seven times the level it had achieved on the eve of the publicized announcement in 1962 of the formation of the Surgeon General's Advisory Committee.

But the Big Six did not rely totally on the research grants awarded by this formal joint venture. In addition, they pooled other resources to make special grants to particular institutions. For instance, in 1963, during the time the FTC was formulating its proposal to require health warning labels on all cigarette packages and advertisements, the Big Six awarded an unrestricted research grant of $10 million (more than its total previous funding to the Tobacco Research Council) to the American Medical Association (AMA). It was not surprising, therefore, according to Fritschler (1975), to find that the AMA was not active in its support of the FTC's initiative during the labeling-regulation hearings that took place early the next year. By 1975, Big Six grants to the AMA had climbed to a total of $18 million (Fritschler, 1975).

In 1971, Washington University Medical School in St. Louis also received

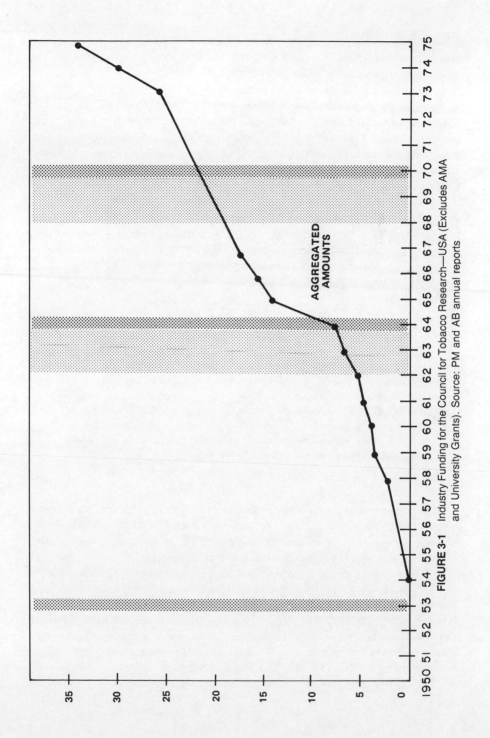

FIGURE 3-1 Industry Funding for the Council for Tobacco Research—USA (Excludes AMA and University Grants). Source: PM and AB annual reports

AGGREGATED AMOUNTS

a pooled research grant from the Big Six in the amount of $2 million for cancer research, and in 1972, Harvard was granted $2.8 million for cardiovascular and pulmonary research. In 1973, when UCLA was granted $1.7 million for research related to smoking and health, the industry reported that some $48 million had been provided for health research in "independent" laboratories. That same year, the Big Six announced that not only had they "funded more scientific research on smoking and health problems than any other source, government or private," but that "the tobacco industry is now providing more financial support for smoking and health research than all of the private health agencies *combined*" (RJR, *Annual Reports,* 1970, 1972).

What were the Big Six hoping to accomplish with their pooled investment in health research? For one thing, the industry was becoming the most knowledgeable source concerning the relation between smoking and health, which also made it the "first to know." It is generally recognized that the inability of regulatory agencies to acquire information about the activities of the corporations they regulate hampers the development and implementation of public policy:

> *Information control . . . is an important mechanism for both the exercise and the avoidance of influence. . . . The limited staff of commissions and their reliance on the regulated firms for viturally all the data permits the regulated organizations additional control over regulatory outcomes. It can be seen why regulation is so desirable. The regulatory commission buffers the organization from influence attempts since the commission ostensibly controls the organization's behavior; yet, because of the information and visibility advantages accruing to the regulated organization, it can actually retain much discretion and influence over regulatory results.* [Pfeffer and Salancik, 1978:105−6]

The reorientation and pooling of the research strategy of the Big Six does not appear to be an exception. The accumulation of research findings into a massive data bank represented an investment in an asset that would, first, strengthen the industry's position in the continuing debate on smoking and health, and second, provide valuable lead time for adapting to any new evidence in the controversy. Substantial industry commitment to research on the smoking-and-health question obliged the antismoking forces to do the same to legitimize their claims. The time it would take to come up with definitive answers to this complex question would be time gained by the industry to invent a set of contingency plans and to implement strategies for its long-term survival. In fact, the industry was so successful in becoming a major center of knowledge on this subject that its Research Council was eventually persuaded by government agencies to submit an annual report to the U.S. Department of Health, Education and Welfare on the current status of smoking-and-health findings from industry-sponsored research. Finally, both the pervasiveness and the timing of the research grants awarded to major medical centers and research organizations leave little doubt that resource dependences were being established that might in many subtle ways tend to coopt the interests of influential organizations in the medical and scientific communities.

LOBBYING AND COOPTING THE INSTITUTIONAL ENVIRONMENT[1]

The history of lobbying in the U.S. tobacco industry is rooted in a tradition of joint effort among manufacturing competitors and other industry participants. As early as 1915, the Tobacco Merchants Association was founded by member firms to collect and analyze information about state, federal, and special agency or department reports and activities of relevance to the tobacco industry. Since then, tobacco growers, warehousers, wholesalers, retailers, and manufacturers have often joined forces to anticipate or react to both potential and real environmental threats.

The industry created the Tobacco Tax Council in 1949 to deal with a common concern of members of the tobacco subsystem over continuing federal and increasing state taxation on cigarettes. The council was to report to sponsoring organizations on taxes relating to tobacco products. This organization is currently supported by virtually all the elements of the tobacco industry, and it has lobbied vigorously for a reduction in what it labels "discriminating taxes on American smokers."[2] Its existence also serves to remind politicians at all levels of how much their coffers depend on the tax revenues from the sale of tobacco products.

By the late 1950s, however, it had become evident to members of the tobacco subsystem that a far more serious threat to their well-being than taxation was being mounted by certain elements of the federal government in collaboration with other interest groups. By this time, the antismoking forces had begun to coalesce around the mounting evidence linking the tobacco habit to health disorders; and this group was getting enough press and media coverage to raise serious concerns not only in the investment community surrounding the tobacco industry but among smokers and nonsmokers alike. This attention escalated the smoking-and-health controversy from a "weak signal" to an issue of national prominence, and at least one major administrative agency, the Federal Trade Commission, had taken the ball and was about to make an end sweep with it.

This rather exponential increase in both activity and attention in the industry's institutional environment aroused the latent tobacco subsystem. One of the broadest and wealthiest political subsystems in U.S. history began to stir. In a political system pioneered by the spirit of free enterprise, one of the best indicators of the potential strength of this particular subsystem is financial dependence of many important constituencies on the industry under threat. Another indicator, in this specific case, is human habituation with the primary product of the threatened industry.

U.S. smokers spent an estimated $7 billion on cigarettes during 1963, the year in which the federal government began mounting a campaign to require health warning labels on cigarette packages and advertisements. That same year, more than 34,000 workers were employed in cigarette manufacturing plants, and over 600,000 families, dispersed among 26 states, were dependent upon tobacco farm crops as their primary source of income. By 1967, advertising outlays to promote tobacco products exceeded $300 million (Fritschler, 1975).

Although the Big Six and their lobbying arms have persistently bemoaned the state and municipal tax burdens borne by their cigarette brands, these payments have probably served them well by creating revenue dependences in legislatures that could potentially do harm to the industry. National, state, and municipal taxes on tobacco retail sales amounted to $3.25 billion per year by the mid-1960s, although this tax revenue dependence is not distributed evenly among the states. For instance, in 1975, ten states collected over $100 million each in cigarette tax revenues.

Tobacco farming has become an institution in the states in which the controversial leaf is grown. Tobacco allotments (parcels of land that carry a license from the U.S. Department of Agriculture to grow tobacco) have become an important part of a farmer's estate, one that the farmer can sell at retirement or pass on to heirs. The rent alone on one acre of tobacco allotment has reached $1,000 a year in some areas, compared to a rent of less than $100 annually for an acre on which soybeans are grown. This extremely high financial yield per acre, combined with the taxes raised from cigarette sales and manufacture in certain states, creates a potentially broad and powerful prosmoking constituency. Indeed, actions taken to outlaw cigarettes by elected officials in North Carolina or Virginia would be about as helpful in ensuring their reelection as outlawing cars, gambling, or sunshine would be to their political counterparts in Michigan, Nevada, and Florida. Members of Congress from tobacco states were in powerful positions in the early 1960s. "In the Senate, nearly one-fourth of the committees were chaired by men from the six tobacco states. Of the twenty-one committees in the House, tobacco state congressmen chaired seven" (Fritschler, 1975:26).

What the Big Six needed most as the battle over smoking and health heated up was an organization and a strategy for assembling and orchestrating the mutual interests of all these potential supporters. They first formed a joint lobbying venture to organize these interest groups. Using this joint political venture, they developed a concerted strategy aimed away from the smoking-and-health issue itself and, instead, at the process by which administrative agencies of the federal government were attempting to force it upon the tobacco industry.

CREATION OF THE TOBACCO INSTITUTE

The creation of the Tobacco Institute, Inc., in 1958 was the industry's response to the need for an organized lobbying effort. The Institute's activities are controlled by the chief executive officers of the sponsoring tobacco companies, who serve on its board of directors. It draws its revenues from participating tobacco companies in exact proportion to the share of the domestic cigarette market held by each in the preceding year. From the time of its creation, the Institute has borne the delegated responsibility for managing the industry's programs on public issues. Its primary activities have involved efforts to deny the cause—effect implications of the Surgeon General's Report and to mount an active campaign against any government legislation and administrative initiatives whose intent is to limit the discretion of the Big Six.

The Institute was headed initially by a former U.S. ambassador, who left to become the director of the Foreign Service Institute. He was succeeded by Earle G. Clements, former U.S. congressman, U.S. senator, and governor of Kentucky, who was close to the Johnson administration in the White House at the time. Indeed, Clement's daughter, Bess Abell, served as Lady Bird Johnson's social secretary (Fritschler, 1975).

The Tobacco Institute had worked for some time to develop the case for smoking by emphasizing the inconclusiveness of the research evidence, the contribution of tobacco products to the national economy, and the individual rights of smokers. But the initial efforts in 1963 of one federal administrative agency to restrict cigarette advertising and label cigarette products with health warnings created the need for an intensified and concerted lobbying effort directed at various instrumentalities of the federal government. The initiative taken by the Federal Trade Commission was the first of its kind for the tobacco industry. If it could not be checked or at least eased at its inception, the prospects for the Big Six were going to be bleak. The efforts of Lee Fritschler in his book, *Smoking and Politics* (1975), to recount and analyze the events that followed the FTC's first move provide a window into the lobbying strategy and the tactics used to achieve a limited victory by the tobacco interests.

THE TOBACCO LOBBY: STRATEGIES AND TACTICS

The Federal Trade Commission announced its proposal to restrict cigarette advertising and to mandate health-warning statements on all cigarette packages in 1963. In doing so, it was operating on its own initiative under the traditional principal of "delegated authority" as an administrative agency of Congress. Its commissioners believed that such a regulatory move was within the FTC's charter and that the mounting evidence linking smoking to ill health provided sufficient justification for it to proceed against the industry. At the time of their public announcement, the commissioners of the FTC informed interested groups, including the Big Six, that three days of open hearings on the proposed cigarette-and-advertising rule would be conducted in March of the following year.

Former Senator Clements was hired by the Big Six in 1964 to develop and direct, through the Tobacco Institute, the industry's lobbying strategy against the FTC's attempts to initiate and enforce its health-warning labeling rule. Several elements of the strategy developed by Clements warrant special attention.

Switch the Issues.   First, Clements directed his lobbying attack away from the smoking-and-health issues, focusing instead on the legitimacy of the FTC's rule-making authority. His tactic was one of having the labeling issue wrestled away from that regulatory agency to be taken up by a more sympathetic Congress. Thus, the earlier public-relations emphasis on the criticism of the correlational findings of medical researchers was played down. Instead, as Fritschler (1975:54) observed, "the strategy of the tobacco men was to question Federal Trade *authority to make policy* involving a cigarette health warning and thereby insure that the final policy decision would be made by Congress, not the FTC. Consequently, . . . the tobacco interests raised with skill and eloquence some of the most basic questions that have stalked the growth of agency policymaking powers."

Under Clements's leadership, the tobacco lobby based its complaints on the clear language of Article I of the Constitution, which states, "All legislative powers herein granted shall be vested in a Congress of the United States . . ." Accordingly, the tobacco lobbyists argued that a democratic form of government was threatened when nonelected bureaucrats in administrative agencies were permitted to exercise policy-making powers of the government that are constitutionally the responsibility of elected representatives of the people. They argued that those associated with the tobacco interests were being denied participation in policy making that was being proposed by the FTC. And they argued further that, when an administrative agency is permitted to set national policy, there are no electoral means to hold administrative decision makers responsible for their decisions.

In reality, however, a tradition of "delegated authority" had emerged between Congress and its administrative agencies. A number of factors help explain this tradition. As a practical matter, Congress had become overloaded with complex policy issues and had entrusted many of them to agencies. Moreover, career experts in the federal bureaucracy are often in a better position to devote continued attention to particular problems and to develop and evolve policies and standards for coping with them than are members of Congress. As Fritschler has noted, "In delegating policymaking powers to agencies, Congress relieves itself of the burden of detailed work and frees itself to devote time to issues of basic policy" (p. 55). Despite this general precedent, the question of limits on delegation can never be defined for all times with precision. The strategy of the prosmoking interests, therefore, was based in part on the claim that Congress had stopped short of providing authority to the FTC to issue regulations for the tobacco industry.

This major position was expressed in excerpts of a written communication from the Tobacco Institute to the FTC:

> . . . in terms of policy and discretion, whatever substantive regulation may be believed to be necessary in the area of smoking and health, Congress alone should enact it. . . .
>
> . . . We respectfully submit that in these Trade Regulation Rules the Commission is not exercising authority conferred upon it by Congress in the Federal Trade Commission Act. It is plainly legislating." [Fritschler, 1975:58]

This, then, was the primary lobbying strategy of the tobacco interests. By pressing hard on the delegated-authority issue, they hoped to rally important segments of public opinion against administrative regulatory agencies in general. Powerful industrial and commercial interests could also be expected to be sympathetic to the tobacco lobby's major argument. But just as important, by arguing the delegation issue, they hoped to gain the attention of Congress and have the FTC's effort taken up there, where it could be killed, or at least postponed.

Mobilize a Concerted Front. To accomplish this strategy, Clements had to organize a united front among all elements of the tobacco subsystem that, according to Fritschler (1975:4):

> . . . cuts across institutional lines and includes within it all groups and individuals who are making and influencing government decisions concern-

> *ing cigarettes and tobacco. . . . The tobacco subsystem included the paid*
> *representatives of tobacco growers, marketing organizations, and cigarette*
> *manufacturers; congressmen representing tobacco constituencies; the lead-*
> *ing members of four subcommittees in Congress . . . that handle tobacco*
> *legislation and related appropriations; and certain officials within the*
> *Department of Agriculture who were involved with the various tobacco*
> *programs of the department. This was a small group of people well known to*
> *each other and knowledgeable about all aspects of the tobacco industry and*
> *its relationship with the government.*

In addition, Clements sought to appeal for the sympathetic support, or at least nonopposition, of individual-freedom, pro-private-sector and anti-federal-regulation sentiments of the public at large and of other big businesses in particular. By focusing away from the substance of the smoking-and-health controversy and toward the general legitimacy of policy making by bureaucrats instead of elected representatives, he succeeded in maximizing the breadth and power of his prosmoking lobby while minimizing the opposition of marginally interested groups. As a result, antismoking lobbyist David Cohen characterized the contest between the cigarette lobby and the health lobby as being:

> *. . . similar to a match between the Green Bay Packers and a high school*
> *football team. The tobacco state congressmen had powerful reasons to*
> *reverse the Federal Trade Commission action, namely, their constituent's*
> *support. On the other hand, there were few if any "health" congressmen.*
> *Those members who did champion the health cause had no substantial*
> *constituent interest to back them up.* [Fritschler, 1975:129]

Next, Clements rightly sensed that the Big Six were going to have to give up something. The evidence accumulated by the health forces and the media attention it received had generated too much momentum to be dismissed or stonewalled. Therefore, with some difficulty but eventual success, Clements persuaded the Big Six to accept health-warning labels on cigarette packages in exchange for unfettered media advertising and a prohibition against states' developing their own health warnings.

Clements, relying on agreement among his constituencies, focused the attention on Congress, and in particular on the Senate Commerce Committee and the House Interstate and Foreign Commerce Committee that had FTC oversight responsibility. The House Committee was stacked with Southerners, one of the most influential of whom (Kornegay, D., North Carolina) later decided not to run for Congress and assumed, instead, the position of vice-president and general council of the Tobacco Institute (Fritschler, 1975). He later succeeded Clements as head of the Institute.

Finally, Clements was an old friend and political ally of Lyndon B. Johnson, then president of the United States. Indeed, Clements had once served as the executive director of the Senate Democratic Campaign Fund. According to Fritschler, Clements was therefore one of the few people who could keep President Johnson out of the controversy:

> *Mr. Johnson had a good, if not a better, record on consumer legislation than any president in memory. Yet he made no public attempt to support the Federal Trade Commission in its struggle on the Hill. He was uncharacteristically silent during the whole affair. . . . [1975:125]*

These were the elements of the Tobacco Institute's lobbying strategy. The tactics employed by the prosmoking lobby accounted for the fact that the strategy of the Big Six was not only successful but actually resulted in what many would describe as a "limited victory."

FTC HEARINGS AND CONGRESSIONAL OVERSIGHT

On March 16, 1964, the commissioners of the FTC began three days of hearings on the proposed cigarette-labeling and -advertising rule. Only one of the commissioners—MacIntyre, from North Carolina—opposed the rule.

The first witnesses to appear were in favor of the rule. Later came a representative of the Tobacco Institute, who was followed by still others who favored the rule. The second day included the trade interests; advertising and tobacco growers' associations testified. On the third day, congressional and gubernatorial elected officials from the tobacco states vigorously protested the proposal that directly threatened their constituents. They, too, hoped to get the issue transferred from the FTC to Congress.

The Big Six themselves chose to publicly ignore the FTC by not appearing at the hearings. Instead, an attorney named Austern was retained by the Tobacco Institute to represent manufacturers. He avoided the smoking-and-health controversy and focused on the illegality of the general rule-making authority that had been assumed by the FTC. The commissioners, as expected, responded that rule making was in their jurisdiction under the tradition of delegated authority from Congress.

The FTC's cigarette-labeling rule was to take effect nine months after the hearings. But within a month after the conclusion of the hearings, the Big Six created another joint venture, the Cigarette Advertising Code, Inc. The purpose of this association was to establish and maintain a self-policing advertising code. According to Fritschler:

> . . . creation of the voluntary code was intended to signify to Congress and the public that the industry was interested in regulating itself, and that the action of the Federal Trade Commission was an unnecessary obstacle to self-regulation. [1975:107]

To give clout to the Code, the Big Six hired former New Jersey Governor Robert B. Meyner as its administrator and empowered him to levy fines against violators up to $100,000. The Code prohibited advertising targeted at persons under 21 and cigarette-advertising health claims. The Code lasted six years, until the cigarette advertising ban on radio and television.

Also before the FTC's rule was to take effect, Congressman Oren Harris of Arkansas, then chairman of the House Interstate and Foreign Commerce Committee, requested that the FTC delay implementation of the rule until the next session of Congress had an opportunity to review it. "Harris' arguments," according to Fritschler (1975:109), "were the same as those made by Mr. Austern at the commission hearings." The FTC complied. The labeling issue was transferred from the FTC to its overseeing congressional committees, which were populated by senior elected officials representing the tobacco states.

Congress Steals the Ball and Redefines the Game.   Movement of the labeling controversy from the administrative agency that sponsored it to the mainstream of political Americana was a battle won by the tobacco industry and its allies; and they wasted little time in escalating a visible presence before and during the congressional committee hearings that they so carefully avoided during the FTC hearings.

The cigarette lobby now appeared in full force, with each witness rolling out a broad set of issues at stake: the inconclusiveness of the Surgeon General's Report; the importance to the national economy of unfettered competition; the proper role of Congress in national policy making as outlined in Article I of the Constitution; the contributions of tobacco to everything from employment and tax revenues to the nation's balance-of-payments situation. Scientists and professionals were marshaled by the Tobacco Institute into the hearing room to criticize the evidence linking smoking to health.

The support of "friends" of the tobacco industry also got into the act. The American Newspaper Publishers Association, the Advertising Federation of America, the Association of National Advertisers, the Radio Advertising Bureau, and the National Association of Broadcasters, all fearing loss of revenues from proposed cigarette-advertising restrictions, aligned themselves with the tobacco interests (Fritschler, 1975). The National Association of Broadcasters, an ally of the smoking lobby, entertained more than 400 of the 535 members of Congress at a reception, held at its annual convention in Washington, D.C., during the week of the hearings. Moreover, it has been estimated that at the time, more than one-third of those members of Congress owned major stockholdings in radio and television stations (Parker, 1965). Guiding all these activities was the Tobacco Institute's carefully orchestrated and skillfully played lobbying strategy.

The FTC and its loose confederation of health and special-interest groups were no match for the resources and unity that supported and guided the tobacco lobby. Indeed, the major difficulty that plagued the health groups throughout the congressional hearings was a lack of agreement about what they wanted Congress to do (Fritschler, 1975). All they could seem to agree on was that smoking was harmful to health and that the federal government should do something about it. Their inability to develop an action plan comparable to that of Clements's strategy resulted in a disunity that became evident as the health groups testified before the congressional committee.

For instance, the FTC argued that it was the most appropriate agency to enforce the labeling and advertising rules, whereas the Surgeon General argued that the Department of Health, Education and Welfare was best prepared for this task. The health groups were also in disagreement over the wording of proposed health-warning labels.

> Their failure to agree on a plan of action reflected their lack of political know-how and inability to organize a cohesive campaign. . . . These disputes were in sharp contrast to the ultra-smooth coordination and scenario employed by the cigarette interests. The case that the cigarette people made in support of their position was a good one. Their arguments were detailed, coherent, and generally persuasive. . . . The strategy of the cigarette interests was to play off various agencies of the bureaucracy against each other or against Congress to prevent the smoking and health controversy from expanding. [Fritschler, 1975:10]

But disunity was only one of the weaknesses that characterized the health lobby. They also had little or no political support from powerful constituencies, and their financial viability was either uncertain or contingent upon the sympathetic support of the Congress that wanted to wrestle the labeling issue away from them. The FTC, for instance, had virtually no support from the industries it regulated, all of which feared greater policy-making powers on the part of nonelected, career bureaucrats in federal administrative agencies. Moreover, the funding of both federal (e.g., Public Health Service) and nonprofit (e.g., American Cancer Society, American Heart Association, and so on) health groups has always been precarious and to some extent influenced by congressional appropriations and corporate-donation programs. Therefore, when the congressional contest was waged, the smoking forces simply overwhelmed the nonsmoking forces.

"The resulting congressional reprimand of the Federal Trade Commission," Fritschler (1975:119) said, "was unexpectedly severe in its intensity. . . ." The following excerpt from *Smoking and Politics* summarizes the battle that was waged in the congressional committee hearings, as well as the losses that were sustained by both sides:

"NO VICTORY FOR HEALTH"

Congress was not acting alone when it moved against the Federal Trade Commission. It was assisted by the skills, rhetorical and organizational, of the Tobacco Institute and the allies recruited by the Institute. The lobbying effort mounted by this group was brilliantly conceived; it indicated that the cigarette manufacturers had the good sense to adapt their approach to the changing tides of public demand in the health field. The manufacturers saw the beginning of a breakdown in the tobacco [political] subsystem, and they had the political acumen and sensibility to shift their tactics to cope with it. They turned what could have been a substantial threat to the steady expansion of cigarette sales into a limited victory. The Cigarette Labeling and Advertising Act passed by Congress *in 1965 was more of a victory for cigarettes than it was for health.*

The cigarette manufacturers realized that public demands for action in response to the research on smoking and health were much stronger than they had been in the past. The health forces had been strengthened by the Surgeon General's 1964 report, Smoking and Health. *And it was becoming increasingly clear that the cigarette manufacturers would no longer be able to bury or ignore the criticisms of the health people as they had in the past. The industry's attempt to find a safer cigarette and to mitigate the adverse findings of health research by counter, pro-cigarette research had resulted in very little data favoring smoking. Consequently, promises for even more research, voluntary advertising codes, and a less dangerous cigarette could no longer be used to stay the momentum that the antismoking people had been able to build. Armed with the Federal Trade Commission rule, the Surgeon General's report, and some public support, the health groups had many things going for them in 1965. The carefully constructed walls of tobacco defense were beginning to crack.*

. . . In the face of mounting concern over cigarette smoking as a health hazard, there was genius in the Cigarette Labeling and Advertising bill from the

industry point of view. The bill contained just enough regulation to pass as a health measure; and while the bill required a health warning, it also contained provisions to dismantle an important part of the work of the Federal Trade Commission. Its most significant provision in these terms was the section that temporarily eliminated the FTC's rulemaking power in the cigarette advertising field.

. . . Another provision of the bill prohibited other federal agencies, for example, the Federal Communications Commission, from taking any action to require health warnings in advertising. State and local action was also blocked or preempted by congressional action. Foreclosing the possibility of state and local regulation was a major attraction of the bill for the cigarette manufacturers.

. . . As the final votes neared, there was virtually no opposition to the bill from the cigarette manufacturers. On the contrary, they seemed to be supporting it. The bill passed the Senate by a vote of 72 to 5, with most of the tobacco state senators voting for it.

. . . The House adopted the bill by voice vote under circumstances that were designed to limit debate and discussion. The bill was brought to the floor and passed on a Tuesday afternoon when there were only a few members present. The chief opponent of the bill, John Moss (D., California), had been informed earlier that the vote would come on the following Thursday. When the vote was taken, he was in a commercial aircraft over the Atlantic flying back from Europe. This switch in scheduling violated the gentlemen's agreement that governs such matters in Congress.

. . . The passage of the Cigarette Labeling and Advertising Act was a major victory for cigarette manufacturers and their allies. . . . Cigarette manufacturers needed some legislation from Congress, *or the much more onerous Federal Trade Commission rule would stand. The ruling could have been challenged in the courts, but the success of any such challenge was questionable.*

. . . One observer commented upon the cigarette triumph in these terms: "In fact . . . the bill is not, as its sponsors suggested, an example of congressional initiative to protect public health; it is an unashamed act to protect private industry from government regulation." *

If Congress had not acted, the stronger and broader FTC rule would have taken effect. In addition, more legitimacy would have been associated with the

*Reprinted by permission from A. Lee Fritschler, *Smoking and Politics: Policymaking and the Federal Bureaucracy*, 2nd ed. (Englewood Cliffs, N.J.: Prentice-Hall, 1975), pp. 120–25.

FTC's delegated authority, and the Big Six could expect, as a result, an increasingly stiff regulatory agenda from this agency governing its market activities. But Congress did act, and:

> . . . the bill went to President Johnson on July 13, and he maintained his silence on the legislation as he had done throughout the controversy. On July 27, within hours of the time the bill would have become law automatically without the president's signature, it was signed . . . in the privacy of his office. There were no guests, no glitter, and no souvenir pens, which ordinarily accompany the signing of a major piece of legislation. The bill was signed without ceremony, and the president's press secretary released the news without benefit of comment. . . . [Fritschler, 1975:25]

The legislation that emerged from hearings in both houses of Congress and was signed by the president specifically voided the Federal Trade Commission's labeling rule and took away for several years its delegated authority to make new regulations relating to cigarette advertising. The commission, other administrative agencies, and individual states were prohibited from requiring or even considering the requirement of a health warning in cigarette advertising for four years. Later, Congress extended this moratorium on the FTC to six years! The diluted label proposed in the bill was to be required only on cigarette packages, not in cigarette advertising in the broadcast and printed media. "The pinpoint accuracy of the congressional oversight [regarding tobacco industry rule making by the FTC] was so unusual," according to Fritschler, "that old-timers on Capitol Hill could not remember when or if it had ever happened that way before."

Antismoking Movement: Derailment and Delay.   Clements's strategy had been quite effective. The Tobacco Institute had been successful in building a well-financed campaign that united and articulated the shared interests not only of the Big Six but of a broad set of constituencies that made up the latent but potentially powerful tobacco subsystem. Although the tobacco lobby was unable to prevent a health-labeling regulation—indeed, Clements's strategy from the beginning was not to try—it was effective in getting Congress to overrule one of its administrative agencies by diluting its proposed package-labeling statement and eliminating the other half of its regulatory proposal pertaining to cigarette advertising in general. The congressional oversight committee also temporarily neutralized the FTC's plans for further regulation of the industry and preempted the efforts of other federal agencies, as well as individual states, to press forward on their own antismoking initiatives.

To be sure, the victory for the Big Six was a limited one. The boundaries surrounding the tobacco subsystem had been breached, and further influence from the institutional environment awaited only the expiration of the temporary restrictions placed on the FTC's antismoking activities and the emergence of organized public opinion of the antismoking variety. For a period lasting several years, however, the lobbying strategy employed by the Tobacco Institute had derailed the antismoking forces and had bought precious time for the Big Six to develop other strategies for coping with the smoking-and-health threat to their primary domain of operations.

MEDIA AND ADVERTISING STRATEGIES

The congressionally imposed four-year moratorium on the FTC's rule-making authority over the tobacco industry did not prevent that Commission from moving forward with the smoking-and-health issue short of rule making itself. Indeed, in the years following Congress's rebuke, the FTC continued to keep the smoking-and-health issue before the public eye and build support for health warnings in all cigarette advertising even though the four-year moratorium on its rule making power had been extended by Congress to six years, ending in 1971.

Support of the Federal Communications Commission (FCC), which licensed and regulated broadcasters using the public airwaves, and the U.S. Department of Health, Education and Welfare (HEW) was also enlisted during this period. The FTC quickly set up its cigarette tar and nicotine laboratory and then began to submit a long series of hard-hitting annual reports to Congress. The FTC's 1966 Report to Congress called for a stronger health-warning label and more appropriations for the FTC and HEW so they could step up their public antismoking campaigns. The 1967 report vigorously attacked the advertising tactics of the Big Six, which the FTC argued were misleading to the public. In the 1968 report, the FTC first recommended that cigarette advertising be banned from the public broadcast media entirely. But the most important event during the FTC's state of moratorium was the *unexpectedly sudden* and *unique* entry of the Federal Communications Commission into the smoking-and-health controversy in 1967.

THE FCC AND THE "FAIRNESS DOCTRINE"

The FCC was prompted to act when it received a letter from a young attorney, John F. Banzhaf, requesting that the Commission require a New York City television station to give free, to responsible health groups, the same amount of air time as that sold to the Big Six for the purpose of promoting the virtues and values of smoking. In doing this, Banzhaf was requesting that the FCC apply its "Fairness Doctrine" in an unprecedented manner. The FCC's response did not require that exactly equal time be given to both views, but it did require stations licensed to operate over the public airwaves to provide "a significant amount of time for the other viewpoint" (Fritschler, 1975:145).

Heretofore, the Fairness Doctrine had been applied to situations in which expressed viewpoints of a personal nature, particularly statements about politicians, obligated broadcasters to give "equal time" to opposing points of view. Because only the four-year, congressionally imposed moratorium governed the rule-making authority of the FCC, this commission was not constrained as was the FTC beyond 1968. Its creative application of the Fairness Doctrine to the public broadcast advertisements of a major consumer product caught both the Big Six and Congress off guard. Before examining the responses of the Big Six, we will review briefly the media strategies and advertising themes that set the stage for this dramatic event.

Media Choices and Advertising Themes.   Throughout the 1950s and into the early 1960s, unfettered cigarette advertising prevailed in the public broadcast media in the United States. Few readers will recall the slogans that were used to promote cigarettes in the prime-time radio programs that preceded the era of television. For those who can, the recollection is likely to conjure up visions of "Johnny," the little guy who chanted, "Call for Philip Morris!" and the attention-getting R.J. Reynolds slogan, "LS/MFT, Lucky Strike Means Fine Tobacco." But although the Big Six were major advertisers during the era of radio, they clearly dominated all other U.S. industries in their advertising expenditures in the television medium that emerged during the early 1950s.

During this period, the annual reports of all members of the Big Six contained major sections describing with pride their sponsorship of a broad variety of popular television programs; and each year, tobacco firms added more programs to their lists. Table 3-1, using R.J. Reynolds as a typical example, reveals just how pervasive was the reliance on broadcast-media advertising for the promotion of cigarettes. The Big Six were all invested heavily in the sponsorship of a number of prime-time weekly shows, many of which (e.g., family shows and sports programs) appealed to a potential audience much larger than the adult-age population in the U.S. market. However, with the continuing criticism of cigarette advertising in particular and the rising public concern about the issue of smoking and health in general, the question of the dominance of television advertising by tobacco companies had become a topic of more than passing concern. It was not surprising to discover, therefore, that the traditional sections proudly displaying television-program sponsorship in the annual reports of all members of the Big Six had been scrapped three to four years before Congress passed the broadcast ban on cigarette advertising.

TABLE 3-1 R.J. REYNOLDS'S LIST OF SPONSORED TELEVISION PROGRAMS

Musical variety shows:	"The Andy Williams Show"
	"The Jonathan Winters Variety Show"
	"Hollywood Palace"
	"The Danny Kaye Show"
	"The Jimmy Dean Show"
Comedy shows:	"Get Smart"
	"McHale's Navy"
	"The Beverly Hillbillies"
	"Mona McCluskey"
Western/adventure shows:	"The Virginian"
	"F Troop"
	"The Legend of Jesse James"
Panel shows:	"To Tell the Truth"
	"Password"
	"I've Got a Secret"
Feature film programs:	"Saturday Night at the Movies"
	"The Sunday Night Movie"
Sports shows:	"Wide World of Sports"
	"AFL Football"
	"American Sportsman"
News/current events:	"The Today Show"

Source: RJR, *Annual Report,* 1965

Throughout our entire study period, and quite remarkably during the tumultuous 1960s and early 1970s, cigarette-advertising themes remained relatively constant. Three primary themes have persisted: (1) appeals to satisfying taste (e.g., mildness, smoothness, genuineness); (2) association of cigarette smoking with pleasing personality traits (e.g., sex appeal, good health, independence, self-assurance); and (3) reduction of anxiety concerning smoking-and-health issues (e.g., emphasis on "safer" smoking).

Continued Control over Vital Information. During the years separating the labeling hearings and the eventual broadcast ban, the FTC continued to press for more information from the Big Six regarding both their advertising expenditures and their research on the effects of cigarette advertising—an initiative begun long before the labeling controversy, and one not affected by the congressional moratorium. But the FTC had been successful in obtaining only advertising-expenditure data that were broken down by general media categories. HEW had also been active in monitoring the industry's accumulating smoking-and-health research findings. Indeed, it had succeeded in persuading the Big Six to release annual reports summarizing those findings. But during the late 1960s, the FTC filed subpoenas against all members of the Big Six to require them to divulge both more specific data on advertising expenditures and more sensitive marketing-research data on the effects of cigarette advertising on a broad range of consumer behaviors, especially regarding the decision to start smoking. The Big Six responded with litigation that, again, served to postpone a potential threat posed by their institutional environment. They argued that detailed marketing data of the types sought by the FTC were proprietary, and that by seeking to incorporate them in its annual reports to Congress, the FTC could not guarantee confidentiality.

Once again, the joint defensive strategies of the Big Six were successful in delaying a threat to their primary domain, because they controlled access to vital information that federal regulators required in order to proceed against them. It was not until 1977 that a federal judge ruled against the Big Six in favor of the FTC's subpoenas for detailed advertising information; but even that victory was unrealized. The immediate response of the Big Six was to mount an appeal of the court decision that would cause, at the very least, several more years of delay for the FTC.

A New Congress Acts. By the close of the 1970s, the breakdown in the defense of the tobacco subsystem was becoming more visible. The smoking-and-health issue had continued to build momentum, and the growth in the domestic cigarette market had plateaued. Moreover, the FTC and other federal administrative agencies had become smarter. The use of subpoenas and the court system by the FTC, and the FCC's creative application of the Fairness Doctrine with support, again, from the court system, enabled both agencies to avoid direct oversight by a Congress that had been all too sensitive to the demands of the industry they threatened. By the time the broadcast-advertising ban was proposed as a congressional bill, even the forces within that institution had shifted. Senator Moss (D., Utah), the key antismoking figure who had been outmaneuvered in 1963 with the unusual floor vote on the labeling bill, was now the chairman of the Senate committee having oversight responsibility for the FTC. It was not surprising, therefore, that although the oversight committee in the House of Representatives failed to pass the bill, the Senate committee overruled. At the Senate hearings, the representative of the Tobacco Institute announced that the Big Six were willing to withdraw all radio and television advertising beginning January 1, 1970. In exchange, the tobacco lobby requested that the FTC continue to be required to give Congress six months' notice of any rule-making activity affecting cigarettes. The bill was passed. The ban was to become effective January 2, 1970, and a stronger health-warning label was prescribed.

BROADCAST-ADVERTISING BAN: A VICTORY FOR WHOM?

But how serious was the loss of access to the broadcast-advertising media to the Big Six? First, the Big Six's joint defensive strategies had postponed potentially immediate threats for almost a decade. As the subsequent chapters will reveal, this period was sufficiently long to enable the Big Six to engage in the formation and implementation of new strategic directions, involving major reallocations of resources, to ensure their survival. Moreover, subsequent research has demonstrated that the victory for the health forces was more apparent than real and that the tobacco interests, as well as the investment community, recognized the advertising ban as such *before* the fact.

The loss of major advertising media to any consumer-products industry could reasonably be predicted to have severe consequences for the prospects of continued growth and prosperity of member firms. In the present case, approximately 80 percent of the Big Six's advertising expenditures in 1969 had been allocated to the broadcast media (radio and television), as shown in Figure 3-2. Moreover, from the mid-1960s until the 1971 broadcast-advertising ban, cigarette companies had been the largest television advertisers in the United States.

Failing to avert the broadcast-media ban, the Big Six reacted with neither resignation nor panic. They adapted to this unprecedented handicap, first, by shifting advertising expenditures to formerly minor media. Because they had experienced regulations in several European countries that had prohibited cigarette advertisements in broadcast media for a number of years prior to 1971, the Big Six were already practiced in the use of alternative promotional strategies for introducing new cigarette products. They turned this experience to their advantage after the U.S. ban.

Domestic cigarette-advertising expenditures in printed media (newspapers and magazines) and outdoor media (billboards), for instance, jumped 277 percent between 1970 and 1971. The sponsoring of special events such as the Virginia Slims Tennis Tournament, the Doral Open Golf Tournament, the "Win With Winston" Sweepstakes, and others, became commonplace. The television advertisement of "little cigars" between 1970 and 1972 was also an attempt to skirt the cigarette-advertising ban, a tactic that was cut short by Congress's "Little Cigar Act" of 1973. Several firms even toyed with the idea of introducing pipe tobacco or cigars with the same names as their traditional cigarette brands in order to maintain broadcast-media exposure of these brand images.

Second, the oligopolistic market of the Big Six had locked them into huge outlays for broadcast advertising that for many firms did not substantially alter

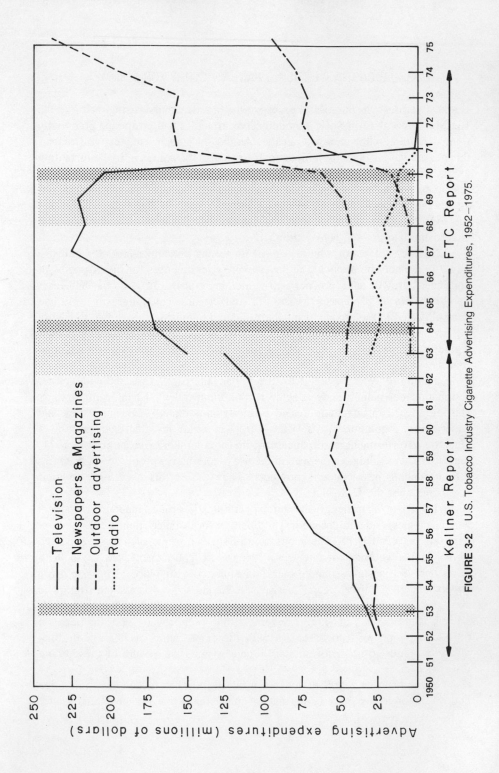

FIGURE 3-2 U.S. Tobacco Industry Cigarette Advertising Expenditures, 1952–1975.

their market shares. It was conceivable, therefore, that the elimination of access to this medium might result in greatly reduced costs for the Big Six without commensurately affecting any member's competitive strength. Analysis of the annual advertising outlays of the Big Six reveals that substantial cost savings were, indeed, realized from the ban.

From the time of the announcement of the formation of the Surgeon General's Advisory Committee in 1963 until the eve of the broadcast-media ban on cigarette advertising that went into effect on January 1, 1971, the gross domestic expenditures of cigarette advertising increased from $250 million to just under $315 million per year, as revealed in Figure 3-3. But during the first three years under the ban, gross industry expenditures on cigarette advertising fell back and momentarily stabilized at around $250 million per year. Thus, one of the potential industry benefits of the broadcast advertising ban was a virtual gift of approximately $200 million in reduced advertising expenditures from 1971 to 1973. Indeed, this potential benefit was *anticipated* three years before the advertising ban, in a 1968 public release to investors made by the research department of Smith, Barney and Company, members of the New York Stock Exchange:

> . . . *in spite of 225 million dollars spent yearly on advertising cigarettes via television and radio, domestic per capital consumption of cigarettes has declined modestly. There seems to be, furthermore, some incentive for the cigarette industry voluntarily to discontinue radio and television commercials. It may lessen the pressures on Congress for more stringent antismoking measures, and may end antismoking messages themselves. It would, on the other hand, free large sums of money to support acquisitions and diversification, utilize other forms of promotion or increase earnings.* [*Smith, Barney and Company, 1968:1−2*]

The reprieve granted the Big Six from a deadlocked broadcast-advertising strategy, although enormous in terms of cash savings, was not long-lived. By the end of the fourth year after the ban, annual cigarette-advertising expenditures had jumped again, from the $250-million range to an all-time high of $330 million. The Big Six had mastered the switch to printed, outdoor, and point-of-purchase advertising, and the early success of innovative low-tar brands (i.e., allegedly "safer" cigarettes) was creating new opportunities for market-share growth by way of aggressive advertising. Indeed, by 1978, the FTC's *Report to Congress* would reveal that low-tar cigarettes had achieved a 28 percent share of the domestic market and were being backed by almost 50 percent of total cigarette-advertising expenditures.

A far more serious by-product of the broadcast advertising ban, however,

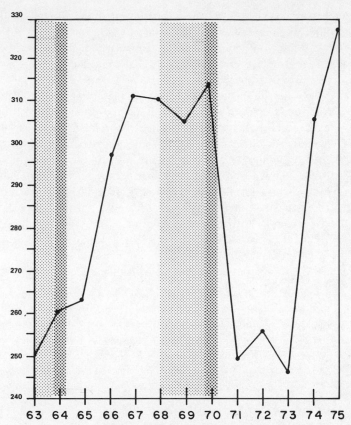

FIGURE 3-3 Domestic Cigarette Advertising Expenditures, 1963–1975.
NOTE: Total Domestic Cigarette Advertising Expenditures per Year Include Advertising via Television, Newspapers and Magazines, Radio, Direct, and Other Advertising. Source: Federal Trade Commission, *Statistical Supplement to Report to Congress: Pursuant to the Public Health Cigarette Smoking Act, for the Year 1975,* May 3, 1978.

was the fact that it voided the application of the Fairness Doctrine to the promotion of cigarettes. Because there were no more cigarette commercials, no obligation was imposed on broadcasters to air antismoking spots. During the two-year (1969–70) life of the Fairness Doctrine, about 1,200 antismoking messages were aired by the three major U.S. television networks; but during the first two years (1971–72) of the broadcast ban, the number of antismoking messages delivered by these networks totaled less than 250 (Doron, 1979:17).

Hindsight analysis reveals that the flurry of antismoking commercials during the three years preceding the ban had a far more dramatic impact on cigarette consumption than the ban itself. The Big Six, apparently in possession of this foresight, actually *volunteered* to withdraw from broadcast advertising before the ban was to become law.

Through the use of econometric modeling, Doron (1979) has demonstrated that the Big Six were better off after the ban. He estimates that they lost 2.7 billion packages of cigarettes during the three years under the Fairness Doctrine, owing to the combined effect of the antismoking commericals and other antismoking activities, but lost only 1.7 billion during the first five years of the ban.[3] Indeed, the American Cancer Society (1976:29) later admitted that it overlooked the fact that the imposition of the ban would result in the removal of the Fairness Doctrine:

> *While this law was hailed as a victory for the antismoking forces, it could not be foreseen that it would also produce a serious drawback. Since the broadcasters could no longer advertise cigarettes, they no longer were required to carry anti-cigarette messages. How powerful these messages had really been was demonstrated by what happened when they were no longer there. By the end of 1971, the per capita consumption curve for cigarettes had begun to point upward again, then it continued to move up gradually through 1972, 1973, and 1974.*

Doron also argued that because of the ban on cigarette advertising, the difficulty presented to potential new entries into the industry increased enormously; thus, this effort by the government may actually have served to increase the market power of the Big Six. Moreover, because there are apparently no close substitutes for cigarettes to smokers, the continued ability of other industries to broadcast-advertise their products would have a relatively inconsequential effect on the profitability and market size of the domestic tobacco industry. In short, one industry observer summarized the apparent victory of the health forces as follows:

> *The prohibition of cigarette advertising on television was actually followed by increased sales of cigarettes. Even more striking, the prohibition enormously strengthened the financial resources of the producers so that they have presumably become better able to distribute their wares, hardly a circumstance that discourages smoking. [Riker, 1979:xiii]*

Thus, once again, a combination of collaborative efforts and formal joint ventures had been used by the Big Six to ward off and postpone a major threat to the legitimacy and autonomy of their primary business operations. Together, the domain-defense strategies and tactics summarized in this chapter not only reveal that competitive firms may and do create joint political ventures to advance their interests and to protect their domain, but provide some insight into the conditions under which such ventures take precedence over behavior of individual firms.

TRADE ASSOCIATIONS AND DEFENSE OF DOMAIN

The literature on the formation of formal joint ventures among competitive firms is thin, to say the least. Although some attention has been focused on discoveries of tacit, and therefore illegal, collusion among competitors (e.g., Staw and Szwajkowski, 1975; Sonnenfeld and Lawrence, 1978), virtually no investigations have been reported on the conditions under which competitive firms may and do initiate formal collaborative ventures. The importance of such ventures, as evidenced in the political activities of the Big Six to ward off and postpone external threats, therefore, warrants closer attention.

The type of joint ventures created by the Big Six to manage their domain-defense strategies are generally referred to as "trade associations." The major purpose of trade associations has been described as follows:

> . . . to exchange information and exert political influence for the benefit of their members. The formation of such associations has frequently coincided with major changes in the industry caused either by unexpected growth or decline or by threats from new external competition or the government. [Pfeffer and Salancik, 1978:177]

In one of the few published studies on this type of joint venture, it was shown that active support of a trade association tends to vary directly with the strength of political threat from an industry's institutional environment. Gable (1953) observed that membership activity in the large and heterogeneous National Association of Manufacturers swelled when major legislation of interest to its members (e.g., the Taft-Hartley collective-bargaining legislation) was being contested in Congress, but declined in the absence of relevant political activity. Thus, trade associations tend to be formed within industries in anticipation of, or response to, a *major external stimulus*. But beyond that stimulus situation, a number of external conditions, as well as factors at the level of individual firms, help explain when and why this form of joint political venture emerges or declines.

The legality of joint ventures, as expressed in the antitrust laws of the

United States, is quite explicit. No collaborative effort may be permitted among competitors within a given industry if that effort would tend to reduce competition in that industry. The burden of proof, however, falls not upon the collaborators but upon the plaintiff who wishes to prevent or terminate such collaboration; the latter is almost always an outsider, and in many cases has been the Antitrust Department of the U.S. Department of Justice. But proof of a reduction in competition is often more elusive than the law implies.

After discovering the extensiveness of the Big Six's reliance on joint ventures to mount their domain-defense strategies, we inquired into the legality of such ventures at the U.S. Department of Justice. The following reply expresses the Antitrust Department's current position on the legality of the joint research and lobbying ventures that have emerged in the U.S. tobacco industry:

> *With respect to . . . questions about the industry's adaptation to anti-smoking campaigns through such ventures as The Tobacco Institute, . . . such activities do not fall within any exemption to the federal antitrust laws. However, where the type of competition eliminated by a joint venture does not involve or lead directly to market control, the courts have been fairly lenient in not interfering with the joint venture's activities, even where each firm, but for the joint action, would have done the work of the venture independently. Joint research (and for that matter, joint lobbying) is a common form of cooperation within this category. The reason that the cigarette industry has been able to operate such ventures without the censure of the antitrust laws is that we have been unable to identify any direct and substantial anticompetitive market impact caused by them. [Poole, 1978]*

The stated purposes of the Big Six's joint ventures have always been to create a more favorable set of relationships between their industry and elements of its broader institutional environment. Their public goals have been political, not market goals. The extent to which tacit collusion, directly affecting the market structure of the industry, has also been achieved remains only a subject of conjecture. So far, the industry's joint ventures have not been challenged on these grounds.

But *legal norms* constitute only one of the contextual factors that help explain and predict the formation of joint political ventures among competitive firms. In addition, the *size* of the industry population of firms and the degree of *heterogeneity* among its member firms also seem to play important roles. In industries consisting of relatively few competitive firms, as by definition in oligopolistic markets, it should be an easier matter to coordinate the efforts and objectives of member firms than in industries comprising a large population of firms. More important, though, the formation of joint political ventures is more feasible in industries characterized by a homogeneous population of firms. Where member firms compete with the same product lines for similar market segments, the relevance and potential effect of external influences and threats, as well as opportunities, should affect them similarly. In contrast, where industries are populated by a heterogeneous assortment of firms, each having its own product lines and serving different segments of the total market (such as in the U.S. insurance industry), where a high degree of population heterogeneity forces firms to take different positions in response to a given external threat (Miles and Bhambri, 1980), the feasibility of industry wide joint political ventures is greatly reduced. Thus, certain contextual conditions, including the legal framework in which all corporations must operate, as well as characteristics of the industry in which a population of corporations exist, are important factors influencing whether corporate political activities will be managed by individual firms or on their behalf by joint political ventures.

Beyond these contextual factors is the actual choice that firms must make between mounting their own political activities or pooling their activities with those of competitors. Three firm-level factors appear to influence this choice. Joint political ventures, or, in our case, trade associations, will be formed to the extent that competitors believe they can achieve greater *economies of scale* and/or greater *concentration of power* by pooling their resources and taking a united stand to deal with an external threat—but only to the extent that their individual thresholds of discretionary behavior are not exceeded. As Pfeffer and Salancik have observed:

> . . . *organizations may engage in their political activities alone through their own resources or collectively pooling their resources with organizations which have similar interests. As with any collective effort, the danger exists that the interorganizational organization may not represent the interests of all the members, and for those coordinating mechanisms that develop formal staffs and structures, control of the lobbying organization itself becomes, at times, an organizational objective.* [1978:218]

Therefore, members of a potential or existing joint political venture face a dilemma. Each must weigh the benefits that accrue from collaborative effort (e.g., greater power at less cost) against the potential loss in organizational autonomy.

In the case of the U.S. tobacco industry, under siege during the smoking-and-health controversy, all four contextual conditions existed. A basic threat to the legitimacy of the primary domain of the Big Six warranted serious political response. Because the Big Six were highly homogeneous with respect to their product markets, the threat amounted to a shared-fate condition that potentially affected all six firms with roughly equal and substantially negative consequences. Because the Big Six were few in number, together accounting for over 98 percent of the domestic cigarette market, coordination was relatively easy to accomplish. Finally, because the threat was a nonmarket one, emanating from the industry's institutional environment, the required response was a political one and therefore lawful in the U.S. economy. In summary, all the contextual conditions surrounding the members of this oligopoly favored the formation of joint ventures to mount a political response to the legitimacy threat. But what of the immediate factors influencing organizational choice?

Mounting a research program to create and control information vital to the resolution of the smoking-and-health controversy provided a clear opportunity for individual tobacco manufacturers to obtain certain economies and leverage from pooling their resources. After all, they still continued to fund their in-house programs of research that focused on production efficiencies and new-product innovations. Similarly, the direct threats posed by the FTC, the FCC, the Congress, and antismoking interest groups warranted a strong, united industry response that could benefit from a pooling of lobbying resources. This primary threat to the legitimacy of the industry upon which the survival of the Big Six depended cut deep enough into the intersts of each firm to substantially raise their thresholds of discretion. Therefore, all members of the Big Six participated in the formation of the Tobacco Research Council and the Tobacco Institute, and their active support of these joint ventures continued throughout the period studied. The same, however, was not the case for the joint venture designed to manage the industry's attempt to self-police its advertising strategies.

The Cigarette Advertising Code, Inc., did not have a broad purpose, and the loss of organizational discretion had different implications for the firms that participated in it. Indeed, two members of the Big Six, American Brands and Lorillard, pulled out of this venture shortly after its creation. The fact that during that time both were suffering erosion in market share and one was having difficulty in introducing new low-tar cigarettes may indicate that, at least for them, the potential benefits of membership were insufficient to compensate for the advertising discretion they lost from participation.

SUMMARY

A number of effective collaborative efforts and formal joint ventures were employed by the Big Six to mount a broad range of anticipatory and reactive strategies whose purpose was to defend the traditional tobacco domain from threats to its legitimacy and efficacy from the broader institutional environment. On the anticipatory side, the defense was mounted with pooled resources and a unified strategy that simply overwhelmed the antismoking forces for a period long enough for the Big Six to develop the longer-term strategies that will be discussed in the next two chapters. When reaction to unavoidable institutional threats was called for, the joint positions of the Big Six were generally well conceived in advance and resulted in a skillful and orderly retreat that was always accompanied by the negotiation of important regulatory concessions. One cannot help being struck by the political sensitivity of this group of traditional competitors, and in particular by the acute sense of timing that was exhibited in all their efforts to defend a very profitable domain. But vanguard became rear guard as the joint political ventures encountered greater and greater antismoking sentiment during the 1960s and struggled to give the Big Six the time to engage in major organizational adaptations that would ensure their survival. Other strategic behaviors would be required to get the most out of, and to avoid overdependence on, the declining domestic domain.

FOOTNOTES

[1]We have relied primarily on the following work of political scientist A. Lee Fritschler for this account of the tactics used by the tobacco industry to influence its institutional environment: *Smoking and Politics: Policymaking and the Federal Bureaucracy* (Englewood Cliffs, N.J.: Prentice-Hall, 1975).

[2]The effectiveness of the Tobacco Tax Council may be judged in part by the fact that the *federal* excise tax of 8¢ per pack of twenty cigarettes has remained unchanged since 1952. This means that the federal tax *rate* on cigarettes has fallen from 35 percent of the retail price of a pack in the mid-1950s to 15 percent in 1977 (Warner, 1978).

[3]Similar conclusions were reached in an analysis of per capita cigarette consumption by the U.S. Department of Agriculture (Miller, 1974a). This report revealed that actual per capita cigarette consumption lagged behind an estimated path of potential by about 4.5 percent in 1964−67, widened sharply to a 14−15 percent lag with the antismoking advertisements on radio and television in 1968−69, and then began to close the gap between actual and forecasted consumption by 1973. Warner (1978) and Hamilton (1972) have reported similar findings.

4

Domain Offense

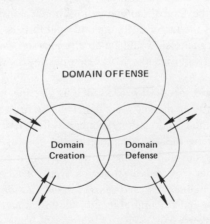

The Big Six were not simply biding their time in their immediate product-market domain as their joint political ventures sallied forth to battle forces in the broader institutional environment. Despite the incredible sacrifice of discretion and resources required of these organizations to create and sustain a unified strategy of domain defense, they were also competing more intensively than ever in the marketplace that was the target of the institutional threats. As the growth of the domestic industry began to slow and eventually plateau, each member of the Big Six began to allocate significantly more resources to its own strategy of *domain offense*.

Since they were faced with a pernicious decline in domestic cigarette-market growth, significant market-share gains by one firm would have to come in large measure from the traditional market shares of its five competitors. Indeed, by the later stages of the smoking-and-health controversy, domain-offense strategies were being developed under virtual zero-sum conditions.

The two primary offensive strategies were *product innovation*, in the direction of "safer" cigarettes, and *market segmentation*, which required the tailoring of both new and existing brands to the tastes and preferences of target populations of smokers and potential smokers. Thus, in response to the smoking-and-health threat, the Big Six engaged *simultaneously* in defensive and offensive strategies that involved the partitioning of their domain into largely independent arenas of cooperation and conflict. These arenas were not, however, totally independent. For example, the direction of product innovation was responsive to both the political threat and the domain-defense strategy, because it involved the introduction of allegedly "safer" cigarette brands that contained reduced levels of harmful tar and nicotine. Also, the efforts of some members of the Big Six to collaborate in defense of domain broke down, because to do so created difficulties for the successful implementation of their competitive strategies, as in the case of the withdrawal of American Brands and Lorillard from the Cigarette Advertising Code, Inc.

To our knowledge, no major industry study has examined this combination of defensive and offensive responses of corporations to an external threat. Industrial economists have focused primarily on the responses of one firm to market changes (e.g., price, supply, demand) induced by other firms either within the industry or in other industries. To the extent that institutional forces have impinged upon the marketplace, economists have tended to focus their investigations on the impact on competitive relationships within the affected industry. Political scientists, on the other hand, have tended to focus on the institutional threat (i.e., public policy) and the political strategies of defense mounted by a population of firms. Each discipline, therefore, has tended to follow its own instincts and thereby to render only a partial picture of the strategic process of organizational adaptation. By considering a broader range of possible organizational coping behaviors, we were free to document and interpret a more complete description of the organizational adaptation process that unfolded within our population of firms. In order to build that broader picture, this chapter turns from the political responses to the economic responses of the Big Six.

PRODUCT INNOVATION AND BRAND PROLIFERATION

The smoking-and-health threat stimulated a proliferation of new cigarette brands that, by the end of our study period, had saturated the domestic market (Table 4-1). Although the domestic cigarette market (measured by the number of cigarettes sold) increased by less than 70 percent during this 25-year period, the number of cigarette brands introduced successfully into the domestic market increased by a whopping 450 percent. A total of only 18 traditional brands were produced by the Big Six in 1950. However, between that time and the announcement of the formation of the Surgeon General's Advisory Committee on Smoking and Health in 1962, the number of cigarette brands on the domestic market had increased to 47. And in just the four years following that public announcement, the number of Big Six cigarette brands on the domestic market increased by 78 percent, to 82 brands. By 1975, 100 brands populated the domestic market, which had become so saturated that Big Six firms were pursuing a policy of eliminating marginal brands to make shelf space available to yet more new-product introductions (Ramirez, 1980b).

These estimates of brand proliferation, although large in magnitude, are conservative, since they include only those brands that were *successfully* introduced into the domestic market.[1] It is conceivable that just as many brands were introduced on a limited scale but failed to gain market acceptance. And because each new cigarette brand introduction can cost $100—$200 million for advertising alone (Sease, 1978b), this rate of product innovation signals a major

TABLE 4-1 BRAND PROLIFERATION
IN THE DOMESTIC CIGARETTE MARKET: 1950-1974

Year	RJR	PM	B&W	AB	L	LM	Total
1950	2	5	4	3	1	3	18
1951	2	5	4	3	1	3	18
1952	2	5	4	3	2	4	20
1953	2	6	4	3	4	5	24
1954	3	7	5	4	5	5	29
1955	3	7	5	4	4	5	28
1956	4	7	6	5	4	5	31
1957	4	7	6	5	5	6	33
1958	4	6	6	5	5	6	32
1959	4	7	7	6	6	7	37
1960	4	7	9	6	6	7	39
1961	5	10	10	6	8	8	47
1962	5	10	10	6	8	8	47
1963	5	9	10	5	8	9	46
1964	6	10	10	8	8	10	52
1965	6	12	9	9	8	11	55
1966	6	14	9	12	10	10	61
1967	9	16	13	17	13	14	82
1968	9	19	14	18	12	11	83
1969	10	19	13	15	13	11	81
1970	12	20	18	16	14	13	93
1971	13	21	13	17	16	13	93
1972	13	21	14	17	14	13	92
1973	13	21	14	18	14	13	93
1974	16	21	16	18	17	12	100
1950-74 % Change:	+700%	+320%	+300%	+500%	+1600%	+300%	+450%

Source: Maxwell Report, July 31, 1975.

Big Six firms:

RJR:	R. J. Reynolds
PM:	Philip Morris
B&W:	Brown & Williamson
AB:	American Brands
L:	Lorillard
LM:	Liggett & Meyers

reallocation of resources away from traditional brands to new ones and away from broad market categories to narrower, better-defined market segments. Therefore, product competition must be considered another major strategy of the Big Six during the smoking-and-health threat. But quantitative indices of product-innovation rates do not reveal much about the *quality* of this strategic adaptive response and its relation to the external threat to the tobacco domain.

Both the *nature* and the *timing* of major waves of product innovation among the Big Six were pegged closely to the major 1953 and 1962−64 institutional threats to the tobacco industry. In this chapter we will concentrate mainly on these two aspects of product innovation, inferring where possible the market-segmentation strategy implied by each class of brand introduction. It should be recognized, however, that market-segmentation data are perhaps the most sensitive and proprietary information controlled by the Big Six. It is this kind of data that, although required by the FTC almost a decade ago, is still hotly contested in the courts by the tobacco companies.

HISTORICAL MARKET TRENDS

Beginning before World War II and continuing through the 1950s, the strategies of the Big Six became increasingly focused on expanding the industry's domestic market. Efforts, successfully initiated during the war, were made to bring women into the market, and direct solicitation of a growing young-adult population in the United States was emphasized. Beginning about the time of the 1964 Surgeon General's Report, however, the growth rate in this young-adult population began to taper off, and the percentage of smokers in the domestic population similarly began to decline. The maturation of the domestic market forced each tobacco-products manufacturer to devote more of its energy to the expansion of its market share and to exploit other market potentialities at home and abroad. Thus, a combination of domestic-market stagnation, the relative ease of new product promotion via television, and new technological developments that made possible detailed product differentiation (on the basis of taste, size, packaging, and composition) all contributed to the strategy of product innovation and brand proliferation that characterized most of the period under observation. A broad product mix enabled firms to "squeeze out" what demand remained in the home market. A product was designed, therefore, for each substantial domestic-market segment.

THE MEANING OF "PRODUCT"

Before discussing the strategy of product innovation, it is important to be clear about what is meant by the term *product*. The meaning of the term varies according to the level of aggregation to which it is applied. At the highest level of aggregation, product refers to a *product category*. A product category is defined as "all products, produced by all competing producers, which, despite differences in appearance and performance, are all essentially serving a set of functional needs in roughly a similar manner" (Capon, 1978:1). In our case, tobacco products constitute the category of products that have been the mainstay of the Big Six. Within this broad classification are usually product subcategories; in our case, cigarettes, cigars, and smoking and chewing tobacco. But because the controversy centered on cigarettes, which have dominated the revenues and profits in the industry, our analysis will treat cigarettes as the product subcategory of interest.

At a finer level of aggregation, product may refer to a *product type,* such as a two-door coupe, station wagon, or four-door sedan. In the U.S. tobacco industry, three primary types of cigarette products have emerged through two and half decades of product innovation: nonfilter regular brands, regular filter-tip brands, and low-tar-low-nicotine filter-tip brands. Finally, there can be *product extensions* or "brands" that emerge out of one of the product types within a product category. Extensions do not depart from the fundamental character of the product type from which they emerge; instead, they offer small variations that are targeted to meet the particular preferences of a segment of the product market.

It will be demonstrated that, under conditions of environmental stress and market maturation, the Big Six resorted increasingly to innovation in both product type and brands in order to compete effectively in their traditional product-market domain. Both forms of innovation will be treated in our discussion in this chapter as "product innovation." The Big Six also engaged in what might be classified as product-category innovation, but this activity resulted from their entry into entirely new business domains and therefore is treated in the next chapter, under the subject of diversification.

PRODUCT-INNOVATION STRATEGIES

Our analysis of the product-innovation strategies of the Big Six will focus first on the identification of patterns that emerged from the industry as a whole. It will be shown that two major waves of product innovation characterized the industry population, and that each wave emerged during a concentrated period of antismoking activity. As the smoking-and-health controversy took on momentum, the product-innovation strategies of the Big Six produced waves of new cigarette brands that were lower in harmful tar and nicotine content and, consequently, more responsive to changing attitudes and regulations in the industry's institutional environment. But the subsequent analysis of the product-innovation strategies of individual firms will reveal variations that led to major shifts in market share among the Big Six and that encouraged some firms to seek alternative product-market domains while committing others more heavily to a dependence on the threatened cigarette business.

INDUSTRY-LEVEL STRATEGIC ANALYSIS

In general, the stormier the health-and-smoking controversy, the lower in tar and allegedly "safer" the new cigarette brands became. The Sloan-Kettering report and its subsequent publicity similarly stimulated a major change in the product-mix strategies of the other firms in the industry. Nonfilter brands, which were high in harmful tar and nicotine content, began a decline from which they never recovered (Figure 4-1), and the first wave of product innovation was under way. At the same time, filter-tip cigarettes were introduced across the industry and began their sharp rise over the remainder of the period. Every tobacco company introduced at least one filter cigarette in either 1953 or 1954. Whereas the 1953 health-and-smoking scare had unanticipated negative consequences for the industry's sales, the rebound was rapid as cigarette manufacturers responded with both filter introductions and an emphasis on "safer smoking." By 1957, filter brands could be loosely categorized into high- and low-filtration categories,

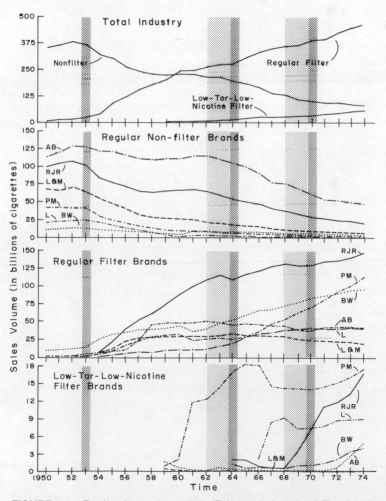

FIGURE 4-1   Product Innovations at the Tobacco Industry and Firm Levels:
1950-74. Source: Maxwell Report, July 31, 1975

and by 1959, filter-cigarette sales had surpassed nonfilter sales (Figure 4-1). In contrast to the meager attention to product innovation prior to 1954, at least 42 new brands were introduced by the Big Six between 1954 and 1964.[2]

The marked rise of the low-tar-low-nicotine brands of the mid- to late 1960s closely accompanied the release of the 1964 Surgeon General's Report.[3] In the cases of both waves of new product types, their trivial volumes before major environmental inductions can be attributed almost wholly to market testing. Thus, the overall strategic response of the industry in terms of its products was to gradually evolve allegedly "safer" cigarettes that would appeal to the growing market segments of smokers switching from high-tar regular brands to brands containing less harmful substances. Indeed, to reinforce this adaptive response, John Banzhaf, the head of Action on Smoking and Health and promoter of the application of the Fairness Doctrine to cigarette advertising, has recently suggested that the broadcast ban be lifted in order to allow the Big Six to advertise only low-tar cigarettes.[4]

Discontinuities in product-innovation waves during major events in the institutional environment were even more pronounced at the level of the individual firms. Note, for example, in Figure 4-1 how the regular, nonfilter brands of the Big Six all began their declines at or about the same time as the Sloan-Kettering release; and how the introduction of filter brands by the Big Six closely followed that same antismoking release. It is as though the product-development and marketing staffs of the Big Six used the pressure placed on the industry as a whole for less hazardous cigarette products to introduce into the domestic market just what the doctors ordered.

Product Innovation and Natural Selection.   A natural-selection process appeared to govern the success of new-product introductions. Product type and market epoch were closely coupled in the determination of success or failure of a new cigarette brand. New regular brands of the high-tar type suffered progressively greater mortality as the Big Six attempted to introduce them into a marketplace that was becoming more and more health-conscious. Although nine regular, nonfilter brands were introduced by the Big Six between 1950 and 1974, this product type suffered eight market casualties over that period. The same mortality pattern occurred for filter cigarettes as they were displaced by low-tar brands at later stages in the development of health-consciousness in the market. But the mortality pattern also worked in the reverse direction. Innovative product types (especially low-tar products) that were introduced too early (that is, before consumer preference for "taste" was eroded by a preference for "safer" smoking) suffered a higher mortality rate than conventional brands. In short, the product introductions and failures, summarized in Table 4-2, reveal that innovations that were timed to be responsive to the increasing pressures of the smoking-and-health controversy had a much higher empirical probability of success.[5] Once again, the three major environmental events were useful in distinguishing among the market epochs and product innovation waves of the U.S. tobacco industry.

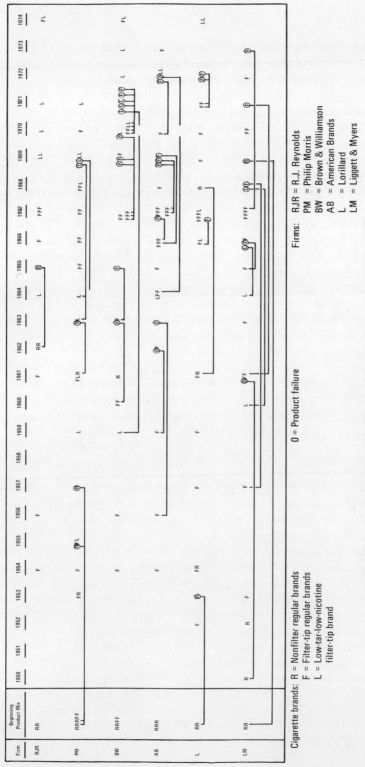

TABLE 4-2 PRODUCT INNOVATIONS AND FAILURES OF THE BIG SIX, 1950-1974
Source: Maxwell Report, July 31, 1945

Nature and Timing of Product Innovations. A closer inspection of Table 4-2 will reveal the importance of *timing* in product innovations and failures. For instance, only six regular, *high-tar* cigarette brands were introduced by the Big Six during the twenty one years following the Sloan-Kettering report, whereas sixteen brands in this category had been introduced prior to it. More important, only 30 percent of the early sixteen introductions eventually failed, compared to a failure rate of 50 percent for the high-tar regular brands introduced afterwards. Similar patterns of market selection emerged for the other two product categories.

Of the 22 *filter* brands introduced between the Sloan-Kettering report (1953) and the formation of the Surgeon General's Advisory Committee (1962), only 23 percent eventually failed. Of the filter brands introduced between the formation of the committee and the 1970 broadcast-advertising ban, 27 percent failed. And the filter brands that were not introduced until after the ad ban suffered a 40 percent failure rate. During that last period (1970–74), the number of low-tar brands introduced exceeded the number of new filter cigarettes. Only 22 percent of all *low-tar* product innovations had failed by the end of our study period; and only 15 percent of the low-tar brands introduced before the ad ban had failed. In contrast, 50 percent of the low-tar brands introduced *before* the Surgeon General's Report eventually failed.

These results reveal a pattern of success in product innovation for the Big Six. The most successful firms were those that timed the nature and intensity of their product innovations to the changing environmental conditions. Both tardiness and eagerness in the introduction of new-product types were penalized by the market that was moving, slowly at first but later rapidly, toward the "safer" cigarettes demanded by both smokers and the antismoking institutional environment.

Safer, but Also Cheaper Cigarettes. Innovations in filter cigarettes were accompanied by an industrywide move to the use of greater proportions of reconstituted tobacco sheet, shorter tobacco columns, and a freeze-drying process, all of which decreased the actual quantity of tobacco, and thus the tar and nicotine levels, contained in a cigarette. Most filter brands contained about one-third less tobacco than nonfilter brands, owing to shorter and thinner tobacco columns, and a "puffing" process gave the tobacco more filling capacity (Miller, 1972). Figure 4-2 shows the decrease in tobacco used per 1,000 cigarettes since 1950 as a result of the industry's emphasis on product innovation. That the industry was hard at work in producing "safer" cigarettes is evidenced by Philip Morris's announcement to its stockholders in 1969 that the tar and nicotine content of all its brands had been "substantially reduced over the past 15 years [an average of 46 percent]." In addition, a reconstituted-tobacco-sheet process made it possible to use both less and lower-quality tobacco in cigarette manufacture. Thus, product innovation toward allegedly "safer" cigarettes also resulted in reduced cost of manufacture and in higher profit

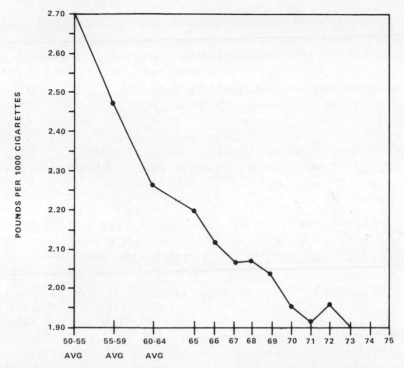

FIGURE 4-2 Pounds of Tobacco Used per 1,000 Cigarettes. Source: *Tobacco Situation,* September, 1976

margins per unit of cigarettes sold.[6] Once again, the Big Six had turned a threat to an advantage.

Industry Summary. In the intervening years between the first health-scare publicity in 1953 and the 1964 Surgeon General's Report, the industry evolved from a highly "reactive" posture to an "anticipatory" stance. Whereas little product innovation occurred until the first major environmental induction, the industry as a whole became accurate in reading the environmental climate and judging the necessity for filter and low-tar cigarettes to counter the increasingly publicized research linking smoking to health disorders. The introduction of an entirely new product type, the low-tar cigarette, at least four years prior to the Surgeon General's 1964 report, for example, provides evidence of the adoption of an industrywide anticipatory stance. In addition, one firm—American Brands—began to publish the tar and nicotine content of its Carlton and Montclair brands on the cigarette packages as early as 1963, a move initially prohibited by the industry's Cigarette Advertising Code, Inc., but later required of all brands as a result of the 1970 legislation.

There seems to be little doubt that the tobacco industry has been successful in producing new products that have been responsive to the trend in its market and institutional environments for "safer" smoking. As a result, despite setbacks on several occasions, the industry has remained viable, but its population of firms has continued to build financial resources needed to continue their adaptation to a decline in their primary domain. Individual firms, however, have chosen somewhat diverse strategies in their product-innovation efforts over this 25-year period, and the first 1953 health scare served to highlight their differences.

A SAMPLING OF FIRM INNOVATION STRATEGIES

Despite the overall patterns that emerged in the *nature* of product innovation within the tobacco industry, member firms exhibited substantial variety in *timing* of their domain-offense strategies. We will concentrate our analysis of this variety on the behaviors of the four independent tobacco firms. Throughout the study period, Brown & Williamson was a wholly owned subsidiary of the British-American Tobacco Company, based in the United Kingdom, and during 1969, Lorillard was acquired by the U.S.-based Loews Corporation to provide cash needed to finance its hotel expansion program. Because these members of the Big Six were not independent companies during the entire study period, some important data on their market performance are embedded in the information about their parent companies, and the explanation of their strategic behaviors is limited because of the overriding portfolio strategy of their conglomerate parents.

Among the four remaining Big Six firms, we may distinguish four general strategic orientations. These orientations were identified by Miles and Snow (1978) to describe the predispositions of competitors within a given product-market domain. Indeed, a subsequent study (Snow and Hrebiniak, 1980) revealed that the best discriminator among those of this strategic typology was a firm's competence in the area of product research and development. Therefore, the Miles and Snow typology was examined for potential fit with the competitive behaviors of the four tobacco independents. Although the generalizability and comprehensiveness of this typology across industries has not been established conclusively, its fit with the four tobacco independents was a good one. The four strategic types—Prospector, Analyzer, Defender, and Reactor—appeared to describe the primary domain-offense strategies of Philip Morris, R.J. Reynolds, American Brands, and Liggett & Meyers, respectively.[7]

PHILIP MORRIS: THE *PROSPECTOR*

The product-market strategy of a Prospector is one of continual search for market opportunities. Prospectors regularly experiment with potential responses to emerging environmental trends. As a result, they are often the creators of market change and uncertainty to which their competitors must adapt. However, because of their strong orientation toward innovation within the existing product-market domain, their financial performance may not achieve the level and reliability of less impetuous competitors operating in the same domain. Instead, they tend to capitalize on the advantages of being the industry "first mover," but they are prone to lose much of the benefit of their early entry as the market segments they open up become attractive to more generalist competitors who may enter with the backing of more resources.

If ever there was an archetype of the Prospector, it has to be Philip Morris. In 1950, PM was at the bottom of the heap in terms of relative market share; consequently, it had little to lose and much to gain from innovation. Also, the company is unique among the Big Six, as its senior officers are prone to emphasize. For instance, PM was not part of the "trust bust" at the turn of the century that created its competitors. Instead, it began modestly as an independent also-ran.

During the Great Depression, its representatives peddled unheard-of "economy" brands on the streets. It pioneered cigarette advertising in the radio medium because it could not afford the high cost of newspaper advertising. It was the first to develop advertising and products designed to bring women into the smoking market. Philip Morris anticipated its competitors by four years in introducing the first low-tar (high-filtration) cigarette. Moreover, during the 1950s, Philip Morris introduced each of its new brands with a packaging innovation. Much of the early success of the filter-tipped Marlboro brand, introduced in 1955, was attributed to the unique "flip-top" box and red tear-tape, both regarded in the tobacco industry as major packaging innovations.

It is as though Miles and Snow, when they were defining the strategic orientation of the Prospector, had been present at the public address of George Weissman, president of Philip Morris. In Weissman's own words:

> . . . we have never felt inhibited by the traditions of the big five. We've felt we could buck the industry and succeed. We've also figured Philip Morris could never compete dollar for dollar with Reynolds and American; we've had to innovate, to accept the risk of higher costs and lower margins that accompany the introduction of many new products in our businesses.

R.J. REYNOLDS: THE *ANALYZER*

The Analyzer, according to Miles and Snow, is an organization that operates simultaneously in two product-market spheres, one relatively stable, the other changing. In its stable sphere, this type of organization operates routinely with great financial success. In its more turbulent sphere, top managers watch their competitors closely for new ideas, and then they rapidly adopt those that appear to be the most promising. For R.J. Reynolds, as in the case of Philip Morris, the fit between strategic orientation and domain-offense strategy was a neat one.

Sharing the top position in domestic-market cigarette sales with American Brands in 1950, Reynolds had much to lose from product innovation and very little to gain—that is, until the emergence of the smoking-and-health controversy. In the absence of demand for "safer" cigarettes, the introduction of early innovations by Reynolds would have generated as much competition against its established product lines as it would against those of its competitors holding smaller market shares. Therefore, Reynolds never was first mover in the product-innovation waves; but it was always an early adopter of the successful innovations of its competitors. The process by which filter cigarettes were introduced into the domestic market during the early 1950s provides some insight into Reynolds's domain-offense strategy.

Prior to 1950, only Philip Morris and Brown & Williamson produced filter cigarettes, and these early innovators ranked sixth and fifth, respectively, in domestic market share. Their filter-tip brands were slightly ahead of the times. Before the 1950s, filter-cigarette sales accounted for less than 1 percent of the market, and there seemed to be little pressure for filtered-cigarette innovation. However, by the time of the 1953 health-and-smoking scare, Reynolds, then the industry sales leader, had acknowledged a gradual market acceptance of the filter brands introduced by its competitors. RJR's annual reports during that time indicated that these innovations were being carefully monitored by its marketing-research staff. The 1953 report noted that filter-tip brands had moved from a 1¼ percent share of the domestic market in 1952 to a 3¼ percent share by 1953, and that the company had for some time been developing its own filter-tip product for distribution should market demand increase. With this marketing intelligence and the lead time it provided, coupled with the Sloan-Kettering report of 1953 linking cigarette smoking with heart and lung disease, RJR introduced the Winston filter-tip cigarette in 1954. A new strategic emphasis on "safer smoking" was in the making.

By 1956, RJR was predicting in its annual report a permanent decline in the volume of regular cigarettes sold and an overall increasing trend in the domestic consumption of filter-tip cigarettes. That same year, filter brands had acquired a 30 percent share of the domestic market; by 1958, 46 percent; by 1959, 50 percent. By 1974, RJR was selling seventeen filter-tip cigarettes for every two regular cigarettes it sold.

Throughout the study period, therefore, Reynolds was content to monitor the developments of its competitors' new-product innovations. As shown in Table 4-2, it followed Philip Morris, Brown & Williamson, and Lorillard in the introduction of filter cigarettes; yet Winston, its first filter cigarette (1954), and Vantage, its first low-tar brand (1963), both captured the number 1 position in share of market within their product types by the end of the first year in which they were introduced. Also, both product types were introduced during a year that a major event occurred in the institutional environment surrounding the tobacco industry.

Partly as a result of this "wait-and-see" policy, of the seventeen brands introduced by RJR over the period 1950–74, only one was a failure, and that was a regular, nonfiltered brand introduced on the eve of the 1964 Surgeon General's Report (Maxwell, 1975). Thus, the RJR product failure rate was 6 percent over this quarter century, compared to a failure rate of 53 percent for American Brands.

AMERICAN BRANDS: THE *DEFENDER*

In the same quarter century in which Philip Morris had prospected its way from the bottom to the second industry rank in market share, American Brands had moved from first place to fourth, leaving Reynolds, the Analyzer, in the first place. The reason is quite simple. American Brands played for too long the strategic role of Defender in a domain that was undergoing rapid change in a new direction as the result of the confluence of market and nonmarket forces. The singular unique feature of the Defender strategic orientation is the focus on a narrow product-market segment. According to Miles and Snow:

> *Top managers in this type of organization are highly expert in their organization's limited area of operation but do not tend to search outside of their domains for new opportunities. As a result of this narrow focus, these organizations seldom need to make major adjustments in their technology, structure, or methods of operation. Instead, they devote primary attention to improving the efficiency of their existing operations. [1978:29]*

American Brands historically had been invested heavily in the nonfilter product type, and had started late in developing filtered products. As late as 1957, the company's continued emphasis on nonfilter cigarettes was revealed in its annual report, which boasted that the company produced two of the three leading nonfilter brands (Pall Mall and Lucky Strike), and that these high-tar brands accounted for 45 percent of nonfilter cigarette sales in the United States. Whereas plans were announced in 1957 to increase the company's competitiveness in the filter market, over 90 percent of cigarette sales at AB was in the nonfilter category until 1963. A change in AB's chief executive officers in 1963 finally brought about an emphasis on product innovation.[8] In a statement made to investors, the new CEO revealed his product strategy: "At the 1963 Annual Meeting I set as a prime goal the improvement of our position in the filter cigarette market. Filter brands accounted for about 12% of our cigarette sales in 1963 as against 9.5% in 1962."

An all-out effort was mounted to move up in the filter market. Five new brands were introduced in 1964. By 1966, the president of American Brands reported that 30 percent of company sales was accounted for by filter brands but that a renewed effort was needed to overcome the long-time reliance on nonfilter brands:

> *Despite the decided progress which has been made in advancing our filter business, I must concurrently report that, as measured in unit sales, the decrease in our non-filter volume was not offset by our increased filter volume. Your Management is fully cognizant of the necessity to further increase its share of the filter market, now representing almost 70% of the industry's total cigarette sales. . . . While our total filter cigarette sales have increased from . . . 1962 to . . . 1966, it is evident that further progress must be made in this direction. This will be done.*

During the same period, filter brands at Philip Morris increased from 84 percent of company sales in 1963 to 91 percent in 1966, and President Joseph Cullman reported to his stockholders that ''the trend to filter cigarettes resulted in this category capturing approximately 70% of the market, a development that augurs well for Philip Morris because of our strong position in the filter cigarette field.''

LIGGETT & MEYERS: THE *REACTOR*

We have reserved the Reactor strategic orientation for Liggett & Meyers. In the Reactor organization, top managers frequently perceive change and uncertainty occurring in their product-market domain but are unable to respond effectively. According to Miles and Snow:

> *. . . the Reactor is an unstable organization type because it lacks a set of consistent response mechanisms that it can put into effect when faced with a changing environment. This inconsistency potentially may stem from at least three sources: (1) management fails to articulate a viable organizational strategy; (2) a strategy is articulated but technology, structure, and process are not linked to it in an appropriate manner; or (3) management adheres to a particular strategy-structure relationship even though it is no longer relevant to environmental conditions.* [1978:82]

Industry observers are prone to fault Liggett for all three of these factors (Koten, 1979). During this quarter century, Liggett exhibited substantially less internal consistency that did its competitors. Until R.J. Mulligan, a former marketing executive with one of Liggett's acquisitions, took over as chief executive officer in 1973, Liggett management had been dominated by production-oriented managers who had grown up in the traditional tobacco industry. The credibility of marketing managers within Liggett had been lost with the market failures of the early product innovations. The company experienced only two successful brand introductions during the 1950−60 period. It was still trying to introduce filter cigarettes as late as 1972, and by 1975, it had not successfully introduced a low-tar brand.

In a *Wall Street Journal* account of the plight of Liggett, an unidentified manager in a rival Big Six firm observed that "Liggett is always too late with too little," and that the firm's attempted move to low-tar cigarettes was no exception (Sease, 1978a). Indeed, Liggett's first low-tar brand was not introduced until 1977. By that time, Liggett's share of the market had dwindled from 18 percent to less than 4 percent, and the market had become saturated with the low-tar brands of its competitors. The $20 million that Liggett allocated to the promotion of this entry amounted to only one-third to one-half the normal expenditures made by its competitors to introduce their new brands. By the end of the 1970s, Liggett was searching for someone to purchase its tobacco business.[9]

DOMAIN OFFENSE: ACHIEVEMENTS AND FAILURES

The achievements and failures of the strategies we have described as domain offense may be discussed at both industry and firm levels. As the Big Six pursued strategies of product innovation, brand proliferation, and market segmentation in an attempt to preserve and increase their shares of a maturing and threatened domain, the industry as a whole benefited, because the nature and timing of these aggregated firm strategies resulted in overall responsiveness to the demand for "safer" smoking. By moving toward cigarette product types with lower tar and nicotine content, the industry was able to engage in a positive manner the threat from the institutional environment to its legitimacy. But not all members of the industry population received the same benefit from this general trend.

TRACK RECORDS OF THE BIG SIX:
SPRINTS, HURDLES, AND MARATHON

Evaluation of the relative effectiveness of a group of organizations is usually a difficult undertaking and one that is sure to encourage its critics. In the present case, however, we are able to rule out a number of typical criticisms by focusing on a relatively homogeneous population of firms that operated under virtually identical environmental conditions. Moreover, we will not, at least at this stage of our investigation, grapple with the total concept of organizational effectiveness. Instead, we will focus on the competitive performance among the Big Six within their traditional domain, the cigarette business. For this purpose, we will make a distinction, suggested by Miles (1980c:366), between organizational goals and organizational strategies.

All members of the Big Six were pursuing a common goal of *domain offense*: achieving the greatest possible share of the maturing domestic market for cigarettes. This fact was established through interviews with senior corporate executives and corporate development officers, conducted by the senior author in 1980.[10] The interviews focused on what the companies had learned from their efforts to diversify, but the question that inevitably surfaced was why the companies began to diversify *away* from the traditional tobacco industry. Although a host of precipitating factors were identified, all companies responded that virtually no other legal business in the United States is as profitable and generates as much stable cash flow as the cigarette business. It was true that growth in cigarette demand had plateaued and that the legitimacy and ultimate survival of the cigarette industry was uncertain; but it is important to recognize that *none* of the companies sought to leave what remained of their traditional domain *without a fight*.

As Miles (1980c) has cautioned, the first element in the determination of organizational effectiveness is the appropriateness of the organization's goals, given the nature of the environment in which it must operate. One may certainly question the appropriateness of the domain-offense goal that was shared among the Big Six, because its successful achievement could make some firms overdependent on a domain that might not survive in the long run. Nevertheless, the success that the industry had achieved with its collaborative domain-*defense* strategies was sufficiently encouraging to the senior managers of the Big Six to cause them to commit their resources first to the traditional domain (i.e., to domain-*offense* strategies) and then to apply the excess resources generated by the lack of growth in that domain to the development and acquisition of other businesses (i.e., to domain-*creation* strategies). With a common goal of domain offense identified, it remains to be determined how successful were the strategies employed by the member firms to achieve that goal.

Domain-Offense Strategies and Financial Performance. We have linked four major domain-offense strategies with the behaviors of the tobacco independents over our quarter-century period. Three of these strategies—Prospector, Analyzer and Defender—are almost always viable, according to Miles and Snow (1978); that is, companies pursuing any one of these competitive strategies may be able to perform "effectively" in the same industry or domain. Reactors, these theorists assert, almost never perform effectively in the company of industry rivals pursuing the other three strategies.

Preliminary tests of these hypotheses were reported in 1980 (Snow and Hrebiniak), based on a survey of senior officers in single-business firms representing four industries. Their results revealed, first, that Defenders were more prevalent in industries characterized by relatively low market uncertainty (i.e., automotive manufacture and air transport), and that the Prospector was the dominant form in high-uncertainty industries (i.e., plastics and, especially, semiconductors). Second, they found that (1) Analyzers were more profitable than the other three strategic types in all industries, and that (2) Prospectors and Defenders were more profitable than Reactors except in the industry where competitive relations were mandated by federal government regulation (i.e., air transport).

Given these preliminary findings from single-business organizations, we decided to investigate whether the financial performance among the tobacco independents varied according to the strategy each pursued. Theoretically, the Analyzer should outperform, in financial terms, the Prospector and the Defender, which, in turn, should outperform the Reactor. Moreover, because the tobacco market has been a dynamic and uncertain one during our quarter-century period, we should expect the Defender, with its focus on the maintenance of the status quo, to achieve less profitability than the innovative Prospector.

On all counts, the overall financial performance of the tobacco independents achieved a perfect fit with these predictions. During this quarter century, the compounded average growth rate in earnings per share of common stock for the four tobacco independents, as shown in Table 4-3, reveals that Reynolds (the Analyzer) achieved the best profitability record, followed in order by Philip Morris (the Prospector), American Brands (the Defender), and Liggett & Meyers (the Reactor). These results, however, should be treated with caution because many factors, not necessarily encompassed by this typology, may influence a firm's overall profitability.

By the mid-1960s, as the next chapter will reveal, these organizations were no longer single-business companies. The success of yet another major strategy, which we will refer to as *domain creation*, had transformed the Big Six into multibusiness conglomerates, whose nontobacco businesses were beginning to influence their overall financial performance in significant ways. Therefore, a

TABLE 4-3 COMPOUNDED AVERAGE GROWTH RATE IN EARNINGS PER SHARE, U.S. TOBACCO INDEPENDENTS (1950–1975)

Independent Firms	Domain Offense Strategy	Compounded Average Growth Rate in EPS[a]
R.J. Reynolds	Analyzer	9.16%
Philip Morris	Prospector	8.35%
American Brands	Defender	5.61%
Liggett & Meyers	Reactor	0.75%

[a]Earnings per share (EPS) is calculated for each firm by dividing net annual earnings by the number of common-stock shares outstanding.

Source: *Moody's*

more precise assessment of the domain-offense strategies of the Big Six must come from an analysis of their immediate market performance.

Domain-Offense Strategies and Market Performance. Market performance may be measured in terms of both product-innovation success rate and relative market share. As shown in Table 4-4, Reynolds, the Analyzer, experienced the lowest number of product failures over the quarter-century period. It was followed by the prospecting Philip Morris, which introduced the largest number (28) of new products. Both American Brands and Liggett & Meyers suffered eight product failures. So, on this measure of market performance, both Defender and Reactor achieved the same degree of ineffectiveness. In terms of total rate of failures, American Brands (53 percent) performed even worse than Liggett (40 percent).

Closer examination reveals that American Brands had its greatest failure rate with filter cigarettes. Recall that it was toward the end of the filter-cigarette market era that executive succession within American Brands brought about a recognition of the need for innovation in this product type. But by that time, competitors had already captured that market, and a new market period emphasizing low-tar cigarettes was beginning to unfold. The Defender was simply too late in responding. Its strategy was not viable in the dynamic cigarette marketplace. More telling, however, is the impact that these product failure rates had on the market shares acquired or lost by the Big Six.

Table 4-5 summarizes the relative market shares achieved by the Big Six at the beginning and end of the quarter-century period. Although the overall degree of concentration in the tobacco industry remained stable, a major reshuffling in market shares occurred among the industry population.

By 1974, American Brands, the Defender, had moved from first to fourth place in market standing, and Liggett, the Reactor, had moved from third to last

TABLE 4-4 PRODUCT INNOVATION FAILURE RATES, 1950-1974

Big Six Firms	Failure Rates				
	Regular Brands	Filter Brands	Low-Tar Brands	All Brands	Total Failures
Independent Firms:					
Reynolds	(4)[a] 25%	(8) 0%	(5) 0%	(17) 6%	1
Philip Morris	(5) 60%	(14) 0%	(9) 22%	(28) 18%	5
American Brands	(3) 0%	(19) 42%	(3) 0%	(15) 53%	8
Liggett & Meyers	(4) 59%	(14) 29%	(2)100%	(20) 40%	8
Captive Firms:					
Lorillard	(4) 50%	(13) 23%	(4) 0%	(21) 24%	5
Brown & Williamson	(3) 0%	(16) 44%	(7) 43%	(26) 38%	10

[a]Number of attempts to introduce new cigarette brands of this product type.

Source: Maxwell Report, 1974

TABLE 4-5 CONCENTRATION AND MARKET-SHARE DISTRIBUTION
IN THE U.S. TOBACCO INDUSTRY, 1950 AND 1974

Members of the Industry Population	Share of Domestic Cigarette Market			
	1950		1974	
	Share	Rank	Share	Rank
American Brands	31.1%	1	15.7%	4
R.J. Reynolds	27.4	2	31.5	1
Liggett & Meyers	18.6	3	4.6	6
Philip Morris	11.3	4	22.5	2
Lorillard	5.5	5	8.2	5
Brown & Williamson	5.2	6	17.4	3
Industry Concentration Ratio:[a]	88.4%		87.1%	

[a]Industry concentration is computed for a given year by dividing the total industry net revenues by the combined net revenues of the largest four member firms.

Source: Maxwell Report, 1974

place. Both had suffered a loss of 14—15 percent of the total domestic cigarette market, while the Analyzer and the Prospector had thrived. Reynolds had moved from second to first place, and Philip Morris from fourth to second in relative market standing. Brown & Williamson, a captive Prospector that rivaled Philip Morris in product innovation rate but with less success, had also advanced strongly, from sixth to third in market share, during this turbulent period in the tobacco industry. These results argue that competitive strategy makes a difference, but they also suggest an amendment to the Miles and Snow propositions.

A Second Look at the Defender. The major distinction between Defender and Reactor is that the former has a coherent strategy, whereas the latter does not—a distinction, Miles and Snow argue, that makes it possible for Defenders to survive under conditions in which Reactors cannot:

> . . . *Defenders enact an environment of greater stability than do their counterparts within the same industry. Even in industries widely noted for their rapidly changing conditions, there are potential pockets of stability within which a Defender can thrive. Thus . . . we have argued that the Defender* deliberately *creates and maintains an environment for which a stable form of organization is appropriate.* [1978:47]

To the extent that the demands of the product-market environment are rapidly changing in unpredictable directions, however, it would appear that the Defender strategy is also a reactive one that may not guarantee more than a temporary assurance of organizational survival. Indeed, somewhat contrary to the position taken above, Miles and Snow have observed that:

. . . *the primary risk faced by a Defender is* . . . *the inability to locate new product or market opportunities. Indeed, in times of crisis, the typical Defender is probably both unable and unwilling to search for solutions to its adaptive problems by scanning the environment for potential opportunities.* [*1978:92*]

Thus, the effectiveness of Defenders is likely to hinge on the degree of unpredictable dynamism in the product market. Fortunately for American Brands, the tobacco industry during the time of the smoking-and-health controversy was *predictably* dynamic. The pattern of changing market demands for new-product innovations assumed a definite direction, one oriented more and more toward lower-tar cigarettes and "safer" smoking. We would argue, therefore, that this directionality made the market dynamics in the tobacco industry somewhat more amenable to tardy responsiveness on the part of member firms. Thus, although the late attempts by American Brands to enter the filter-cigarette market resulted in near-disaster (i.e., American Brands suffered the highest failure rate among the Big Six in new filter-cigarette products), its new management was eventually able to make a strong entry into the low-tar-cigarette market. By that time, we would argue further, this Defender had learned its lessons the hard way and had achieved a reorientation in its competitive strategy toward that of an Analyzer.

In summary, we have found the Miles and Snow typology to be quite helpful in sorting among the domain-offense or competitive strategies of the Big Six. Indeed, their four strategic orientations appeared to be remarkably stable over the quarter century of changes that occurred in the U.S. tobacco industry. The only evidence we discovered of an organizational shift in competitive strategy among the member firms was what happened within American Brands after a period of prolonged environmental uncertainty and organizational underachievement, and then only after a rather complete transition in executive leadership. But the results of the present study, as well as those of subsequent applications of this typology (e.g., Snow and Hrebiniak, 1980), cast doubt on the proposition that three of the four strategic orientations will always be viable in a given industry. These results suggest that across a variety of situations the Analyzer may do relatively well and the Reactor relatively poorly; but the relative performance of the extreme orientations of the Prospector and the Defender may vary widely, depending on the rate and unpredictability of change in the environment surrounding their industry.

Beyond these important considerations is the question of the generalizability of the relationships uncovered between competitive strategy and organizational performance. As we shall review in the next chapter, there has been a dramatic increase in the number of U.S. corporations that operate in more than one product-market domain, and the Big Six are no exception. But the Miles and Snow model was built and subsequently tested by relying on the analysis of single-business organizations. It remains to be determined, therefore, whether the strategic orientation that a firm chooses within its traditional domain also guides its competitive behavior in other business domains in which it operates as a result of internal development and external acquisition programs. It will also be important to determine whether and how these multibusiness organizations choose industries and acquire firms to fit their traditional strategic orientation, or whether and how they adapt their orientation to fit conditions in new industries and acquired companies. We will return to these issues after we have reviewed the domain-creation strategies of the Big Six in the next two chapters.

SUMMARY

Economists have focused traditionally on the *competitive* responses of member firms to market changes within an industry that are induced by endogenous or exogenous factors. Political scientists, on the other hand, have typically studied the *collaborative* responses of industry populations to political threats to their autonomy or legitimacy. As a result, the study by both traditions of the behavior of complex organizations under conditions of environmental stress have failed to capture the full scope of organizational adaptation or the interdependences among its components.

So far, we have demonstrated that an industry population not only is capable of pursuing simultaneously strategies involving intense conflict and cooperation under conditions of extreme environmental press, but may be very successful in doing so. Indeed, the Big Six were able to partition their environment into economic and political spheres and to tailor and pursue simultaneously strategies of intense competition and intense collaboration. Moreover, these components of organizational adaptation have often been mutually reinforcing. The domain-offense strategies that were mounted by member firms created a product that responded to the threat to the legitimacy of their traditional domain and, therefore, contributed to their joint political strategies of domain defense.

The evidence from the story of the Big Six also raises serious doubts about the traditional assumption made by economists that industry competition and concentration are opposites. The fewer the number of member firms that control the majority of the share of market, they have argued, the less will be the intensity of competition. In our oligopoly, although there has been little evidence of price competition, rivalry among the Big Six has been intense in the areas of product innovation and promotion.[11] Drawing upon the story so far told, we are led to believe that conditions of market maturity and outside threat (either from the institutional environment or from other industries producing close product substitutes), but particularly both conditions, are sufficient to stimulate the stereotypically lethargic, highly concentrated oligopoly to engage in intense competition.

Finally, the increase in competition among the Big Six did not occur, as "natural-selection" theorists assert, from the entry of new firms into the industry. Instead, the industry may be characterized as highly responsive to the threats to its survival. Only certain traditional firms exhibited signs of inertia, as evidenced by the lag in reorientation among alternative domain-offense strategies that separated the most adaptive firms from the others.

But success in achieving the domain-offense goals of member firms has a paradoxical quality. Firms that succeeded in maintaining and enhancing their shares of the maturing domestic cigarette market could actually find that their futures had become tied more tightly to a threatened domain whose survival remained in question, particularly if the strategies that we have defined as domain offense and defense were the only ones they pursued. Such was not the case, however. A third major strategy—one made possible by the first two—also characterized the process of strategic adaptation that was pursued by the Big Six. It is to the strategy of *domain creation* that we must turn before completing our analysis of organizational adaptation in the U.S. tobacco industry.

FOOTNOTES

[1]Product innovation is based on the Maxwell Report (1975), which records the volume of all cigarette brands whose volume reaches a minimum of 500,000 units in a given year. Product failure is adjudged where the brand's volume dips below 500,000 units and, consequently, the brand is removed from the Maxwell Report statistical summary—and also, typically, from the product portfolio of the tobacco firm.

[2]Many firms simply repackaged or renamed existing brands during this period (e.g., the Parliament brand name was changed to Benson & Hedges in 1956), but these "cosmetic" changes are not included among our product-innovation statistics.

[3]"Low-tar" brands were defined initially by the industry as those brands containing less than 15 milligrams of tar per cigarette. This definition was adopted later by the Federal Trade Commission.

[4]This proposal would also expose the Big Six to another volley of antismoking commercials.

[5]In Table 4-2, the letters R, F, and L identify the introduction of particular types of brand innovations: R=regular, nonfilter brands; F=filter-tip brands; and L=low-tar filter brands. Circled letters indicate dates of brand failures.

[6]Similar results were achieved by the product-innovation strategies of British tobacco companies during the 1960s. According to the report of the Monopolies Commission in Great Britain, "the filter tip enables the manufacturer to produce a cigarette with a smaller tobacco content while maintaining overall dimensions and avoiding waste of tobacco in the unsmoked fag-end" (1969:1). Thus, the British counterparts to the Big Six were able to produce cigarettes that were responsive to the smoking-and-health issue and that resulted in cost reductions without loss of market price.

[7]The application of the Miles (no relation to the senior author) and Snow (1978) strategic typology came as a result of a serendipitous occasion. The senior author was presenting some preliminary findings from this study in a 1977 colloquium sponsored by the Wharton School at the University of Pennsylvania, where Snow was a visiting faculty member. After the colloquium, the two researchers met, at which time Snow revealed the remarkable fit between his unpublished strategic typology and the domain-offense strategies of the tobacco independents. As a result, the early descriptors we used have been replaced by the Miles and Snow terminology.

[8]This transition in executive leadership in American Brands was a radical departure from the industry's traditional pattern of executive succession. In the 1963 transition, the former president was not retained as a member of the board of directors. Thus, the transition to new executive leadership at American Brands was a complete one.

[9]By that time, however, Liggett's market share had dropped to $3-4$ percent, a level that made its tobacco operations unattractive to overseas investors. And since U.S. antitrust laws prohibited sale of these operations to domestic competitors, Liggett was effectively "stuck" with its failing tobacco business.

[10]A full discussion of these findings will be discussed in the next chapter, "Domain Creation."

[11]To a large extent, institutional forces constrain price competition in the tobacco industry. Two primary constraints are the uniform prices required by cigarette vending machines and the potential sensitivity of taxation to changes in cigarette prices.

5

Domain Creation

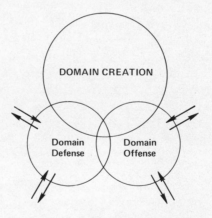

The domain defense and offense strategies employed by the Big Six not only served to protect the tobacco industry from some important institutional threats and to shape the prosperity that member firms derived from their traditional line of business, but also provided an opportunity to engage in yet another set of strategies designed to create new domains of opportunity characterized by less political risk and higher economic growth. The lead time derived from the successful defense of domain generated sufficient slack for members of the Big Six to engage in bold new ventures at home and abroad. The successful lobbying effort, bolstered by the development of tobacco products that were responsive to the legitimacy threat, created a "space" for organizational adaptation that lasted almost a decade. During that time, the Big Six were able to explore the potentials of new domains of operation, to experiment in them before committing major reallocations of resources into unknown areas, and to orchestrate an orderly transfer of capital and talent away from the threatened domain to alternative domains that evinced more potential.

To some extent, the domain offense strategies employed by members of the Big Six also shaped the direction and intensity of each firm's movement into new operating domains. For example, Liggett & Meyers's lackluster performance as a Reactor in the competition for domestic market share compelled it to seek aggressively new product markets in distilled liquor and pet food that offered more potential. Similarly, American Brands' Defender strategy had resulted in severe market-share erosion, a condition that caused it to acquire a major British tobacco company and thereby to make a bold entry into the international market for tobacco products.

In one sense, these domain-creation strategies of diversification and overseas expansion tell us more about the *character* of our firms than does either their domain defense or domain offense strategies. The latter two involved collaboration and competition among the industry players—a situation of strategic interdependence—in which the choices and behaviors of one player were shaped in part by those of the others. In contrast, each member of the Big

Six pursued independently its strategies of domain creation. Particularly in the case of diversification, strategic choices made by traditional players in the tobacco industry led them into very different product markets, each presenting a new set of rivals. But only scant systematic knowledge about diversification and overseas expansion was available at the time the Big Six embarked on their independent strategies of domain creation. Therefore, this set of strategies provides a unique window into each firm's capabilities for learning, experimenting, and adapting to changing external forces.

DOMAIN CREATION: LEARNING FROM ENACTING

The Big Six did not invent the strategies of domain creation; however, it is fair to say that the social technology of domain creation was at a primitive stage of development when members of the tobacco industry embarked on their programs of overseas expansion and diversification. No coherent body of practical knowledge existed in the late 1950s and early 1960s to provide reliable guidelines for embarking on the path of domain creation. As in so many other cases, practicing managers had been experimenting with new approaches in this case to the corporate problems of market stagnation and political risk, which organizational scholars and researchers would understand only after the results of practical experimental variation had stood the test of time.

The first major studies of corporate diversification did not appear until Penrose (1959) and Gort (1962). Although prescient, these highly theoretical treatises would hardly be on the reading lists, much less capture the attention, of practicing managers. By this time, diversification was well under way at Reynolds and Philip Morris, and an active search was being pursued by most of the other tobacco companies. It was not until the mid-1970s that a practical body of literature (e.g., Wrigley, 1970; Markham, 1973; Rumelt, 1974; Biggadike, 1976; Salter and Weinhold, 1979; Leontiades, 1980) emerged to help provide an informed choice to potential diversifiers that was based on the track records of pioneers in this movement.

The state of practical knowledge was somewhat better for firms attempting to expand overseas during the late 1950s. Many U.S. corporations had operated overseas for decades, and others had begun foreign operations from outposts set up during World War II. But firms attempting to escape the confines of a stagnant domestic market for the first time were faced with a variety of difficult choices, many of which were hard to reverse once resources had been committed.

As will be shown, many U.S. firms began international expansion very tentatively, but their experimental commitment ran counter to the emergence of multinational free-trade areas (e.g., the European Economic Community) that erected high tariff walls in the path of domestically produced exports. Gradually, export sales agreements gave way to licensing agreements for overseas manufacture that, in time, were replaced by outright ownership of overseas manufacturing subsidiaries. The result was a gradual but significant increase in the commitment of organizational resources to a global strategy. As with the diversification movement, systematic knowledge lagged organizational practice. The first major study (Stopford and Wells, 1972) of the patterns of overseas expansion employed by U.S. firms was not published until a decade and a half after the Big Six had embarked on this strategy of domain creation.

What was available to the Big Six, as they groped for ways of coping with their dependence on the threatened tobacco domain, was evidence that major companies in other industries were engaging in overseas expansion and were beginning to experiment with domestic product-market diversification. But the absence of a body of knowledge to guide strategies of domain creation was amplified for the Big Six by the fact that their managers had grown up within the traditional tobacco business. Very few among the senior ranks of this industry had logged significant management experience in other industries, and frequently, those who had were linked through several generations to the executive suites of these traditional tobacco companies. Thus, strategic managers in the Big Six had much to learn about the domain-creation process; but because of the lack of systematic knowledge in this area, much of that learning had to come from the experience gained by each company as it enacted (Miles and Randolph, 1980) its programs of overseas expansion and domestic diversification.

In summary, although the strategy of domain creation did not begin with the Big Six, it did represent a major organizational innovation, a strategic choice that committed them to untested assumptions and subjected them to uncertain risks, a condition that one organizational sociologist (Stinchcombe, 1965) has characterized as "the liability of newness." For these reasons, it is important to scrutinize the decisions and behaviors of the Big Six as they embarked on what was for them a brave new redeployment of strategic resources. In doing this, we will want to pay attention not only to what they did to create new domains of business opportunity and when they did it, but to how well they accomplished their goals, how and why they proceeded along their own paths, and whether they would do so again. As we move from *when* to *whether*, we will shift from an archival description of events as they unfolded as strategic patterns to in-depth reflections on what has been learned by the strategic managers who have guided these major organizational transformations.

In this chapter, we will trace the evolution of overseas expansion and domestic diversification among the Big Six over the quarter century of 1950−1975. In the next chapter, we will focus on what senior managers in some of the tobacco independents have learned from their programs of corporate diversification.

OVERSEAS EXPANSION: PATTERNS AND CHOICES

Expansion into overseas markets by U.S. firms has not been an overnight phenomenon, but rather a protracted evolutionary process. The results of the Harvard Multinational Enterprise Project, a study of the international experiences of 170 U.S. multinational firms, identified successive stages in the development of both corporate strategy and structure of domestic firms choosing to enter foreign markets (Stopford and Wells, 1972). Many of the pioneers of this strategy found themselves with products already in place in Europe at the end of World War II. Some had established primitive distribution systems and networks of contacts abroad that were holdovers from the war. So most of the pioneers simply let things develop from there.

First, there was reliance on exports produced in the United States and loose licensing agreements with foreign assemblers or distributors. But the rise of both cost-effective competition abroad and tariff walls around newly organized free-trade areas caused U.S. producers to gradually acquire a majority interest in foreign manufacturing subsidiaries. As the contribution to the "bottom line" of overseas operations became significant, international divisions were created to manage them. Thus, the early emphasis on experimentation and learning was gradually replaced by growth in the control of foreign operations as they began to create greater stakes for their U.S. parents.With continued growth in importance, the role of the international division gave way to more comprehensive planning and control on a global basis in the domestic headquarters of the parent corporation. These general patterns have characterized the evolution of the overseas-expansion strategies of the tobacco Big Six.

Before the 1950s, U.S. tobacco companies felt no urgency to expand into foreign markets on a large scale. Most firms exported tobacco products to a limited extent prior to 1953, and export statistics were accounted for mostly by cigarette sales to U.S. armed-services personnel overseas. Only a little over 15 million cigarettes were exported in 1950 (see Figure 5-1), compared to the 375 million sold domestically that year. It was not until the health-and-smoking scare of 1953, which depressed demand at home, that active strategies geared toward opening and expanding foreign cigarette markets were initiated. Overseas expansion, however, was not without its own challenges.

DIFFICULTIES POSED BY A GLOBAL STRATEGY

Many problems face a firm wishing to pursue a global strategy in the tobacco-products field. In RJR's address in 1976 to security analysts, Tylee Wilson, executive vice-president of RJR's international subsidiary, illuminated some of the unique aspects of operating in the world tobacco market:

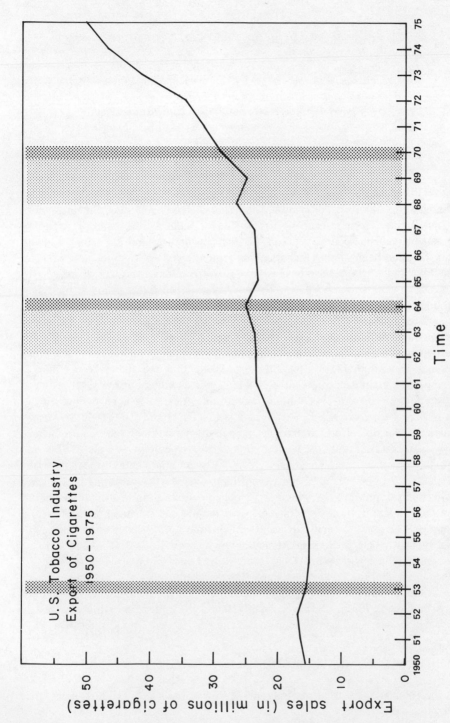

Figure 5-1 Source: U.S. Department of Agriculture, Annual Reports, 1955–76.

In 1975 worldwide unit sales of cigarettes totaled 3.8 trillion, up 2.2 percent from 1974. Not all of this total is available to us in the short term. First we must remove the Communist-bloc countries. These nations represent long-term potential markets, but we cannot call them an immediate opportunity for us or anyone else. We also eliminate the strong monopoly countries. These are countries like Korea, where you can get no footing at all, or like Japan, where you can get a very, very minor footing at best. Finally we take away the U.S. market. This leaves us with an available market of about 1.2 trillion cigarettes a year. [1]

In the same address, Wilson outlined the following factors that differentiate the various foreign markets: culture, tobacco blends, economic climate, investment climate, foreign-exchange rates, government control and restrictions, voluntary industry codes, taxation, political instability, and the salience of the smoking-and-health issues and attendant regulations. As examples, the inflation rate may range from as low as 5 percent in Germany to as high as 40 percent in Brazil. Government control may be much more or much less severe abroad than at home. Many countries had a total ban on consumer communication regarding cigarette products. "Smoking-and-health has not yet become an issue in Latin America or the Far East," said Wilson. "But in Europe, the smoking-and-health issue is much more advanced in the consumer's mind and the mind of the press than it is here in the United States." Thus, although the overseas market possessed a great deal of potential in terms of sales volume, successful overseas operations would add uncertainties and complexities to the management of the Big Six. Nevertheless, U.S. tobacco firms embarked on serious overseas market-expansion efforts for the sale and manufacture of their tobacco products.

At least four types of overseas strategies have been used by the Big Six: (1) *exports* of tobacco products made in the United States and shipped to U.S. armed-services personnel or other nonresident citizens; (2) *marketing agreements* with foreign countries, by which U.S. tobacco products are distributed and sold by the foreign firm along with their own brands but are manufactured in the United States; (3) *licensing agreements* with foreign companies that, although not owned by the U.S. firms, manufacture, distribute, and sell U.S. tobacco products along with other local brands; and (4) *foreign manufacturing or production affiliates,* wholly or partially owned by the U.S. firms, where both U.S. brands and products designed specifically for the local or national market are produced. Philip Morris currently leads the industry in these overseas strategies, and American Brands and Liggett & Meyers bring up the rear.

BIG SIX OVERSEAS STRATEGIES

Philip Morris's Overseas Strategy.   Philip Morris was out of the blocks first, creating a purchasing subsidiary in Syria in 1953 and a manufacturing subsidiary in Australia in 1954. Consolidation of Benson & Hedges with its Canadian subsidiary also took place that year. PM's annual report in 1954 announced an increased emphasis on developing foreign markets and the beginning of plans to establish local cigarette-assembly operations supervised by its own employees in several foreign countries.

By 1955, PM had consolidated its foreign operations under an international division, and by 1961, 104 countries received PM cigarette exports. By 1971, 140 brands were sold in 162 countries, and more units of cigarettes were sold overseas by PM than in the domestic market. In 1972, the company's annual report announced:

During 1972, Philip Morris became the leading exporter of cigarettes from the United States, and Marlboro now ranks as the number one cigarette brand around the world. Philip Morris International's growth is due in part to the demand for Philip Morris brands generated by our international affiliates, licensees, and marketing companies in their own markets. [p. 23]

The international holdings of the U.S.-based tobacco companies as of 1975 are shown in Table 5-1. In that year, Philip Morris held more agreements in more parts of the world than any other U.S.-based tobacco firm, and company revenues had increased from $6.6 million in 1950 to over $1 billion by 1975. As with the strategies for product innovation and diversification, Philip Morris adopted the early-innovator role and chose to expand more rapidly than its domestic competitors in overseas markets. The success of PM's strategy is dramatically illustrated in Figure 5-2.

Reynolds's Overseas Strategy. The first mention of RJR's efforts to develop and promote foreign markets for its cigarette products came in its 1958 *Annual Report* (five years after PM's Syrian acquisition), at the end of a four-year lull in domestic cigarette sales. Until 1960, the company had relied upon export sales of domestically produced tobacco products. However, because of the greater protectionist sentiment evidenced by the increasing tariff walls and restrictive import quotas of countries in Europe's free-trade areas, RJR sought to complement its overseas expansion by export sales with the establishment of manufacturing subsidiaries located within foreign customs walls. So, in 1960, RJR acquired a majority interest in a European cigarette-manufacturing firm. This $10 million acquisition established a company-controlled cigarette manufacturing facility within the European Common Market, in an agreement that established a wholly owned Swiss manufacturing company producing cigarettes for the European Free Trade Association nations. Thereafter, overseas manufacturing facilities were acquired in rapid succession in the Canary Islands, Indonesia, Ecuador, Malaysia, Brazil, and Canada. Throughout this period,

TABLE 5-1 OVERSEAS MARKET EXPANSION OF U.S.-BASED TOBACCO COMPANIES: A SUMMARY OF HOLDINGS

Country	PM	RJR	L&M	L	AB
AFRICA					
Algeria			√		
Canary Islands	√	√			
Morocco			√		
Nigeria	√				
So. Africa				√	
SOUTH AMERICA					
Bolivia	√		√	√	
Brazil	√	√	√		
Colombia	√				
Mexico	√	√		√	
Neth. Antilles	√				
Trinidad	√				
Venezuela	√			√	
Peru		√	√	√	
Puerto Rico	√	√		√	
Argentina	√		√	√	
Panama	√			√	
Guatemala	√			√	
Ecuador	√	√			
Dominican Rep.	√				
Costa Rica	√		√		
CANADA	√	√			
ASIA, PACIFIC					
Hong Kong	√	√		√	
Philippines	√	√	√	√	√
Pakistan	√			√	
Japan	√				
Iran		√			
New Zealand	√	√			
Malaysia	√	√			
Indonesia	√	√			√
Australia	√	√	√	√	
India	√				
Singapore	√				
EUROPE					
England	√	√			√
France	√			√	
Netherlands	√	√	√		√
Belgium	√		√		
Austria	√	√	√	√	
Andora			√		
Bulgaria	√	√			
W. Germany	√	√	√	√	
E. Germany	√	√			
Finland	√	√		√	
Switzerland	√	√	√	√	
Greece	√	√		√	
Italy	√		√		
Luxembourg				√	
Poland	√				
Spain	√				
Denmark				√	
Sweden	√				
Yugoslavia	√	√	√	√	
TOTALS					
AFRICA	2	1	2	1	0
SOUTH AMERICA	14	5	5	8	0
CANADA	1	1	0	0	0
ASIA-PACIFIC	10	7	2	4	2
EUROPE	16	10	8	9	2
GRAND TOTAL	43	24	17	22	4

NOTE: These figures include license agreements as well as financial interests. Brown & Williamson has not been included since it does not hold any interest in any company overseas; however, its British parent company, BAT, holds interests in 39 countries.

Source: *Tobacco Reporter,* 1976

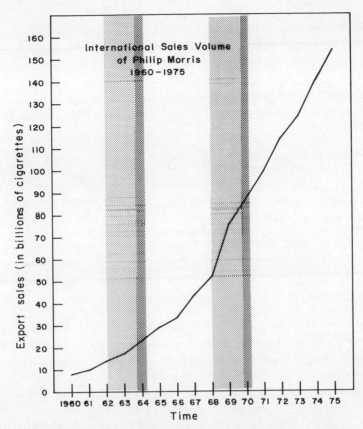

FIGURE 5-2　Source: Philip Morris, Inc., Annual Reports, 1960–76.

capital expenditures not earmarked for the company's domestic diversification program were allocated in the main toward expansion of overseas tobacco-products production capacity. Only token additions were made to domestic production facilities.

Overseas growth by the acquisition of production facilities was complemented with an extensive system of licensing agreements, and by 1974, RJR was exporting cigarettes to more than 140 countries, with over 25 percent of its tobacco-products sales accounted for by overseas markets. Furthermore, RJR had negotiated a joint agreement with the Soviet Union to experiment with the growth of tobacco crops on Russian soil.

By 1975, the international division of RJR had divided the world and its overseas operations into four areas: (1) Area I: Europe, Africa, and the Middle East; (2) Area II: Canada; (3) Area III: Latin America; and (4) Area IV: Asia and the Pacific. Recent major investments have been placed in Area III, where the smoking-and-health issue is not currently emphasized, and in Area II, a market quite similar to the U.S. domestic market in which RJR has traditionally been so successful. A statement in the 1974 *Annual Report* sums up RJR's overseas-expansion strategy during the past decade and a half:

> *The dusty road that led from the "little red factory" a hundred years ago has circled the earth. A third of our employees now live outside the United States, and the number is growing rapidly; a third of our revenue is generated abroad.* [p. 2]

American Brands' Overseas Strategy.   According to the right-hand column of Table 5-1, it would appear that, in terms of the relative number of foreign activities, American Brands has been the laggard in overseas expansion. The company consolidated a minor British tobacco firm as early as 1957, but it was not until 1968 that AB acquired part ownership in its first overseas company, the Gallaher Tobacco Company. It was not until 1974 that American Brands took 100 percent ownership of the Gallaher stock, and this holding remains AB's only major foreign investment in tobacco. But closer investigation of this strategic departure among the Big Six revealed that American Brands' choices of expansion into overseas domains was limited by legal precedents that had been established half a century earlier.

The 1921 "trust bust" in the U.S. tobacco industry broke the American Brands monopoly into several component companies, among which are Reynolds, Lorillard, and Liggett & Meyers. The U.S. Justice Department ruled that American Brands at that time possessed an effective monopoly in the United States. As part of the disaggregation of this monopoly, American Brands developed a joint venture with the Imperial Tobacco Company in the United Kingdom, which became the British-American Tobacco Company (BAT). As part of this agreement, BAT acquired the rights to sell all existing American Brands cigarettes throughout the world except in the United States. So, one important reason why American Brands had not been as active as other members of the Big Six in overseas expansion during the 1960s was that the international distribution of most of AB's traditional brands was controlled already by BAT, the parent of Brown & Williamson.

Given this unusual constraint on domain choice, American Brands purchased Gallaher to give it an overseas outlet. Since that purchase, Gallaher has acquired other companies in different parts of the world, thereby extending American Brands' global reach. But even now, BAT owns the overseas rights to American Brands' traditional cigarette brands, even though AB has been forced to divest itself of its 50 percent ownership of BAT. With the recent market acceptance of some of AB's newer brands, notably the "super-low-tar" Carleton cigarette, American Brands has been able to gradually develop its overseas business. Despite these constraints, however, by 1975, through the unusual combination of a declining domestic cigarette market and the purchase of a single, large, and expanding overseas tobacco company, American Brands was achieving over 60 percent of its tobacco sales and products from its overseas operation. Once again, the limits on domain choice had been creatively managed and effectively avoided by a member of the Big Six.

Liggett's Overseas Strategy.   Although Liggett & Meyers enjoyed sales in many countries by the end of our study period, its commitment to these new domains was never as great as those of the other U.S. tobacco independents. The great majority of its overseas sales came from exports and licensing agreements, not from direct investment in overseas manufacturing subsidiaries. Indeed, because of its poor domain-offense performance at home, it had less financial slack and fewer cigarette brands to apply to its overseas activities. Therefore, it placed almost all its excess cash from the domestic tobacco operation into its diversification program. Indeed, a few years after our study period ended, Liggett sold its overseas operations to the international division of Philip Morris, in order to generate cash to support the continued development of its domestic diversification effort.

OVERSEAS SUMMARY

The foregoing brief descriptions of international activities indicate that the predispositions of the tobacco independents that were identified with their domain-offense strategies parallel the choices and timing that characterized each firm's entry into the global domain. Philip Morris, the Prospector in the domestic competition for market share, emerged as the pioneer that moved boldly into overseas tobacco markets. As a result, its overseas sales and its resource commitments to the international market for cigarettes greatly exceeded, in absolute terms, those of its traditional competitors by the end of the study period.

R. J. Reynolds also moved into foreign markets, but more cautiously than Philip Morris. After successful experimentation with export and licensing agreements, it gradually began to shift its international portfolio toward direct ownership of manufacturing subsidiaries abroad. American Brands arrived late on the international scene, primarily because of legal complications that were embedded deeply in its history. However, the acquisition of a major cigarette-manufacturing company in Great Britain, together with this subsidiary's ability to make further tobacco acquisitions on its own, enabled AB to proceed thereafter more rapidly with its shift from dependence on the domestic cigarette market.

Finally, Liggett was forced to narrow its choices for domain creation because of the reduced slack provided by its unsuccessful domain-offense strategies. It simply could not keep up in the global race for new cigarette markets, and opted instead to place its limited supply of excess cash in a domestic diversification program. It is to this other strategy of domain creation that we now must turn to complete our analysis of the process of strategic adaptation among the traditional Big Six.

DIVERSIFICATION: PATTERNS AND CHOICES

Before getting into the analysis of the diversification strategies of the Big Six, we need to take a look at how this strategy had been developing in the U.S. economy during the first three-quarters of the twentieth century. This brief survey will reveal several important trends that provide a framework for understanding the behaviors of our industry population.

U.S. MERGER ACTIVITY: THREE MAJOR WAVES

The history of merger activities in the United States may be divided into three distinct waves, as shown in Figure 5-3. All three waves occurred during periods of expansion in the U.S. economy and declined during periods of economic downturn. The waves differed in terms of both their impact on the distribution of market power among firms competing in the same industry and the degree of diversity they created within acquiring organizations. These differences have been characterized as follows: the first wave, "merging for monopoly"; the second, "merging for oligopoly"; and the third, "merging for growth" (Salter and Weinhold, 1979).

The first two waves did not result in substantially more diversity for acquisition-oriented corporations, but they did enhance their market power. The first discernible wave occurred from 1898 to 1902, with a peak of merger activity during 1899 (Reid, 1968). It involved vertical and horizontal integration within industries and created many of our industrial giants. The second wave, which took place between 1925 and 1931, continued the focus on the concentration of major industries, through vertical integration of buyer−seller relationships and horizontal product and geographical expansion. Together, the two merger movements were instrumental in altering the structure of corporate enterprise in the United States (Leontiades, 1980).

Nearly 70 percent of these mergers involved the elimination of direct competitors (Federal Trade Commission, 1969). The first wave created monopolies in important industries; the second spawned a number of second-most-powerful industry competitors. Horizontal mergers eliminated competitors, and vertical mergers facilitated the achievement of scale efficiencies in production and distribution, permitting lower unit costs and thereby strengthening competitive positions. The ultimate effect of the first two merger waves was to

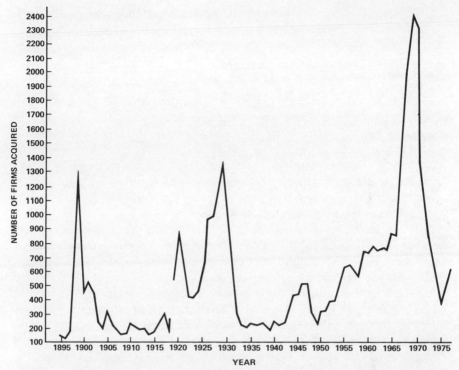

FIGURE 5-3   Number of U.S. Manufacturing and Mining Firms Acquired; 1895–1978. Source: M. Salter and W. Weinhold, *Diversification Through Acquisition: Strategies for Maximizing Economic Value.* The Free Press (1979), p. 10. Reprinted by permission.

increase the concentration of market share and power among a few corporations in a number of industries; although, in general, these acquisitive corporations tended to remain in their traditional domains. Further efforts to increase industry concentration and market power, however, were blunted by the enactment of the Celler-Kefauver Amendment to the Clayton Act in 1950, giving authority to the Antitrust Division of the U.S. Department of Justice to deny attempts by corporations to increase their power within their primary industries of operation.

The third wave of U.S. mergers, by contrast, led to an increase in organizational and product diversity without adding substantially to market power or concentration within industries. This wave, which began in the mid-1950s after the Celler-Kefauver Amendment and continued into the early 1970s, involved corporate acquisition of companies operating outside the traditional or primary industry. In contrast to the first two waves, which may be characterized as merger for *concentration*, this most recent wave might be labeled merger for *diversification*. It was merger for diversification that the Big

Six pursued during the years following the emergence of the smoking-and-health controversy.

DIVERSIFICATION: A FRAMEWORK FROM HINDSIGHT

As studies of diversification were reported during the mid- and late 1970s, several major themes emerged. First, there appeared to be a variety of *motives* or reasons for diversification. Some—those we will refer to as *rational* motives— related to improved efficiency, effectiveness, or survivability of the organization as a whole. Rational motives, therefore, pertained to the welfare of the organization's stockholders. Others, which we will refer to as *political* motives, related to the outcomes sought or experienced by the professional managers who operated the corporation on behalf of its owners.

A second theme had to do with the *types* of diversification firms chose to pursue. Some diversifying companies chose to acquire predominantly *related* businesses, hoping to achieve the benefits of synergy as they applied their traditional expertise to new domains or achieved economies of scale and integration. Others pursued a conglomerate strategy of diversifying into a broad range of businesses largely *unrelated* to their traditional businesses. Often they hoped to counterbalance the cyclical nature of their traditional business or to otherwise spread their risk exposure over a portfolio of independent but complementary businesses. Studies based on the experience of firms pursuing conglomerate versus integrated diversification strategies began to produce consistent evidence that, in particular, these choices eventually led to different levels of performance in terms of organizational profitability.

A third theme relates to the *mode* of diversification. It became clear that firms in general could achieve many of their diversification objectives more quickly by pursuing a strategy of *external acquisition* of existing businesses than by one of *internal development* of new businesses. In many cases, an acquiring firm can consolidate external acquisitions that already hold significant positions in other industries many years sooner than they could develop internally new businesses into similar positions of market leadership. Indeed, a recent study of forty large U.S. companies has suggested that for internal diversifiers, it took on average eight years before their new ventures generated a positive return on investment (Biggadike, 1976). In addition, if payment is made in stock and if the acquirer's stock commands a higher price—earnings multiple than that of the acquiree, the result is an immediate earnings-per-share gain for the acquirer (Pitts, 1979).

By pursuing the external route, a diversifier also may avoid many of the barriers to new entry into an established industry. It does so by purchasing rather than creating brand images, by paying for depreciated capital equipment rather than buying new facilities at fully inflated prices, and so forth. Finally, external acquisition may enable top management to avoid some of the internal political obstacles to adding a rival business to the traditional operations of the enterprise. For instance, by the acquisition of major companies in other industries, the viability of these new businesses may be enhanced because they tend to contribute enough to overall corporate performance and consume enough of its human and capital resources to capture the attention of strategic managers.

Internally developed businesses, by contrast, can tend to languish for lack of senior management attention because they may not contribute importantly to overall corporate performance, especially during the startup and early developmental stages of their life cycle. However, internal diversification does possess one potential advantage: It may be less risky. Gradual internal development of new businesses may give a firm time to experiment, to test its capabilities in new areas, without the threat of large losses.

A fourth theme from the diversification studies relates to the *entry* strategy chosen by acquisition-minded companies. The evidence produced by Biggadike's (1976) study in particular suggested, but did not demonstrate conclusively, that the most successful diversifiers were those that acquired major companies in rapid-growth industries. He reported that only 15 percent of his sample of *Fortune* 500 firms had chosen to acquire companies that operated in markets that had reached a mature stage of development. Instead, the major emphasis had been on acquiring businesses in rapid-growth industries to give new life to the largest U.S. corporations, many of which had been operating as industry leaders in low-growth, mature industries.

In addition, Biggadike observed that the tactic of bold entry into new domains was related more often to ultimate success than was tentative, experimental entry. Indeed, by the end of this merger wave, the rate of major as opposed to minor acquisitions in other U.S. industries was on the rise. The final years of the third merger wave were characterized by an increasing number of large-company acquisitions per year.[2] Thus, the evidence regarding entry strategy suggested by these findings poses a dilemma for strategic managers. On the one hand, we have reviewed several arguments supporting a careful, experimental approach to this new and uncertain strategy; on the other, a bold entry involving a heavy commitment of resources would ensure the diversifier a major foothold with established brands in the entered market.

Although these themes were not well understood by managers at the early stages of the U.S. diversification movement, subsequent research had demonstrated that they account for a considerable portion of the variance experienced by diversifying companies in the strategic choices they made, the behaviors they engaged in, and the outcomes they achieved. Before we move into the review of the diversification achievements of the Big Six during the last quarter century, however, the first two themes require further development.

Diversification Motives. A variety of motives or objectives have been associated with the strategic choice of diversification. At the most general level, the relationship between an organization and its environment may be thought of as a system of mutual dependences whose direction determines the degree of organizational autonomy and managerial discretion. From this perspective, diversification is a means by which organizations may manage their interdependence with environmental elements. In general, diversification alters this situation of interdependence, and in particular, it reduces the organization's dependence on traditional environmental exchanges. As Pfeffer and Salancik (1978) have observed:

> *A firm dependent on a single, critical exchange can reduce its dependence on any single exchange through diversification by engaging in activities in a variety of different domains [p. 115]. . . . Diversification is a way of avoiding the domination that comes from asymmetric exchanges when it is not possible to absorb or in some way gain increased control over the powerful external exchange partner. . . . One organization which can create significant problematic interdependence for other organizations is the government, particularly the federal government. [p. 127]*

Indeed, Pfeffer and Salancik assert that shifting external interdependencies, and thereby increasing organizational autonomy and managerial discretion, is the predominant motive for diversification: "... merger is undertaken to accomplish a restructuring of the organization's interdependence and to achieve stability in the organization's environment, rather than for reasons of profitability or efficiency as has sometimes been suggested" (p. 114).

Other authors, however, have identified a number of more specific reasons for diversification; and as in any organizational decision-making setting, the strategic choice of whether and how to diversify is subject to both rational and political influences (Pettigrew, 1973; Pfeffer, 1977, Miles, 1980c). Indeed, the relative importance of these motives is hotly debated in the contemporary literature on corporate diversification and performance.

Business-policy theorists have tended to develop conservative explanations of the diversification phenomenon, emphasizing the rational analysis of the financial costs and benefits to a firm considering the choice of remaining in a single product-market domain or spreading organizational resources over a variety of domains. Among the diversification motives most frequently considered by these theorists are increased profitability and growth rate, decreased risk exposure, increased managerial career opportunity and hence motivation, ability to captialize on economies of scale in one of more of the firm's functions (e.g., production, marketing, research), increased financial leverage, and greater market intelligence derived from intimate knowledge from working in a variety of industries. An important concept for the business-policy perspective is the organization's "distinctive competence," and whether acquired businesses can profit from the transfer of this competence from the parent so that from the combination of businesses, the whole organization can achieve a competitive advantage in the form of enhanced synergy. Thus, from the business-policy perspective, diversification has the potential for enhancing the efficiency, effectiveness, and survivability of the organization and, consequently, the welfare of its stockholders.

Economists (e.g., Baumol, 1959; Firth, 1980; Marris, 1964; Mueller, 1969; Penrose, 1959; Williamson, 1964), in contrast, have tended to be more skeptical about the rational motives of diversification, especially in cases of "conglomerate" diversification involving the accumulation of unrelated businesses by a large holding company. For example, Mueller (1969) has discussed two rival hypotheses that have been used in attempts to explain the managerial decision to diversify. The first is that managers choose to diversify in order to *maximize profits* or stockholder welfare. This hypothesis, according to Mueller, is correct only if either additional economies of synergy may be obtained from the combination of one firm with another or the acquiring managers correctly perceive an economic potential unrealized by the stockholders of the acquired firm and consequently unrealized in its market price. "Alternatively," Mueller reasons, "mergers can be explained by the hypothesis that managers *maximize the growth rate* of their firm, not stockholder welfare" (1969:654—55). The growth-maximizing hypothesis is one Mueller regards as benefiting primarily the professional managers of the enterprise, not its owners. Moreover, he identifies one clue as to whether managers' motivation to acquire other firms is based primarily on growth, and hence self-interest motives, or profit or shareholder-interest motives. Companies that acquire firms already having strong management that subsequently is left to operate autonomously would not appear to profit from the synergy that Mueller argues is the essence of shareholder benefit from acquisition.

Thus, economists have taken a more liberal position on the question of diversification; they have raised the issue of whether rational decision making has been undermined by the political motives of those who manage corporations on behalf of their owners.[3]

Although some combination of rational and political motives is probably behind almost any diversification decision, it is worth noting that traditional economic models of firm behavior have been built on the assumption that a firm exists within one given product market or industry. The emergence of the diversified company operating simultaneously in multiple industries places severe limits on this major assumption underlying the economic theory of the firm. It is noteworthy also that the studies reported so far have paid scant attention to the "profit-protection" motive that characterized the diversification strategies of the Big Six as they faced legitimacy threats and market stagnation in their traditional domain of operations.

Related vs. Unrelated Diversification.   By the time our study period ended, the evidence generated by research in business policy and economics revealed that U.S. firms had engaged in two different types of diversification strategies and that their choices had tended over time to result in different performance outcomes.

Two dissertation research projects conducted at the Harvard Business School (Wrigley, 1970, and Rumelt, 1974) traced the emergence of different types of corporations during the third U.S. merger wave. The typology of corporate diversification in both projects was based on the firm's specialization ratio (SR), "the proportion of a firm's revenues that is attributable to its largest discrete product-market activity" (Rumelt, 1974:29). With this rough guide, firms were classified into four types: (1) single-business firms (SR≥95%), (2) dominant-business firms (95%>SR≥70%), and (3) diversified firms (SR<70%). Using this classification scheme, Rumelt conducted a study of the evolution of corporate diversification during the time of the third U.S. merger wave.

The overall patterns he found among *Fortune* 500 firms from 1949 to 1969 revealed two important trends. First, there was a dramatic shift from reliance on single-business strategies toward a strategy of diversification into multiple businesses operating in a variety of product markets. Among the firms that appeared in both the 1949 and 1969 *Fortune* 500 lists, 51.3 percent had made a strategic shift from 1949 to 1969, and 95 percent of these moves were in the direction of increased diversification. Of all the firms that were in the single-business or dominant-business categories in 1949 and that remained in the largest 500 in 1969, 79 percent of the former and 45 percent of the latter had moved into categories of greater diversification by 1969. Rumelt also demonstrated that the two decades between 1949 and 1969 contrasted sharply in the diversification patterns that emerged. During the first decade, diversification was much more tentative and was often confined to product markets that were highly related to a diversifying firm's traditional business. During the period 1959−69, however, firms showed an increasing willingness to look farther afield for opportunities.

The second trend that Rumelt discovered was that the highest levels of corporate financial performance were found among firms employing strategies of "controlled diversity," diversification that preserved and built upon some central skill or distinctive competence of the acquiring firm. In contrast, the lowest levels of financial performance were found among conglomerate firms that had chosen to operate in areas completely unrelated to their traditional product markets and distinctive competences.[4] Rumelt interpreted his findings as follows:

> . . .firms that have diversified to some extent but have restricted their range
> of activities to a central skill of competence have shown substantially higher

rates of profitability and growth than other types of firms [*p. 8*] . . . the task of matching opportunity with corporate skills and strengths *is the most important of top management's responsibilities and may be taken as* the primary component of diversification strategy. [*p. 10*]

By 1974, Porter and Salter (1979) reported that only 13 percent of the *Fortune* 500 companies were in single businesses. About 24 percent of the firms on this list of America's largest corporations could be classified as dominant-business companies, and over 60 percent as diversified companies. Moreover, a sharp increase in the number of "unrelated" acquisitions had occurred as the last merger wave unfolded; and this latest trend had created many of the industrial conglomerates that have emerged in the U.S. economy.

The Concept of "Relatedness."   Because of these performance differences in the strategies of related versus unrelated diversification, it is important to arrive at a conceptual definition of the "relatedness" concept. Early attempts to measure the degree of business relatedness were grounded in either economic theory or published archival standards. From the economist's perspective, two businesses were unrelated to the extent that their products were poor substitutes for one another. If these products served different consumer needs, the industries in which they were produced were viewed as unrelated; demand for the product of business A would not affect demand for the product of Business B.

But the cross-elasticity of product demand is a theoretical concept that in practice is difficult to estimate. So economists turned to more concrete estimates of industry differences in their early studies of diversification. The most common index was the Standard Industrial Classification Code employed by the federal government to distinguish among U.S. industries. By relying on the prefixes in this code, economists were able to estimate, albeit very crudely, the degree of industry relatedness. As research on diversification unfolded, however, it became evident—at least to scholars in business policy—that a more sensitive, if less concrete, measure of relatedness was needed to capture the true significance of differences in the growing portfolios of diversified companies.

For these researchers, the matter of *distinctive competence,* an integral component in their conceptualization of the corporate strategy-formulation process, is closer to the essence of the diversification decision and its outcomes. Kenneth Andrews (1971), proponent of the business-policy perspective and author of *The Concept of Corporate Strategy,* represented this view when he asserted that companies develop their resources into a distinctive competence. In his opinion, any major extension in a firm's activities should be related to this competence in order for satisfactory performance to be attained. Porter and Salter have expressed this connection between organizational competence and diversification strategy as follows:

> . . . *diversification can offer potentially significant benefits to the firm and its shareholders. The most significant shareholder benefits from* related *diversification accrue when the special skills and industry knowledge of one merger partner can be applied to the competitive problems and opportunities facing the other. It is worth stressing that not only must these special skills and resources exist in one of the two partners, but they must also be transferable and usable by the other. Shareholder benefits from* unrelated *or conglomerate diversification can occur where more efficient capital management leads to a larger return for corporate investors than that available from a diversified portfolio of securities of comparable systematic risk.* . . .
>
> *In general, the operating benefits of related diversification tend to have the greatest potential for improving corporate performance. As one moves from related diversification towards unrelated diversification, the nature of the potential benefits changes with their potential impact. Operating "synergies" related to integrating functional activities fade into benefits stemming from general management efficiencies. Eventually, when the totally unrelated diversifying acquisition is made, only financial benefits can be achieved.* [1979:22−23][5]

From this perspective, businesses may be considered to be related if they have the potential for creating greater operating synergy within the diversified company. This increased synergy will result if the businesses share common functional skills and "critical success factors," as in such instances as (1) businesses serving similar markets or relying on similar distribution channels, (2) businesses employing similar production technologies, (3) businesses exploiting similar science-based research, or (4) businesses that operate at different stages of the same commerical chain (Salter and Weinhold, 1979: 134−35). It is around the concept of synergy and managers' beliefs about its utility that many strategic decisions to diversify have turned.

Indeed, researchers have observed very different beliefs systems among managers who have opted for related instead of unrelated diversification. For example, in their book, *Diversification through Acquisition*, Salter and Weinhold summarized the differences they encountered among managerial beliefs in diversified companies:

> . . . *our experience indicates that what often appears as arbitrary preferences for either related or unrelated diversification turns out, upon inspection, to be based on one or two common perceptions of the transferability of corporate resources and the risks of diversification. Managers who profess a preference or inclination for* related *diversification will often argue that successful companies develop distinctive competences and skills that are transferable to companies operating in allied businesses. They will also argue that risks of diversification can be reduced if companies apply their skills and resources to businesses they can understand and in which they can*

exercise informed judgment. In contrast, managers who show an interest in unrelated *diversification often argue that the existence and transferability of distinctive corporate skills is irrelevant as long as one acquires a strong company and that operating risk can be reduced by integrating a recent acquisition into the company's planning and control system. They will also argue that portfolio diversification, not portfolio specialization, reduces investment risk. Such propositions by themselves are not sufficiently rigorous to support a major commitment of capital and management time to a diversification program, . . . but they can form the basis of a set of working hypotheses about what kind of diversification makes sense for a given company and its inevitably unique package of corporate resources.* [1979:152–53]

Under the condition of related diversification, therefore, it is argued that the organization is able to capitalize on the potential synergy it can obtain from the integration of a related business. Diversified firms may also be able to achieve greater financial leverage and flexibility and lower overall investment risk than single-business companies. By diversifying, the firm may be able not only to balance its investment portfolio and the cyclicality of its businesses, but thereby to reduce the variability of its income stream as well as the risk premium it would otherwise have to pay for debt.[6] Moreover, it may be able to more efficiently transfer cash from profitable but mature businesses to businesses in rapid-growth stages of development with heavy cash needs, a process referred to as "cross-subsidization." These financial and investment advantages may be more tightly associated with *unrelated* as opposed to related diversification strategies.[7] But Leontiades, drawing upon the work of Stigler and other economists, has observed:

The completely unrelated *merger is regarded by economists as an act of pure investment (Stigler, 1962). In effect, current [economic] theory tends to deny conglomerates or unrelated mergers as economic justification for existence. If the theory is true, conglomerate organizations are economic dinosaurs doomed to extinction.* [1980:17]

In summary, the choices among the ideal types of corporate diversification may be thought of as resting along a continuum from the fully integrated, related-business company to the decentralized, financially controlled, unrelated-business conglomerate. In practice, few diversifed companies fall at either extreme, and the availability of desired acquisitions has probably been a major factor underlying the business mix of multidivisional corporations. In theory, the more related the captive business, the greater will be the opportunity for the parent to capitalize on the competitive advantage of synergy. But synergy requires, first, the selection of the right types of businesses, and second, the ability and willingness of the parent to transfer its distinctive competence to the acquired businesses. Inadequate understanding of the candidate business, its critical success factors and its potential fit with existing businesses, as well as the inability, inappropriateness, or unwillingness to transfer distinctive competence, may negate many of the anticipated benefits of related-business diversification.[8]

In the remainder of this chapter, we will develop an overview of the diversification strategies of the Big Six that unfolded during our quarter-century study period. We will pay particular attention to the key choices made as each company pursued its own version of diversification, and we will examine the effect these strategies had on the extent to which our population of firms were dependent on their traditional domain. This discussion will round out our description of the domain-creation strategies of the Big Six. In the next chapter, we will return to the analysis of diversification by focusing on what strategic managers in the Big Six had learned form their experience, based on interviews with them conducted five years after the end of our study period.

DIVERSIFICATION AMONG THE BIG SIX

For all the reasons covered so far, diversification was the most substantial and innovative strategy pursued by the Big Six as they attempted to adapt to events in their institutional environment. Other strategies involving domain defense and offense took place in the context of a familiar setting and could be intitiated almost immediately in response to the environmental threat. Even with overseas expansion, the Big Six could rely on their traditional products, their network of export licensing agreements, and their experience with distributing tobacco products in foreign theaters of war. Indeed, some of their earlier experience with cigarette regulation in other countries helped prepare them to cope with antismoking developments at home.[9]

But a serious program of diversification constituted a massive reallocation and a long-term commitment of organizational resources to what were for traditional managers in the Big Six new domains of operations. Consequently, there was a three- to four-year lag after the Sloan-Kettering publicity in the initiation of diversification programs even among the industry leaders, Philip Morris and Reynolds, and a somewhat more delayed response on the part of other member firms. Indeed, American Brands, the competitive "Defender," did not initiate its diversification strategy until well after the 1964 Surgeon General's Report. However, by the end of the 1970s, all six firms had become diversified holding companies with varying degrees of dependence on the threatened tobacco domain, and two of them had been acquired by other companies as the third U.S. merger wave had drawn to a close.

DIVERSIFICATION AT R.J. REYNOLDS

The development of the diversification strategy at R.J. Reynolds, which is particularly well documented, shows how its managers attempted to spread risks associated with traditional dependence on a single domain and create growth opportunities in new domains.

From all the evidence we were able to gather about the Big Six, Reynolds took the most formal and systematic approach to the initiation of its diversification strategy. Within three years of the Sloan-Kettering release, Reynolds had taken a major step toward spreading its risks by establishing a formal "Diversification Committee." Commenting on the company's reasons for such a commitment, a company official said, "It was felt at that time that all of Reynolds' eggs, for practical reasons, were in the tobacco basket. Cigarettes constituted 95 percent of Reynolds' volume, and the company had 28% of the total U.S. cigarette market."

The official continued by enumerating a number of specific factors supporting the diversification decision: "A health issue in smoking had been raised. It had to be considered that it might slow down growth or possibly produce a decline in cigarette volume. Even assuming this issue would be overcome, a single-product business was open to unforeseen challenges." Moreover, market acceptance of cigarettes had largely been achieved for both men and women in the domestic market; therefore, the only significant increase in sales volume was expected from "population growth in the smoking-age groups." Income also was tied to cigarette sales. Thus, the restriction of market potential put pressure on the development of new-product alternatives both within the tobacco line, stimulating cigarette-product innovation to reach specific market segments, and outside the tobacco line, calling for diversification into nontobacco products.

RJR's Diversification Committee quickly began to develop a long-range plan, guided by the following premises:[10]

1 Generally, only successful companies can diversify successfully. Reynolds met this requirement.

2 *Diversification should utilize the strengths of the company.* Reynolds's marketing and financial strengths were available to be utilized to the fullest.

3 *Diversification* should be regarded by Reynolds management *as a form of insurance*, similar to other risk-minimizing measures already customary in the company.

4 *Profit protection should be the primary goal of the diversification.* Although diversification should lead to improvement in the profit picture, its goals should be the protection of the profit base through adding new sources of income.

With these premises firmly in mind, diversification at RJR proceeded cautiously at first with internal development as opposed to external acquisition. It began in the late 1950s on a small scale with the expansion of the Archer Aluminum subsidiary, a captive producer of foils and packages for RJR tobacco products. The primary motive for the development of this subsidiary was to meet demand created by the overnight success of RJR's first two filter-tip products, Winston and Salem; but the operation quickly developed excess capacity. It was hoped that the expanded capacity would find a market in the growing industrial and consumer packaging and wrapping businesses, a hope that was realized in a very few years.

From the humble expansion of the aluminum-foil division, diversification at RJR continued along the external-acquisition route. The planned acquisition strategy eliminated industries, markets, and products outside RJR's area of "distinctive competence"—the packaged consumer-goods field—but did not exclude the growth possibilities of "young industries" with high growth potential in unrelated businesses.

The company first moved rapidly into the consumer-foods industry with a number of acquisitions involving small companies that marketed relatively narrow product lines. The acquisition of Pacific Hawaiian Products, producer of the popular Hawaiian Punch fruit drink, in 1963 was followed by Penick & Ford Ltd., then the Chun King Corporation, and finally Filler Products, Inc., in 1966. Rough estimates of the capital expenditures, expressed either in cash or exchanges of treasury stock, on these non-tobacco-product acquisitions reveal that outlays for the acquisitions dwarfed the amounts spent on expansion of manufacturing capacity for new filter-tip cigarettes during the much-publicized plant-expansion program of 1957−62. Total annual capital expenditures during the plant-expansion and the diversification eras are shown in stark contrast in Figure 5-4.[11]

Although not all expenditures shown in Figure 5-4 during the 1966−74 period were for acquisitions of nontobacco-products companies (some went for overseas expansion of the tobacco business), virtually none of these expenditures went for expansion of new domestic cigarette-production capacity. Furthermore, the acquisition figures are heavily understated, since several major companies, including Pacific Hawaiian, were acquired through exchanges of treasury stock rather than cash.

In 1964, the year of the Surgeon General's Report and the year after the first major external acquisition, the "Plant Expansion" section in RJR's annual report was replaced by a "Diversification" section. By 1966, the company had realigned its structure, creating two new subsidiaries to consolidate its expanding interests in the consumer-foods industry and in the aluminum and packaging industries. That same year, nontobacco products accounted for 10 percent of total RJR sales.

In 1967, further penetration into the consumer-foods domain was achieved

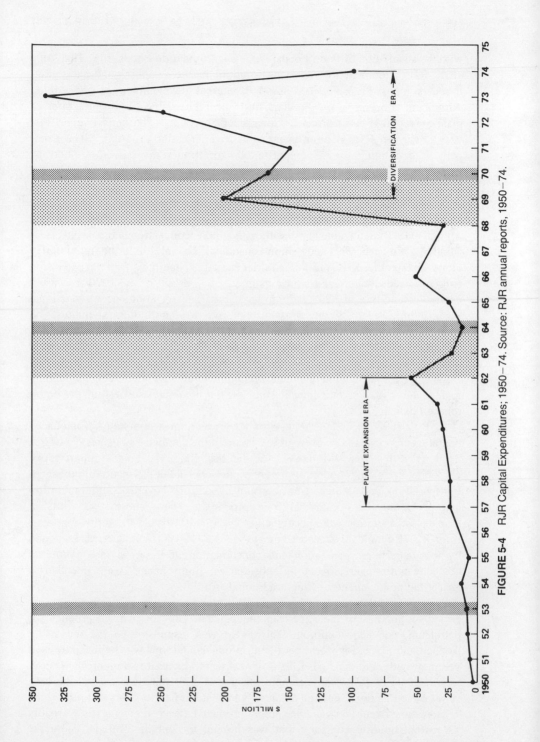

FIGURE 5-4 RJR Capital Expenditures; 1950–74. Source: RJR annual reports, 1950–74.

with the acquisition of Patio Foods, Inc., and Coronation Foods, Inc. That same year, RJR attempted to secure its foothold in the wrapping-and-packaging-products industry, established through internal development of the Archer Aluminum subsidiary, by the acquisition of Filmco, Inc., a manufacturer of plastic wrappings used primarily for grocery products. The annual report that year reaffirmed RJR's commitment to its diversification program: "The Company is continuing to seek opportunities for further diversification, both to expand the product lines of its subsidiaries and to acquire additional businesses having sound profitable growth potentials."

And so it went. Two years later, RJR purchased McLean Industries, Inc., owner of Sea-Land, the largest containerized sea-freight service in the world and a bona fide "young industry" within the more conventional break-bulk sea-freighting industry. This acquisition consumed $115 million in the initial outlay alone, and another $172 million in initial capital expenditures for fleet expansion and equipment modernization. An estimated 93 percent of the 1970 forecasted capital expenditure of $245 million was earmarked for nontobacco operations. Against this awesome financial backdrop of over $500 million in expenditures on RJR's new nontobacco businesses was the company's planned tobacco-plant expansion of $7 million, the alleged purpose of which (betrayed by the dollar comparison) was publicly announced as follows: "This program is further evidence of the Company's determination to remain the nation's leading manufacturer of cigarettes and its faith in the continued success of the entire tobacco industry."

By 1969, the metamorphosis of RJR was almost complete. Nontobacco operations represented an even greater share of the company's business, rising to 24 percent that year. Moreover, for the first time, the annual report broke corporate sales and operating figures into contributions made by tobacco, transportation, and "other" (i.e., consumer foods and beverages, aluminum foil and packaging, and industrial food products). These substantive shifts in domains of operation were accompanied by a name change the following year, from R.J. Reynolds Tobacco Company to R.J. Reynolds Industries, Inc., and by a structural reorganization and consolidation of the firm into a holding company with several operating subsidiaries. Both changes were intended to reflect the new character of this traditional firm.

In 1970, the company made its last major acquisition during our study period by purchasing the American Independent Oil Company, a producer of petroleum, for $55.5 million. This event was responsive to the increasing demand and prices for world petroleum products and thus was believed to have greath growth potential. Also, its products would be used to support the energy requirements of RJR's new shipping business. This purchase capped the long series of acquisitions, entered tentatively at first but later boldly, that moved the organization from a vulnerable, single-product tobacco company to a broadly diversified holding company that was hoping to capitalize on its distinctive competence in consumer-products markets as well as on the growth potential of unrelated "young industries."

The consumer-products acquisitions formed the basis of RJR's diversification into businesses related to its traditional business. These companies manufactured products that were marketed through some of the same distribution channels as cigarettes. They were low-price, high-turnover, branded products that were purchased directly by the ultimate consumer in retail food stores. In contrast, the containerized shipping acquisition represented a potentially high-growth business that related to industrial clients and that was about as unrelated as could be to the traditional tobacco business. The oil-company acquisition was also unrelated to RJR's traditional business, but it too represented high profit potential, and it tended to support the energy requirements of the new shipping business. Thus, RJR's diversification strategy involved a mixture of related and unrelated businesses, with related acquisitions representing a series of relatively small outlays and unrelated acquisitions involving major redeployments of capital. It is noteworthy that, for Reynolds as well as many of the other Big Six members, much of the capital required to support the broad diversification strategy was generated not by the sale of equity or the issuance of debt, but by the huge cash spinoff from the stagnating tobacco domain.

By 1974, contributions to earnings from nontobacco operations of the company had increased substantially and the annual report revealed with pride the role assumed by the diversification program in the life of the corporation:

> . . . 1974 is the first year that really points up the advantages of our diversification. The way the non-tobacco subsidiaries performed and grew more profitable played a big part in the total results. Because we made more money in those businesses, we were able to put more money into the tobacco business. That is a good example of how your Company's expansion into other areas is beginning to pay off.

The Diversification Committee was dissolved in 1974, but only after this remarkable series of acquisitions that resulted in a shared contribution to earnings by tobacco and nontobacco products. By this time, the holding company consisted of six operating divisions: domestic tobacco products, foods and beverages, aluminum products and packaging, containerized shipping, petroleum, and international tobacco operations. Moreover, even with the committee's formal dissolution, the function continues, with former committee members intact under a new vice-president of corporate development.

Two years later, Reynolds hosted a two-day seminar in its Winston-Salem, North Carolina, headquarters for 114 securities analysts and bankers from across the country.[12] Among the purposes of that seminar were attempts to allay the concerns of the investment community about the risks associated with RJR's involvement in the threatened tobacco business and communication of the results of its diversification effort. As Paul Sticht, RJR's president and chief operating officer, explained to his audience:

> It appears that in the 10-year period during which we diversified, many people took a somewhat jaundiced view of our Company. They had in their minds the problems of smoking-and-health and punitive taxation confronting our Tobacco Company, and added to them the historic problem areas facing the shipping and petroleum industries into which we had entered. I think they focused only on the problems and neglected the opportunity for success that solving these problems would offer. . . .
>
> . . . we don't think we have a hodgepodge. We have several solid, well-managed companies which, brought together, are stronger than the individual pieces.

DIVERSIFICATION ELSEWHERE IN THE TOBACCO INDUSTRY

All other members of the Big Six likewise began to diversify their domains of operation, as summarized in Table 5-2. Their initial reasons and planning premises were essentially the same as those that guided RJR. We will treat the diversification strategies of some of these firms in greater detail in the next chapter; for now, we wish only to provide a broad overview of their accomplishments by the end of our study period.

Philip Morris was the first of the Big Six to diversify via external acquisition. Instead of expanding its own packaging division beyond the needs of its tobacco products as in the case of RJR, PM acquired Milprint, Inc., a packaging-products firm, in 1957. This Big Six first in external acquisition by PM was followed by those of RJR in 1963, Liggett & Meyers and Lorillard in 1964, American Brands in 1965, and Brown & Williamson in 1969.

Four of the Big Six even went so far as to change their traditional names to better reflect their diminishing dependence on tobacco products as a result of their diversified operations. Aside from RJR's name change, the American Tobacco Company became American Brands in 1969, Liggett & Meyers Tobacco Company became The Liggett Group in 1973, and Brown & Williamson Tobacco Company became Brown & Williamson Industries, Inc., in 1974. Only Philip Morris, which did not include the word *tobacco* in its corporate identity, continued with its traditional corporate name.

The evidence presented in Table 5-2 also reveals that most of the early diversification attempts across tobacco companies were designed to capitalize on the industry's traditional distinctive competence: the management and, particularly, the marketing of packaged consumer goods. The most notable exceptions—RJR's acquisitions of shipping and petroleum companies in 1969 and 1970, and PM's purchase of a land-development company in 1970—fall into the second category: "young" industries with high growth potential. In addition, the cash-rich Lorillard, a late adopter of the diversification strategy, was eventually acquired by Loews, Inc., the asset-rich, cash-hungry worldwide theatre and hotel chain.

Domain Dependence and Diversification. As a long-term effort, the strategy of diversification did not begin to reflect itself in the composition of net sales and income until the mid-1960s, the time of the Surgeon General's Report, as shown for the U.S. tobacco independents in Figure 5-5. With the Report's release in 1964, marked discontinuities may be observed in the amount of net tobacco-products sales in each of the Big Six firms. Furthermore, the figure also reveals that the actual results of diversification were quite different from firm to firm.

One way to capture this evolution in the nature of the tobacco independents is to cast their diversification results into the scheme developed by Rumelt (1974) that classifies corporations into categories based on the diversity of their business lines (see above, under "Related vs. Unrelated Diversification"). According to Rumelt's "specialization ratio," and referring to Figure 5-5, it can be seen that with the exception of Philip Morris, the tobacco independents were single-business corporations even into the early 1960s.[13] Indeed, Philip Morris remained in this category throughout the study period even though it was the first industry major to embark on a diversification strategy.

By the mid-1960s, however, all the independents had achieved the status of dominant-business corporations, as shown in Table 5-3. Although they still relied heavily on the tobacco-product market, their diversification efforts were moving them more and more toward being fully diversified firms. Only Philip Morris, the industry innovator in diversification, showed continued heavy reliance on the threatened tobacco domain. Two reasons account for this departure. First, Philip Morris had been *very* successful as a product innovator, enjoying early marketing success based on the introduction of cigarettes that continued to decline in allegedly harmful "tar" content. Second, Philip Morris had diversified into product markets that were outside its traditional areas of competence (e.g., hospital-supply firms) and was in the process of divesting itself of some poor choices.

By the end of the study period, Liggett, American Brands, and Reynolds had moved into the diversified-business category, according to Rumelt's specialization ratio. But the tobacco industry was not failing. Although it was stagnating and its legitimacy was in question, it was still very profitable, providing a huge cash throwoff that could be used to fuel each firm's entry into more promising domains. Therefore, the real domain-dependence criterion in the case of the Big Six was one of income dependence, not sales dependence, which Rumelt and others have used in their diversification typologies.

Viewing domain dependence in terms of earnings sources, Table 5-4 reveals that Philip Morris was considerably more dependent on the threatened

TABLE 5-2 DIVERSIFICATION IN THE U.S. TOBACCO INDUSTRY, 1950–1974

Firm	Major Product Categories					
	1950	1955	1960	1965	1970	1974
Philip Morris	Cigarettes and other tobacco products	Cigarettes and other tobacco products	Cigarettes and other tobacco products Packaging products Industrial products Shaving products Paper products	Cigarettes and other tobacco products Packaging products Industrial products Shaving products Chewing gum Paper products	Cigarettes and other tobacco products Packaging products Industrial products Shaving products Chewing gum Hospital supply Beer Community/land development Paper products	Cigarettes and other tobacco products Packaging products Industrial products Shaving products Beer Community/land development Paper products Chemicals
R.J. Reynolds	Cigarettes and other tobacco products	Cigarettes and other tobacco products	Cigarettes and other tobacco products Wrapping materials	Cigarettes and other tobacco products Wrapping materials Food and beverages	Cigarettes and other tobacco products Wrapping materials Food and beverages Containerized freight and sea transportation Petroleum	Cigarettes and other tobacco products Wrapping materials Food and beverages Containerized freight and sea transportation Petroleum
Lorillard	Cigarettes and other tobacco products	Cigarettes and other tobacco products	Cigarettes and other tobacco products	Cigarettes and other tobacco products Pet foods Candy	[P. Lorillard was acquired by another U.S. corporation in 1969.]	

	1951	1956	1961	1966	1971	1975
British-American[a]	Cigarettes and other tobacco products	Cigarettes and other tobacco products	Cigarettes and other tobacco products	Cigarettes and other tobacco products Paper products Cosmetics	Cigarettes and other tobacco products Paper products Cosmetics Food products	Cigarettes and other tobacco products Paper products Cosmetics Food products Retailing Grocery chains
Liggett & Myers	Cigarettes and other tobacco products	Cigarettes and other tobacco products	Cigarettes and other tobacco products	Cigarettes and other tobacco products Pet foods	Cigarettes and other tobacco products Pet foods Alcoholic beverages Cereal products Watchbands Household cleaners	Cigarettes and other tobacco products Pet foods Alcoholic beverages Cereal products Watchbands Household cleaners Rugs
American Brands	Cigarettes and other tobacco products	Cigarettes and other tobacco products	Cigarettes and other tobacco products	Cigarettes and other tobacco products	Cigarettes and other tobacco products Food products Alcoholic beverages Office services and supplies Hardware Toiletries	Cigarettes and other tobacco products Food products Alcoholic beverages Office services and supplies Toiletries Lighting

[a]British-American Tobacco Co., Ltd. acquired Brown & Williamson Tobacco Corp. in 1929.

Source: *Moody's Industrial Manual*, 1951, 1956, 1961, 1966, 1971, 1975

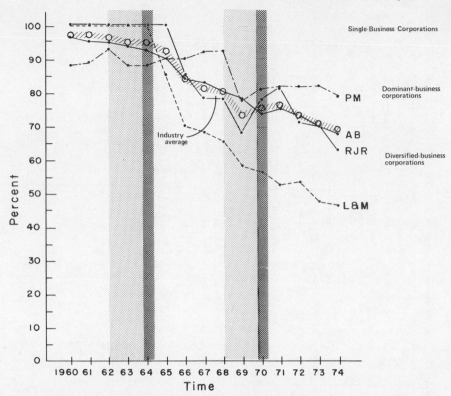

FIGURE 5-5 Percentage of Net Sales Accounted for by Tobacco Business of industry Independents, 1960–74. Source: Annual reports, 1960–1974; Rumelt (1974).

tobacco domain than its specialization ratios would indicate. By contrast, the income-dependence ratios reveal that Liggett & Meyers was less dependent on its tobacco business than the analysis of its sources of sales would indicate. Indeed, by 1974, Liggett's share of the domestic cigarette market had dwindled to about 3 percent, a level that many market analysts believed was too low to sustain profitable operations.

These ratios point to yet another interaction among our clusters of domain-management strategies. Success with domain offense kept firms wedded to the traditional tobacco business, whereas strategic failure in domain offense stimulated the active search for alternative domains of operation. In the case of American Brands, by 1975 the majority of its tobacco sales and earnings came from its overseas Gallaher subsidiary. For Liggett, utter competitive disaster in the domestic cigarette market propelled it into a series of related businesses. Indeed, within a few years after the end of our study period, Liggett had sold the rights to overseas manufacture and sales of its cigarette brands to Philip Morris in

TABLE 5-3 DIVERSIFICATION IN THE U.S. TOBACCO INDUSTRY: TRENDS IN THE SPECIALIZATION RATIO

Independent Firms	Specialization Ratio[a]			
	Pre-1960	1965	1970	1975
Liggett & Meyers	100%	81%	57%	49%
American Brands	100%	100%	77%	65%
		(98%)[b]	(38%)[b]	(26%)[b]
R.J. Reynolds	> 95%	89%	74%	68%
				(50%)[b]
Philip Morris	> 90%	n.a.	73%	76%
			(50%)	(47%)[b]

[a]The specialization ratio is the percentage of annual net sales accounted for by the primary tobacco business of the industry independents. The lower the specialization ratio, the more diversified the firm.

[b]Domestic tobacco sales only.

NOTE: All firms except Philip Morris report revenues and operating income on the basis of tobacco and nontobacco businesses. Philip Morris, however, only reports these figures on the basis of domestic and international division performance. Their domestic tobacco figures are therefore somewhat overstated, because the domestic division also included some non-tobacco product lines during their early stages of development.
Source: Annual reports, 1950–1975

TABLE 5-4 DOMAIN DEPENDENCE IN THE U.S. TOBACCO INDUSTRY: TRENDS IN THE CONTRIBUTION TO OPERATING INCOME OF THE PRIMARY TOBACCO BUSINESS

Industry Independents	Income Dependence Ratio[a]			
	Pre-1960	1965	1970	1975
Liggett & Meyers	> 95%	90%	46%	42%
R.J. Reynolds	> 95%	92%	86%	74%
				(70%)[b]
American Brands	100%	100%	78%	70%
			(61%)[b]	(26%)[b]
Philip Morris	> 95%	n.a.	95%	91%
			(68%)[b]	(68%)[b]

[a]Income-dependence ratio is calculated by dividing the annual operating income generated from the primary tobacco business by the total annual operating income.
[b]Domestic tobacco operating income only.
Source: Annual reports, 1950–1975

an attempt to generate cash, which could not be done by its shrinking tobacco operations, to sustain its strategic exit from the traditional industry.

Obvious from these results is that diversification has been most complete for L&M, quite substantial for RJR and AB, and least effective in spreading the risks of PM. Philip Morris has become the independent most committed to the core tobacco industry, because its acquisitions have been substantially offset by a series of successful filter- and low-tar-cigarette innovations that have enabled it to climb from the bottom of the domestic industry in market share to a close second place behind RJR, the industry leader. Rapid expansion of cigarette sales abroad is another factor contributing to PM's present stance. In contrast, with repeated brand-innovation failures, L&M's diversification effort had brought it to the point where the majority of its net sales and income by 1973 was being contributed by its nontobacco products.

Philip Morris's commitment appears deliberate. By 1970, PM's board chairman, Joseph Cullman, had gone on record stating, "I don't foresee a pressing need for moving off into further new directions" (Fienning, 1971). The following year, when several other tobacco companies were still highly active in searching for diversification opportunities, PM was divesting itself of two hospital-supply companies (outside its area of distinctive competence) and later, in 1973, a chewing-gum company.

By contrast, Liggett & Meyers did not actively begin diversification until 1964, a full seven years after PM, but almost overnight it became heavily involved in the pet-food industry. In fact, L&M quickly became the target of litigation alleging that it was becoming a monopoly in the dog-food business. As early as 1966, the annual report announced, "Liggett & Meyers is no longer solely a tobacco company," and by 1969, L&M depended on nontobacco products for over 50 percent of its net earnings. That same year, L&M President Milton Harrington, in a letter to his stockholders, reported, "The record sales and higher earnings achieved by your company in 1969 were primarily due to the continuation of our aggressive diversification program. . . ."

By way of comparison with Philip Morris, Liggett's heavy investment in diversification was no doubt influenced by an almost yearly decline in cigarette sales since 1952 ($603,000 in 1952, compared to lows of $366,000 in 1973 and $397,000 in 1975). In stark contrast, PM's persistent growth in cigarette sales over the same period ($307,000 in 1952, compared to $2.7 million in 1975), fired by a series of well-timed product innovations in the filter and low-tar brand categories, made it less dependent on diversification, at least for short-term survival.

Lorillard and Brown & Williamson, the Big Six "nonindependents" (firms held by parent corporations), also engaged in diversification efforts of their own, but Lorillard started very late. Beginning in 1964 with the creation of its own Corporate Planning and Development Group, Lorillard began acquiring other consumer-goods firms in an effort to diversify its holdings—first a pet-food company, then two candy companies. But in 1967, Lorillard announced that only 5 percent of its total business was accounted for by nontobacco products, and "it is our objective to increase this percentage substantially. Our overall goal has been, and is, to seek entry in business fields that inherently enjoy faster growth than the tobacco industry. . . ."

The realization of that goal took a unique turn the following year, with the acquisition of Lorillard by Loew's Theatres. Lorillard thereby became a subsidiary of a company formerly only a quarter the size of the tobacco firm. Tobacco sales from Lorillard produced approximately 75 percent of Loew's revenues annually, and until 1974 when a financial corporation was acquired (CNA), it served as the primary means by which new theatres and hotels could be internally financed and built by the growth-minded Loew's corporation.

Brown & Williamson, a subsidiary of British-American Tobacco Company since 1927, also made its own acquisitions, even though its parent firm, the largest tobacco company in the world, was itself diversified. With the purchase of Vita Food Products (1969), Aleutian King Crab, Inc. (1969), Sea Pass Corporation (1970), the Kohl Corporation (1972), Gimbel Brothers (1973), and Saks Fifth Avenue (1973), B&W became a multiproduct company; and, following the lead of other U.S. tobacco independents, it changed its name from the Brown & Williamson Tobacco Company to Brown & Williamson Industries.

The strategy of diversification, whether into domains demanding the industry's distinctive competence or into "young" industries with high growth potential and cash needs, has played a key role in enabling the Big Six to avoid some of the uncertainties posed by the increasing complexity and turbulence in their traditional domain of operations. In addition to strategies designed to specifically act upon the changing environment of the core tobacco industry, the diversification strategy has made it possible for member firms to move into new domains posing less potential risk and, in many cases, greater potential growth.

SUMMARY

In terms of spreading total company risk and creating growth opportunity through diversification, by 1975 Liggett had been the most successful, with less than 50 percent of its sales and income being derived from the tobacco business. American Brands came in second, with 65 percent of its sales and 70 percent of its earnings coming from tobacco operations; and R.J. Reynolds followed, with 68 percent of sales and 74 percent of profits coming from its tobacco products. Philip Morris, with its huge successes in both domestic and overseas market expansions for cigarettes, remained the most dependent of the four companies, with 76 percent of its revenues and a whopping 91 percent of its income being derived from its tobacco businesses at home and abroad. Thus, to a large extent, success or failure in one strategy of domain management has greatly influenced the development of other strategies.

Similar patterns emerged from the attempts of these firms to spread risks and create opportunities through the strategy of overseas expansion. By 1975, over 60 percent of American Brands' tobacco revenues and profits were generated by overseas operations. Philip Morris, although the industry leader in terms of the magnitude of its international operations, fell second to American Brands, with over a third of its tobacco sales and a quarter of its tobacco earnings coming from abroad. In 1975, R.J. Reynolds, although obtaining a quarter of its tobacco sales from abroad, received only 5 percent of its profits from overseas tobacco operations. And finally, within a few years of the end of our study period, Liggett had divested itself of the majority of its international tobacco holdings. Again, it is obvious that for each company, the strategies chosen for domain offense and defense have interacted with their strategies of domain creation, with the result that, although the Big Six have shared the overall patterns of organizational adaptation, each has tailored the many choices to meet its own needs and to fit its own circumstances.

But our story of domain creation is not over. A study of corporate diversification, conducted by the senior author five years after the study period covered in this chapter, provided an opportunity to take a closer look at not only what these companies had done to diversify, but why they made important choices and what they would have done differently if they could start from scratch. This retrospective study, based primarily on interviews with senior managers who have guided their firms' diversification strategies, provides an unusual occasion to understand, in general, the process of organizational learning and, in particular, the knowledge these organizations gained from their diversification experience. The results of the study will be discussed in Chapter 6.

FOOTNOTES

[1]R.J. Reynolds Industries, Inc., *Analysts Meeting,* Winston-Salem, North Carolina, September 19–21, 1976, p. 21.

[2]Salter and Weinhold (1979:3) reported the following figures on the number of U.S. corporate acquisitions costing $10 million or more: 1973, 137; 1974, 129; 1975, 112; 1976, 159; 1977, 195; 1978 (estimate), 260.

[3]For instance, Marris (1964), noting the separation of owners and professional managers in modern corporations, has argued that the primary motive for diversification may be the maximization of benefits to the managers themselves rather than the maximization of shareholder wealth, as the traditional economic theory of the firm would predict. In support of his argument, Marris has presented evidence that both pecuniary and nonpecuniary rewards received by senior managers are more closely tied to the growth of the firm than to its profitability. In his study, managerial salaries and bonuses, stock options, and promotions, not to mention intrinsic rewards such as greater job responsibility, satisfaction, power, and status, were all correlated more closely to the size or changes in the size of the firm than to its profits. Similar results for diversifying firms in Great Britain have been reported by Firth (1980).

[4]One important exception to this conclusion has been observed by Porter and Salter, who have noted that "defensive diversification (diversification out of industries with low profitability) has often enabled firms to increase their profitability from inferior to average levels" (1979:6).

[5]For a more detailed analysis of the tradeoffs among related versus unrelated diversification strategies, refer to Reid (1976), Porter and Salter (1979), Salter and Weinhold (1979), and Leontiades (1980).

[6]As Salter and Weinhold have summarized, the potential benefits of income stability and capital efficiency are "in particular great in the *unrelated* diversified firm. With its operations at different levels of production and in different stages of seasonal or business cycles, the diversified corporation through centralizing cash balances can act as a banker for its operating subsidiaries" (1979:139).

[7]Even Porter and Salter have pointed to the poor track record of unrelated or conglomerate diversifiers: "Several empirical studies based on capital market data have found that while conglomerates may have achieved some risk reduction relative to individual firms, it typically came through reducing company-specific risk and *increasing* the more relevant market-related risks of the firm. These studies concluded that in every comparison made, mutual funds provided more efficient diversification than unrelated corporate diversifiers, as well as better risk/return payoffs." [Porter and Salter, 1979:6]

[8]In practice, financial benefits may outweigh operating synergies as the results of the third merger waves are recorded. As Salter and Weinhold have observed: "Unfortunately, those benefits of diversification that offer the greatest potential are usually those least likely to be implemented. Of the synergies usually claimed possible in a diversifying aquisition, financial synergies are often unnoted while operating synergies are widely trumpeted. Yet, the overwhelming evidence is that the benefits most commonly achieved have occurred in the financial area. It is not hard to understand why this is so. All one has to do is to reflect on the nature of the corporation. Most managers will agree that the greatest impediment to change is the inflexibility of the organization itself. Ironically enough, the realization of operating benefits accompanying diversification usually requires significant changes in the company's organizational format and administrative behavior. These changes are typically slow to come; so are the accompanying benefits of changes in bureaucratic practices." [1979:146]

[9]For instance, several members of the Big Six had engaged in outdoor advertising and sponsorship of sporting events in Europe before the U.S. broadcast-advertising ban.

[10]Much of this internal information was provided in a letter from RJR's Director of Business Planning and Development, November 15, 1976 (Miles and Cameron, 1977:48−54). Other major points are matters of record in the company's annual reports and other public documents.

[11]Profit protection was distinguished from profit improvement in the following manner: "Profit *improvement* may be accomplished either through improved operations, integration, or diversification. Profit *protection* is more fundamental and may be accomplished through diversification into other products."

[12]This meeting is summarized in R.J. Reynolds Industries, Inc., *Analysts Meeting*, Winston-Salem, N.C., September 19−21, 1976, 91 pp.

[13]Again, because the operating data of Lorillard and Brown & Williamson are aggregated with those of other subsidiaries of their parent companies, we had to confine our financial analysis to the four tobacco independents, for which data were available.

6

Learning from Diversifying

By involving itself in a diversified, complicated and demanding environment,
a company hastens the development of knowledge within itself and increases
the likelihood that it will be able to adapt to a variety of situations.
[Normann, 1977:84]

The long-term development of a strategy of diversification by member firms of the tobacco Big Six provides us with a unique opportunity to understand some important aspects of the processes of strategy formation and organizational learning. Each firm approached the initial occasion of diversification experimentally. They all tended to begin with small resource commitments and with businesses that were closely related to their traditional operations. By trial and error, they gradually built a base of knowledge about diversification and a repertoire of skills for choosing and managing their new domains before committing themselves to a full-blown diversification strategy. There is little evidence that their initial search was exhaustive or that the analysis of the limited range of alternatives they considered was complete. As a result, their experimental trials were different, as were their particular resources, competences, competitive situations, and internal politics; and their learning from diversifying was, at least at first, uneven.

By the time these companies had accumulated fifteen to twenty years of experience with their diversification strategies, however, some common patterns and beliefs had emerged from the learning each had mustered. This is not to say that the learning was the same in all cases. Indeed, each company appeared to learn as much about itself, its resources, competences, weaknesses, and predispositions as it did about diversification. Put another way, diversification as a strategy could not be separated from the unique characters of the companies choosing to employ it.

Because we had carefully analyzed the context and behaviors of the Big Six over an extended quarter-century period, as reviewed in the first five chapters, we believed that a retrospective study would be capable of revealing some important aspects of how diversification strategy and organizational learning unfolded within some of the Big Six firms. A research project on corporate diversification funded by the Harvard Business School in the spring of 1980, five years after the end of our quarter-century period, provided an opportunity to extend our archival findings.

Because we already knew so much about the tobacco industry, the project began with a pilot study of the tobacco independents. This preliminary project consisted of a series of focused, in-depth interviews with senior executives in several of the Big Six independents. The interviews were with the senior manager in charge of the corporation's diversification program and others who had been part of the initial decision to diversify. The results of the interviews were summarized in a detailed research note (Miles, 1980b), which is included later in this chapter. Before we move to these findings, however, let us first review what is known about the processes of organizational learning and then build an agenda of important diversification concepts and choices to frame the company histories that follow.

ORGANIZATIONAL LEARNING:
AN INTRODUCTORY FRAMEWORK

A major factor in the persistence or decline of organizations under changing environmental conditions is the process of organizational learning. Regardless of whether changes occur within an organization or are imposed upon it from outside, effective adaptation to the new circumstances requires the acquisition or creation of knowledge about cause and effect, about relative strengths and weaknesses, and about the feasibility and viability of options for adaptation. Such an occasion often requires also an adjustment in relative priorities and beliefs, and the development of new skills and resources. The creation of new domains by the tobacco Big Six was such an occasion.

Their choice to enter new domains exposed the Big Six to different markets and technologies. It forced them to respond to new expectations that accompanied each new venture. And, to varying degrees, it put at risk investments of capital and human resources.

To some extent, these corporations had access to the existing knowledge about diversification. But, as we have observed, not much practical knowledge on the subject was available at the time senior managers in these companies had to make their initial decisions about whether and how to diversify. Therefore, much of the knowledge they acquired had to come, not from consultants or the management literature, but from the enactment of the strategy itself.[1] Indeed, in this chapter we will use the single term strategy *formation,* instead of the more conventional dichotomy between strategy formulation and implementation. As business-policy theorists have cautioned:

> *In real life the process of formulation and implementation [of strategy] are intertwined. Feedback from operations gives notice of changing environmental factors to which strategy should be adjusted. The formulation of strategy is not finished when implementation begins. A business organization is always changing in response to its own makeup and past development.* [Christensen, Andrews, and Bower, 1973:619]

As Kimberly, Miles, and associates have observed in their book, *The Organizational Life Cycle* (1980), the dichotomy between formulation and implementation—between advance planning and doing—is especially artificial in the creation and early development of new but particularly innovative ventures. Because diversification among the tobacco independents committed them to some new and different settings, the initiation of this strategy exacerbated the normal problems of strategy formation.

This problem of inadequate knowledge was one with which we, as researchers, were also confronted. Not much research has been conducted on the process of organizational learning, especially as it applies to strategy formation in complex enterprises. What was evident from the literature at the time the interview study was being designed was that at least three factors could be identified as important conditions under which organizational learning could be expected to occur.

CONDITIONS FOR ORGANIZATIONAL LEARNING

The first condition is one of negative performance feedback. Consistent throughout the preliminary literature was the finding that "the stress produced by negative performance feedback is an important condition for organizational learning" (Miles and Randolph, 1980:49). For instance, studies of decision making in government administration, international economic development, and research and engineering programs led Hirschman and Lindblom (1962) to conclude that organizational learning occurs in response to immediate problems, imbalances, and difficulty, or to what Downs (1967) has referred to as "performance gaps," much more than it does in response to deliberate planning. They argue that the intraorganizational conflicts and tensions created by these immediate problems serve a constructive function in stimulating search behaviors that lead to organizational learning. But other researchers (e.g., March and Simon, 1958; McKenney, 1978) have cautioned that the negative feedback must generate "reasonable stress" for the organization.[2] Too little stress or performance gap (whether potential or actual) may be insufficient to encourage organizational members to call into question their traditional beliefs or strategies or to engage in the search for alternatives. Too much stress or performance gap, in contrast, may overwhelm the organization to the point that its members find themselves clinging to the false security of old beliefs and accustomed ways.

A second important condition for organizational learning is that of "catalytic leadership." A number of management theorists (e.g., Barnard, 1938; Selznick, 1957; Normann, 1977; McKenney, 1978; Andrews, 1980) have insisted that, even in the absence of actual performance gap, executive leaders, who are responsible for guiding the overall purposes and strategies of an enterprise and who have considerable authority to do so, play a major role not only in whether organizational learning occurs but in the focus of such learning. Based on his study of technological innovation the U.S. Forestry Service, McKenney (1978) reported that an important condition for successful innovation was "a leader's catalytic action that both facilitates and legitimizes change." In addition, other researchers have noted that sometimes a turnover in executive leadership is required before an organization can begin to break from outmoded traditions and beliefs that persist even in the presence of unequivocally negative performance feedback (Pfeffer and Salancik, 1978). Such occasions of executive succession may result in the accession of new strategic managers who possess either the knowledge and experience needed to bring dysfunctional organizational goals or practices into line with reality, or the vision and stature to cause a fundamental search and assessment process to occur.[3]

Finally, the creation or utilization of "slack" (Cyert and March, 1963) appears to be required by almost any occasion of organizational reflection, experimentation, and problem solving. Slack may be created by bringing new competences or skills into the organization, by diverting resources internally so as to develop new competences or skills, or by attempting to generalize existing core competences or skills to new situations. In any event, the creation or utilization of slack normally requires the temporary relaxation of performance standards, a decision that must be managed very carefully in highly competitive situations.

No doubt other important conditions for organizational learning will be uncovered as our understanding of the process advances. But these three elements—negative performance feedback, catalytic leadership, and the creation of slack—provided a beginning framework for studying the learning that occurred within our tobacco companies as the formation of their diversification strategies unfolded.

DECOMPOSING THE PROCESS OF ORGANIZATIONAL LEARNING

We borrowed from the work of earlier theorists (e.g., Simon, 1945; Duncan, 1974; Argyris and Schön, 1978) to define organizational learning for this study as "a *process* by which growing insights and successful restructurings of organizational problems by the individuals dealing with them reflect themselves in the structural elements and outcomes of the organization itself'' (Miles and Randolph, 1980:50). In addition, the *content* produced by this learning process—organizational knowledge—was defined as "the patterns of cognitive association that develop among the context, structures, processes, and outcomes of a membership's organizational experience'' (Miles and Randolph, 1980:50). These definitions were operationalized for our study of the tobacco independents in the following ways.

First, *whether* learning occurred among our study organizations was demonstrated in terms of the outcomes of the diversification strategy. These outcomes included not only the relative frequency and importance over time of acquisition successes and failures (divestitures), but also the degree to which each organization had realized the goals for which its diversification strategy had been initiated (e.g., risk minimization, growth enhancement, profit stability, and so on).[4] Both forms of evidence provided insight into the degree of mastery of the performance situation and hence the degree of organizational learning.

Second, *how* learning occurred was revealed in the unique organizational histories that were recorded in the interviews with senior managers who had participated in the strategy-formation process. Important to this analysis were the archives that revealed the degree of formalization characterizing the strategy-formation process as it developed over time, the structures and processes that were developed to guide the process from initiation to institutionalization, and the roles played by different coalitions within the organization in generating diversification alternatives and in making acquisition and divestiture choices. In addition, it was important to examine the pattern and timing of executive succession within each company.

Finally, the content of organizational learning about diversification, or *what* the organizations learned, was gathered from the perceptions and beliefs that were expressed in 1980 by those who guided the strategy and who now are responsible for its success and continued development. More important, however, much of the knowledge gained from the diversification experience had been institutionalized in the form of formal acquisition criteria and guidelines and in the patterned approaches each organization had developed for assimilating its acquisitions. The retrospective interview study conducted in the spring of 1980 provided insight into all three of these aspects of organizational learning in general.

HISTORICAL ANALYSIS OF STRATEGY FORMATION: AN AGENDA

This retrospective study also permitted us to examine more closely some important concepts and choices associated with the formation of a diversification strategy. Because of their different initial choices, the histories of our three tobacco companies provided new insights into (1) the concept of "distinctive competence" as it applies to complex organizations, (2) the type of diversification chosen (i.e., "related" versus "unrelated"), (3) the modes of diversification (i.e., internal development versus external acquisition), (4) the alternative approaches to the organization and management of a growing portfolio of businesses (e.g., centralization versus decentralization), and (5) the objectives of diversification (i.e., return on investment versus growth). These histories also revealed how organizations may attempt to tailor either strategy to accommodate existing structures and competences, or structures and competences to fit emerging strategies. Finally, the histories revealed how decisions made early in the strategy-formation process, at a time when the management was least informed to make strategic choices, served to constrain an organization's options later on and to shape, in many ways unanticipated at the time of initiation, the ultimate strategy that was realized fifteen to twenty years later.

"LEARNING FROM DIVERSIFYING"*

The strategy of corporate diversification has been with us for almost three decades as part of what economists and business historians have labeled the "Third U.S. Merger Wave." At the core of this strategy is management's attempt to create new domains of opportunity for a company. The reasons for diversification have been as varied as the types of strategies that have been tried. Diversification, it is said, can rejuvenate a company that has been suffering from a maturing or declining business by enabling it to enter markets with greater growth and profit potentials. Diversification can provide a place to invest excess managerial capacity and organizational capability as well as surplus earnings. It can help a company spread its risks across businesses with complementary cycles and thereby enhance the stability of its performance. Diversification is also a vehicle by which organizations grow, and with that growth there is the potential for satisfying managerial needs and for increasing organizational discretion. But for many corporations that have attempted some form of diversification, the potential benefits of domain creation have been elusive.

At this point in the diversification movement, an extensive body of knowledge about the subject has been accumulated. But for corporations that were among the first to embark on this strategy, the wisdom available at the time they initiated their programs of diversification was sadly lacking. Instead, these innovators had to learn from doing. Most of their preliminary attempts, therefore, were experimental. In the beginning, they risked relatively small

*Reprinted from R.H. Miles, "Learning from Diversifying," (ICCH: 9-481-060). Boston: Intercollegiate Case Clearing House, Graduate School of Business Administration, Harvard University. Copyright © 1981 by the President and Fellows of Harvard College. Reprinted by permission.

investments that typically involved entry into domains which were related to the traditional business or particular competencies of the innovator. As managers in these innovative firms enacted their new strategies, they began to learn more and more about diversification and how to tailor this strategy to their own resources and talents. With time and with success, which often was uneven in the beginning, knowledge accumulated in each innovative firm that gradually became institutionalized within both the management belief sytem and the formal statements of corporate purpose. By the time they had invested 15–20 years in a strategy of diversification, managers in each company had developed a general consensus about where they would and would not diversify and how they would consolidate amd manage both their new and existing holdings. Such was the case, at least, for the companies that had diversified successfully.

The purpose of this study, as the title implies, was to discover what several companies have learned, and how they have learned, about the process of diversification. The experience of three companies, all operating in the same single-business domain in the 1950s, was studied by interviewing the senior executives in charge of each company's diversification program. Prior to the interviews, an intensive review was made of the diversification record of each company in order to focus the discussions that would follow and to raise issues that should be covered. Particular attention was paid to the nature and timing of major acquisitions and divestitures and to how each was related to the traditional business of the diversifier.

THE INTERVIEW STUDY

The interview study was conducted in mid-1980. Three of the independent U.S. tobacco companies, the Liggett Group, Philip Morris, and R.J. Reynolds, agreed to participate. An interview protocol (Appendix) was forwarded to the senior executive having overall responsibility for each company's diversification program. This advance set of questions enabled those who ultimately represented each company to prepare in advance and to seek required information if necessary.

The impression of the interviewer was that all senior management representatives participated fully in the in-depth, focused interviews that were conducted on site and which lasted normally half a day apiece. They spoke quite freely about the historical evolution of their diversification strategies, the factors that precipitated this reallocation of resources, the roles played by different subgroups as the strategy unfolded, and the failures and successes their companies had experienced. By the end of each interview it was clear that these managers and organizations had learned much about not only the process of diversification, but about themselves and about their company's strengths and weaknesses. In all three cases, the knowledge gained had been translated into a

*set of refined criteria to guide future acquisitions (and divestitures) that now
constituted an important element of each organization's belief system.*

*It was evident also that the process of diversification was far from over for
these firms. All three companies were making plans to capitalize on their
hard-earned knowledge about diversification strategy. Even Liggett, which was
in the process of being taken over, had been encouraged by its new British parent
to continue to pursue acquisition opportunities in the United States. In terms of
specifics regarding future acquisitions, all three companies declined to comment, owing to the proprietary and highly sensitive nature of that kind of
information. But all agreed that the criteria each had developed over the past
twenty years from experience with dozens of acquisitions and divestitures would
figure heavily in their domain-creation choices in the future.*

*The purposes of this study were to summarize these organizational
experiences and to interpret what each company has learned about diversification. In the process, a search was made for patterns within the accumulated wisdom
of these companies that have implications for other organizations embarking on
this avenue of domain creation. First, a brief review will be made of the
precipitating factors that senior managers associated with the initiation of the
diversification strategy. Next, each company's unique history with respect to
diversification is summarized. Included in this review is an analysis of the
choices made early in each program, the roles played by different organizational
subgroups, the successes and frustrations each company experienced, and the
organizational learning that eventually occurred. Finally, an attempt is made to
relate the combined experience of these companies to the literature on the
strategy of diversification.*

THE BIRTH OF A STRATEGY

*Each interview began with the question, "What were the factors that precipitated
the initial decision to diversify?" The responses of senior managers in each
company are summarized in Exhibit 1. Where the responses differed from
company to company, the interviewer probed to determine if omissions were the
result of oversight or deliberation. Two categories of precipitating factors
emerged.*

Overdependence on a Single Domain. *The first response given was that the
company had become overdependent on a single operating domain—the traditional tobacco business. The domestic industry's annual growth rate had
decreased from 5 percent in the 1950s to 2−3 percent during the late 1960s,
and now the domestic tobacco business had become a no-growth industry. Thus,
all three companies made as their first priority the search for acquisition
candidates operating in markets with higher actual or potential growth rates
than their traditional one.*

EXHIBIT 1 PRECIPITATING FACTORS IN THE STRATEGY TO DIVERSIFY

Precipitating Factors	Philip Morris	Reynolds	Liggett
1. *Overdependence on a single domain*			
a. Decline in industry growth rate	x	x	x
b. Risk from smoking-and-health controversy		x	x
c. Market-share erosion in traditional business			x
2. *Financial liquidity*			
a. Needed to reinvest excess cash from traditional business	x	x	x
b. Needed to avoid risk of takeover			x

Senior managers in two of the companies also reported that the smoking-and-health controversy had been a major factor in increasing the perceived risk, especially among stockholders and members of the investment community, which was associated with continued reliance on tobacco products for future growth and earnings. As one senior manager explained, "There was an overdependence on a primary source of earnings which had become more risky as a result of the smoking-and-health controversy." The consequence, observed another company official, was that risk-averse investors overreacted, and price—earnings ratios plummeted. Only the managers at Philip Morris, a company whose successful competitive and overseas expansion strategies had increased substantially its stakes in tobacco products, did not view the smoking-and-health controversy as a significant factor in stimulating the birth and development of its diversification program.

Finally, Liggett associated overdependence with an erosion of its share of the domestic cigarette market. For this company, overdependence meant not only a slower growth rate, but an actual performance decline. Thus, although all companies diversified to avoid the risk associated with overdependence on their traditional domain, their interpretations of the implications of this condition varied by the success each had achieved in the competition for market share within the maturing domestic tobacco business, a business which, although maturing and uncertain, remained a lucrative one.

Condition of Extreme Liquidity. *The second cluster of precipitating factors related to the condition of extreme liquidity that existed within all three firms at the time they first decided to diversify. Members of the U.S. tobacco industry generated annually an enormous cash flow from operations that was not subject to cyclical uncertainties. So great was the cash spinoff from the tobacco business that it could not be reinvested profitably in this stagnating industry. To make matters worse or better, depending on the options available to each firm, U.S. tobacco companies maintained large inventories of tobacco leaves that had to be cured for three years before being used in the manufacture of cigarettes. Because* *tobacco leaves had a ready market worldwide, these inventories were considered as near-cash assets which together with the excess cash that could not be reinvested in tobacco operations, constituted a large pool of liquid but idle corporate assets within each company. For these reasons, senior managers in all three companies agreed that by the end of the 1950s they needed to invest their excess cash in new businesses which had the potential for generating returns in excess of those that could be earned from simple portfolio investments alone.*

To complicate matters, the high degree of cash and near-cash holdings exposed these companies to involuntary takeover, an activity that was becoming more popular as the third U.S. merger wave unfolded and a possibility that became a reality in 1968 for Lorillard, the laggard among U.S. tobacco companies in the area of diversification. Liggett managers, in particular, were concerned that if they let idle cash sit too long, the potential for hostile takeover would be heightened. But this was not recalled as a major factor by senior managers who had participated in the initial decisions to diversify at the other two companies.

THE DEVELOPMENT AND INSTITUTIONALIZATION
OF THE DIVERSIFICATION STRATEGY

Philip Morris

The approach to diversification, as well as to almost any strategy that Philip Morris had pursued, may be traced to the origins of the company. In almost every endeavor, PM has been an innovator among its traditional competitors. It was an early pioneer of filter-tip cigarettes, first to move boldly overseas with cigarette manufacturing subsidiaries, and first to make an external acquisition. Because Philip Morris was not a product of the tobacco trust bust, it has always viewed itself as "the odd man out" among the U.S. tobacco companies. A dual emphasis on innovation and marketing can be traced back to its early years and to the stamp left on the company by an early leader, Alfred E. Lyon.

The Legacy of Company Leaders. *Alfred E. Lyon, the English-born chief executive officer who ushered Philip Morris into the 1950s, was an industry maverick who had been with the company since 1912. After World War I, his company, until then known as the Tobacco Products Corporation, acquired the United States business of the British-based Philip Morris & Company, Ltd., and "Al" was made the company's international representative. He traveled through Europe, Asia, and Africa, acquiring along the way a working knowledge of French, German, Dutch, Italian, and, having lived for two years in India, Hindustani.*

Lyon was known as a dealer and a salesman. In a 1953 New York Times *interview, Lyon recalled that one of his biggest transactions in those years was his sale of several million cigarettes in Poland. The hitch was that Lyon could not receive payment in money; the only exchange of value available was geese, thousands and thousands of them. But the cost of transporting them would have removed any element of profit from the deal. Not to be outdone, Lyon hit upon the idea that a good market existed in the United States for goose feathers that cost very little to transport overseas. So he hired a group of Polish workers to pluck the feathers in return for a half-pound of precious coffee and every goose they plucked. This story of Al Lyon reveals a lot about the management culture and distinctive competence of Philip Morris today.*

When Lyon returned to the United States in 1929, he was sent to the West Coast to build a sales force. He was named executive vice-president of Philip Morris in 1936, was elected president in 1945, and had become chairman of the board before mid-century. His biography appeared in a book entitled, America's Twelve Master Salesmen. *It is said that in front of this master salesman's desk at 100 Park Avenue hung an old adage: "There are a hundred thousand reasons for failure, but not a single excuse." Alfred Lyon retired from Philip Morris in 1957.*

He was succeeded by O. Parker McComas, one of the first outsiders to assume a senior management role in the tobacco "Big Six," who had begun his career as a Wall Street foreign-exchange trader after graduating from Princeton with A.B. and M.A. degrees in 1917. For twenty-seven years he had worked in foreign exchange and finance, serving tours in Paris and London, before becoming associated with Philip Morris in 1946 as a member of its board of directors while serving as vice-president of the commercial banking and foreign departments of Bankers Trust Company. McComas, who had been invited to join the board by Lyon only a few months after he had been elected president of Philip Morris, was to become the company's executive vice-president in 1947, chief administrative officer in 1949, and chief executive officer, succeeding Lyon, in 1955.

McComas was succeeded in 1957 by Joseph F. Cullman III, a Yale graduate and a third-generation tobacco executive, who had spent his entire career in the tobacco business. He started as a tobacco sales representative, gradually worked his way up through the Benson and Hedges subsidiary, and was marketing director of the parent company before becoming chief executive officer of Philip Morris. By the late 1960s, Cullman had been named for an unprecedented fourth year as one of Financial World's *"Ten Top CEOs."*

With Lyon had come the all-encompassing marketing focus of Philip Morris; with McComas, the emphasis on financial control and the first move into diversification. Both brought an international experience to complement Philip Morris's domestic expertise. With Cullman came the building of a strong management team which attempted to balance the two perspectives–marketing and finance–already imprinted deeply in the organizational character of the modern Philip Morris.

The current CEO, George Weissman, took over in 1978. A former journalist and public relations advisor, who spent time early in his career as a press agent for Hollywood's Samuel Goldwyn, Weissman has spent most of the past quarter century working within the strategic echelon of Philip Morris. In the early 1950s he joined the company as an assistant to McComas, and within fifteen years he was running the domestic tobacco marketing. Along the way, Weissman was assigned by Cullman to head up the fledgling international division. Under his leadership, which began in 1960, the overseas tobacco business grew enormously. He recommended the Miller acquisition and, for a period, was relieved of formal tobacco responsibilities by Mr. Cullman so he could concentrate on Miller. He brought John Murphy, whom he had trained in Philip Morris International, to Milwaukee as head of Miller. Thus, because of Weissman's long exposure to strategic decision making at Philip Morris, industry observers expect that he will emphasize the overall thrust carefully developed by his predecessors, which combines marketing and growth, at home and abroad, with strong financial controls.

Points of View and Acquisition Choices. *Two primary points of view have been reflected in the evolution of Philip Morris's diversification strategy. The financial viewpoint during the McComas era was emphasized in the early years of diversification. Acquisitions were screened on the basis of their potential for providing good gross margins and a hedge against inflation. But later, after several divestitures, the marketing perspectives moved into prominence. The focus shifted from earnings stability to growth, first in market-share penetration and later in earnings. Acquisitions under the marketing-driven strategy were sought in industries characterized by a very large market, but in which the acquired firm was not already dominant. Instead, Philip Morris looked for firms with quality products but undeveloped management and marketing functions; ones it could turn around by transferring personnel from its headquarters if necessary, to build a strong subsidiary team, and excess capital from its tobacco business, to improve production efficiencies and to build market share in the acquired firm.*

The early acquisitions, under the financially driven diversification strategy, were not very successful, and several were divested. The more recent Miller Brewing Company acquisition, brought into Philip Morris during the marketing-driven strategy, has been highly successful, and has assumed legendary proportion in the minds of Wall Street observers.

Early Acquisitions: The Financial Orientation. *The early acquisitions were guided by a senior management belief that the stable tobacco business provided "good ballast as well as good cash flow": assets thought to be important for successful diversification. The active search for alternatives, followed by the rejection of several candidates, led in 1957 to the acquisition of Milprint, a packaging company that would support in part the company's growing filter-tip* *cigarette market. In 1960, the American Safety Razor Company (ASR) was acquired. This acquisition took place during the peak of the "blue blade" era, which was characterized by a product that would provide only a couple of shaves before disposing of the blade.*

On the surface, ASR's products resembled in many ways the company's traditional tobacco products. They were repeat-purchase, packaged and branded consumer goods that were sold through many of the same distribution channels as cigarettes. However, the industry was never enormous and, as one senior executive remarked, "the technology got ahead of the economics of this industry." Several waves of product innovation in the razor-blade industry left the "blue blade" a relic of the past. First, Wilkinson developed a blade that would last several weeks. Next came the coated blade that could last as long as a month. The result was that ASR turned out not to be the high-volume business that Philip Morris believed it to be at the time of acquisition; so it was divested.

The next acquisition was Clark Gum. Philip Morris tripled its business volume by hitchhiking its advertising on the budget normally devoted to cigarettes. But, again, industry competitors thwarted Philip Morris's attempt to build profitably the market share of its acquisition. Wrigley held down the prices of its chewing-gum products until Philip Morris got out of the industry. When senior managers were asked if any benefits had been realized because of the "relatedness" of the ASR and Clark Gum product lines to their traditional products, they reported that this was not a particularly effective advantage. Before they were divested, each of these businesses had established its own sales force.

The Mission Viejo real estate venture, acquired in 1970, is the purest example of a financially oriented acquisition. It provided a hedge against inflation for surplus cash from the tobacco business, and it bore virtually none of the product characteristics of the company's traditional business. This acquisition was followed by the purchase of two small hospital-supply firms, whose business also was unrelated to the company's traditional business. Both of these firms were subsequently divested; but the Mission Viejo venture, profiting from rapid appreciation in West Coast real estate, has continued to serve its purpose as a successful hedge against inflation.

Turnaround at Miller Brewing: The Marketing Orientation. *The best example of Philip Morris's marketing-oriented approach to diversification was its highly publicized acquisition of Miller Brewing Company in 1970. The degree to which the product-market characteristics of this business overlap those of the company's traditional business has been striking, right down to the innovation of "LITE" as opposed to the conventional regular beer.*

By 1977, a complete turnaround in Miller Brewing had been achieved. As shown in Exhibit 2, between the date of acquisition and 1977, this subsidiary had moved from seventh to a strong second in market share within the U.S. brewing industry. In doing so, it had transformed a traditional, relatively stable industry

EXHIBIT 2 PERFORMANCE OF MILLER BREWING AFTER TAKEOVER

Year	Miller Brewing Performance			
	Sales ($ mil.)	Profits ($ mil.)	Market Share	Market Rank
1970	$ 198	$ 11.4	4%	7th
1971	204	1.3	4%	7th
1972	210	0.2	4%	7th
1973	276	(2.4)	5%	5th
1974	404	6.3	6%	5th
1975	658	28.6	9%	4th
1976	983	76.1	12%	3rd
1977	1,323	106.5	15%	2nd

Source: Ralph Biggadike, "The Risky Business of Diversification," *Harvard Business Review,* May-June, 1979, p. 110.

into an innovative and competitive marketplace. Its product innovations and quality controls set new industry standards. But how was all this accomplished?

First, Philip Morris placed its initial emphasis on growth in market share rather than immediate profits. Now preferring "capital-intensive" acquisitions, the company spent more than $500 million expanding and updating Miller's production capacity. This infusion of surplus cash resulted in huge, efficient breweries by industry standards. Second, marketing expertise was applied to Miller Brewing by the transfer of experienced Philip Morris managers who displaced the subsidiary's traditional team. The advertising budget for Miller's products reached an estimated level of three times that of the nearest competitor. And finally, Miller innovated, introducing "LITE," the industry's first successful lower-calorie beer, which set off a wave of product imitations by traditional competitors in the beer industry.

The result was a decrease in profitability for Miller Brewing immediately following acquisition that actually resulted in a net loss by the end of the third year. But by the fourth year, profits began to rebound; and by the fifth year, the profit rate exceeded that during the year Miller was acquired. Between 1970 and 1978, Miller's share of the domestic beer market had increased from 4 to 15 percent, and its annual sales had increased sixfold, exceeding $1 billion for the first time in 1977.

By 1980, there was evidence that Philip Morris was trying to duplicate this dramatic turnaround performance in its 7-Up soft-drink acquisition. The marketing-driven approach was a carbon copy of the one employed at Miller Brewing. Family management at 7-Up was replaced by an experienced Philip Morris team, and PM's own brand of marketing expertise was felt quickly by traditional industry rivals. Even the broadcast advertising copy was built around well-known sports figures, a promotional technique that had been pioneered by Philip Morris in the turnaround of Miller Brewing. Moreover, 7-Up was beginning to make headway in increasing international market share.

Learning from Diversifying. *At the time of the interviews, Philip Morris had logged over 20 years of experience with a strategy of diversification. In 1980, its senior managers described the distinctive competence of their company as "marketing, followed closely by good financial controls." Over the years they had learned to make extensive use of personnel transfers from the core business to acquired businesses to ensure the diffusion of their marketing expertise and to get control of acquisitions. In their most successful acquisitions, the existing management team had been too weak, and the resource base too inadequate, to take advantage of the potentials offered by the large domestic markets in which they operated. Therefore, PM's marketing-driven, capital-intensive strategy, which looked for profitability only after the first five years in a turnaround situation, was well suited to this kind of acquisition.*

On the basis of over two decades of experience with the strategy of diversification, Philip Morris had generated several criteria to guide future acquisition choices. The first priority related to the size of the industry *in which a potential subsidiary operated, expressed in terms of the estimated total pre-tax income of its domestic market. The industry has to be large enough to enable an acquisition that benefits from the infusion of PM talent and capital to contribute substantially to the earnings of the parent company. This criterion was used to identify the brewing and soft-drink industries that led to the acquisitions of Miller Brewing and 7-Up. Second, because Philip Morris has always considered itself to be growth company, its acquisitions have to satisfy a growth objective of 20 percent per annum. A corollary to this criterion, therefore, is that an acquisition candidate should not already hold the dominant share of its product market. Instead, it should be appropriate for a* "turnaround" *strategy oriented toward rapid market-share improvement. Again, both Miller Brewing and 7-Up were suited ideally to this criterion.*

Third, Philip Morris managers have decided that when they take over a firm in an existing market, they "have to do something different"; they have to innovate. *They do not want to put themselves in a position where they have to compete head-to-head with established rivals, as they did when they made the ill-fated American Safety Razor and Clark Gum acquisitions. Innovation was a major aspect of PM's competitive strategy later with the Miller Brewing acquisition. Finally, Philip Morris managers believe it is important that acquisitions have the* potential for worldwide distribution, *to capitalize on the parent's long history of success in overseas marketing. Both Miller Brewing and 7-Up meet this criterion, which is unique among the diversification strategies of the tobacco independents.*

In addition to enabling senior managers to formulate both criteria and tactics for diversification, the track record of early acquisitions and divestitures has led Philip Morris to conclude that the potential benefits of common distribution channels among its diversified product lines are seldom realized. In their view, there are many unique aspects of each product market that the company has entered through external acquisition, even though many might fall under the rubric of consumer goods. Philip Morris, for example, originally included the ASR and Clark Gum acquisitions within the traditional tobacco division, but they were separated shortly thereafter into independent sub-sidiaries, each with its own sales force. Whatever synergy PM has realized, therefore, has not come from specific redundancies but from the selection of product markets that are sensitive to capital infusion and to intensive marketing, especially the product innovation and promotional and advertising techniques that Philip Morris had perfected in its traditional tobacco domain.

Integrating the Diversified Portfolio. *With the exception of the ill-fated attempt to combine the initial ASR and Clark acquisitions with the domestic tobacco division, Philip Morris has chosen to keep its acquisitions separate. Instead of consolidating them into core business areas under a "group" structure, each subsidiary operates as an independent business and reports to the corporate headquarters in New York City.*

The first stage in the evolution of the company's structure involved the split between the domestic and international divisions of the tobacco business. The international division began as an export company, but was transformed into an international division during the late 1950s, an event that coincided with the vision, shared among top managers, that future growth in the traditional business would come from international markets.

The next stage involved the birth of corporate planning within the company in the early 1960s. Since that time, corporate planning has been the home for the company's diversification program. This department not only screens acquisition and divestiture candidates, but it supports the monitoring by corporate head-quarters of the performance of the company's semiautonomous divisions. Each division is evaluated on the bases of profit growth and market-share penetration, both of which are reviewed under a system of short- and long-range plans. There is no pressure for a quick turnaround of new acquisitions; instead, Philip Morris prefers to think in terms of the long run, which it defines as more than five years.

But when asked why this company has been so successful with its diversified portfolio of businesses, Philip Morris managers point mainly to the integrative roles of their organizational culture. As a senior official explained:

> Senior managers at Philip Morris are close. They have a "small organization view" of themselves. They are all located centrally in New York, assorted among three floors at 100 Park Avenue. They have worked for many decades together. There have been few outsiders. And they really do their homework; they take work home at night. They're City people, and the diffusion of marketing know-how and management expertise has been accomplished primarily through internal transfers out of the core tobacco business into the acquired businesses.

Diversification Outcomes. *The outcomes of Philip Morris's diversification program are perhaps best reflected in the comments that George Weissman, PM's chairman, made in a 1980 address to the company's stockholders. Summarizing the progress Philip Morris had achieved during the past quarter century, he said:*

> In the first [*Fortune*] 500 listing back in 1955, we ranked 218th in sales. Twenty-five years later, we now rank 49th. Over the 25 years, Philip Morris has been one of the fastest growing of the 500, ranking in the top ten in annual average sales growth, and in the top 20 in earnings growth—reaching 32nd place in net earnings among the 500 in 1979.[5]

Indeed, not only had Philip Morris achieved its sales growth objectives, but during the past ten years its net earnings had grown at a compounded rate of more than 24 percent. Moreover, its nontobacco holdings, though still small by comparison to its domestic and international tobacco business, were substantial. "By themselves," Weissman observed, "this group of products and operating companies would rank Number 111 in the Fortune 500.*"*

Philip Morris's unique brand of diversification, emphasizing turnaround situations and the transfer of experienced personnel, also had contributed greatly to the development and opportunities available to its general managers. Finally, although specific operating synergies had not been realized, financial synergy as well as the transfer of Philip Morris's distinctive competencies in marketing, general management, and international expertise were recognized as important elements in its most successful acquisitions.

The Liggett Group

The diversification strategy at Liggett contrasts sharply in many respects with the approach taken at Philip Morris. For one thing, the experience of the two firms in the domestic tobacco market had been quite different. The training and orientations of managers who guided the companies' initial attempts to diversify also were different. So too were the primary criteria and approaches each company employed in making and managing new acquisitions.

The vice-president of corporate development, James Adams, had joined Liggett in 1973. Since that time, he had been involved in all of Liggett's acquisitions, and for the last two and a half years he has been in charge of the company's diversification program. This responsibility had encouraged him to make an effort to understand the early evolution of the program, and he believed that he was well-informed about the lessons learned from Liggett's diversification experience. Ironically, at the time of this interview, he was preparing a presentation summarizing Liggett's portfolio of businesses and future plans for acquisition and divestiture, to be given to the visiting senior executive group from Grand Metropolitan, a British-based holding company that had acquired Liggett only a few weeks earlier. So the time was especially ripe for a discussion of the subject of corporate diversification as this acquisitive firm was in the process of being acquired.

On Management and Motive. *The principal ladder of executive succession preceding and during the early stages of diversification at Liggett had been production experience. As a result, there had been a great degree of vacillation within the company about the role of marketing. Marketing strategy suffered as a consequence. For instance, although Liggett was early in the development of filter cigarettes, industry analysts have observed that the company was unable to capitalize on this innovation because the themes in their advertising copy were changed too frequently. The pernicious market-share decline which resulted, coupled with the company's exposure to hostile takeover because of its large holding of cash and near-cash assets, forced Liggett to attempt to transfer some of its liquidity into more promising businesses.*

The Surgeon General's Report tended to exacerbate the problems that confronted the company and raised additional concerns within the investment community. This event catalyzed a group decision among Liggett's senior managers to, first, diversify, and, second, to try to turn things around in the tobacco business. Indeed, the company's first acquisition was completed by the end of 1964; the Surgeon General's Report had been released in January of the same year.

An Informal Beginning. *Given these circumstances and the climate of growth and prosperity of the 1960s, Liggett's initial approach to diversification was quite informal. Regarding the initial attempt to diversify, Adams said, "I've never seen a formal document regarding diversification." By that time, marketing had developed a tarnished image, because of its lackluster perform- ance in the competition for cigarette market share; consequently, marketing had not been influential in the early acquisition decisions. At the same time, financial controls for managing the company's growing diversity were not sophisticated.*

Early Acquisitions: 1964–1970. *Liggett was the first tobacco independent to achieve the status of a "diversified" company.*[6] *Its first acquisition in November 1964 of Allen Products, the manufacturer of Alpo dog food, was accomplished with an outlay of $10–12 million.*[7] *The chief executive officer of Allen was nearing retirement and wanted to ensure the perpetuation of his company. Therefore, although Allen Products received several attractive bids for takeover, its owner chose Liggett because this suitor would enable Allen to operate autonomously; a promise made good by Liggett's offer of a payout scheme to Allen's senior officers for performance over a period of several years. The acquisition was very successful. During the next ten years, revenues from Alpo products grew tenfold.*

Next, Liggett acquired the Paddington Corporation, maker of J&B scotch, in 1966 for approximately $60 million. It too was a very successful acquisition. Paddington contributed about 40 percent to Liggett's 1979 operating income and was a primary reason for the Grand Metropolitan takeover in 1980. Although the first two acquisitions were regarded by Liggett executives as very successful, some of the subsequent ones were not.

Carillon Importers Ltd., the licensee for U.S. sales of Grand Marnier liqueur, was also purchased in 1966. This acquisition was considered quite successful due to the strong growth of its popular liqueur brand, Grand Marnier. Four nonliquor and non-pet-food acquisitions made between 1966 and 1970, however, were relatively less successful.

Early Divestitures. *The first divestiture was the National Oats Company, manufacturer of oatmeal and popcorn products, that had been acquired in 1967. Experience with this subsidiary eventually caused Liggett managers to view it as a commodity business. Its products did not have strong brand names and were vulnerable to price competition. Moreover, it was so small that it did not command much of the attention of top management. In the final analysis, its product line did not fit into the four core business areas that developed eventually within the Liggett Group. So it was divested in 1980.*

Brite Industries, Inc., a small manufacturer of watchbands that was acquired in 1968, also was divested. It too was unable to find a home among the core business areas within the company. And Perk Foods Company, a pet-food producer acquired in 1969, became a forced divestiture. Liggett was hoping to extend the low end of Alpo's pet-food line with the acquisition of Perk, but ran into a complaint from the Federal Trade Commission alleging that the combination of Perk with Allen Products would tend to create a monopoly in the dog-food business.

The fourth acquisition during this period involved the 1969 purchase of Austin, Nichols & Company, producers of Wild Turkey bourbon and other branded, imported wines, aperitifs, and spirits. Its products had the potential for complementing the existing bourbon and liquor lines. Although successful, it too was divested in 1980 as part of Liggett's successful attempt to improve the Grand Metropolitan tender offer.

Among the acquisitions completed during the ten-year period, 1967–1978, were a household cleaning-products company (1970), a firm producing branded physical-fitness equipment and sporting goods (1977), and three large Pepsi-Cola soft-drink franchises (1977–79). All remain in the Liggett portfolio.

Acquisition Criteria Distilled from Experience. *From its experience with diversification, Liggett had developed by 1980 several fundamental criteria to guide its future acquisitions. These criteria along with supporting rationale were* *formalized into a planning document in the spring of 1979.*[8] *As an introduction to this document, the following general statement of acquisition policy was made by Raymond Mulligan, president and chief executive officer:*

> As a matter of major corporate policy, Liggett plans further to broaden its consumer products base by acquiring well-managed, growing and profitable businesses selling quality branded goods or services in anticipated growth market segments of the 1980s and beyond. Although we are most familiar with repetitive-purchase packaged products, such items are not the only ones suitable for our consideration. . . . Acquisitions must have both a favorable short-term and long-term impact on net income and generate a satisfactory return measured in terms of our cost of capital. Each acquisition should be judged by the investment community as advantageous, i.e., to have a positive impact upon Liggett's price—earnings multiple and in due course its common-stock price. Accordingly, we must believe each acquisition will have a very high degree of predictable, planned future earnings and cash-flow growth.

By 1980, four "core businesses" had been identified within Liggett's diversified portfolio. Among them were the following lines: spirits and wines; soft drinks; pet foods; and recreational and leisure-time products. The company also had identified the broadcast industry (e.g., television and radio stations and cable television) as a high priority for future acquisitions. But certain special constraints on acquisition policy also had been formalized by Liggett. For example, the acquisition document included the following caveat: "Because of governmental or Liggett's own self-imposed restraints, companies engaged in the cigarette, dog food, beer, and retail or local wholesale wine and spirits businesses are not suitable acquisition candidates." Finally, the company formally expressed a view of its distinctive competence, as follows: "Liggett's management and marketing expertise is in branded repetitive-purchase consumer products responsive to advertising *and other forms of promotion and marketing effort."*

With the identification of these core-business boundary conditions, together with their experience with acquisitions and divestitures, Liggett management was able to agree on four criteria to guide the future development of their diversification strategy. First, Liggett would avoid acquisitions of small companies *if they represented a departure from the four core businesses. As the acquisition planning document states, "Except in acquisitions that are well related to current Liggett activities, net income after tax should exceed $5.0 million." There were several reasons for this criterion. Liggett had learned that certain operational synergies or economies could be gained from aggregating related acquisitions into core businesses. One important source of synergy under* *this criterion was the possibility of extending the product line and market segment coverage of a core business, as in the case of the Carillon products to the Paddington liquor line. As one manager explained the company's own adaptation of the concept of relatedness, "Liggett seeks to add enough similar businesses together to get some marketing muscle." Thus the concept of relatedness for Liggett was not restricted to the traditional tobacco business, but was defined instead with respect to each of the core businesses that had emerged from its diversification program. Moreover, by aggregating small acquisitions into core businesses, the company could be assured that each new business would receive adequate attention from senior management. Experience had revealed that small, unrelated acquisitions could languish without a home in one of Liggett's four product families.*

The second criterion was that acquired businesses must be at least number one or number two in market-share *position within a growing industry in the consumer packaged-goods area. According to the 1980 planning document, "Liggett is not interested in acquiring turnarounds or bail-outs. Nor are we interested in 'patient money' acquisitions requiring a long period of time to generate a satisfactory return on investment." This criterion also emphasized Liggett's distinctive competence in the area of consumer packaged goods.*

Third, the management of the acquired organization must intend to stay. Liggett does not believe in replacing managers in an acquired subsidiary by transplanting managers from its traditional business or from its headquarters. Indeed, Liggett's current CEO had come from the company's first acquisition. This emphasis on strong *existing* subsidiary *management permits Liggett to operate its subsidiaries on a "self-managed, decentralized basis."*

To round out the guidelines for future diversification, Liggett included the following additional caveats on its 1979 acquisition-planning document:

> The business should not be dependent upon one or only a very few large customers; it should not be capital or labor intensive or unusually seasonal; it should not have "fad" characteristics. Preferably the business will have high inventory turnover.

By 1980, therefore, it was obvious that Liggett management had learned a great deal not only about the strategy of diversification, but about its own strengths and weaknesses and how they could be managed effectively in future diversification activities.

Evolution of Management and Structure. *Although the origins of Liggett's diversification program can be identified with the production-oriented managers of the traditional tobacco business, the vice-president of corporate development described the current management of this strategy as a "hybrid of finance and* *marketing orientations." He observed that the most recent trend within Liggett had been the development of more of a marketing-oriented acquisition policy.*

By 1980, the company had adopted a modified group structure, shown in Exhibit 3, to manage its diversified portfolio of businesses. This represented a relatively recent departure from the traditional policy of having subsidiaries report directly to corporate headquarters. With the reorganization came the company's first long-range plan. It included a refined system for allocating capital resources and a budgeting and quarterly review process. Capital allocations for nonnecessities were now subject to a criterion of 15 percent return on investment. New acquisitions also must be able to generate this level of earnings during their first few years with the company.

But the reorganization was not complete. It still did not reflect the four core businesses that had been identified a year earlier. The agglomeration of several different businesses under one group vice-president was evidence that Liggett still had more work ahead. In particular, Liggett's current diversification criteria are oriented toward building on the four existing core businesses in order to amass enough related subsidiaries to justify the overhead required for separate, homogeneous business groups.

Diversification Outcomes. *In contrast to the other tobacco independents, profitability had increased, both absolutely and as a ratio, with Liggett's diversification strategy because of the decline this company had experienced in its tobacco business. Risk exposure had been reduced substantially, because the company had successfully transferred its capital out of the declining domain into industries that had greater growth and profit potential. Regarding the realization of additional synergy from diversification, Liggett currently was not so much complementing its traditional tobacco business as attempting to achieve synergy within each of the four core businesses identified in the long-range planning exercise in 1979. Finally, the feeling within Liggett was that the company had to grow to survive. This strong growth ethic among senior managers was congruent with the continuation of Liggett's diversification strategy.*

The Fate of the Declining Tobacco Business. *For some time, Liggett had adopted what investment analysts had referred to as a "milking posture" with respect to its traditional tobacco business. Because of market-share erosion in the cigarette industry, Liggett had decided to transfer excess cash from this business to its domestic diversification program. It had gradually phased out excess tobacco production capacity and it had sold its European tobacco business to Philip Morris. It also had searched for someone to purchase what remained of the domestic tobacco operations, but had encountered a number of obstacles. It could not sell the business to other domestic competitors because of antitrust restrictions, and its domestic tobacco business was not particularly attractive to foreign competitors because it held such a small share of the domestic market. One highly publicized attempt, by a North Carolina construc-*

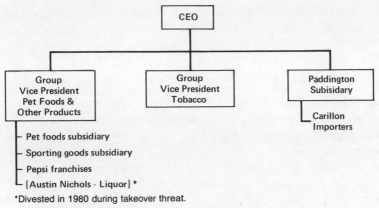

*Divested in 1980 during takeover threat.

EXHIBIT 3 Organization of the Liggett Group, Inc, 1980

tion executive, Dolph Overton, to purchase the business in the late 1970s fell through when it was learned that the suitor could not arrange financing.

On Being Acquired. *Wall Street observers had for some time viewed Liggett as a candidate for hostile takeover, because its size was not large enough to discourage potential parents and because of the attractiveness of its holdings, especially in the spirits and liquors area. With time, Liggett senior managers had decided that takeover might not be a bad prospect if they received an appropriate offer. In preparation, they sought to divest low-return-on-investment businesses in an effort to enhance the company's price—earnings ratio, thereby ensuring that their stockholders would benefit in any takeover attempt.*

When Grand Metropolitan made a bid in 1980 of $50 per share for the company's common stock, Liggett management felt that the offer would be detrimental to its stockholders. So they maneuvered to enhance Grand Met's bid. First, they sold Austin Nichols, a prize sought by the aggressive suitor for close to $100 million, or about one-sixth of the initial Grand Metropolitan tender offer. (Austin Nichols accounted for less than one-fifteenth of Liggett's profits.) Next, they encouraged Standard Brands to enter the contest. The result was that Grand Met boosted its bid to $69 per share and the May 21, 1980, edition of The Wall Street Journal *published the formal notice of takeover to Liggett's stockholders. The maneuver had worked: Liggett's price—earnings ratio jumped from 6:1 to 12:1 with the Grand Met takeover.*

Would the takeover of Liggett mean an end to this company's diversification strategy? The opinion of Liggett managers was that they would continue to diversify, only now to serve the requirements of their new British-based parent for acquisitions of U.S. firms. Indeed, a Grand Met team was making an initial tour of Liggett's tobacco operations in North Carolina on the same day that the interviews for this study were conducted, and was expected to return by the end of the week to the company's New Jersey headquarters for a briefing on Liggett's future acquisition plans.

R. J. Reynolds

Diversification began early at R. J. Reynolds as a result of the almost overnight success of its first filter-tip cigarette brands, Winston and Salem, which were introduced in 1953 and 1954. Shortly thereafter, Archer Products, the internal packaging facility of the tobacco operation, came under pressure from the rapidly increasing demand for Winston and Salem cigarettes. By 1957, the facility had been expanded to the point that it had developed excess capacity, and Reynolds had decided to allow this facility to begin selling its products outside the company. Thus, Reynold's first experience with operating in new markets came as an unanticipated consequence of the internal development of an operation closely related to its traditional cigarette business.

Some Early Experiments. *Although company officials are quick to indicate that "Archer was not really viewed as a diversification effort within R.J. Reynolds," the internal development of this subsidiary provided an initial, albeit small, window into the strategy of diversification; and it is obvious that they learned quite a bit from this preview.*

Soon after the decision to seek outside markets for Archer's packaging products, RJR management decided to permit this subsidiary to complement its operations by integrating backwards and horizontally. As Archer expanded, it bought an aluminum-ingot supplier and a plant for converting ingot into aluminum-foil products. Next, Archer expanded its packaging line by acquiring a wrapping-paper business, producing paper products for Christmas and gift wrapping, and a ribbon-and-bow company. It was not long after this episode of small acquisitions that Reynolds managers began to learn some early lessons about the strategy of diversification.

Almost as soon as the integrated Archer subsidiary had been assembled, it was dismantled. First, Reynolds managers found that the seasonal nature of the gift-wrapping business created more problems than benefits; Reynolds's traditional cigarette business was not subject to seasonal or cyclical fluctuations in demand. Therefore, the entire wrapping-paper operation, together with the ribbon-and-bow line, was sold to American Greeting Cards, an event that required Federal Trade Commission clearance. Next, the household aluminum-foil line was divested because it became viewed as a "commodity" item. By that time Reynolds managers had begun to recognize that they could not compete against fully integrated competitors who were "taking products from the ground to the consumer." As Rex Baker, vice-president of corporate development, explained, the major learning from this divestiture was that "you can't be an intermediate convertor of a commodity product . . . you can't compete in a commodity line if you aren't integrated backwards." For similar reasons, the aluminum-ingot plant was divested. "You can't just be a fabricator," Baker explained. "You can't compete against people who are fully integrated." By 1980, the streamlined Archer subsidiary was dividing its sales of packaging products between the corporation's cigarette operations and its outside markets.

Creation of the Diversification Committee. *Reynolds established a diversification committee in 1957. The committee process was described by Baker as quite informal. Each member had his own ideas, which were expressed freely at the committee meetings. In terms of organizational politics, production never had been very influential. Instead, throughout the early history of RJR's diversification strategy, the two major forces had been the top management group, composed almost exclusively of people who were major stockholders in the company and whose experience was primarily in the tobacco business, and the financial function. In fact, the financial function had been quite influential in the 1960s and early 1970s, the period of greatest intensity in the company's search for and accumulation of external acquisitions. During this time, the corporate legal staff had also been influential in the choice process. In contrast, the marketing function had not played a major role in the choices that shaped the diversified portfolio that exists within R.J. Reynolds today.*

When asked why RJR had relied primarily on the external-acquisition mode of diversification, Baker explained, "We were in a very narrow area of technology—tobacco processing—that couldn't go elsewhere except Archer. We tried flavoring by acquiring Aeromatics International, but we found, subsequently, that there were very few opportunities for utilizing tobacco flavoring expertise." This small company also was sold in the late 1970s. Because of the early experiments with internal development and with attempts to expand the narrow technology of tobacco processing, the diversification committee embarked on an initial strategy of diversification into related businesses, relying exclusively on the external-acquisition route. Moreover, the committee would guide this far-reaching program until 1974, when its corporate development function was combined with the business planning function in what continues as the corporate-level department of business planning and development.

Initiation of Purposive Diversification. *The company's first major attempt to diversify came at the time of the Surgeon General's Report. As Baker observed, there had been a rush among all tobacco companies to diversify. He said, "There was some perceived risk to a primary source of earnings, as a result of the smoking-and-health controversy." In addition, the cash flow from the tobacco business exceeded internal requirements, resulting in the need for external investments.*

The first series of acquisitions brought RJR into the consumer packaged-foods business. RJR managers believed that food products were distributed through channels similar to those of their traditional cigarette lines. In terms of final distribution, both product lines were sold to ultimate consumers through retail food outlets. The only difference was that cigarettes were sold directly to an intermediary, the wholesale jobber, who then made final distribution to retail grocery stores and other outlets. RJR managers also believed that food products responded well to advertising, an activity for which they believed they possessed a good deal of competence, based on their advertising successes in the cigarette business.[9]

Through a series of relatively small acquisitions, between 1957 and 1974, Reynolds became committed heavily to the food-products business. Among these early acquisitions were Pacific-Hawaiian (1963), Penick & Ford (1965), Chun King (1966), Filler Products (1966), and Patio Foods (1967). Part of the Penick & Ford subsidiary was divested subsequently because of antitrust complications. In addition to being small, many of these companies had established branded products. But they also had relatively narrow product lines that were difficult to build upon; therefore, their growth potential was limited. RJR managers soon discovered that the food business was subject to seasonal variations, from such things as crop failures, and to price sensitivities that were not shared with the traditional tobacco business. In addition, the growth of this industry was found to be not among the highest of industry alternatives.

As R.L. Remke, chairman and chief executive officer of RJR Foods, Inc., explained to a meeting of investment analysts in 1976:

> Our task in the 1960s was to take these five separate and disparate businesses with different sales organizations, manufacturing facilities, and business philosophies and merge them into one company—RJR Foods, Inc.
>
> What happened during the consolidation phase in the Foods Company history, from the late 1960s through the early 1970s, was, I believe, predictable. We found ourselves competing in a business that corporately we knew relatively little about. We had a conglomeration of brands to be consolidated into a single business. So for about five years we went through the difficult and trying process of consolidation and learning. . . .
>
> With the benefit of hindsight, it is clear that we made our share of mistakes during this period. It is also clear that it was a period of real accomplishment. We learned about the food business; we built our organization; we cleaned up our product line, eliminating about half our items; we consolidated our manufacturing and distribution system; and importantly, we attracted and held strong managers with a food industry background.[10]

Early Lessons. *From this early episode of small acquisitions, RJR management learned a couple of things that helped them refine their diversification strategy. First, subsequent acquisitions had to be* attractive. *The industry into which entry is made must be characterized by high growth potential and stable* *profits. Moreover, each acquired company had to possess a "critical mass"; it had to be well positioned in its industry. No longer, for example, would the search for new food businesses focus on the aggregation of many small companies with narrow product lines. Instead, RJR waited until 1979, when its search for a company to complement its food-products portfolio finally resulted in the $621 million acquisition of Del Monte, a U.S. industry leader with a broad product line and recognized clout in the competition for retail grocery shelf space. During its first year with RJR, Del Monte generated over $2 billion in sales (all four earlier food acquisitions generated only $85 million in total 1966 volume), contributed a strong consumer franchise system, and operated with branded goods worldwide.*

Second, from the early diversification emerged the criterion of affordability. *Because many of the acquisitions were accomplished through stock transfers, a potential problem concerning the structuring of stock deals had to be managed carefully as RJR's diversification strategy took on momentum. RJR's price—earnings ratio was generally lower than those of most of the companies it sought to acquire. If RJR had made those acquisitions without regard for this consideration, it would have diluted its own shareholders' net worth. "If you're looking after the welfare of your stockholders," Baker explained, "you have to pay attention to the affordability criterion." The P/E ratio, therefore, was a significant acquisition constraint during the early years of the search for diversification opportunities.*

Finally, Baker noted that the criterion of availability *obviously was important throughout the diversification era. Many companies that met the attractiveness and affordability criteria simply were not on the market for takeover. Moreover, when such companies did come on the market, the time available to any prospective parent for analyzing its merits was usually severely constrained.*

Diversification into Unrelated Areas. *After an initial period of diversifying into the related food-products business, Reynolds began to acquire businesses that were unrelated to its traditional domain. Because of their high perceived growth potential, the shipping and petroleum businesses became the focus of RJR's diversification committee. But if undercommitment to the foods business was an early liability to the "related" side of RJR's diversification, overcommitment on the "unrelated" side has also brought mixed blessings.*

In 1969, Reynolds acquired McLean Industries, Inc., owner of Sea-Land, the largest sea-freight service in the world operating with the new "containerized" shipping technology. Not only was this a new industry, but it was a very different one from the traditional business of R.J. Reynolds. It provided an industrial service as opposed to a consumer product. Moreover, it exposed the company to far more uncertainty than its traditional business, from such sources as world trade volatility, dock strikes, and currency revaluations.[11] And by

1980, it had consumed over $2 billion of RJR's resources needed not only to make the purchase but to refurbish and expand the Sea-Land fleet. By 1980, this investment had resulted in a strong increase in revenue growth, but the uncertainties of this unusual business had created an erratic earnings record. By the time Paul Sticht, the current chairman of the board, took over as company president in 1973, he recalled, "Sea-Land was out of control. The business was being run by a traditional management organization without the benefit of normal systems and controls." [12]

In 1970, R.J. Reynolds went even farther afield by acquiring the American Independent Oil Company, a small petroleum exploration and production company based in the Middle East. Although this acquisition was well timed, given the dramatic rise in world oil prices and the need to ensure that Sea-Land had a hedge against rising fuel costs, it also exposed the company to a new form of uncertainty—political risk—because its primary operations were based in the unstable Middle East.

In the fall of 1977, Kuwait nationalized Aminoil's properties, paying RJR in reparation the $55 million that it had initially invested in the acquisition. [13] *But by this time, Reynolds had made a much larger commitment to the petroleum business. In June of 1976, the company had acquired the domestically based Burmah Oil Company for $522 million, a figure that was reported to be less than its book value, but which represented the largest single cash acquisition in U.S. business history. As a company spokesperson at the time explained:*

> Our reasons for the Burmah acquisition were to diversify further into an area where we had already achieved success and had expertise. We sought to improve the quality of our petroleum earnings and achieve a good return on investment and substantial cash flow. We viewed the Burmah acquisition as a unique opportunity to acquire at an attractive price proven domestic petroleum reserves, which are bound to appreciate in value with time. The Burmah acquisition brings us geographical balance and political security; a substantial inventory of exploratory leases with prospects of further discoveries; staff strength and balance; and growth potential in the United States, which has a virtually unlimited market for domestic oil and gas, since consumption is almost twice domestic production. [14]

Since 1976, RJR has invested close to $450 million in petroleum exploration and development, bringing its total investment in the Burmah acquisition up to $1 billion. But the petroleum reserves now controlled by this RJR subsidiary are estimated in the billions of dollars. [15]

Learning from Diversifying. *By 1980, the diversification strategy begun almost twenty-five years earlier at R.J. Reynolds had become the most complex of those of the major U.S. tobacco companies. At that time, much of what the* *company had learned from its broad experience had become institutionalized in the form of general guidelines that would govern its future diversification activities.*

First, new acquisitions must be related to the existing competencies of the corporation. "The company or the acquisition must be something we know how to run," said Baker. "Our early competence was marketing in consumer products. We moved away from the marketing competence, but we're moving back again. The foods area is clearly an area in which we now feel that we have distinctive competence." When asked what principles he would offer managers attempting diversification for the first time, Baker recommended that in making acquisition choices, they rely heavily on the backgrounds, expertise and special competencies of the existing management team. *He said, "When you buy a company like Sea-Land, it takes management a long time to learn the key elements of its business success."*

Second, RJR management recognized quite early in its diversification program that "you can't do things in a small way." As Baker observed, "We've been fiddling in the food business for seventeen years." Both size and positioning *of an acquired company were important factors in its success after acquisition. Third, acquisitions must have product lines that can be built upon. Fourth, an acquisition must be "a good investment" on the basis of discounted cash flow as measured against the corporation's cost of capital. It also should be characterized by both stability and growth.*

The top-management team was in consensus over the next steps in diversification and about what they had learned from the past. In general, they would be emphasizing related, as opposed to unrelated, acquisitions. First in priority would be major companies handling consumer packaged goods. Baker indicated that although Sea-Land does not fit this configuration, it is complemented by the oil subsidiary. He said there also was a desire to build on the corporation's oil and natural gas reserves.

Managing the Diversified Portfolio. *The gradual increase in both diversity of the business portfolio and dependence of the parent corporation on the sales and earnings of acquired businesses led ultimately to the development of a new system of organization and management. At Reynolds, these changes were reflected in the politics, the structure, and the operating mechanisms of the expanding enterprise.*

The most important organizational response to increasing diversity and dependence took place within the top-management team. First, a notable shift in the political structure occurred, beginning in the early 1970s. The marketing function gradually took hold of the diversification program as the current chief executive officer and board chairman, J. Paul Sticht, and other marketing-oriented senior executives joined the company. Indeed, a 1978 Business Week *report on the metamorphosis at the top in R.J. Reynolds observed that:*

Sticht, who came to Reynolds in 1972, after taking early retirement as president of Federated Department Stores, Inc., has recast Reynolds with outsiders—a decisive change for a company that had been led by tight-knit groups of men who worked their way up through the tobacco business. So radical have the changes been that when Stokes [the chairman of the board who hired Sticht] steps down, the senior management of RJR will lack anyone who came up through tobacco.[16]

The transition from a single-business operation had created the need for managers who differed from the traditional ones. Not only was marketing experience emphasized, but there was a need to have managers who knew the critical success factors unique to each new business. Therefore rather than rely on general management talent or on the development of people whose experience had been primarily in the tobacco business, RJR sought managerial expertise specific to each of its core businesses. When asked how the company obtained the necessary expertise, Baker replied, "We generally had to buy it."

The evolution from single-business to multibusiness corporate strategy also was followed by a series of structural reorganizations. Before diversification, RJR had been a functionally organized tobacco company. As early acquisitions were assimilated into the corporation, they were managed as subsidiaries of the tobacco company itself, rather than treated as independent profit centers. Each subsidiary reported to a different senior executive within the tobacco operation.

In 1969, twelve years after the diversification committee had been established six years after the acquisition of the first food company, a major reorganization took place. The company moved from a functional to a divisional structure. RJR Archer, the packaging subsidiary, was set up as a separate company. The small food companies were combined under RJR Foods, also a separate company.

With even greater diversity caused by subsequent diversification into unrelated fields, the company reorganized again in 1970, this time changing its name, to R.J. Reynolds Industries, Inc., as well as its corporate structure. The new holding-company structure centralized certain corporate functions, including legal, treasurer, tax, cash management, planning, and public relations, at the Industries level. The reorganization also created an Office of Chairman and President, with the next level of management consisting of executive vice-presidents who were responsible for the operating companies.

This Office lasted only a few years. It was replaced in 1979 by a top-management structure that eliminated the executive vice-president level which had separated senior corporate management from the operating companies. Now, company presidents reported directly to the chairman, the vice-chairman, or the president of RJR Industries. Although this final shift gave more autonomy to the diverse operating companies, RJR's approach to managing its diversity is described as "active corporate management of subsidiaries." All major decisions, according to Baker, are made at the headquarters board meetings. Moreover, he said, "Subsidiaries make recommendations for acquisition, but the approval rests on the corporate level."

Finally, a realignment of the overall corporate control function toward greater sophistication and formalization also followed the pace of diversification. Presently, the corporate control system consists of a set of operating guidelines that spell out in great detail the levels of subsidiary authority and the dollar amounts that go with them. Monthly reviews, consisting of actual performance against budget, are used to complement five-year strategic plans and one-year operating budgets. A management-by-objectives system is the primary mechanism by which subsidiary managers make various dollar and nondollar commitments to corporate headquarters. These commitments include such areas as growth, profitability, and managerial succession and development. An ongoing management replacement plan had been developed five years earlier. Finally, there is no overall mandatory financial objective. Growth and profit objectives are tailored to each subsidiary based on its unique characteristics, particulary the kind of market in which it operates.

Diversification Outcomes. *In 1980, the current vice-president of corporate development surveyed the outcomes from the diversification strategy at R.J. Reynolds as follows. First, increased profits had been achieved in absolute terms but not in terms of profit ratios. Return on assets, for example, had declined with diversification. As Baker explained, this was so because of the profits in the tobacco industry that were difficult to achieve in other industries. Second, risk exposure had decreased as a result of diversification, at least insofar as the long-term declining tobacco market was concerned. But there was one qualification. "We're in a more volatile industry setting than the tobacco industry, at least in the short term," Baker said. "Therefore, our risk has increased somewhat by moving into less stable industries, but I believe our long-term risks are substantially lower." Third, corporate growth from diversification definitely had increased managerial career opportunities, according to Baker.*

Fourth, the results in terms of potential "synergy" gains from diversification were mixed. When asked whether additional synergy had been achieved, Baker replied, "For the most part, no"; there was no in-house expertise that the company could readily apply across all of its businesses. But he also observed that "there has been some synergy in expertise in the foods business, born out of the early acquisitions, that is now being applied to the management of Del Monte." Finally, when asked if the company had been able to capitalize on its distinctive competencies, Baker replied, "Not much, up to this point, except in the area of international tobacco."

DEVELOPMENTAL PATTERNS AMONG THE DIVERSIFICATION STRATEGIES

Several general patterns may be identified in these corporate histories that should be of use to students and managers of the strategy of diversification. These patterns illustrate important features of both the process of organizational learning and the content of organizational knowledge upon which these firms created, developed, and eventually institutionalized their diversification strategies. They also provide specific insight into the dynamics of strategy formation and structural alignment, and they suggest important refinements in some critical but elusive concepts that link corporate strategy, structure, and effectiveness.

1. **Decisions made early in the strategy-formation process, although appropriate given the initial learning situation, later served to constrain the range of strategic choices.** *All three companies approached the initiation of their diversification strategies with appropriate caution. They began tentatively, experimentally, and conservatively by developing or acquiring small businesses that were closely tied or related to their traditional business and that led them into the fields of packaging or consumer packaged goods. Although each had several good reasons for diversifying, they were not operating under immediate crisis conditions. Therefore, each company was able to ease itself into a multibusiness mode.*

Based on these early experiments, senior managers in all three companies were able to learn some early lessons that would help them refine the future development of their diversification strategies. They soon recognized, for instance, that small acquisitions, even companies selling branded products, did not possess much "clout" in the markets they served. Many operated with specialized product lines that proved to be difficult to build upon, a factor which limited their growth potential. Just as serious, these early, isolated acquisitions were too small to attract and maintain the attention of corporate management. They simply could not contribute very much to the overall performance of the companies, and the minimal investments made to acquire them posed insignificant risks to senior managers. As a result of this knowledge, either the small isolates were divested or similar companies were acquired as management attempted to attain a "critical mass" in the new businesses. As late as 1980, Liggett was still searching for acquisitions that would enable it to complement its emerging core businesses, and Reynolds had searched for almost a decade before it acquired Del Monte to provide the critical mass needed to anchor its five small food subsidiaries.

2. **The meaning of business "relatedness" became clarified only after experience in new business domains.** *The apparent similarities between traditional and new businesses at the time the diversification strategy was* *initiated proved to be more illusory than expected. Although all three companies moved into repetitive-purchase, packaged consumer-goods fields, a domain also populated by the cigarette market each had traditionally served, all discovered that their "distinctive competence" was not always applied with equal success. Business practices varied widely, technologies were difficult to assimilate, and volatilities in market price, demand, and supply were greater than anticipated. For Reynolds, the food industry offered more uncertainty than the stable tobacco market; and for Philip Morris, the "technology got ahead of the economics" in the razor-blade business. Although many of the early acquisitions shared the same final customer and distribution channel with the traditional cigarette business, subtle differences in selling technique or in earlier links in the channel made it difficult to realize the benefits of a common sales force. Indeed, early attempts to consolidate the selling effort soon broke down into separate sales forces for each new subsidiary. Thus, operating "synergy" was elusive, especially during the early stages of development of these diversification strategies.*

With time, the concept of "relatedness" took on more dimensions. In addition to the nature of the product, companies were later screened more carefully in terms of their market characteristics–price sensitivity, supply and demand volatility, earnings stability, and growth potential. More emphasis also was placed on the development or recruitment of managers with specific expertise and intensive experience in the businesses that were acquired. Less reliance was placed on the matchup of general relatedness and general management skills. (This was true more for Liggett and Reynolds than for Philip Morris, an observation to which we will return in the discussion of another pattern.)

3. **"Related" acquisitions were more easily assimilated than "unrelated" acquisitions.** *Even without the refinements discussed above, acquisitions that were generally related to the core tobacco business proved to be more successful than those which were generally unrelated. The divestiture rate was much higher and the earnings stream was much less predictable for industrial-product acquisitions than for consumer-product acquisitions. Philip Morris, for example, quickly divested both of its hospital-supply acquisitions, and both Liggett and Reynolds soon divested companies that they discovered operated in commodity (i.e., high-volume, nonbranded, price-sensitive) businesses. Moreover, Reynolds found itself caught up in market uncertainties to which it was not accustomed, a technology that it did not understand, and in a commitment of capital (e.g., to fleet modernization and expansion) that it did not anticipate, with its bold entry into the containerized shipping business.*

But the identification of core industries by Liggett and Reynolds has put a new twist on the concept of "relatedness." By accumulating similar acquisitions into core businesses, senior managers in these holding companies have been able to apply the knowledge they gained from early acquisitions to industry groups of companies. The adoption of divisional or group structures, in turn, has enabled these companies to achieve some economies (e.g., central staff services at group and corporate levels) and synergies (e.g., the market clout Reynolds obtained by aggregating its small specialty-food companies under RJR Archer). It should be mentioned, however, that this need to build "critical mass" around early product-market decisions also served to constrain the range of acquisition choices later in the life cycle of the diversification strategy. Nevertheless, this emergent twist raises some important issues about the conventional meaning of "relatedness" in diversification, which typically has been used to refer to the relationship between an acquisition candidate and the traditional or dominant business of the enterprise. As a minimum, future attempts to classify diversification strategies must take into account both the proactive and the reactive aspects of the "relatedness" concept, a requirement that imposes upon the analyst a longitudinal investigation of strategy formation.

4. **Structural adjustment lagged behind strategy.** *No doubt "structure" in the narrow sense influenced the early diversification choices. The predispositions and functional points of view of those in authority influenced, as we shall see, the early acquisition criteria and choices as well as the approaches adopted for assimilating and managing the growing business portfolio. But major reorganizations of corporate structure and fundamental alterations in control systems and other basic operating mechanisms lagged far behind the pace of diversification.*

For an extended period, all three companies simply had their new subsidiaries report directly to senior executives in the tobacco operation. But with increasing financial commitment to nontobacco businesses and with increasing diversity within the business portfolio, the need for structural realignment became apparent. Gradually, financial controls and planning and review systems evolved toward greater sophistication. As new core businesses began to contribute in a significant way to corporate revenues and earnings, a separation between tobacco-company management and subsidiary management occurred in all three companies. The portfolios became segmented by business division or industry group, with each component eventually reporting directly to corporate management.

Thus, in this overall sense, structure followed strategy. But the causal direction was not as unilateral as this general conclusion would imply. For example, the requirement for building "critical mass" in order to achieve the economy and control features of the group structure also influenced, as we have discussed, the shape of the diversification strategy that was being formed.

5. **More accurate knowledge of "other" and of "self" came with experience in new businesses.** *Hindsight revealed to these companies that diversification required a more thorough assessment of the context and critical success factors of new businesses than originally anticipated. In the beginning, most senior managers in the three companies were not in the best position to*

make accurate assessments of acquisition candidates because their business experience had been confined largely to the tobacco industry. In addition, the conditions under which potential acquisitions became available did not encourage systematic, in-depth industry analysis prior to takeover. Attractive acquisitions came on the market rather suddenly and were taken out of the running just as quickly. Therefore, acquisitive executives had to act fast if they wanted their bids to be considered favorably.

With time and experience, however, our companies learned what to look for in the markets, management, and product lines of acquisition candidates. More important, they soon established the diversification function within a specialized corporate-level unit, usually in the corporate development or corporate planning department. Here the acquisition process gradually assumed a more rational and proactive thrust, as specialists developed industry and company profiles that would prepare the corporation for action should a high-potential acquisition candidate become available.

Just as important, diversification required a more thorough assessment of the strengths and weaknesses of the parent organization than anticipated initially. Some companies discovered that general management expertise developed out of experience in the tobacco business was not sufficient to understand and harness new businesses. Seasoned veterans in the entered business were often required to complement existing management expertise in the parent companies. All began to realize that marketing was at the center of their distinctive competence, and power realignments were often required to capitalize on this critical resource. Thus, in all three histories it is evident that an appreciation of the strengths and weaknesses of both acquisition candidates and the parents themselves developed out of the actual enactment of the diversification strategy and the process by which new businesses were assimilated, organized, and managed. Indeed, by 1980 the wisdom gained by all three companies could be sorted into two categories—acquisition criteria and assimilation approaches—both of which reflected far more knowledge of ''others'' and ''self'' than was evident at the time the strategy of diversification was initiated.

*6. **Wisdom from experience.** After 15−20 years of experience with a diversification strategy, senior executives in these companies had acquired a substantial base of knowledge that was now firmly established in the management belief system and institutionalized in the formal planning documents that guided each firm's future development. One product of this learning process stood out and was shared by all. Future acquisitions would be, with few exceptions (notably Reynolds's desire to increase its petroleum reserves and Liggett's plans to explore opportunities in the broadcasting industry), related to the distinctive competence of these companies, which was based on the marketing of high-quality, branded, repeat-purchase, packaged consumer products. For some companies this fundamental requirement had been particularized to the needs of core businesses within their diversified portfolio. This commit-*

ment had been affirmed in all three companies by the rise to executive leadership of the marketing function.

In addition, all three corporations sought to acquire firms with high growth potential and expandable product lines as a way of offsetting the stagnating domestic cigarette market. Finally, it was obvious that all three companies had opted exclusively for external acquisitions as opposed to internal development as the vehicle for diversification. All had realized the severe limits to the generalizability of their core technology and the expandability of their tobacco-product line. Moreover, their primary objective of diversification had been to find new growth opportunities to offset the decline in their domestic tobacco market. The acquisition route could accomplish this objective much faster, with the added benefits of access to established branded goods and existing management expertise, and avoidance of entry barriers to new markets. But beyond these similarities were some important differences.

The companies parted ways when it came to the entry tactics and short-term performance expectations that they applied to new acquisitions. The basic approach of Philip Morris has been far more aggressive than those taken by Reynolds and Liggett.

Philip Morris has oriented its diversification toward capital-intensive "turnaround" situations. It prefers to acquire companies in large markets, but firms which do not already command market leadership. Instead, the ideal acquisition candidate usually has a high-quality branded product and an expandable product line, but often suffers from inadequate capital or weak general management and marketing expertise. Given these raw materials, Philip Morris focuses its turnaround strategy on rapid market-share growth. Indeed, its growth objective of 20 percent per annum is the highest among the tobacco independents.

Turnaround is accomplished by transferring both capital and experienced management and marketing personnel from headquarters to the new subsidiary. Capital is used to modernize and expand the subsidiary's operating facilities and to increase its advertising budget. With the transfer of senior personnel, Philip Morris is able (1) to rapidly assimilate and integrate the new subsidiary into the corporate family, and (2) to apply the innovation and promotion techniques that have become the parent's hallmarks. Finally, to facilitate the realization of its turnaround strategy, Philip Morris management is patient; it is willing to defer earning expectations during the first five years following acquisition.

The entry tactics and performance expectations of Reynolds and Liggett have been considerably more conservative. Because these firms have had to operate with price-earnings ratios below that of Philip Morris, both have had to consider the "affordability" of acquisition candidates in order to protect the net worth of their stockholders. Both firms have placed a higher emphasis than Philip Morris on the current market position and the historical earnings predictability of acquisition candidates. Neither has been interested in "patient money" situations. Both have sought companies with strong existing management teams that can generate their own capital requirements and, hence, "stand alone."

Both Liggett and Reynolds have adopted a decentralized approach to subsidiary management. Indeed, one of the reasons the makers of Alpo dog food chose Liggett among many suitors was the promise that this subsidiary would be able to continue as a semiautonomous operating company. In addition, rather than impose corporate management on subsidiaries, both Liggett and Reynolds have benefited from the transfer of experienced subsidiary managers to headquarters, where many now hold senior corporate positions.

7. **Executive succession and organizational politics.** *In all three cases, executive succession was not a major catalyst to diversification. Instead, declining opportunities in the traditional domestic market, together with potential missed opportunities from idle cash, stimulated the diversification initiative. Executive succession did play a major role in organizational alignment to evolving strategy. By the end of the study period, all three companies were headed by marketing-oriented senior executives under whose leadership the marketing function played a central role in both diversification choice and acquisition assimilation and management. Thus, the major role of executive succession was one of* consolidation.

Organizational politics also played a role in the strategy-formation process. During the early period, the financial and operations functions were far more influential than the marketing functions, especially in Liggett and Reynolds. Under their regime, acquisitions were selected more for their presumed stability of earnings and inflation-hedging characteristics. A higher proportion of unrelated acquisitions was made during this period, which was characterized also by some nontrivial misperceptions of the true nature of acquired businesses and the markets they served.

After a series of early acquisitions and divestitures, marketing–the core function in the companies' distinctive competence–assumed leadership in the diversification choice and acquisition assimilation and management processes. With the rise of marketing came much closer scrutiny of the nature of the businesses and markets served by acquisition candidates, as well as a renewed emphasis on business "relatedness." The financial function assumed a close support role to marketing because of the increasing diversity of the business portfolio within each company. Thus, all three political structures in 1980 could be described generally as "marketing, followed closely by good financial controls."

These discontinuities in the patterns of executive succession and organizational politics appeared to be responsive to some strengths and weaknesses discovered early in the formation of each company's diversification strategy. It was through these processes, together with structural realignment, that the companies were able to adapt to the new contingencies imposed by their increasingly diverse portfolios.

ORGANIZATIONAL LEARNING AND STRATEGY FORMATION

In closing this chapter in the history of diversification strategy, it is important to add what we have discovered to the preliminary evidence on organizational learning by examining the period of transformation that separated the initiation and institutionalization stages of strategy formation.

Our company histories reveal that all three conditions for organizational learning were at work in the U.S. tobacco industry, although two figured more prominently in the formation of diversification strategy. *Performance gap,* both potential and realized, was brought forcefully to these companies by the smoking-and-health controversy and its effects on the growth rate of their traditional domain. As a result, executives in each company had little difficulty in the area of problem identification; instead, their efforts were focused on problem solving.

But this performance gap was not cataclysmic. It did not portend a complete and swift end to the tobacco business. Rather, it left tobacco executives with the prospect of depressed, even negative, growth in the short run, and a sense of general uncertainty about the long run of their traditional industry. In this sense, the smoking-and-health threat initially exposed the Big Six to "reasonable" stress, which was high enough to rally the joint response of internal organizational coalitions, but was not so intense as to encourage resignation or panic. For companies that failed to heed the early warning, however, the stress became more intense.

The creation and application of *organizational slack* was also a major feature of the problem-solving approach adopted by these companies. Indeed, most of the potential sources of slack were applied in one form or another by the tobacco independents to help cope with the crisis they all faced. The fact that the tobacco industry was not destined for immediate doom, therefore, meant that diversification could be achieved by an orderly transfer of resources from the threatened domain into others with higher performance potential and less political risk.

In addition, diversification committees were created at the senior corporate level to help these organizations understand diversification and to frame their initial decisions to diversify. In a sense, these units were agents of organizational learning in which senior representatives from diverse organizational functions collaborated to determine whether and how to redeploy slack financial resources. In many respects, these units resembled the marketing-research and technical research-and-development functions that had been institutionalized in corporations wishing to respond more effectively to market and technological uncertainties.

Finally, the companies differed in the sources of slack they created for assimilating and managing their new and different businesses. Philip Morris preferred to stick closely to its traditional skills in marketing by relying on the transfer of excess managerial and marketing capacity to new acquisitions. The price PM was willing to pay for this strategic choice was the suspension of normal profit expectations during the first five years after acquisition. Reynolds and Liggett, in contrast, created slack in the form of new management skills, by either acquiring companies with seasoned management teams or hiring outsiders with proven track records in the new businesses within their increasingly diverse portfolios.

This combination of unequivocal performance gap, with its reduction in the need for problem identification, and abundant slack for problem solving probably accounts for the relatively smaller role played initially by *catalytic leadership,* at least in the three companies for which detailed diversification histories were available. Instead, in Liggett and Reynolds, the rise to executive leadership of marketing-oriented managers from outside or from acquisitions was instrumental (1) in consolidating their diversified portfolios, (2) in realigning their organizational and political structures, and (3) in developing or acquiring the skills needed to cope with new multibusiness contingencies. Under conditions of less definitive threat and organizational slack, no doubt the catalytic, as opposed to the consolidative, role of executive leadership would have been required to focus managerial attention and to redeploy organizational resources. In the situation they faced, however, tobacco executives encountered little sustained opposition to their early experiments in domain creation that, with time, provided the basis for the evolution of a broad-reaching diversification strategy.

In the final analysis, patterns revealed by these company histories confirm the suspected artificiality of the traditional separation of strategy formulation and implementation—of planning and doing. Instead, they demonstrate that the initiation and institutionalization stages in the formation of a new and different strategy are linked, if at all, by the process of organizational learning from enactment. It is in the facilitation and nurturance of this always demanding, often frustrating process that the quality of executive leadership in organizations attempting to cope with stressful conditions is perhaps most visible.

FOOTNOTES

[1] In a recent review of the literature on organizational learning, Miles and Randolph (1980) identified two basic approaches to learning, which they describe as "proactive" and "enactive." The former relies heavily on the acquisition of required knowledge before initiating a new program or venture—knowledge obtained primarily from the previous experience of the managers directly involved, but also from their access to the literature on the subject and to consultants. Based on the existence and availability of relevant knowledge, the *proactive* approach emphasizes planning in advance of a new program or strategy. The *enactive* approach to learning, in contrast, occurs from the process of initiation itself, by which managers rely on trial and error, together with performance feedback, to understand and refine a new program or strategy. Although these authors observed that these extremes of organizational learning seldom obtain in reality, they predict that the proactive approach will predominate in the initiation of conventional programs or ventures and that the enactive approach will of necessity prevail during the development of innovative projects.

[2] As March and Simon have observed, "To explain the occasions of innovation is to explain why a program of action that has been regarded as satisfying certain criteria no longer does so . . . innovation will be most rapid and vigorous when the 'stress' on the organization is neither too high nor too low. By stress is meant the discrepancy between the level of aspiration and the level of achievement" (1958:182−84).

[3] As Miles (1980c:313) has observed, ". . . organizational memory may be systematically built, acquired, or erased. Members can gradually learn through trial-and-error what to pay attention to and which strategy to employ in one situation as opposed to another. An organization can also expedite this learning process by hiring individuals or groups with the relevant experiences it needs to effectively cope. . . . Studies linking biographical information on successive chief executives of an organization to changes in both its environment and its effectiveness would probably be quite revealing in this regard."

[4] An extension of the test of how much learning occurred is presented in the subsequent chapter in which a comparative analysis is made of the financial performance of traditional (tobacco) versus diversified (nontobacco) operations of the tobacco independents.

[5] Excerpts included in Philip Morris, Inc., *Call News*, May 1980, p. 1.

[6] A generally accepted operational definition of a "diversified" company is one whose annual operating revenue from its traditional business is less than 70 percent of its total operating revenues (Rumelt, 1974).

[7] In September 1966, Milton Harrington, Liggett's new chief executive officer, was quoted in a *Fortune* magazine article as saying, "If we diversify, it will be into something either related to the tobacco industry or in the consumer-products area."

[8] Raymond J. Mulligan, "Liggett Group Inc.: Statement of Acquisition Policy and Criteria," spring 1979.

[9] In an address to M.B.A. students at the University of North Carolina, the current chief executive officer of R.J. Reynolds described the company's first major food-product acquisition, Pacific-Hawaiian, as follows: "It seemed like familiar territory to us. We were dealing with consumer packaged goods, just as we were with cigarettes. The marketing approach, distribution network and advertising were all similar to the cigarette industry. Plus we identified it as a growth strategy." T. Eleazer, "Planning Diversification at RJR," in *The Bottom Line* (Chapel Hill, N.C.: Graduate School of Business Administration, University of North Carolina, December 1977, p. 1.

[10] Comments of R.L. Remke, Chairman and Chief Executive Officer, RJR Foods, Inc., contained in R.J. Reynolds Industries, Inc., *Analysts Meeting,* Winston-Salem, N.C., September 19−21, 1976, p. 60.

[11] Comments from Charles I. Hiltzheimer, President, Sea-Land Service, Inc., in *Analysts Meeting,* pp. 35−44.

[12]"When Marketing Takes Over at R.J. Reynolds," *Business Week,* November 13, 1978, p. 88.

[13]"When Marketing Takes Over," p. 89.

[14]Comments of Jack B. Sunderland, President and Chief Operating Officer, Aminoil International, Inc., *Analysts Meeting,* p. 49.

[15]H. Rudnitsky, "Cigarettes with an Oil Chaser," *Forbes,* May 26, 1980, p. 67.

[16]"When Marketing Takes Over," p. 82.

III

ASSESSMENTS, ISSUES, AND IMPLICATIONS

7

Patterns of Strategic Organizational Adaptation

an assessment

Our story now told, we must return to the issues of organizational efficiency and legitimacy that helped to frame this investigation. In this chapter, an attempt will be made to assess the patterns of strategic organizational adaptation that characterized the political economy of the tobacco industry and distinguished its member firms over the past quarter century.

Three major adaptive patterns emerged during this period, as shown in Figure 7–1. First, the Big Six joined forces to defend their traditional domain against a legitimacy threat from its institutional environment. Second, they engaged in an intense competitive battle for market share within the threatened domestic industry. And finally, each company attempted to create new domains of opportunity and to minimize risk exposure through overseas expansion and domestic diversification. Although the evidence demonstrates that *all* members of the industry contributed to these overall patterns, we have revealed and compared the differences among the Big Six in how they went about implementing these strategic choices. Moreover, in the preceding chapters, we have attempted to assess the relative effectiveness of some of these strategies in terms of the outcomes each was intended to achieve.

This chapter contains an overall economic and sociopolitical assessment of the Big Six and their industry. The results of each of the strategies that characterized the adaptive response of the organizational population will be summarized briefly before we proceed with an overall assessment of the relative efficiency of each firm and the performance and legitimacy of the industry.

STRATEGIC ORGANIZATIONAL ADAPTATION: AN ECONOMIC ASSESSMENT

We have discussed already in some detail the degree of success the industry and its member firms achieved with their early political and competitive struggles in the traditional tobacco domain; therefore, we will only briefly summarize these

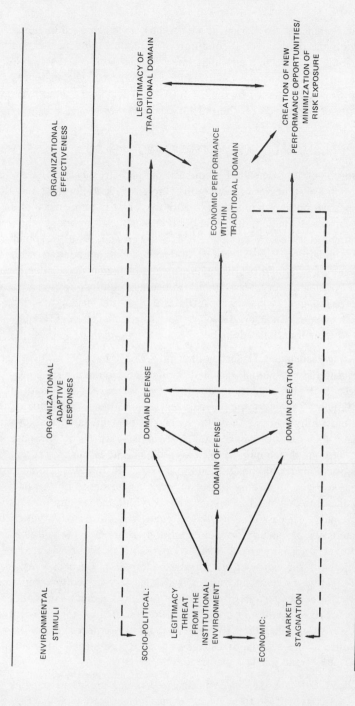

FIGURE 7-1 Model of Organizational Adaptation among the Tobacco Big Six

201

accomplishments here. We will focus more on the results achieved in the area of domain creation and on the overall condition of the tobacco independents at the end of the study period. In particular, this section will serve to highlight differences in the relative efficiency—financial performance, dependence, and slack—that have been achieved by these companies. The next section will take up the question of legitimacy for the industry as a whole.

DOMAIN DEFENSE, OFFENSE, AND CREATION

The Early Defense of Domain. About the immediate success of the early joint domain-defense strategies of the Big Six, there is little doubt. Not only does the industry persist, but it remains a very profitable one for companies holding a major share in its stagnating domestic market. Just as important, the joint political ventures mounted by the Big Six have been successful in sometimes overturning, sometimes circumventing, and otherwise negotiating with the institutional agents of administrative authority that threatened their legitimacy and livelihood. At the very least, their immediate political response to the smoking-and-health controversy was sufficient to create slack time, thereby enabling the Big Six to initiate and develop more substantial strategic adaptations to the threat to their traditional domain.

Maintaining Position in a Stagnating Domain. As we have seen, the tobacco independents differed substantially in their approach to competitive strategy and in the success each achieved in maintaining or increasing its share of the stagnating domain. Reynolds, the "Analyzer," was able to maintain market dominance, and Philip Morris, the "Prospector," enjoyed rapid market-share growth during the industry shakeout. In contrast, American Brands, the "Defender," fell out of step with the pace of product innovation and, as a result, out of its historical leadership position in the industry. It finally had to acquire a large overseas tobacco subsidiary to bolster its sagging domestic business, an event which occurred only after a complete break with the company's traditional pattern of executive succession. Finally, Liggett, the "Reactor," which had been dominated by a production-oriented coalition, dropped to the bottom of the industry and even sold its overseas tobacco operations to Philip Morris.[1]

An important secondary effect of these domain-offense choices (e.g., less-harmful-cigarette product innovations) was that they tended to complement the joint domain-defense strategy. Beyond these immediate consequences, however, the success or failure of these competitive strategies, together with the general predispositions that they illustrated about the companies, influenced substantially the choices and relative successes that distinguished other adaptive strategies pursued by the tobacco independents.

Domestic vs. Overseas Tobacco Businesses. Domain-creation strategies also contributed to the overall performance and survival potential of the Big Six.

Among these strategies was the attempt to avoid some of the negative effects of stagnation in the domestic industry by creating new markets for tobacco products abroad. As we will review later in this assessment, most of the Big Six were quite successful in loosening their traditional dependence on the domestic cigarette market. But here we wish to focus on the relative financial performance of their overseas and domestic tobacco businesses.

As Table 7−1 reveals, the tobacco independents (those among the Big Six for which information was available) have not achieved financial performance abroad that approximates the successes realized by their domestic tobacco businesses. Throughout the period following their rapid buildup of international markets for tobacco products, return on sales abroad has lagged far behind domestic returns. Moreover, there has been a discernible decrease in performance returns with experience in the overseas tobacco business, which may be attributed in part to increasing volatility in the world money market. Finally, Philip Morris has generally outperformed its domestic rivals abroad, a finding that is associated with this company's heavy investment in overseas manufacturing capacity instead of a more tentative reliance on domestic exports and international licensing agreements. In contrast, Liggett, which has never reported separate financial data on its domestic and overseas tobacco businesses, withdrew from international cigarette competitions when it sold most of its overseas operation to Philip Morris in the late 1970s.

Tobacco vs. Nontobacco Businesses. The financial success of the diversification strategy may be estimated for each of the tobacco independents by comparing the operating performances of their tobacco and nontobacco businesses, as illustrated in Figure 7−2. The most obvious difference among the

TABLE 7-1 COMPARATIVE OPERATING PERFORMANCE, DOMESTIC VS. OVERSEAS TOBACCO BUSINESSES

Company	Tobacco Business	Operating Income/Net Sales %	
		1970–1974 Average	1975–1979 Average
Philip Morris	Domestic	16.8%	22.1%
	Overseas	12.2	11.0
Reynolds	Domestic	19.3%	21.9%
	Overseas	7.7	6.4
American Brands	Domestic	19.0%	21.6%
	Overseas	5.4	3.8

Sources: Annual reports, 1970-1979

Note: Liggett does not report operating earnings and net sales on a geographic basis for its tobacco businesses.

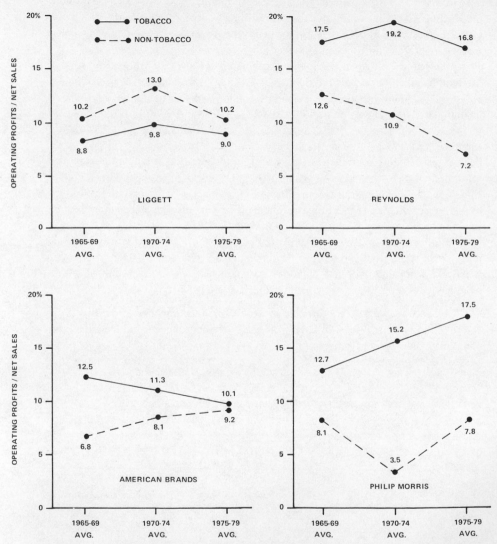

FIGURE 7-2 Comparative Operating Performance, Tobacco vs. Nontobacco Businesses
Sources: Annual Reports, 1965–1979

companies is the fact that Liggett has achieved the highest nontobacco performance and is the only company among the independents whose nontobacco
performance exceeds the performance of the traditional business. This and
several other differences appear to be related to the amount of tobacco business,
particularly to the domestic market share, realized by each company. The
industry leaders, Reynolds and Philip Morris, have been able to generate
unusually high rates of return from tobacco products compared to American
Brands and Liggett, which have suffered pernicious market-share erosion
because of their tardiness in responding to cigarette innovations.

Finally, nontobacco business performance has been lowest for Philip
Morris and Reynolds. The former has been pursuing a patient strategy of
diversification by deferring normal profit expectations for five years after
acquisition in order to achieve its dramatic "turnaround" approach. However,
the upward trend in the performance of Philip Morris's nontobacco businesses
may be a signal that the longer-term financial benefits of its "patient" approach
are being realized. Reynolds, on the other hand, has continued to suffer from its
hodgepodge of small foods and unrelated shipping acquisitions. However, it too
may be due for a turnaround, because of the recent acquisition of Del Monte and
because a release on the market of its vast oil and natural gas reserves could
generate an enormous income stream.

Thus, with the unusual exception of Liggett, which now holds less than 3
percent of the domestic cigarette market and which has sold its overseas tobacco
operations, diversification has not been able in the intermediate term (15−20
years) to achieve a financial performance comparable to that generated by the
traditional business, even under conditions of stagnation. Moreover, for this
intermediate term, the acquisitions of Liggett and American Brands, relying on
strong existing management teams and operating in businesses closely related to
the traditional domain, have achieved the highest financial performance. It
remains to be seen, however, if the more diversified approach of Reynolds and
the turnaround approach of Philip Morris will equal or exceed the performance of
the more traditional approaches over the longer term.

Domain Creation and Dependence.   Overseas expansion and domestic diversification have also made it possible for those tobacco companies to restructure
their interdependences with the threatened traditional market. Although all four
were single-business companies at the beginning of this study, each had
substantially reduced its overall dependence on the domestic cigarette market by
1979. As Table 7−2 reveals, each company's specialization ratio had decreased
to a range from 34 percent for Liggett to 64 percent for Philip Morris. Income
dependence had also fallen, but to a lesser degree, owing to the unusually high
profitability of the domestic cigarette market. By 1980, income dependence
ranged from 29 percent for Liggett to 81 percent for Philip Morris. Thus,
dependence on the traditional domain had been reduced by all four companies,
but its degree was conditioned by the relative success of the domain-offense and

TABLE 7-2 STRATEGIC DEPENDENCE ON THE TRADITIONAL DOMAIN

A. SPECIALIZATION RATIOS:
Percentage of Net Sales Accounted for by the Tobacco Business

Company	1973	1974	1975	1976	1977	1978	1979
Liggett	51%	49%	49%	48%	46%	39%	34%
American Brands	69	67	65	63	64	63	62
Reynolds	71	64	68	64	63	67	55
Philip Morris	82	79	76	71	67	64	64

B. INCOME-DEPENDENCE RATIOS:
Percentage of Operating Income Accounted for by the Tobacco Business

Company	1973	1974	1975	1976	1977	1978	1979
Liggett	52%	44%	42%	42%	62%	35%	29%
American Brands	74	71	70	67	67	66	59
Reynolds	83	63	74	76	83	82	77
Philip Morris	97	94	91	84	80	78	81

Sources: Annual reports, 1973-1979

overseas-expansion strategies each company had developed to support its tobacco business.

ECONOMIC-GOAL ATTAINMENT: INDIVIDUAL FIRMS

Comparisons among the tobacco independents in terms of overall economic performance can be made along four important dimensions: (1) growth, (2) profitability, (3) financial slack, and (4) investment risk. The first two dimensions provide a retrospective view of each firm's economic performance, whereas the last two reflect more their future prospects for organizational performance.

Growth. About the attainment of one goal there is little doubt. Regardless of whether size of profits, sales, or assets is considered, the domain-creation strategies of the Big Six have generated enormous corporate growth. This growth has been realized despite the fact that the compounded average growth rate in the U.S. market for cigarettes was only 1.8 percent per year from 1950 to 1979, and had dropped during the previous ten years to 1.6 percent per annum.

In the face of primary-domain stagnation, the size in terms of total assets of the Big Six had increased remarkably from 1950 to 1979. Reynolds, the largest company, is now twelve times its 1950 size. Philip Morris, the pace leader, is now thirty-four times larger than it was at the beginning of our study period. American Brands, which has been unable to recover the ground lost in its domain-offense battle, has nevertheless grown sixfold in assets, primarily because of its overseas-expansion and domestic-diversification programs. Liggett, on the other hand, has had far less excess cash to play around with because of its steep decline from prominence in the tobacco business. Nevertheless, Liggett has been able to double its size based on the assets of acquired small businesses.

Not only are they bigger physically, but the tobacco independents have recorded substantial gains in sales and earnings. As Table 7−3 illustrates, the growth leader, Philip Morris, has been able to consistently exceed the average sales and earnings-per-share growth rates of both an all-industries composite and other multi-industry companies during the past fifteen years. Reynolds, followed by American Brands, has been able to maintain the pace of growth set by these industry and conglomerate composites, whereas Liggett generally has not been able to keep up with the growth of its traditional rivals or with U.S. industry as a whole. Thus, for the tobacco companies whose domain-offense or overseas-expansion strategies were sufficient to secure their cigarette volume under domestic-market stagnation, diversification enabled them to keep pace with or exceed the growth rate of firms across U.S. industries. Among these firms, Philip Morris, with its marketing-driven "turnaround" approach, has grown the fastest. For Liggett, which failed to maintain its domestic and overseas tobacco businesses, diversification has not been sufficient to achieve normal corporate growth.

Profitability. During the last decade and a half, the tobacco independents have become diversified companies operating a number of different businesses both overseas and at home. Despite this metamorphosis, the profitability patterns that distinguished each company during the past fifteen years of diversification resembled closely the patterns that distinguished the Prospector, Analyzer, Defender, and Reactor during their single-business era (refer back to Table 4−3

TABLE 7-3 COMPARATIVE GROWTH OF TOBACCO INDEPENDENTS, 1965–1979

Industry/Company	Sales Growth[a]			Earnings-per-Share Growth[a]		
	1965-69	1970-74	1975-79	1965-69	1970-74	1975-79
All industries (median)	10.1%	11.0%	13.1%	8.0%	5.8%	13.1%
Multi-industry companies (median)	19.1	7.2	9.9	2.9	4.9	13.1
Philip Morris	11.3	19.5	20.1	18.2	19.9	18.9
Reynolds	5.3	10.0	15.0	3.4	9.1	9.1
American Brands	15.5	10.9	9.3	6.1	7.2	8.7
Liggett	6.0	4.9	4.6	−0.2	5.6	3.3

[a]Yearly averages

Source: "Annual Report on American Industry," appearing in the first issue of *Forbes,* 1970, 1975, and 1980

in Chapter 4). As shown in Table 7−4, Reynolds has generally outperformed the three on both average return on equity and average return on investment.[2] Philip Morris has consistently been in second place in terms of profitability, followed by American Brands. Liggett, again, has been the lowest performer.

Just as important, with the exception of Liggett, the tobacco independents have continued to be more profitable than U.S. industry in general or other multi-industry companies. Again, the success of the domain-defense and -offense strategies is a key to explaining the high performance of these companies under adverse conditions. Because of the high profitability of the domestic tobacco business relative to both overseas tobacco operations and diversified businesses at home (as shown in Table 7−2 and Figure 7−1), the success of these companies in protecting the industry from institutional assault and in maintaining or enhancing their share of it has figured heavily in their overall profitability and in their ability to create and to get control of new domains of opportunity.

Financial Slack.　But these comparative figures on organizational dependence, growth, and profitability reveal only where the companies are today and where they have been. Differences in the ways they have expanded overseas and at home have drastically altered the amount of financial slack available for coping with future contingencies. Philip Morris, in particular, has been running close-hauled. Its emphasis on rapid market-share buildup simultaneously in its domestic tobacco and nontobacco businesses has required huge infusions of corporate capital and has demanded patience for the realization of normal returns. Its choice to invest early in overseas cigarette-manufacturing facilities has resulted in much higher performance than its domestic rivals from international operations. But this aggressive Prospector has had to pay the price of its consistent pattern of capital-intensive choices in terms of greatly reduced financial slack.

TABLE 7-4　COMPARATIVE PROFITABILITY OF TOBACCO INDEPENDENTS, 1965-1979

Industry/Company	Average Return on Equity[a]			Average Return on Investment[a]		
	1965-69	1970-74	1975-79	1965-69	1970-74	1975-79
All industries (median)	12.9%	11.6%	15.1%	10.2%	8.7%	11.8%
Multi-industry companies (median)	12.3	10.5	12.6	9.5	7.9	10.1
Reynolds	18.0%	22.0%	20.5%	16.8%	14.8%	14.8%
Philip Morris	17.5	22.3	22.7	11.5	13.6	13.5
American Brands	13.5	14.4	15.8	11.7	10.5	11.3
Liggett	7.8	11.0	10.3	7.7	8.1	8.3

[a] Yearly averages

Source: "Annual Report on American Industry," appearing in the first issue of *Forbes,* 1970, 1975, and 1980

As Figure 7−3 reveals, Philip Morris has highly leveraged its net worth in order to pursue an aggressive approach. By the end of the 1970s, Philip Morris's long-term debt had reached a level that approximated the total value of its stockholders' equity. In contrast, by pursuing a less patient and capital-intensive approach, especially toward diversification, the other three tobacco independents currently enjoy approximately one-half the liquidity-risk exposure of Philip Morris. Instead of searching for "turnaround situations," which had become the hallmark of PM's approach, the other three had emphasized the acquisition of companies with strong existing management teams already well positioned in their respective industries. It was feasible, therefore, for these companies to expect normal operating returns within the first year after most of their acquisitions.

The only major exception to this pattern was Reynolds's entry into the shipping and petroleum businesses, both of which (1) were unrelated to its traditional business and distinctive competences, (2) were capital-intensive, and

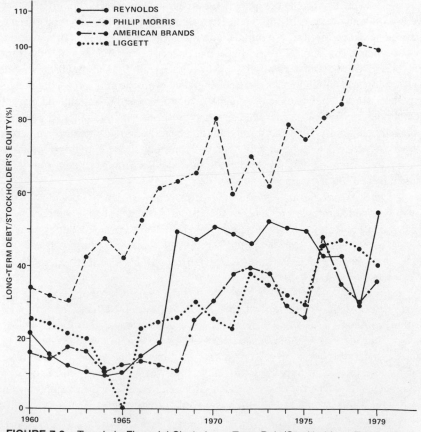

FIGURE 7-3   Trends in Financial Slack: Long-Term-Debt/Stockholders'-Equity Ratios
Sources: Annual reports, 1960−1979

(3) required the deferment of immediate operating returns. This exception is reflected in Figure 7−3 by Reynolds's upward departure from the pattern set by American Brands and Liggett between 1968 and 1978.

The question that remains, therefore, is whether Philip Morris will suffer in the long term from its highly leveraged strategies or will eventually outperform its more conservative traditional rivals. The substantially higher returns that have been achieved by Philip Morris from overseas tobacco operations (Table 7−1), together with a recent turnaround in the performances of its nontobacco businesses (Figure 7−2), suggest that the latter fate is more likely. But this prediction presumes that Philip Morris will not encounter a major crisis over the next half decade in any of its businesses that might require the creation or application of financial slack, a resource that is currently in short supply.

Investment Risk. The most widely cited index of investor confidence in the future performance of a corporation is the price−earnings ratio. Presumably, the more an investor is willing to pay now for a share of common stock in a company, relative to its current earnings per share, the smaller the perceived risk he or she associates with the company's future earnings potential. As Figure 7−4 reveals, since the release of the Sloan-Kettering report in 1953, all four tobacco independents have fared worse on this index than the Standard & Poor's average for U.S. industrials. Only Philip Morris has exceeded this index, and only for a brief period during the last decade. However, as all four companies moved heavily into diversification to reduce dependence on the risky and stagnating cigarette business, they have encountered lower returns and unanticipated market uncertainties in new businesses. In addition, Philip Morris had reached a highly leveraged position by 1979. And, of course, the smoking-and-health issue is still with us. No doubt these developments have contributed to the regression of the tobacco independents toward or below the price−earnings index for U.S. industrials as a whole.

Beyond these overall patterns, the price−earnings ratios reflect that the growth-oriented strategies of Philip Morris have been able to capture more investor confidence than have those employed by the other independents during the most recent decade. But the abrupt decline in its price−earnings ratio during the last half decade suggests that Philip Morris may be losing its comparative advantage.

In summary, there is ample evidence that the Big Six have made significant progress toward the attainment of their goals of domain defense and domain creation, although important differences have been identified for the goal of domain offense. In the process, all members of this industry have undergone dramatic metamorphoses. By any yardstick, none today could be classified properly as "tobacco companies." Even Philip Morris, whose sale of tobacco worldwide is the largest of the industry, has a commitment to nontobacco business that alone would rank it in the top fifth of the *Fortune* 500 list of largest U.S. corporations.

The new company histories have also revealed a remarkable ability, the

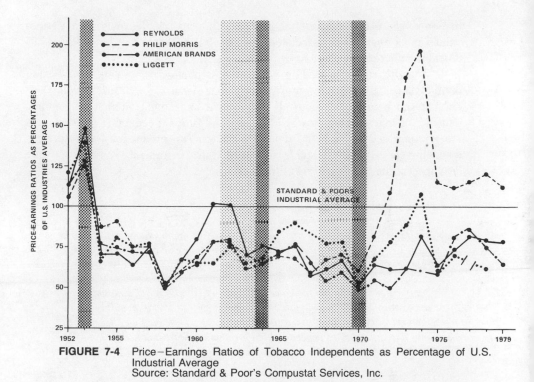

FIGURE 7-4 Price–Earnings Ratios of Tobacco Independents as Percentage of U.S.
Industrial Average
Source: Standard & Poor's Compustat Services, Inc.

normal caveats of internal organizational inertia and politics notwithstanding,
to enter new domains, transform organizational designs and operating
mechanisms, build or acquire new skills, transfer distinctive competences, and
rearrange political structures and career ladders. Indeed, most of these companies
have demonstrated a capacity for operating along the full range of options for
organizational adaptation and for pursuing many goals and strategies simultaneously. But we have still made only occasional reference to the economic viability
of the tobacco industry as a whole. It is to this overall assessment that we now
turn.

OVERALL ECONOMIC ASSESSMENT: INDUSTRY LEVEL

There is no dearth of alternatives for assessing the overall economic performance
of an industry. Indeed, in many of the analyses we have attempted at the firm
level, one can draw conclusions that the overall performance of the tobacco
industry, which is now composed of firms whose portfolios include many
businesses related and unrelated to tobacco, has been both high and stable
relative to all-industry and multibusiness-conglomerate composites. Moreover,
these results have been achieved despite the persistent stagnation of the domestic
tobacco domain. A recent multi-industry study by the Bureau of Industrial
Economics (BIE) at the U.S. Department of Commerce provides some confir-

211

mation of the economic well-being of this industry, and reveals some of the values other than those associated with health that help bolster its survival potential (Vaccara and MacAuley, 1980).

The BIE study focused on the relative economic performances, over the period 1966–1978, of twenty-two U.S. manufacturing industries producing durable and nondurable goods. It represented an explicit attempt to identify industry "winners" and "losers" based on a historical economic performance index composed of growth, return to factors of production, and foreign competitiveness.[3] The rationale for using this performance composite was described in the BIE report as follows:

> *Stated in the most basic terms, industries are expected to produce marketable goods and services and to pay competitive returns to the labor and capital used in production. Growth is also an important objective, with increasing GNP a commonly used measure of economic development. Given that inflation is one of our most pressing economic problems, keeping prices down must also be a characteristic of well-performing industries. Successful competition with foreign producers is another component of good performance. More exports mean more jobs, a stronger dollar and an ability to pay for necessary imports; increasing import penetration may entail a loss of jobs and an excessive dependence on foreign suppliers and hence should be counted as poor performance. [Vaccara and MacAuley, 1980:6]*

On the basis of this study, the tobacco industry was rated a "winner." Its actual standing was third place, closely following the lead of the chemicals and the instruments and photographic-equipment industries. From a look at the economic factors independently, tobacco leads all U.S. industries in profitability, or return to investors,[4] and in the minimization of import penetration. It exported a considerably larger share of its output than manufacturing industries generally, and its product price increases were among the lowest. It ranked unfavorably (low), however, on both net output growth and return to labor. (No industry ranked high on all six economic performance factors.) Thus, despite its exposure to political risk and economic market stagnation over the past quarter century, on most grounds deemed important to the U.S. economy, the tobacco industry has continued to do *very well*.

THE QUESTION OF LEGITIMACY: A SOCIOPOLITICAL ASSESSMENT

Having concluded that the Big Six have done very well for themselves despite a quarter century of adversity, we now turn to the issue of doing "good." We have warned readers that the issue of legitimacy has been considerably more difficult than efficiency to measure—so much so that few organizational observers have made the attempt. Nevertheless, this study would be incomplete if we skirted the legitimacy issue on the grounds of its apparent intractability.

Fortunately, in the case of the U.S. tobacco industry, there are concrete manifestations of several important aspects of the legitimacy construct. Each signals a definite "direction" in actions or values with respect to the smoking-and-health controversy. First, the various legal restrictions placed on the industry during the last two decades remain in force today. Although they could have been much worse were it not for the domain-defense strategies of the Big Six, the laws and trade regulations developed by Congress and its administrative agencies have continued to constrain the traditional autonomy and prestige of the U.S. tobacco industry. Moreover, this mix of federally imposed constraints has been expanded by restrictions—especially those regarding the rights of nonsmokers and the prohibition or segregation of smokers in municipal offices, transportation, and other public places—imposed by state governments and private establishments. Although no new federal restrictions appear imminent, state and local restrictions continue to proliferate.

Second, there is evidence from the trend in the aggregate and per capita levels of cigarette consumption in the United States that the declining legitimacy of smoking is being reflected in the economics of the tobacco industry. Ironically, these data come from the U.S. Department of Agriculture, one of the major pro-tobacco agencies in the federal government.

Third, we were able to discover systematic evidence, spanning the last decade and a half, on the shifting values in U.S. society concerning the social and health aspects of cigarette consumption. These public-opinion polls reveal that smokers as well as nonsmokers are taking a more jaundiced view of the tobacco industry and are more firmly of the belief that smoking is damaging to the health of smoker and nonsmoker alike.

Finally, to explain the persistence of the industry in spite of these legal and social trends, we examine the role of various institutional props that complete the picture of the political economy in which the smoking-and-health confrontation has been waged and that continue to counterbalance the efforts of the antismoking forces.

CIGARETTE-CONSUMPTION TRENDS

A recent (1975) report from HEW revealed that more than 90 percent of all adults now believe that smoking is hazardous to health. The most recent Surgeon General's Report (Public Health Service, 1978) concluded that there have been significant reductions in smoking prevalence among almost all segments of the population. The U.S. per capita usage of cigarettes was 195 packs in 1979, a figure that was 30 percent below the 1963 peak on the eve of the 1964 Surgeon General's Report (Miller, 1979:6). According to the 1978 FTC *Report to Congress:*

> *The percentage of all adults who smoke regularly was 33% in 1978. The*
> *percentage of adult men who regularly smoke declined from 53% to 38%*
> *between 1955 and 1978, and while the percentage of adult women who*

regularly smoke had increased from 25% to 32% between 1955 and 1965, it decreased to 30% by 1978. Nevertheless, in one category, women aged 18–25, smoking prevalence is increasing.

Most of the decrease in adult smoking is explained by quitting, rather than a lower rate of initiation. Since 1964 some 30 million people have quit smoking, and the great majority of smokers have either tried to quit or would if they could find an effective way to do so. [FTC, 1979:2]

"Gradual Chinese Water Torture." In a speech prepared for the Tobacco Association of America in 1980, Robert Miller, a leading economist for the U.S. Department of Agriculture, concluded that "the domestic tobacco market is declining both on an absolute and relative basis." Alluding to the diversified status of the Big Six, he said, ". . . this shift by U.S. consumers impacts as much or more on tobacco growers and processors than on major manufacturers" (Miller, 1980). That same year, a New York investment analyst specializing in the cigarette industry was quoted in *The Wall Street Journal* as follows: "The cigarette industry appears to be on the brink of a long, slow decline. It's going to be a gradual Chinese water torture. . . . It used to be 'in' to smoke. But now it's the other way around. There's a lot of negative social pressure being put on smokers. Some are even beginning to feel guilty about lighting up in public" (Ramirez, 1980a:17).

Shift toward "Safer" Cigarettes. In addition to declining consumption trends, there has been a fundamental shift in the nature of the cigarette product consumed in the United States, as shown in Figure 7-5. Although senior managers in the Big Six have not recognized officially the connection between smoking and disease, their response has been to develop and market allegedly "safer" cigarettes.[5] This product-market shift reflects both the effects of the cigarette health warnings and the responsiveness of the U.S. tobacco companies.

As our review of the domain-offense strategies of the Big Six has revealed, two distinct product-innovation waves were associated with each of the major health-warning inductions from the institutional environment. With the Sloan-Kettering release in the early 1950s came the emergence of the filter-tip cigarette, which was allegedly lower in tar and nicotine content than the traditional regular brands. By 1978, filtertips represented 90 percent of the domestic cigarette market.

The first Surgeon General's Report in 1964 ushered in the era of the low-tar-cigarette category, cigarettes having 15 milligrams or less of tar. By 1967, low-tar cigarettes had achieved a 2 percent share of the domestic market and were backed by 5.5 percent of the Big Six advertising expenditures; but this share increased rapidly since that time, as shown in Figure 7-6. By 1978, low-tar cigarettes had achieved almost 28 percent of the market and were backed by 43 percent of cigarette advertising expenditures (FTC, 1978:45). In 1980, "low-tars" represented over 40 percent of the total domestic market and remained the most rapidly growing market segment (Ramirez, 1980b:17). Indeed, by that

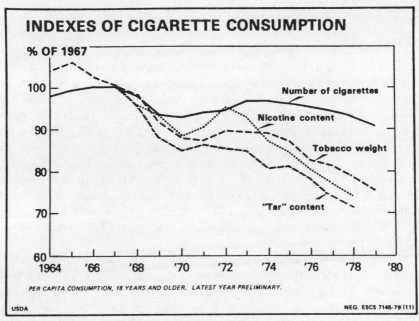

FIGURE 7-5   Trends in U.S. Cigarette Consumption.
Source: U.S. Department of Agriculture, *Tobacco Situation,* TS-169,
September 1979, p. 11

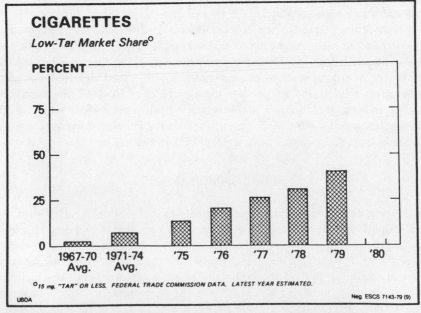

FIGURE 7-6   Cigarette-Consumption Trend: The Low-Tar Market Share
Source: U.S. Department of Agriculture, *Tobacco Situation,* TS-169,
September 1979, p. 12.

time, several "super-low-tar" brands (less than 5 mg tar) were becoming popular in the marketplace.

In contrast to these changes in consumption patterns, the 1978 FTC *Report to Congress* revealed, "In the fifteen years since [the Surgeon General's Report] there has been little change in the character of cigarette advertising. Cigarette ads continued to emphasize the satisfaction to be derived from smoking, to associate smoking with ideas, individuals and activities worthy of emulation, and to attempt to allay anxieties about the hazards of smoking" (FTC, 1978:5). For instance, one of the more controversial advertising campaigns in 1980 was the one Brown & Williamson used to introduce its new 1-mg-tar Barclay brand. Its promotional theme, "99% tar-free," was confusing to staff writers at *Advertising Age* and was almost certain to provoke FTC reaction. Moreover, Brown & Williamson was planning to spend $150 million to introduce the super-low-tar brand, making Barclay the most expensive new entry in the history of the cigarette industry.[6]

Despite all the emphasis on low-tar cigarettes and the declining trend in cigarette consumption, the product-innovation response of the Big Six has raised a number of fresh concerns among the health and antismoking forces. For one thing, the availability of low-tar and super-low-tar brands may discourage health-conscious smokers from quitting (Ramirez, 1980b:52). Although these brands may reduce the health risk of smokers, the 1978 update of the Surgeon General's Report warned that they are still harmful and that the effects of other potentially dangerous "gases" (e.g., carbon monoxide) produced by the lit cigarette may not be adequately controlled.[7]

In addition, there is some concern that easier-to-smoke low-tar cigarettes encourage more young people to take up the habit. In 1980, Congressman Robert F. Drinan (D., Mass.) informed his constituents, "Over the last decade the percentage of girls aged 12 to 14 who smoke has increased eightfold; currently there are six million smokers between the ages of 13 and 19. When we consider that 41 million of America's smokers started when they were under 21, it becomes clear that if our nation is ever to reduce the number of smokers, it must first reduce smoking among teenagers" (Drinan, 1980:1).

PUBLIC-OPINION TRENDS

Underlying the cigarette-consumption trends have been some major shifts in public opinion about smoking, smokers, nonsmokers, and the tobacco industry. As USDA economist Robert Miller has observed, "The attitudes and perceptions of both smokers and nonsmokers provide a description of the environment for individuals as well as the political and social environment in which the tobacco industry must operate" (1980:5). Some insight into these changing attitudes and perceptions was made available when a consultant's report to the Tobacco Institute arrived serendipitously in the offices of the Federal Trade Commission in 1978.

The Roper Report. Subpoenas for information on Big Six advertising practices had been issued by the Federal Trade Commission in the mid-1970s. By 1978, after a series of court challenges by the tobacco lobby that failed, the FTC was beginning to receive this previously undisclosed material. Included in the packages submitted by the tobacco companies was one piece of information, the so-called Roper Report, that reveals much about the shifting values in society regarding smoking and about the present incarnation of the tobacco industry's strategy of domain defense. This report was included in the 1978 FTC *Report to Congress* and thus became part of the public information domain.

The Roper Organization, a national opinion-polling firm, had conducted a series of six biennial national opinion surveys for the Tobacco Institute. The 1978 report summarized findings from these surveys in terms of trends over the twelve-year polling period and recent noteworthy events in the smoking-and-health controversy. It also suggested to the Institute short- and long-term tactics for dealing with the antismoking forces.

The 1978 Roper Report began with an overall assessment of the current status of the smoking-and-health controversy. The writers of the report explained, ". . . we have decided to present the highlights of this report in the form of a balance sheet, measuring the optimistic and pessimistic entries, as it were, on opposite sides of the ledger" (Roper, 1979:3). These current "debits" and "credits" in what might be viewed as the legitimacy ledger of the U.S. tobacco industry revealed a growing antismoking trend in public opinion among smokers as well as nonsmokers.

Smokers and Health. Over the twelve-year polling period, both smokers and nonsmokers had increasingly come to believe (1) that smokers have more illnesses than nonsmokers, (2) that smoking is a significant contributor to the increased incidence of certain diseases in smokers, (3) that smoking makes a "great difference" in how long a person is likely to live, and (4) that smoking in any amount is hazardous to health (an opinion held by 61 percent of nonsmokers and 47 percent of smokers in 1978). The report also revealed that among those smokers who had heard or read something during the last year that worried them about smoking, almost two-thirds gave "I'd like to quit but I don't have the will power" as a reason for continuing (FTC, 1979:Appendix B). But if all this evidence and opinion pointed strongly to the link between smoking and health of *smokers,* a different and far more damaging trend also was uncovered.

Rights of Nonsmokers: The "Passive"-Smoking Issue. The 1978 Roper Report identified a new issue in antismoking advocacy that centered on the rights, not of the smoker, but of the *nonsmoker*—an issue that surfaced from new evidence on the harmful effects of "passive" smoking (i.e., of a nonsmoker's being in the same contaminated air space as a smoker). This passive-smoking issue was singled out in the Roper Organization's 1978 report to the Tobacco Institute as "the most dangerous development to the viability of the tobacco industry that has yet occurred."

TABLE 7-5 CURRENT STATUS OF THE SMOKING-AND-HEALTH CONTROVERSY: THE ROPER "BALANCE SHEET," 1978

"Assets"	"Liabilities"
1. The overall saliency of the "cigarette issue" is low. Compared to crime, drugs, pollution, and half a dozen other items, smoking is at the bottom of the list of personal concerns.	1. More than nine out of every ten Americans believe that smoking is hazardous to a smoker's health.
2. There is little sentiment for a total ban on cigarette smoking in public places (but see #3 under "Liabilities").	2. A majority of Americans believe that it is probably hazardous to be around people who smoke even if they are not smoking themselves.
3. There is overwhelming approval of placing notices *outside* places that restrict cigarette smoking.[a]	3. There is majority sentiment for separate smoking sections in all public places we asked about.
4. Few people favor job discrimination based on cigarette smoking.	4. There is majority acceptance of the idea that the cigarette warning label should be made stronger and more specific.
5. The percentage of smokers in the 17-to-24-year-old age group is up, and the amount smoked per day per young smoker is also up (but see #5 under "Liabilities").	5. The percentage of people who smoke cigarettes is at the lowest level measured in the past ten years.
6. There is broad support for FTC regulation of "public-service" advertising sponsored by non-profit groups like the Cancer Society and Ralph Nader.	6. A steadily increasing majority of Americans believe that the tobacco industry knows that the case against cigarettes is true.
7. There is less than majority sentiment in favor of a graduated-tar cigarette tax.	7. Favorable attitudes toward the tobacco industry are at their lowest ebb.
	8. There is widespread support for anti-smoking education in the schools—and at the very early years.
	9. Two-thirds of smokers would like to give up smoking.
	10. Nearly half the public thinks that smoking is an addiction.
	11. More people say they would vote for than against a political candidate who takes a position favoring a ban on smoking in public places.

[a]Apparently, by placing no-smoking signs outside their establishments, proprietors would have to deal with the consequences of smokers' passing them up for more hospitable alternatives.

Source: Federal Trade Commission, *Report to Congress; Pursuant to the Public Health Cigarette Smoking Act, for the Year 1978,* December 24, 1979, Appendix B, pp. 3-4.

According to the Roper study, over two-thirds of nonsmokers and 40 percent of smokers—most Americans—"are convinced that it is probably hazardous to their health to be around people who are smoking, even if they are not themselves smoking." The Roper Organization attempted to explain to its client the seriousness of this development as follows:

This sharp rise in the number of people who believe that your *smoking harms* my *health has made a whole new ball game out of the antismoking campaign. No matter how many people believe that smoking is injurious to the smoker's own health (more than nine out of ten do), that, in the view of many, is the smoker's own business and thus a matter for personal rather than government control.* But once smoking becomes widely thought of as a health hazard, then the justification for legal measures against sales and use has been established.

Indeed, the Roper Organization emphasized to the Tobacco Institute that "the battle to convince the public of the dangers of passive smoking is in the process of being lost, if indeed it is not already over."

This shift in issues had also been felt by smokers by 1978. Referring to the "inferiority complex of smokers," the Roper Report observed that "a majority of smokers is either frequently or occasionally uncomfortable about smoking in company." Paralleling this development has been the emergence of a more assertive and less sympathetic role for the nonsmoker. In 1978, 58 percent of the nonsmokers replied that when present indoors with a smoker, they would probably ask the smoker to stop, indicate disapproval without saying so, or try to move away from the smoker. Thus, if future scientific evidence reinforces the link between passive smoking and health, there is some chance that smoking may become illegal. However, what is more certain, based on the Roper Report, is that cigarette smoking is becoming socially unacceptable in American society.

Industry Consultant's Suggested Tactics.   What did the Roper Organization recommend that the tobacco industry do to counter these new developments favoring the antismoking and health forces? The transcript of the report's "Implications and Findings" section as it appeared in the appendix of the FTC's *Report to Congress* is reproduced below. We found the suggested short-term tactics, especially items 3 through 6, to be particularly interesting.

"THE ROPER REPORT:"
IMPLICATIONS AND RECOMMENDATIONS

The original Surgeon General's Report, followed by the first "hazard" warning on cigarette packages, the subsequent "danger" warning on packages, the removal of cigarette advertising from television and the inclusion of the danger warning in cigarette advertising were all "blows" of sorts for the tobacco industry. They were, however, blows that the cigarette industry could successfully weather because they were all directed against the smoker himself. While the overwhelming majority of the public has been convinced by the antismoking forces that smoking is dangerous to the smoker's health, this has not persuaded very many smokers to give up smoking.

The antismoking forces' latest tack, however—on the passive smoking issue—*is another matter. What the smoker does to himself may be his business, but what the smoker does to the nonsmoker is quite a different matter. The antismoking forces have not yet convinced anything like as many people that smoking harms the health of the nonsmoker as they have convinced people that smoking harms the health of the smoker. But this study shows that they are well on the way to making the same sale about the effects of smoking on the nonsmoker as they have already made with respect to the effects on the smoker. Nearly six out of ten believe that smoking is hazardous to the nonsmoker's health, up sharply over the last four years. More than two-thirds of nonsmokers believe it, nearly half of all smokers believe it.*

This we see as the most dangerous development to the viability of the tobacco industry that has yet occurred. *While there is little sentiment for an outright ban on smoking in public gathering places, there is already majority sentiment for providing separate facilities for smokers and nonsmokers. As the antismoking forces succeed in their efforts to convince nonsmokers that their health is at stake too, the pressure for segregated facilities will change from a ripple to a tide as we see it.*

It is, of course, possible that once smokers and nonsmokers alike experience all the inconveniences of separate facilities, people will become fed up with the restrictions as they did with the Volstead Act. Smokers who want to work or travel with nonsmokers may become fed up with having to forego smoking. Nonsmokers who want to dine, work or travel with smokers may become fed up with having to endure the extra smoke that exists in segregated smoking facilities. Both could say "to hell with it all" and go back to a smoking-anywhere sentiment.

But if the antismoking forces are successful in convincing nonsmokers that their health is in danger, it's at least as likely that the sentiment for segregated facilities will be strengthened. And if segregated facilities do not accomplish the antismoking forces' desire of making segregated smoking so untenable that smokers will give it up, the next step could be an outright ban. If nonsmokers are by then convinced that it's their health that is at stake, the present sentiment for separate facilities could become support for a total ban.

The strategic and long-run antidote to the passive-smoking issues is, as we see it, developing and widely publicizing clear-cut, credible medical evidence that passive smoking is not harmful to the nonsmoker's health.

While that should be the fundamental objective of the tobacco industry in our opinion, this study suggests that there are some short-term tactical approaches that may slow the efforts of the antismoking forces and buy the industry the necessary time to develop what we see as the fundamental evidence needed to reverse the trend. *But they are tactical and short-term in character. Among these short-range tactics are the following:*

1 Where outright bans on smoking are proposed and appear likely of passage, the industry could propose separate facilities (as the lesser of two evils).

2 Where New Jersey—type legislation appears to be a real possibility, the industry might propose that operators of restaurants, cabs and other public "institutions" be permitted to establish whatever smoking policy they desire—"Smoking permitted anywhere," "No smoking permitted," "Separate facilities for smokers," or "Separate facilities for nonsmokers"—but with the requirement that the smoking conditions that apply be posted outside the premises for the convenience and protection of smokers and nonsmokers alike.

3 In view of the widespread public belief that public service advertising by nonprofit organizations should be subject to the same FTC scrutiny as commercial advertising, we think it might be desirable to noisily file an action with the FTC the next time public-service advertising misquotes the facts about smoking and health, and to further demand that the FTC require the offending organization to run "corrective" advertising as Listerine has been required to do.

4 While the public widely supports government programs to discourage cigarette smoking, a majority opposes spending tax dollars for such a program—which suggests such programs might be vulnerable if people were made aware of their costs.

5 Several questions in this study suggest that where there is substantial support for government action against cigarette smoking, there is a discernible decline of such support when people are made aware of the other government intrusions that might follow. "Where will it all end?" might be effective in blunting antismoking regulation.

6 Another short-range tactic is suggested by the question concerning "fumaphobes." The findings suggest that there is the possibility of dividing those who are relatively unexcited about the passive-smoking issue from the antismoking zealots, by portraying these zealots as people with an unreasonable fear of cigarette smoking.

But we would repeat that since antismoking forces have now gone a long way in convincing the nonsmoker that his health, too, is at stake, the number one objective in our opinion is to develop authoritative and credible evidence with respect to the effects of passive smoking on the nonsmoker's health. The issue, as we see it, is no longer what the smoker does to himself, but what he does to others.*

Based on these tactical suggestions, we were not surprised to find that, by 1979, the Tobacco Institute had added to its traditional advertising theme of

*Source: FTC, *Report to Congress*, 1979, Appendix B, pp. 5–8.

"Freedom of choice is the best choice" another that engaged directly the passive-smoking issue. These new issues-oriented ads, according to Robert Miller of the USDA, "skirt around the pollution of nonsmokers' air by emphasizing tolerance, courtesy and respect of differing viewpoints as well as claiming people as a whole suffer when smokers are segregated" (1980:5). For example, in a 1979 advertisement in the *Boston Globe*, titled "A Word to Nonsmokers (about Smokers)," the Tobacco Institute appeared to be taking tactic #6 from the Roper Report to heart when it explained (to nonsmokers):

> *The trouble is that some people (*anti-*smokers, as distinguished from* non*smokers) don't like those who march to the sound of the different drummer, and want to harass smokers and, if possible, to separate them from your company in just about everything.*

> *And the further trouble is that even the tolerant* non*smokers, and that's most of you, are honestly annoyed by the occasional sniff of tobacco smoke that's a little too pervasive.*

> *It annoys us smokers equally.*

> *But it would be a shame if we allowed a tiny handful of intolerant* anti-*smokers, and a small group of discourteous smokers, to break up the enjoyable harmony we find in each other's personal style.*

> *Maybe if we ignore them both, they'll go away and leave the rest of us to go on playing together.*

Industry Image. The Roper Organization also tracked the public "image" of the tobacco industry, which it found to be steadily declining from 1968 to 1978. Survey respondents holding a favorable image of the industry had declined from 51 percent in 1968 to 36 percent in 1978. In addition, the Roper Organization had asked people their impressions of how interested a few controversial industries are in the safety and welfare of the people who use their products. The results for 1978, summarized in Table 7-6, reveal that the tobacco industry shared with the liquor industry (into which several Big Six firms had diversified) the lowest-rated concern for the ultimate consumer. Moreover, among all the controversial industries for which data spanning 1968–1978 were available, tobacco had declined the most on the consumer-concern index. Finally, although smokers and nonsmokers agreed on their ratings of the first six industries, smokers were more favorable than nonsmokers when it came to the tobacco (37 vs. 20 percent) and liquor (31 vs. 21 percent) industries.

The Roper polls also asked respondents what they perceived the tobacco industry itself believes about the smoking-and-health case against cigarettes, in terms of the following categories: (1) that "they *know* it's true but won't admit it," (2) that "they *suspect* it's true but don't think it has been proven," or (3) that

Controversial Industry	Total Sample	Nonsmokers	Smokers
Drug	66%[a]	66%	64%
Automobile	65	67	65
Food	65	64	64
Chemical	47	47	46
Oil	44	46	44
Asbestos	32	31	31
Tobacco	27	20	37
Liquor	25	21	31

[a]Percentage of respondents rating industry as "very interested" or "moderately interested" in the safety and welfare of the people who use their products or services.

Source: The Roper Organization, Inc., "A Study of Public Attitudes toward Cigarette Smoking and the Tobacco Industry in 1978," Vol. 1, in the Federal Trade Commission, *Report to Congress, Pursuant to the Public Health Cigarette Smoking Act, for the Year 1978,* Appendix B, December 24, 1979, p. 50.

"they *don't believe* it's true." In 1978, 56 percent of the respondents—up from 36 percent in 1968—believed the tobacco industry "knew but wouldn't admit" the health risk of cigarette consumption. Eighty-three percent responded in 1978 that the industry either knew of or suspected the smoking-and-health link, whereas only 8 percent of the sample population thought that the tobacco industry did not believe it is true. Finally, among the respondents who believed the tobacco industry "knows" or "suspects" it is true, only 7 percent also believed that the industry is "working hard to find answers" to the smoking-and-health controversy.

Public Attitudes vs. Government Actions.   Despite all this negative sentiment in the United States today about cigarette smoking and the tobacco industry, when it comes to pressing for more restrictions on cigarette sales and use, the public prefers that government actions be directed at more important social problems. The Roper poll, for example, asked respondents to identify which among a long list of social problems they believed "the government should take more steps against." The results for 1978, shown in Table 7-7, reveal that if the public had its way, increased government action against smoking would receive a relatively low priority.

Indeed, there have been no major trade regulations at the federal level concerning smoking since the early 1970s. Moreover, an attempt made by Joseph Califano to launch an aggressive antismoking campaign, by forming a new office on Smoking and Health in 1978, has been credited by many Washington observers for his abrupt dismissal as head of the U.S. Department of Health, Education and Welfare (Terry, 1979). Califano's announcement of a strong new policy statement on smoking and health in January 1978 was

TABLE 7-7   PARTICIPANT PRIORITIES FOR STRICTER GOVERNMENT CONTROLS:
RESULTS OF THE ROPER POLL (1978)

Social Problem	Percent of Respondents Urging Stricter Government Controls
Crime in the streets	82%
Narcotics addiction	76
Water pollution	58
Exposure to fumes and dust on the job	53
Food additives	53
Air pollution	53
Use of marijuana	49
Prescription drugs and medicines	49
Automobile safety	44
Alcoholic beverages	34
Cigarette smoking	34
Being around people who are smoking	25

Source: Federal Trade Commission, *Report to Congress, Pursuant to the Public Health Cigarette Smoking Act, for the Year 1978*, December 24, 1979, Appendix B, p. 16

immediately assailed by tobacco interests and antismoking forces alike. The latter felt that the initial $23 million budget for his attack on smoking was too little and too late. One article in *Business Week* at the time summarized the cool reception Califano received: "Even the HEW plan to ban smoking in its own offices and other government buildings failed to win support from President Carter, a native of a state with big interests in tobacco growing and cigarette production. Carter refused to issue such a ban in the White House."[8] In addition, the diverse and often conflicting goals of different federal departments surfaced from the antismoking campaign announced by HEW. For instance, in a letter received by Califano, then secretary of HEW, six months before the official announcement, Secretary of Agriculture Robert Bergland noted that his "Department's responsibility begins and ends with the interests of the farmer in a sound production and marketing program. The Department [of Agriculture] cannot involve itself in the health aspects of tobacco."[9] So diametrically opposed are these major departments on the subject of tobacco that in 1980, the federal government spent about $48 million for an antismoking effort run by HEW and $337 million for USDA's pro-tobacco program.[10]

Conflicting Values and Dependences.   Counterbalancing the general public's unfavorable attitudes toward the tobacco industry, and exacerbating the conflicts of values in American society about the proper status of smoking, are a variety of dependences among a number of constituencies that bind them to the cigarette business. These institutional props are largely responsible for the persistence of the tobacco industry despite increasingly unfavorable trends in social attitudes and medical opinions.

Perhaps the major reason that the traditional products of the Big Six have suffered more from social disapproval than government restrictions has been the heavy historical revenue dependence of government institutions at federal, state, and local levels on tobacco taxes. Recent figures released by the Tobacco Institute reveal:

> *Federal, state and local governments collected $6,305,521,000 in direct taxes on tobacco products in FY 1978. Cigarette taxes represented 98.8 percent, or $6,228,168,000. . . . Since 1863, when cigarettes were added to the tobacco products taxed by the federal government, governments at all levels have collected over $131.5 billion in tobacco taxes. Cigarettes have accounted for 94.1 percent of that figure, or more than $123.8 billion.* [1979a:3]

Second, the tobacco industry has been a major U.S. exporter.[11] According to the Tobacco Institute (1979a), more than 74 billion cigarettes were exported to 108 countries in 1978, an 11.3 percent increase over 1977. Moreover, in 1978, U.S. exports of leaf tobacco and manufactured products totaled $2.12 billion, $390 million more than the previous year. Finally, imports to the U.S. tobacco industry amounted to only $428 million in 1978. Therefore as a major net exporter, the domestic tobacco industry makes a positive contribution to the U.S. balance of payments in the world economy.

In addition, the domestic industry is linked to a number of diverse constituencies that are dependent upon it for their livelihood. In 1977, for example, tobacco-industry contributions to gross national product and national employment were estimated at $48.6 billion and 2.3 percent, respectively (Wharton Applied Research Center, 1979:6). Among those directly dependent upon the tobacco business, according to the Tobacco Institute (1979a), are 1.41 million retail outlets, over 2,600 wholesale businesses, some 72,700 employees in tobacco manufacturing operations, and an estimated 276,000 families on tobacco farms. Tobacco remains the sixth largest cash crop.

Finally, the industry has continued to support research projects on smoking and health. According to Tobacco Institute (1979a:6) estimates, "the combined commitment of the tobacco industry for these projects as of June 1, 1979, is $82 million. In many years the industry's smoking/health research funds have exceeded those of any major government department. They surpass the combined grants of the major voluntary health organizations for smoking/health research."

CONCLUSION

An attempt has been made in this chapter to illustrate the political economy in which the modern corporation operates and the interdependence this context creates between the issues of organizational efficiency and legitimacy. Much as the latest Roper Report's balance sheet implies, the current legitimacy ledger of the U.S. tobacco industry is tilted but not completely out of balance. In response to the growing legitimacy threat, the Big Six have activated a number of strategies to help restore equilibrium. They have conformed to overwhelming sentiment and legislation by labeling their products with warnings, by voluntarily withdrawing from the public broadcast media, and by transforming their products to respond to the smoking-and-health issue. But on other occasions, they have attempted to influence the sources of the threat, as in their efforts to create and control the mainstream of research on smoking and health. And most certainly, they have aligned themselves with powerful constituencies and with a number of important values, both social and economic, that are not engaged directly by the smoking-and-health issue. Finally, the Big Six have hedged the political risk in their traditional domain by creating and developing new domains of growth and opportunity. Indeed, it remains to be seen which will be more problematic for the Big Six—the political risks to which they continue to be exposed in their traditional domain or the market risks they have inherited with their strategies of domain creation. For all these reasons, one senses with little doubt that this industry will enjoy a long and profitable senior citizenship.

FOOTNOTES

[1] By 1980, the following market-share ordering achieved by the domain-offense strategies of the Big Six had not changed significantly from the patterns set in 1975 (see Table 4−5 in Chapter 4): Reynolds, 32.8%; Philip Morris, 30.8%; Brown & Williamson, 13.7%; American Brands, 10.7%; Lorillard, 9.8%; and Liggett, 2.2%. Source: *Business Week,* Dec. 15, 1980, p. 52.

[2] The one exception during 1975−79, in which Philip Morris achieved the highest return on equity, can be explained by this company's extraordinarily heavy reliance on long-term debt for financing its expansion and diversification strategies. See subsequent section on ''Financial Slack.''

[3] Included in the growth factors were output growth (measured by growth rate, 1966−78, of real gross product originating in the given industry) and inflation (measured by rate of growth, 1966−78, in the industry producer price indexes); the first growth factor was scored positively, the second negatively. Among the return to factors of production considered were return to labor (measured by 1978 average hourly earnings of production workers) and profitability (measured by the average rate of return on sales and on stockholders' equity, 1969−1978). Finally, foreign competitiveness was assessed in terms of import penetration (measured by the 1978 ratio of imports to new supply and by the change between 1966 and 1978 in this ratio) and export importance (measured by the 1978 export share of domestic output and the change between 1966 and 1978 in this share; the first factor was scored negatively, the latter positively. Industry averages of these six factors were converted into industry rankings, and ''winners,'' ''losers,'' and ''middle-of-the-roaders'' were identified on the basis of the composite ranking of each industry.

[4] Similar results were obtained in a recent study (Hayes, 1980) of the profitability of the *Fortune* 500 largest U.S. corporations over the period 1955 to 1980. Among the five industries registering the highest average annual rates of return on investment were tobacco and beverages—the traditional industry of the Big Six and the business into which many have chosen to diversify.

[5] A 1976 American Cancer Society report, *Task Force on Tobacco and Cancer,* observed, ''While pretending to ignore [the smoking-and-health] evidence, the cigarette companies have been reducing the tar and nicotine content of their products steadily, year after year. . . . The movement,

in the industry, is definitely toward the production of less hazardous cigarettes, by reducing tar and nicotine content, and eventually, by reducing carbon monoxide as well'' (p. 11).

[6]*Business Week,* December 15, 1980, p. 57.

[7]The preface to the 1978 Surgeon General's Report states clearly, "Consumers should be advised to consider not only levels of 'tar' and nicotine but also . . . levels of other tobacco smoke constituents, including carbon monoxide. They should be warned that, in shifting to a less hazardous cigarette, they may in fact increase their hazard if they begin smoking more cigarettes or inhaling more deeply. And most of all, they should be cautioned that even the lowest yield of cigarettes presents health hazards very much higher than would be encountered if they smoked no cigarettes at all, and that the simple most effective way to reduce the hazards associated with smoking is to quit'' (Public Health Service, *Smoking and Health,* 1978).

[8]"An Antismoking Pitch Gets a Cool Reception,"*Business Week,* January 30, 1978, p. 24.

[9]Reported in Kenneth M. Friedman, "Tobacco Agriculture and Health: Towards a Positive Approach," a paper presented to the American Agriculture Economics Association, Blacksburg, Virginia, August 7, 1978.

[10]Blaine Harden, "The Federal World of King Tobacco," *The Boston Globe,* May 5, 1980, p. 3.

[11]By 1980, Philip Morris and R.J. Reynolds ranked among the top twenty-five U.S. exporters (Welles, 1980).

8

Implications for Strategic Management

The time has come for us to discuss the implications of our historical analysis of strategic organizational adaptation. In earlier chapters we have examined prevailing theories and ideas about the strategic behavior of complex organizations. But our frame of reference in these chapters was necessarily narrow, focusing primarily on the specific issue or strategy under investigation. On several occasions we were able to identify some important interdependences among the strategies of these firms; and in the previous chapter we expanded the focus to consider the overall question of how effectively our subject organizations have coped with their shared problem situation. This question required a far-reaching account of the political and economic facets of effectiveness that must be considered in an assessment of the strategic behaviors of large, multibusiness, global corporations. The assessment included an examination of the relationships between the efficiency and legitimacy dimensions of organizational effectiveness. The overall results revealed, first, that the industry population has coped remarkably well with its increasingly unreceptive context but, second, that coping effectiveness has been uneven among the member firms.

From these industry patterns and organizational variations, it is now possible to isolate some of the factors that have contributed to successful adaptation among the Big Six. In this, we hope to reveal several important implications for the strategic management of complex organizations.

MODES OF STRATEGIC ORGANIZATIONAL ADAPTATION: A FUNDAMENTAL TYPOLOGY

Although this has been a study of a single industry attempting to cope with a particular kind of threat, the severity of the problem situation under investigation called for the broadest possible range of adaptive responses from the target organizational population. By the careful tracking of developments within the member firms over a quarter century, we believe it has been possible to identify a fundamental typology of the modes of strategic organizational adaptation that may serve as the basis for understanding and managing a wide variety of problem situations confronting complex organizations.

This typology consists of three conceptually independent modes of adaptation: *domain defense,* for coping with political threats from the institutional environment; *domain offense,* for coping with economic threats from existing and potential rivals in the primary product-market domain; and *domain creation,* for creating new domains potentially offering greater performance opportunity and less risk exposure. These modes have been distinguished on the basis of the goals they serve, the strategies they employ, the domains for which they are relevant, and the targets they engage. But we have also demonstrated that their independence stops at the conceptual level.

Not only were active strategies of domain defense, domain offense, and domain creation uncovered in the cases of all members of the Big Six, but in many instances important influences were observed among these elements of adaptation. Shifts among modes in the pattern of internal resource allocation, for instance, affected—sometimes in unanticipated ways—the progress of strategies contained within different adaptive modes pursued by the Big Six. Successful defense of domain, for instance, can create a temporal space that allows an organization to pursue other modes of adaptation. The strategies employed in domain offense may enhance (or detract from) domain defense efforts, as in the case of the companies' shift toward allegedly "safer" cigarette products. Successful initial domain offense, even in the face of persistent legitimacy threat and market stagnation, may also provide the resources needed to move into new domains offering opportunities no longer available in the traditional domain. Conversely, the failure of one adaptive mode may be expected to influence the progress achieved in other modes of adaptation.

Because of the apparent comprehensiveness, conceptual independence, operational interdependence, and empirical realism of these adaptive modes, executive leaders as well as students of complex organizations may be well advised to develop an appreciation of this typology and the potential interdependences among its elements as a way of beginning to understand and more effectively manage the process of strategic organizational adaptation.

The message for organizational managers and scholars, therefore, appears to be straightforward. Much as complex organizations require an executive function to guide and integrate the overall process of organizational development and adaptation—a process that exceeds the capacities of specialized units performing different parts of the whole—so too does the study of complex organizations require the creation of a legitimate domain of knowledge and inquiry bridging the many academic disciplines that specialize in the various levels of organizational analysis and strategic modes. Indeed, a fundamental purpose of this investigation has been to demonstrate that understanding of the behavior of complex organizations increases dramatically when one takes a holistic view of the adaptive situation.

But this new appreciation cannot be a mechanical one. As we have witnessed, although the full range of adaptive modes was employed by all members of the Big Six, individual firms differed in both the timing of and their initial commitments to new adaptive strategies, in the specific choices about how to implement them, and in the degree to which their objectives were ultimately realized. These variations reflect differences among companies in the extent to which their business strategies or product mixes exposed them to the external threat. These variations also reflect differences in both the resources and capabilities of the focal organizations and the extent to which these features of the adaptive situation were appreciated by executive leaders and responsive to the coping techniques they attempted.

Not all problem situations, for instance, call for the same degree of devotion to all three adaptive modes. A fundamental legitimacy threat, such as the one we have studied, appears to have the potential for raising all three modes to prominence; whereas a threat to a firm's efficiency in a particular market may not fully arouse the politically oriented domain defense mode. Nevertheless, it is important for executive leaders to have a grasp of the full range of options for strategic adaptation if they are to be in a position to engage a wide variety of potential threats to organizational integrity before they become a full-blown reality. Moreover, ensuring that this appreciation is widely shared among the management cadre is a duty that should serve executive leaders well when it comes time for them to initiate new organizational directions.

In addition, the same initial problem situation may not affect the companies with equal force. Even firms operating in a relatively homogeneous industry develop variations in product lines and market segments that create differences in "business exposure" to the economic and political issues that may emerge within or be imposed upon the industry. The outbreak of the smoking-and-health controversy threatened the traditional industry leader, American Brands, more so than it did Philip Morris, the struggling "odd man out." For Philip Morris, the turbulence and uncertainty of the controversy provided an opportunity—a "strategic window"—that enabled this company to increase its market position through the introduction of innovative filter-tip products. For American Brands, however, the same environmental conditions threatened its stake in the primary market segment for traditional cigarette products. Production innovation by American Brands, which was needed to respond to the legitimacy crisis and the ensuing market stagnation, therefore, would have the effect of competing as much or more against its own traditional products than against those of its competitors. Closely related to the issue of business exposure are those of organizational competence and strategic predisposition.

Few organizations are likely to have the capacity and predisposition to engage in all the strategic variations possible within these adaptive modes. A forward-thinking executive leader, therefore, might serve the interests of the organization's constituencies better if he or she had an accurate perception of the basic predispositions and core competences of the organization and the extent to which they might constrain or facilitate the choices of strategic options within different adaptive modes. Indeed, such an executive leader might engage in experimentation with some strategies as a way of either forming an accurate appreciation of what the organization will (can) and will not (cannot) do or developing the organization in such a way that the potential range of strategic options available to it is expanded. Evidence of both forms of experimentation was demonstrated in the review of the knowledge and skills acquired by Big Six senior managers from their early attempts to diversify.

But we are beginning to get ahead of ourselves. Before continuing with these insights into the quality of executive leadership, we must pause to examine in the light of our evidence the relative powers of our extreme models of adaptation in explaining the behavior and development of the tobacco Big Six.

MANAGERIAL CHOICE vs. ENVIRONMENTAL DETERMINISM

The most fundamental issue in this investigation concerns the extent to which the behavior and development of complex organizations may be explained by two competing perspectives, the natural-selection and strategic-choice models of organizational behavior. The problem situation pitted the survival of an industry population of firms against an unprecedented external threat. The primary research questions, concerning the range of strategic options available for organizational coping and the relative effectiveness of different mixes of strategic choices among members of an organizational population, were selected to examine in detail the relative power of these competing models. Therefore, we must examine the underlying assumptions of these perspectives and the implications their advocates have drawn from these assumptions.

NATURAL SELECTION vs. STRATEGIC CHOICE

The natural-selection perspective rests on the integrity of three explicit assumptions: (1) that organizations are *captives* of a specified environment; (2) that the given environment is *immutable* with respect to influence attempts by the organizations it contains; and (3) that organizations are characterized profoundly by *inertia*. A fourth assumption implied by the natural-selection perspective is that organizations tend to possess little slack for coping with imposed change. Based on the apparent validity of these assumptions, natural-selection advocates have advanced a set of implications for organization and management. The first implication is that the direction of causality in organization—environment interactions is controlled almost exclusively by the embedding environment. The second is that organizations and their senior managers are incapable of transforming themselves to meet the demands posed by new and different developments in their environment; that the variation within an organizational population or industry occurs not from managerial choice and organizational change, but from the entry of new organizations into the population of relatively inert ones. In short, the natural-selection perspective implies that the role of executive leadership is largely cosmetic; that organizational fortune is more a function of fate and luck than learning and choice and that the role of strategic management is a myth. The primary limiting factor for the development of an organization is the nature of its embedding environment.

Other, more pervasive disciplines bearing on organizational behavior (e.g., industrial economists' theory of the firm and organizational behaviorists' contingency theory of organization design), while not denying the processes of organizational learning and change and the role of management, have generally ignored these features of organizations in order to focus on more specific questions. For example, economists have assumed a given, immutable market environment in order to specify theoretically optimal production functions. Managerial behavior is noticeably absent in their constrained optimization models of firm behavior. Similarly, contingency theorists have generally assumed both an immutable task environment and a given organizational strategy, and have limited the role of management to the choice of an organization's design, in order to look at the alignment between the structures of an organization and its immediate environment. Thus, through their choice of research questions and designs, these economists and organizational theorists have tended to adopt, at least implicitly, many of the limiting assumptions of the natural-selection perspective.

The extreme contrast to these deterministic models of organizational behavior is the strategic-choice perspective, which assumes (1) that managers exercise considerable choice concerning not only how their organizations will relate to the environment, but what environments they will operate in; (2) that organizations may profoundly influence their embedding environments; and (3) that organizations are capable of fundamental learning and change under the guidance of skillful executive leaders. It follows, then, that the nature of organization−environment interactions may be substantially controlled by complex organizations, depending on the quality of their executive leadership—the primary limiting factor in the process of organizational development from the strategic-choice perspective.

Drawing from Barnard (1938:235), the role of executive leaders involves first "the *sensing* of the organization as a whole and the total situation relative to it." Second, executive leaders must continually develop an effective *alignment* among organizational resources, distinctive competences and predispositions, and environmental constraints and opportunities. This is a never-ending function of executive leadership.

To accomplish this function, according to the strategic-choice perspective, executive leaders have at their disposal three primary sets of options: (1) strategic options, which include the choices of organizational purposes, operations, and domains; (2) structural options, which include the choices of organizational designs, resource-allocation systems, and other operating mechanisms that, in turn, influence the internal political and cultural context of decision making; and (3) performance options, which include the choices of performance dimensions that will be emphasized and where slack resources will be created and committed. From this perspective, an organization's inability to adapt to changed circumstances or its failure to persist over time says more about the quality of its executive leadership than about the nature of its context.[1]

Because the assumptions and implications of these perspectives are almost perfect opposites, we will examine the evidence from this investigation in the light of the natural-selection perspective and draw from this examination some important implications for strategic managers. Because the tests of the first two assumptions are relatively straightforward, they will be examined first.

ORGANIZATIONAL CAPTIVITY AND ENVIRONMENTAL IMMUTABILITY

The results of this investigation provide no support for the most restrictive assumptions of the natural-selection model, which imply that organizations are captured by a given, immutable environment. Instead, these results demonstrate unequivocally that corporations not only are able to influence the environment in which they operate through strategies of domain defense (e.g., lobbying and coopting environmental agents, controlling vital information, activating and marshaling the dependences of primary and secondary constituencies, and aligning themselves with superordinate social and economic values) and domain offense (e.g., product innovation, market segmentation, and advertising), but may exercise considerable choice with respect to the domains in which they will and will not operate (e.g., strategies of diversification and overseas expansion).

Substantial strategic variation together with subsequent structural alignment occurred within all members of the tobacco Big Six despite the fact that no new firms entered the traditional industry during the quarter-century study period. These patterns in the strategic choices made and implemented by Big Six senior managers enabled all member firms to survive and most to prosper, even though one firm eventually failed to compete effectively in the domestic and international tobacco domains. Nor did the economic and legal constraints often cited by natural-selection theorists significantly constrain the processes of domain choice and strategic organizational adaptation. Economic barriers to entry into new markets frequently were skirted through the strategy of external acquisition. Exit was accomplished through divestiture, which left the competing firm in place only under new ownership. Even the occasional interference of antitrust law (as in the cases of Liggett's forced divestiture of its second pet-food acquisition and its ability to divert resources from but not sell its domestic tobacco business) posed little threat to the overall strategy of diversification.

These observations are not to deny, however, the important influence of the traditional environment on an organization or population of organizations. To be sure, there would be little story to tell if it were not for the interactive influences of the legitimacy threat from the tobacco industry's institutional environment and the stagnation that occurred in the domestic market for cigarettes. But the observations we have made about the Big Six raise serious doubts about the relevance to informed strategic managers of the strict assumptions underlying the popular deterministic perspectives on organizational behavior.

Given the enormous gap between these assumptions and the organizational reality, we discovered, it is important to take a closer look at the concept of *domain choice flexibility,* or "the extent to which an organization is free to alter its domain" (Miles, 1980c:233). Theoretically, organizational control over domain choice may range from autonomous to mandated. In addition, the flexibility afforded an organization for choosing what domains it will and will not operate in cannot be regarded as a viable asset if the enterprise possesses neither the slack resources, the competences and predispositions, nor the managerial foresight to take advantage of it when necessary. But the first determination of whether an organization is, in fact, a captive of its existing domain must focus on the broad institutional context that sets an outer limit on the "rules of play."

In the United States, the charters of public- versus private-sector organizations provide the first approximation of domain choice flexibility. The charter of a "corporation," for instance, is a profoundly unremarkable mechanism of social control. Its most important feature, for our immediate purpose, is that it does not limit the domain choice of organizations adopting the corporate form. In contrast, the charter of a public agency specifies by law what it may do, how it may do it, to whom, and where. Thus, the corporate charter and the public-agency charter stake out the theoretical extremes of domain choice flexibility. Neither corporation nor agency, however, is likely to operate at these extremes.

Few public administrators, for example, are likely to resist maneuvering to enlarge or collapse their chartered domain if the persistence of their agency is in doubt. As Wamsley and Zald have observed for public agencies, "these mandates may be vague, ambiguous, and extraordinarily complicated. Therefore, the values and perspectives of the [executive] cadre become the touchstones for interpreting, highlighting and realizing the mandate or policy. There remains room for the kinds of interpretations that mark the political function" (1973:58). To attempt to deny this function of the executive cadre in public agencies is to ignore the well-documented fact that such agencies in the United States tend to enjoy a very long life, often persisting far beyond the reasons for their creation (Kaufman, 1976).

Similarly, corporations are often exposed to a hierarchy of external constraints on domain choice that fall—to a significant extent—below their charter. Some are permitted to operate only in licensed markets; others must abide by rate regulations; still others must cope with a canopy of industry-specific regulations. And all must respond to the universal "social" and "economic" regulations that have evolved in U.S. society. However, even federal antitrust regulations do not prohibit domain choices that involve entry into different markets as long as they do not tend to reduce competition *within* an industry. U.S. antitrust policy, formulated on the basis of traditional economic theories of the firm, has therefore excluded "horizontal" merger for market monopoly and for market concentration (which characterized the first two merger waves in North America); but it has proved to be no barrier to merger for diversification, which has been the primary basis for industrial conglomeration during the last merger wave. Such diversification mergers may tend to increase overall economic concentration and corporate power in the United States, but apparently they have not been shown to lead directly to greater concentration and lesser competition in a particular market or industry. Likewise, the formation of joint political ventures among industry rivals, which does not lead to the reduction of competition within the industry, is sanctioned by current antitrust law.

In summary, for both private and public-sector organizations, there appears to be a far greater degree of domain choice flexibility than the deterministic models of organizational behavior have allowed. The relevant question then becomes whether an organization possesses the predispositions and compe-tences, the slack resources, and the managerial foresight and skills to be able to take advantage of this potential asset when conditions warrant. This question brings us to the third explicit assumption of the natural-selection perspective.

ORGANIZATIONAL INERTIA AND CHARACTER

Three interrelated forms of organizational inertia may be found among the quarter-century histories of the tobacco Big Six. First, each organization exhibited clear signs of a unique *strategic predisposition*. Second, each organiza-tion was guided by an executive cadre whose political structure selectively represented different functional specialities and reflected different *dominant values and beliefs* in the process of critical decision making. Finally, all organizations shared a core *distinctive competency*—the marketing of durable, repeat-purchase consumer products—which was appreciated and expanded in different ways as each organization enacted new and different domains. The peculiar mix of these relatively enduring features of an organization provides a first approximation of "corporate character."

All three elements of organizational inertia appear to have been shaped by the long reinforcement history—particularly experience in the traditional domain—of each industry member. Although the imprint of these internal forces on the substance and progress of strategic organizational adaptation is, in retrospect, quite visible, it has not been as indelible as natural-selection advocates would have predicted. As our review of their effect will reveal, these elements of organizational inertia may be called into question by the performance gaps they create for organizations that are exposed to definitive feedback. They may be altered through the mechanisms of executive succession and personnel development or change. Their assumptions may be tested by the process of organizational enactment—attempts by organizations to try new and different things. Thus, even when viewed as constraints, these forms of inertia are subject to modification in order to meet the demands of new domains and strategies.

But this study has also demonstrated that these forms of inertia may represent opportunities. Because of the wide variety of domain and strategic choices available to complex organizations, in many cases it may be more important for executive leaders to understand the limits of their organizations' distinctive competences and predispositions than to try to change them. Executive leaders who possess an accurate appreciation of what their organizations can and will do may be able to select from among a wide range of potential domains and strategies those that best fit these relatively enduring characteristics of their enterprises. The following evidence from our quarter-century company histories will reveal, therefore, not only that such forms of inertia exist and have an impact, but that the organizational consequences of their existence may be functional or dysfunctional depending on the quality of executive leadership.

Strategic Predisposition. During our analysis of the competitive behaviors of the Big Six, we uncovered four basic strategic orientations among the tobacco independents. These orientations—labeled Prospector, Defender, Analyzer, and Reactor, after the Miles and Snow (1978) typology—provided a neat fit with the characteristic competitive behaviors of Philip Morris, American Brands, Reynolds, and Liggett, respectively. The fundamental continuum underlying this typology was a conservative versus risk-taking propensity in the strategic orientation adopted by each firm to compete in its traditional domain.

Philip Morris, the Prospector, approached the competitive situation aggressively, despite the forecast of market stagnation, by opening up new market segments with successive waves of product innovation. In contrast, American Brands, which occupied a position of industry leader at the beginning of our study period, assumed the role of Defender. It clung tenaciously to the products upon which it had built its historical success, and it suffered as a consequence severe market-share erosion when the segment of traditional cigarette products was displaced by growing filter-tip and low-tar segments. Indeed, it took a complete break in the normal pattern of executive succession before American Brands was able to face up to the problems of its conservative strategic orientation. Thus, only after a prolonged period of unmet performance aspirations, punctuated by a break in executive succession, did this company make a late entry into the segments pioneered by Philip Morris and already occupied by other major competitors.

R.J. Reynolds occupied the status of Analyzer in the competition for cigarette market share. With one foot placed firmly in the traditional market segment, it stood poised to place the other foot in the emerging segments as soon as they had grown to the point at which profitable entry was feasible. Reynolds, therefore, was able to pursue a dual competitive strategy that has enabled it to maintain a leadership position in a changing market by simultaneously profiting from traditional market segments while exploiting the development of new market segments. Finally, industry analysts have observed that Liggett was unable to successfully align strategy and structure in order to be able to pursue the Analyzer orientation. Instead, its new products did not "take," while its old ones declined with the traditional market segment.

Traces of each company's predisposition with regard to this conservative—innovative continuum may also be found within the joint domain defense arena. For instance, American Brands—the Defender—withdrew from the Cigarette Advertising Code, the industry's proactive attempt to police its advertising practices under threat of a possible broadcast-media ban.[2]

Generalizability of Strategic Predisposition. The question that was posed at the beginning of our discussion of the strategies of domain creation, however, has not been answered. Did the strategic orientations adopted by member firms in their traditional competitive domain generalize to the approaches they took in creating new domains of growth opportunity? Miles and Snow (1978), by focusing exclusively on single-business companies, have not addressed this question. So the issue remains: Can we predict the strategies used by traditional competitors to enter different business domains from knowing the strategies they employed to compete against one another in their shared domain? Does the strategic orientation each competitor develops from a long history of competitive relations with traditional rivals transfer to the strategy it adopts for dealing with new and different rivals? The answer, from our analysis of domain creation, appears to be affirmative, at least insofar as the overall strategic orientation of each company is concerned.

Strategic predisposition may be defined generally as *the extent to which an organization exhibits a consistent pattern over time in the choices it makes about the formulation and implementation of its strategies.* For an organization to be described as having a strategic predisposition, it must exhibit such a pattern regardless of the modes of adaptation and the domains for which they are relevant.

Patterns among the tobacco independents, in (1) the timing and degree of commitment to overseas expansion and diversification, (2) the choices made about acquisition candidates, and (3) the approaches taken to assimilate new businesses and enter new markets, all seem to conform to the conservative versus risk-taking orientations each had manifested in its traditional domain.

First, the persistence of strategic predisposition among the tobacco independents may be found in the overall approaches they took to overseas expansion. Firms with a high risk-taking propensity expanded overseas aggressively by acquiring manufacturing facilities in countries where firms with a more conservative predisposition operated more tentatively with export and licensing agreements.[3]

Philip Morris extended its traditional role of Prospector by being the first among the tobacco independents to expand overseas and by adopting a high-risk strategy of acquiring major manufacturing facilities abroad. Reynolds followed Philip Morris's lead soon thereafter but took a more moderate approach, relying on a dual overseas strategy that involved both acquired manufacturing facilities abroad in carefully chosen foreign locations, and export and licensing agreements in other parts of the world—the latter involving substantially less risk of capital than the former. American Brands, the Defender in the traditional domain, was characteristically the last to embark on an overseas-expansion strategy.[4] And Liggett, the Reactor, was no more successful in aligning strategy and structure in the overseas tobacco business than in the domestic market. By the end of our quarter-century period, Liggett had almost completely abandoned its overseas-expansion strategy, having sold most of its international holdings to the aggressively prospecting Philip Morris.

Second, the imprint of strategic predisposition was even more pronounced in the diversification strategies each firm adopted for acquiring and assimilating businesses in new domains. Philip Morris was the first to initiate the strategy of external acquisition, followed immediately by Reynolds and later by Liggett. Diversification at American Brands was not initiated until much later. Paralleling these company differences in the timing of the initiation of diversification were different patterns among the tobacco independents in the criteria they developed for making acquisitions and the approaches they adopted for assimilating and managing new businesses.

Philip Morris remained true to the prospecting orientation in both aspects of its diversification strategy. After a brief flirtation with a financially oriented diversification strategy, which exposed the company to product markets unrelated to its traditional domain, senior managers returned to the company's traditional strategic predisposition, which emphasized a marketing-driven, capital-intensive approach and which subordinated immediate profits to encourage rapid growth in market share. This orientation toward turnaround situations, which differed greatly from the orientations adopted by the other tobacco independents, was coupled with an aggressive approach to the assimilation and management of new subsidiaries. A pattern emerged in which Philip Morris quickly displaced the traditional management of an acquisition by transferring its own marketing-oriented personnel to run the new business. Heavy initial commitments of capital were made to stimulate the development of new products, to mount a characteristically engaging and expensive Philip Morris advertising campaign, and to modernize and expand the capacity of existing production facilities. Having dumped all its unrelated acquisitions except its real estate venture in California, which has continued to flourish as a result of the rapid appreciation in residential housing on the West Coast, Philip Morris aligned its diversification strategy with its traditional structure and distinctive competences. Finally, this high roller's aggressive, risk-taking propensity is reflected in its debt-to-equity ratio, which by 1979 was more than double that of Reynolds, its closest traditional rival.

In many important respects, therefore, the most critical decisions in Philip Morris's domain creation strategies appear to conform to what one would predict from the Prospector type. As Miles and Snow (1978) observed, the Prospector enacts a dynamic environment. Its primary risk is the overextension of its resources, whereas its primary strength is finding and exploiting new domains. It is the creator of change for the industries in which it operates.

Reynolds, the Analyzer in the traditional domain, also carried forward onto its diversification strategy elements of its traditional strategic predisposition. Characteristically, not only was it the first to follow the Prospector into diversification, but its approach was more tentative. Whereas Philip Morris began by acquiring a new packaging subsidiary, Reynolds allowed its own packaging division to expand its operations to serve outside clients. When the internally developed packaging facility did not perform according to expectations, its operations were pared back to serve primarily the production requirements of the company's cigarette operations.

In addition, the design of Reynolds's early diversification program was put together by financial and production executives, assisted by the company's attorneys, not by executives representing the marketing function. As a consequence, an acquisition strategy emphasizing financial return was implemented. Guided by this search for immediately profitable businesses, a dual strategy emerged, which included not only acquisitions related to the distinctive competencies of the firm (i.e., consumer-products businesses) but also unrelated businesses operating in "young" industries with high margin potential. Moreover, this propensity to operate simultaneously in two different arenas has persisted for over two decades.

Finally, Reynolds's approach to subsidiary assimilation and management has tended to be more conservative than that of Philip Morris. Reynolds prefers to avoid what its managers refer to as "turnaround," "bail-out," or "patient-money" acquisitions, focusing instead on companies with large market shares and strong management teams, which can be managed semiautonomously and which can be expected to provide a satisfactory and stable return on investment from the date of acquisition.

In several important respects, therefore, Reynolds has continued to exhibit important characteristics of its traditional predisposition. Its historical risk-taking propensity places it somewhere between the Prospector and the Defender and exposes its managers to two very different arenas, whether the strategy be domain offense, overseas expansion, or diversification.

Little is known publicly about the diversification strategy of American

Brands. The firm's president, who was formerly a journalist, has ironically maintained a policy of minimizing the flow of company information to the public media. But the fact that American Brands was the last of the Big Six to embark on a strategy of diversification—and then only well after experiencing a prolonged period of performance "gap," the impact of the 1964 Surgeon General's report, and a complete break in the traditional pattern of executive succession—suggests that it has not shed its Defender orientation. That its most significant domestic acquisition was the recent purchase of Franklin Life Insurance, a company operating in a financially oriented industry renowned more for predictable financial returns than for sweeping product innovations, provides little indication that the basic approach of the company is moving toward either a more aggressive marketing approach or a greater risk-taking propensity. When one considers that the second largest acquisition in American Brands's history was the large, British-based Gallaher tobacco company, the persistence of this company's Defender predisposition appears to be intact.

Liggett, the competitive Reactor, was never able to rationalize fully its strategies of domain offense and creation. A major factor in Liggett's plight has been the inability to stop a pernicious decline in its share of the traditional market. Liggett coped with this decline by transferring excess tobacco capital to its diversification strategy. But the reduced level of excess cash at Liggett forced its managers to consider only small companies as acquisition candidates. By the end of our study period, Liggett was still attempting to amass enough related small acquisitions to complete its reorganization to a group structure. Thus, our Reactor continued to have difficulty aligning strategy with structure. The declining traditional market also left Liggett with fewer slack resources to apply to its overseas expansion program and to promote new cigarette products. In the final analysis, the cycle linking domestic market decline to other activities tended over time to result in the divestiture of Liggett's overseas business and the involuntary takeover of the company as a whole.

In summary, there is ample evidence to suggest that the basic strategic predispositions formed among these companies in their traditional domain are relatively enduring and that important influences of these predispositions have been reflected in the strategies each company has taken to create new domains of opportunity. Moreover, the diversification arena has provided a rather strong test of the enduring nature of strategic predisposition, because it freed the traditional competitors from their symbiotic relations in the domain they all shared.

Powerful forces have been at work in these companies that have tended to develop and reinforce their unique strategic orientations. Among these influences are each company's reinforcement history; the time-honored career ladder that has rewarded certain behaviors, experiences, and attitudes; and the beliefs held by executive leaders about their company's distinctive competences and their perceptions of the company's role both in its industry and in society. However, if the persistence of strategic predisposition is a relatively enduring feature of complex organization, its influence on organizational effectiveness and adaptiveness is less clearly understood.

Consequences of Strategic Predisposition. From the natural-selection perspective, the persistence of strategic predisposition is a form of organizational inertia that tends to prevent an enterprise from adapting to a changing external context. Business policy and institutional theorists, in contrast, are apt to view strategic predisposition more favorably. For them, a central function of an executive leader is to develop and shape the fit among the organization's strategies and its predispositions and competences. An important part of the performance of this role, therefore, involves constant reexamination, testing, and development of the organization's resources, capabilities, and predispositions. Only then can the leader attempt to maintain an effective alignment between the organization and its relevant environment.

But as our study of the Big Six has demonstrated, alignment may be brought about in different ways. First, executive leaders may attempt to alter their organization in response to a changing environment. If they cannot and if, as the natural-selection perspective asserts, the altered environment represents a given, the persistence of predisposition will be problematic for organizational performance and adaptation. Second, if neither the environment is immutable nor the enterprise totally its captive, the alignment problem may also be engaged by strategic choices designed to influence the existing environment directly or to create new environments to achieve greater compatibility with the organization's capabilities and orientations. Elements of both forms of adaptation characterized the developmental histories of even the most recalcitrant members of the tobacco Big Six.

These organizational histories have provided evidence of both the persistence of strategic predisposition and an ability within some organizations to modify or accommodate their orientations under conditions of actual or anticipated performance gap. More important, however, the findings indicate that *the relatively enduring quality of strategic predisposition is not necessarily a liability.* If understood by senior managers, a company's strategic predisposition may be used as the basis for selecting new environments or niches in which to extend its domain and for deciding how to enter these new areas of opportunity. Indeed, the absence of a clearly articulated strategic orientation and a broadly recognized and accurately perceived mix of distinctive competences may be a far more limiting condition than the "inertia" claimed by the natural-selection perspective to inhibit organizational adaptation. This conclusion is reinforced by the following discussion of the other two elements of organizational character and the roles played by executive leaders in responding to or developing them.

Dominant Values and Executive Succession. The internal political structure of an organization, particularly the extent to which the orientations and values of specialized functions become and remain represented within the dominant coalition of executive leaders, is another primary source of organizational inertia. By tracing carefully the patterns of executive succession and the nature and timing of strategic choices among the Big Six firms, one may observe the distinct imprints of the particular function in favor on the direction and progress of organizational development.

In cases where the values and beliefs of key decision makers representing different functions in the executive cadre—manifested in the strategic choices they made over time—departed significantly from the distinctive competences and strategic predispositions of the firm or the requirements of its operating environments, performance ''gap'' eventually occurred. When this discrepancy between organizational aspiration and achievement persisted, major breaks took place in the organization's traditional pattern of executive succession—breaks that restructured the internal polity, and consequently, the dominant values and beliefs, to facilitate either the initiation of new strategies or the distinctive predispositions and competences of the firm. It is through a careful review of these episodes of organizational transformation that we may begin to understand how influential the internal political structure and the process of executive succession are on the dynamics of organizational development and adaptation.

But, if the internal political structure of the organization was an important source of influence on the process of strategic organizational adaptation, it was not always an enduring one. In three of the four tobacco independents, executive succession proved to be an effective means for correcting outmoded values and beliefs that had created ineffective alignments among strategy, external environment, organizational competences, and predispositions.

For example, after three of the four tobacco independents experienced a period of performance ''gap,'' someone who had not come up through the tobacco-business ranks was invited to lead the company. The appointment of these ''outsiders''—one a former journalist and Hollywood promotional expert, one a marketing-oriented manager from an acquired nontobacco business, and one from early retirement as president of a retail store chain—represented major breaks in the traditional pattern of executive succession in each company.

American Brands, our traditional Defender, experienced a prolonged period of performance gap because of its failure to respond effectively to developments in the traditional tobacco domain. At the time of the major ''break'' in its pattern of executive leadership, which occurred in 1963, this company was still wedded to its high-tar, regular brands and was still dependent almost exclusively on the traditional domain in which it had suffered severe market-share erosion. It is not surprising, therefore, that the break in AB's traditional pattern of executive succession was a complete one. The former chief executive officer was denied the traditional privilege of taking his place on the company's board of directors. The consequences of this break were just as dramatic as the way it was accomplished. Within two years, American Brands introduced the first successful super-low-tar cigarette (Carlton), within four years it had acquired a major British-based tobacco company (Gallaher), and within a decade the company had achieved the status of a diversified major. Thus, in the case of American Brands, new executive leadership was required to *catalyze* a departure from its traditional values and orientations, which may have begun to develop as early as the 1911 trust bust in which the company had been broken apart to create many of the members of the contemporary Big Six. The consequence was the formation of a number of long-overdue adaptive strategies.

The break at Liggett served different purposes. With most strategies operating under various degrees of performance gap, the appointment in 1973 of a marketing-oriented chief executive officer from one of the company's non-tobacco subsidiaries represented a rejection of the leadership provided traditionally by executives who had risen from the ranks of tobacco manufacturing. The impact of this break was intensified by the fact that the new leader installed several other marketing-oriented managers in senior positions in the company's headquarters.

Although the new marketing orientation was not successful in stemming the pernicious decline in Liggett's domestic tobacco business, the company's gross return on sales from diversified operations, which included only consumer-products firms, soon became the highest among the Big Six. In fact, one of the reasons Grand Metropolitan eventually acquired Liggett in 1980 was to use Liggett's expertise in making future acquisitions of domestically based consumer-products firms. Thus, the break in the traditional pattern of executive succession at Liggett served two purposes. First, it elevated to prominence the marketing function, the core of most consumer-products firms' distinctive competence, thereby aligning structure with strategy. Second, it served to *consolidate* under the marketing orientation what remained of Liggett's far-flung holdings.

Finally, the break at Reynolds, although the last to occur among the tobacco independents, was as fundamental as the other two. In this case, not only did an outsider with a marketing orientation assume control of the organization, which had been run traditionally by executives who had come up through the tobacco ranks; he replaced Reynolds's entire senior management cadre with outsiders whose experience had been with other consumer-products companies. The legacy left by traditional managers was a hodgepodge of related and unrelated businesses, many of which were draining more resources from the parent's traditional operations than they contributed. The break in executive succession, therefore, represented a return to the parent company's core distinctive competences and formed the basis for a *consolidation* of the diverse holdings created by the acquisition choices of the preceding executive order.

In contrast to these examples, no major break occurred within Philip Morris, the firm that on many counts achieved the most successful adaptation. Within this company, an unbroken chain of marketing-oriented successors complemented the firm's basic predispositions and competences and provided the basis for tailoring new strategies to fit the relatively enduring properties of the organization. Indeed, the finding that the most "inert" organization achieved the most successful adaptation represents a paradox that challenges the future development of the natural-selection perspective.

In summary, these patterns of executive succession, when coupled with the progress of strategic organizational adaptation, provide insight into the powerful influence of executive leadership on the development of complex organizations. It is by observing these continuities and discontinuities over time that one begins to appreciate the critical role of strategic management.

Distinctive Competence. The concept of distinctive competence, first treated by Selznick, rounds out our discussion of the inertial properties of complex organizations. With experience in a particular performance situation, such as the traditional tobacco domain of the Big Six, organizations tend to develop distinctive competences that set limits on what they can and cannot do *well*. These distinctive competences distinguish among organizations operating in different performance domains, and they tend to take on unique elaborations even among firms occupying the same domain. From the natural-selection perspective, such distinctive competences represent internal constraints to organizational adaptation.

Some evidence to support this view is available from the diversification histories of the tobacco companies. In virtually every case, acquisitions made by the Big Six that were closely related to the distinctive competences developed over decades in the traditional domain fared much better than did unrelated acquisitions. Indeed, in many cases, unrelated acquisitions were quickly divested.

But the same evidence cautions the reader about the limitations of this view. In some cases, executive leaders were able to change and expand the distinctive competences of their firms. In others, they were able to apply their knowledge of the strengths and limitations of their organization to the process of strategic choice and thereby enhance the overall adaptive potential of their enterprise.

Executive leaders expanded the distinctive competences of their organizations in two visible ways. Either they brought in outsiders who possessed the knowledge and skills that would enrich the organization's base of competence, or they created slack in the form of reduced performance expectations in order to allow managers transferred from the parent to develop competences required by the new and different venture. Thus, distinctive competence represents more of a base than a fixed constraint with regard to the process of organizational adaptation.

The case of Philip Morris illustrates one way in which an organization may increase the scope of its distinctive competence. Through years of struggle to capture a significant share of the domestic cigarette market, under a succession of marketing executives, the company developed a unique competence in the area of consumer-products marketing. With the succession of Lyon, who had a flair for international dealings, the genesis of an extension in the core marketing competence was realized. When Lyon was succeeded by McComas, a former Wall Street international banker, the enlarged competence, which by then included an international component, was realized. In addition, because of McComas's background in finance, coupled with the organization's growing need to get control of its increasingly diverse operations, finance was introduced into the core of the firm's distinctive competence, where it now plays a close support role to the international marketing of consumer products. Subsequent succession by Cullman and then by Weissman, both of whom had grown up under these earlier regimes, ensured the nurturance and refinement of the company's expanded distinctive competence, which Philip Morris's senior management cadre now regard as "international consumer-products marketing, followed closely by good financial controls."

Having aligned strategic predisposition and internal political structure within its evolving distinctive competences, Philip Morris created the fit with its diversification strategy through both careful selection and systematic transformation of new acquisitions. It began to aggressively assimilate new subsidiaries whose markets conformed to the needs and objectives of the company, by displacing traditional subsidiary management teams with executives who had been socialized in the thick marketing culture within the parent organization.

The development of distinctive competence within Reynolds and Liggett has taken a different form. To the extent feasible, both companies, as in the case of Philip Morris, have tried to weed out acquisitions completely unrelated to the central requirements of the traditional cigarette business. On this score, Liggett has been more successful than Reynolds, because of the latter's huge sunk costs in the unrelated shipping and petroleum businesses. In addition, both companies finally realigned their internal political structures to reestablish their core marketing competency. However, the difference lies in their approaches to assimilation and management of new subsidiaries.

Liggett and Reynolds, in contrast to Philip Morris, have developed their distinctive competences in a decentralized manner. Rather than homogenize all acquisitions around a central core competence, Reynolds and Liggett have fostered the development of multiple mixes of competences to serve the special needs of internally consistent clusters of their diverse business holdings. In many cases, these competences have come from senior managers in acquired subsidiaries or from executives brought in from outside. To handle all the variations in distinctive competences, these parents have adopted a decentralized-holding-company approach to subsidiary management.

Thus, senior executives at Philip Morris have tended to manipulate corporate strategy to fit corporate character and structure, whereas those at Reynolds and Liggett have tended to manipulate character and structure to fit strategy. Both approaches have made it possible for leaders to expand and refine the scope of distinctive competences within their organizations. But the development of these competences has not been without costs. In all three cases, it has taken considerable experimentation, often accompanied by substantial performance gap and internal politicking to discover both the real base of competence of each organization and the actual requirements of its strategies.

The Character-Defining Properties of Complex Organizations. The focus of the foregoing discussion has been on what Philip Selznick (1957) described as the "character" of an organization and the "character-formation" process. The relatively enduring properties of complex organizations—strategic predisposition, distinctive competence, and dominant values and beliefs—have been relied on as the basic character-defining properties of the corporations profiled in this study. As our developmental analysis has revealed, elements of the character of complex organizations are the products of history; in particular, the early pattern of decisions within an organization and the reinforcing context in which those decisions were enacted. As Selznick observed more than twenty years ago, these products of history tend to become integrated. In every case covered in this study, when inconsistencies among the elements of character persisted, performance gap eventually occurred that stimulated a rethinking of conventional wisdom or a restructuring of the decision-making process. Finally, the elements of character have been shown to be functional when their existence is recognized by executive leaders and when those leaders reflect this recognition in the pattern of strategic decisions they make.

Much as in the case of individuals, the character of an organization sets limits on what it can do well, shapes the values that are pursued and the choices of what shall be done, and influences which behaviors are in the choices of what shall be done, and influences which behaviors are in the organization's repertoire and which are drawn from it. But these character-defining elements may be viewed more appropriately as the basis for, rather than constraints on, organizational behavior.[5] What appears to be most important is not the fact that they exist, but the appreciation of what they are relative to the requirements of a performance situation. Armed with this knowledge, both individuals and organizations are better able to select situations in which their likelihood of success is high, to select behaviors that have a greater potential for coping with the demands of the situation, and to select a limited number of areas of competence that need improvement. Indeed, in many respects, organizations may be in a better position to do these things than individuals are, because the former are constantly exposed to different internal points of view and are capable of replacing and reassembling their parts. The point at which organizations may not match the coping ability of individuals is in the area of integration, and this is why the quality of executive leadership is so important in instances of organizational crisis and externally imposed change.[6]

In summary, these developmental histories indicate that the extent to which executive leaders appreciate the character-defining features of their organization may be a far more powerful predictor of success in adaptation than the fact that those features exist. For example, selective strategic experimentation in new and different domains provides opportunities for executive leaders to understand more fully the limits as well as the potentials of their companies' distinctive competences—an appreciation that could be used to inform more substantive strategic choices made later in the process of adaptation. In this sense, the existence of a clearly articulated and broadly recognized distinctive competence may be regarded as a asset of enormous benefit to executive leaders struggling to create opportunities for successful organizational adaptation.

Taken together with the evidence we have reviewed so far in this chapter, these findings demonstrate that corporations have a wide degree of domain choice flexibility, which, depending on the quality of executive leadership, may be constrained by relatively enduring but hardly immutable organizational features, including their strategic predispositions, the dominant values and beliefs as represented by the internal political structure, and distinctive competences. Beyond these key factors in the adaptive situation, however, lies one remaining factor that may help explain the relative success and apparent rationality with which members of the Big Six were able to respond to externally imposed crisis. This factor is implied in the natural-selection model and is explicitly included in the performance options specified in the strategic-choice model.

ORGANIZATIONAL SLACK

Natural-selection theorists implicitly assume not only that there is a tight coupling between powerless organizations and powerful environments but that organizations possess little slack for coping with substantial environmental change. We have already demonstrated that our organizations had at their disposal considerable domain choice flexibility; but we have also cautioned that this potential asset may not be realized if an organization does not possess the resources to take advantage of it. In the cases of the tobacco Big Six, various forms of organizational slack were available for coping with externally imposed crisis. The three most important forms appear to have been economic, political, and managerial slack.

Economic Slack.   The most visible and tangible type of organizational slack in the case of the Big Six was economic in nature. In general, economic slack may include liquid financial assets, such as cash, marketable securities, current receivables, and easily convertible assets (e.g., inventories for which current demand meets or exceeds supply); and the generalizable capital assets, such as underutilized plant capacity or technologies that may be applied to a variety of alternative production functions. In the case of the Big Six, highly specialized cigarette-production facilities possessed limited generalizability to other product-market alternatives that these firms might otherwise have pursued as part of their portfolio of adaptive strategies. But the existence of a high degree of financial slack characterized all six tobacco companies at the outbreak of the smoking-and-health controversy.

As we have demonstrated, all members of the industry population occupied a very favorable liquidity position at the time of rising institutional threat. Not only were their debt-to-equity ratios extremely low, but the stable although stagnating earnings flow from their traditional operations gave them enormous borrowing capacity. The stagnating domestic market for cigarettes created a situation in which the relatively high profits from cigarette sales could not be reinvested fully in traditional operations. To add further to their condition of extreme liquidity, excess tobacco-leaf inventories of high quality had a ready world market. So both unusual borrowing capacity and large, predictable cash and near-cash spinoffs from the threatened business created an enormous pool of financial slack for adaptive maneuvering. This liquidity could be used to finance the creation of joint political ventures, the support of massive smoking-and-health research programs, the development of product innovations, the burden of large advertising budgets needed to open up new market segments for allegedly "safer" cigarettes, the development of overseas markets for cigarette products, and finally, the acquisition of an impressive portfolio of new businesses.

Political Slack. Another important type of organizational slack, although often less apparent than financial and capital resources, is political in nature. In general, an organization's political slack includes both its social commitments and institutional props, which are manifestations of the vested interests of various constituencies in an enterprise, and the "goodwill" and "consumer loyalty" it has earned on the basis of historical exchanges with these constituencies. If available in sufficient magnitudes, these elements of political slack may generate enough commitment and support to enable an enterprise to successfully weather periods of external threat and actual or potential performance gap.

In the case of the U.S. tobacco industry, we discovered a latent but broad and potentially powerful infrastructure that linked the fates of the Big Six to those of a wide variety of private and public constituencies. It was this infrastructure that, together with the shared-fate condition of the Big Six, made it possible for the tobacco industry to mount a dramatic defense of domain. The initial success of the joint domain defense strategies, in turn, blunted the more ominous initiatives of the antismoking forces and bought precious time to mount more substantive strategies of adaptation. This temporal space made it possible for the Big Six to begin experimentally with their strategies of domain creation and to develop cigarette products that in several respects were responsive to the smoking-and-health challenge.

It is important to recognize, however, that the use of joint political ventures was not invented by the Big Six at the outbreak of the smoking-and-health controversy. Rather, decades of battling with local, state, and federal legislators and agencies over the issue of cigarette taxation had created a latent infrastructure of prosmoking constituencies that could be activated and marshaled under situations of threat to this ancient American industry. The industry's long history of positive contributions to national employment, agriculture, and balance-of-payments issues also guaranteed the support of several important federal agencies, notably the Agriculture and Commerce departments, and of influential actors in the Congress, not to mention the typical quiescence of the executive branch on smoking-and-health issues. This peculiar form of "goodwill," combined with the aggressive defense of domain, therefore, created another important source of slack for the Big Six.

Managerial Slack.   Finally, under conditions of market decline, especially the kind induced by nonmarket forces, it is likely that a surplus of managerial resources and capabilities will accumulate within member firms of the affected industry population. These resources represent a major investment, both emotionally and financially, of the senior managers in the threatened firms; consequently, it may be expected that the executive leadership will do what it can to provide a continuation of the kinds of developmental opportunities that are required to retain and motivate its most capable managers.

But managerial resources are not always as fluid and generalizable as cash and goodwill. To contribute to organizational slack, managerial capabilities must fit the strategic alternatives for organizational coping. Cigarette-production experience possessed restricted generalizability. The more generalizable distinctive competences of the tobacco firms lay in the areas of consumer-products marketing and advertising. So for those firms, such as Philip Morris, that could trade on this strength by diversifying into businesses closely related to their traditional business, this form of slack was realized. For other rivals, who believed that this slack was present in the form of "general" management capability, the results were less encouraging. Believing that executives who had grown up in the tobacco business were generalists who could manage almost anything, these companies embarked on wide-ranging diversification strategies, at least initially, which exposed them to a hodgepodge of business holdings many of which were unrelated to the specific knowledge and skills developed in the traditional business.

For these unrelated diversifiers, the realization of managerial slack was elusive. Not only did their managers have difficulty in anticipating and coping with the new features of different businesses for which they were now responsible, but in numerous cases, corporate management had to pay the price of negative managerial slack. Many of the unrelated diversifiers had to purchase the expertise they needed to manage their new holdings by hiring outsiders instead of relying on the skills and knowledge of managers groomed in the parent company. Thus, an important factor in determining whether the Big Six realized the benefits of managerial slack in responding to industry decline was once again the appreciation among executive leaders of the distinctive managerial competences inherent in their companies and their inclination to make strategic choices, especially in the area of diversification, that reflected this appreciation.

In summary, the organizational, strategic, and environmental factors that have been identified, together with the quality of executive leadership, help explain a considerable portion of the variance in strategic adaptation within the organizational population that served as the focus of this book. Taken together, these facilitating and inhibiting factors may be used to construct a revised model of the behavior and adaptation of complex organizations that includes selected elements of the pioneering models and offers an integration based on evidence from the actual behavior of such enterprises.

TOWARD A DEVELOPMENTAL THEORY OF ORGANIZATIONAL BEHAVIOR AND ADAPTATION

Neither the natural-selection model nor the strategic-choice model is sufficient to explain the behavior and adaptation of the complex organizations in this study. The former tends to exaggerate the potential constraints on organizational behavior and denies the role of organizational learning and executive leadership. The latter, although favored in this study of large corporations, tends to minimize the relatively enduring properties of the complex organization, emphasizing instead the vast range of choices available to strategic managers for coping with crisis and change. Elements of both theories, however, were verified in our account of the tobacco Big Six and were useful in explaining part of the behaviors and outcomes in the efforts of these companies to cope with externally imposed crisis.

By looking at this population of organizations over an extended period of time, however, it has been possible to sketch in broad terms a preliminary framework that includes some elements from each of the two competing models that have demonstrated utility for understanding the adaptive behaviors of the Big Six. This new framework will be referred to as the *developmental* perspective.

The idea that organizations must be understood from a developmental perspective is supported by this study, but it was not invented here. More than twenty years ago, Philip Selznick argued, ''The study of institutions is in some ways comparable to the clinical study of personality. It requires a genetic and developmental approach, an emphasis on historical origins and growth stages. There is a need to see the enterprise as a whole and to see how it is transformed as new ways of dealing with a changing environment evolve'' (1957:141–142).

The comparative and longitudinal nature of this investigation has made it possible to push this long-overdue developmental perspective further along than have either the static-comparative studies or the longitudinal studies of single institutions that preceded and informed the present inquiry. Moreover, by concentrating on a fundamental crisis situation rather than a temporary threat, we have been able to tease out important influences on the process of critical decision making within complex organizations—decisions that have the power to transform the basic purposes and directions of an established enterprise.

The basic elements of this developmental perspective for understanding and managing the process of strategic organizational adaptation are illustrated in Figure 8-1. Among these elements, the degrees of domain choice flexibility and organizational slack available to an organization represent boundary conditions. The extent to which these "potential" assets are available establishes important limits on the breadth and depth of adaptation that it is feasible for an organization to undertake. Adaptation, the reader will recall, was defined in Chapter 2 as "the process by which an organization manages itself or its environment in order to maintain or improve its performance, legitimacy, and, hence, its survival potential." This definition recognizes the potential for both organizational adjustment and environmental manipulation on the part of executive leaders.

Within these boundary conditions lie a set of relatively enduring organizational features or character-defining elements—strategic predisposition, distinctive competence, and dominant values and beliefs—and a range of strategic choices or adaptive modes—domain defense, domain offense, and domain creation—whose development and alignment are shaped by the process of executive leadership.

THE BOUNDARY CONDITIONS

According to the developmental perspective, the ability of complex organizations to adapt to fundamental threats depends, first, upon the degree of domain choice flexibility and organizational slack at their disposal. When domain choice is restricted by mandates imposed by an organization's charter, the matter of adaptation becomes more one of changing the organization, its predispositions,

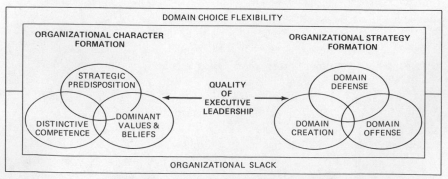

FIGURE 8-1 The developmental perspective

competences, and decision-making structures, to conform to the dictates of a given, relatively powerful external environment. When organizational slack is minimal, fundamental adaptation is either precluded or extremely costly in terms of its propensity to produce visible performance gap. In addition, when little slack exists within an organization, the potential advantages of domain choice flexibility may not be realized. Thus, the first step in understanding the severity of the adaptive situation under conditions of imposed crisis is to examine the domain choice flexibility afforded an organization by the institutional "rules of the game" and the slack resources available within the enterprise. These two factors represent boundary conditions that circumscribe the scope and range of adaptation possible in an organization.

But it would be misleading to view even these two factors as givens. Executive leaders can do much to ensure that their organizations continue to operate under conditions of at least moderate levels of domain choice flexibility and organizational slack. Even the detailed charters of public agencies leave considerable room for strategic maneuvering on the part of executive leaders. Indeed, we are persuaded that the extent of domain choice flexibility is more a function of the creativity and imagination among members of the executive cadre than of formal mandates and informal traditions embedded in their external context.

Organizational slack, similarly, is far from being immune to the quality of executive leadership. Companies exposed to the same degree of domain choice flexibility and possessing equivalent levels of slack resources may perform quite differently, depending on the strategic and structural choices made by their executive leaders. Considering just the tobacco independents from the beginning of the smoking-and-health controversy to the end of this study, the great differences in the performances achieved by the two industry leaders—Reynolds and American Brands—and by the two smaller firms—Philip Morris and Liggett—demonstrate that the relative timing and nature of implementation of each firm's strategic choices accounted for a significant portion of the variance in each firm's success in adaptation.

A number of levers are available to executive leaders for creating and applying slack to meet the demands of a wide variety of adaptive situations. Such leaders can create intelligence-gathering functions that can help their organizations anticipate and initiate preventive or preemptive measures to deal with issues to which their organizations are potentially exposed. Through the use of symbolic behaviors, the modification of the structural context for decision making, the selective focus on particular aspects of the organization or its performance situation, and the dissemination of credible data, executive leaders can cause attention to be focused on issues or problems that might otherwise be ignored or dismissed by organizational members. Indeed, almost every issue of potential relevance to an organization has a prehistory in which early-warning signals are available to organizations that have the receptors to pick them up.

Executive leaders in some of the Big Six companies, for example, were better able than those in others to appreciate the early-warning signals of the 1953 Sloan Kettering Report. As a result, by 1964, when the smoking-and-health controversy finally emerged full blown, these leaders had already positioned their companies for defensive, offensive, and creative adaptation.

Finally, executive leaders often have considerable voice in determining how much of the organization's earnings are to be retained as slack resources as opposed to being returned to investors or plowed back into current operations. Indeed, the separation of ownership and management in publicly held corporations has contributed to an increase in the discretionary power of executive leaders who run corporations on behalf of a multitude of marginally interested owners. As long as the dividend payout of corporations meets the minimal expectations of common stockholders, these constituencies are not likely to become interested in how the enterprise is being operated or to coalesce to call for a major change in executive leadership.

Thus, as a starting point in understanding any adaptive situation, one must look to the two conditions that tend to create boundaries around the breadth and depth of strategic organizational adaptation. In doing so, however, one is cautioned that even these factors are not fixed, but are to some extent under the influence of complex organizations depending on the quality of their executive leaders.

CHARACTER-FORMATION AND STRATEGY-FORMATION PROCESSES

These boundary conditions are necessary but not sufficient conditions for explaining the behavior and adaptation of complex organizations. Not only is strategy formation constrained by the availability of domain choice flexibility and slack resources, but its progress is facilitated or dampened by the extent to which it is congruent with the character of the enterprise.

The elements of organizational or corporate character examined in this study include (1) *strategic predisposition,* which reflects how an organization tends to behave over time and across different situations; (2) *distinctive competence,* which refers to the unique knowledge and skills contained within an organization and which indicates what it can do particularly well; and (3) *dominant values and beliefs,* which are represented by the internal political structure of the enterprise.

Perhaps the most important finding of this study will be judged to be the demonstration of the relatively enduring construct of corporate character and the variety of ways in which it may be shaped or capitalized upon by executive leaders who guide the strategy-formation processes of an enterprise. This study has shown that careful retrospective reconstruction of organizational actions and outcomes under known situational conditions can reveal important differences in the characters of organizations residing in the same organizational population. However, it remains the task of practicing managers and future students of complex enterprise to refine the construct of corporate character and to develop effective processes of real-time diagnosis and intervention.

Armed with the insights and clues from this study, this careful thinking and research will no doubt reveal a richer basis for expressing the multidimensionality of character when applied to complex organizations and its implications for the practice of strategic management. With these needed refinements, we expect that a more complete appreciation of corporate character might include not only this study's findings on risk-taking propensities and distinctive competences, together with the dominant values and orientations of the coalition in power, but other traits, including intelligence, creativity, flexibility, and social awareness. In addition to the breadth of corporate character, differences may also be discovered in its depth—its "thickness," or density. These refinements and extensions appear to be justified by the demonstrated pervasiveness of the character construct in this account of strategic organizational adaptation and, therefore, by their potential for improving the quality of executive leadership in complex organizations.

If corporate character is shaped by one of the visible hands of executive leadership, corporate strategy appears to be even more pliable clay in the other hand. Through the process of strategy formation, executive leaders can facilitate the development of effective, evolving alignments among the features of their organization and its operating domain and institutional environment. Strategy formation—the interaction between the formulation and implementation of strategies—is also the primary process by which organizations learn. It is through the process of trying new and different behaviors and situations that executive leaders begin to appreciate more accurately their organization and its environments and that they expand the knowledge and skills that form the basis of their distinctive competence. It is also through the strategy-formation process that organizations reveal their predispositions and call into question their belief systems—the values and orientations favored in the internal political structure.

In summary, it is primarily through the strategy-formation process guided by executive leaders that the operating domains and institutional environment of an enterprise become defined. It is primarily from the character-formation process, also guided by executive leaders, that the formal aspects of organization, typically referred to as structure or design and systems, and the informal organization, including its myths, norms, and rituals, evolve and become institutionalized or deinstitutionalized. Moreover, it has been demonstrated repeatedly in this study that these two developmental processes are highly interactive. Strategy formation is facilitated or inhibited by the predominant character of the enterprise; yet new and different strategies test and shape the character-formation process. Therefore, from what we have learned, a focus on these core constructs of character and strategy appears to offer greater utility to managers and students of complex organizations than does the more conventional preoccupation with their derivatives—organization design and external environment, respectively.

THE QUALITY OF EXECUTIVE LEADERSHIP

By now it should be obvious that the role played by executive leaders is critical to the performance, adaptation, and persistence of complex organizations. This role includes the sensing of the nature of the enterprise and the total situation relevant to it, the development of organizational resources and environmental opportunities, and the articulation of the alignment among the essential elements of organizational character and strategy—all of which are ongoing role requirements. That executive leaders can and do perform these role requirements has been demonstrated in this quarter-century account of strategic organizational adaptation.

The variety of successful approaches to strategic adaptation taken by executive leaders in the tobacco Big Six is too extensive for complete summary here; but for the great majority of approaches, the processes of organizational learning and managerial choice have figured heavily. In many cases, some combination of definitive performance feedback and catalytic or consolidative leadership was able to powerfully influence the elements of an organization's fundamental character. In other cases, once executive leaders began to appreciate the relatively enduring features of their organization, they were able to capitalize on this knowledge. Some leaders found it less costly to modify strategy to conform with their organization's predispositions, competences, and values than to attempt alterations in the elements of character to fit strategy. Others were able to expand their organization's competence base to better accommodate its political structure, its basic predispositions, or its strategies. And in some cases, the dominant values and beliefs represented by the internal political structure itself were modified through changes in the traditional pattern of executive succession to achieve internal consistency of character or more effective alignment with strategy.

At the core of the developmental perspective, therefore, resides the role of executive leaders and the influence they have on the character-formation and strategy-formation processes in complex organizations. Indeed, the model presented in Figure 8-1 implies that an effective way to begin an assessment of the quality of executive leadership is to examine the fit over time between the character of an enterprise and the mix of strategies it pursues, while controlling for the degrees of domain choice flexibility and slack resources available to it. From what has been gathered in this quarter-century study of a whole industry population of firms, the articulation of the organizational character-formation and strategy-formation processes is both the fundamental requirement imposed upon executive leaders and the essence of organizational adaptation.

FUTURE PROSPECTS AND DIRECTIONS

A number of issues for strategic management that have been raised either directly or indirectly in this investigation, and in the developmental perspective constructed on the basis of the evidence it generated, are beyond the scope of its research design and data-gathering methods. Therefore, in addition to the need for refinements and generalizations of the findings and perspectives in this book, we must rely on future research to come to grips with the issues we could not engage.

First, there is the need to know more about the process of character formation in complex organizations and the intervention strategies that are most useful in helping executive leaders and other organizational members recognize their collective character and make appropriate strategic choices accordingly. The relatively enduring features of organizations discovered in this study appear to provide a useful first approximation of the multidimensional construct of organizational character, one that effectively distinguished among members of an industry population and helped to predict and explain the process and outcomes of their approaches to adaptation. No doubt future research will provide insights into other important dimensions of this powerful construct.

In this regard, the historical analysis of archival information, especially the kind that compares the responses of a focal organization and its peers to different situations of crisis or opportunity, should provide one important source of character-defining information. In addition, there is a complementary need in developmental analysis for in-depth, on-site clinical diagnosis of the forces and actors, and the beliefs and myths, at work within an enterprise. These intensive bases for understanding the character-formation and strategy-formation processes, although often difficult and expensive, appear to be justified on the basis of both the relative importance of these developmental processes for explaining and predicting organizational behavior and the current state of knowledge about them. We are perhaps several decades removed from the time (if ever) in which paper-and-pencil tests, such as the personality inventories and aptitude surveys used to assess the character of individuals, may be relied on as substitutes for the rich comparative-historical and intensive-clinical approaches to organizational assessment encouraged by this study.

This study has also revealed dozens of creative ways in which executive leaders can either shape organizational character or select organizational environments, strategies, and structures to better accommodate it. But the research design we employed, together with the managerial sensitivity to the legitimacy threat, made it infeasible to inquire deeper into the tactical behaviors of executive leaders in guiding the character-formation and strategy-formation processes.

A detailed understanding of the tactical behaviors of strategic managers must await careful research of another kind, research that places the investigator in the midst of the adaptive processes within complex organizations. It is only through this in-depth, real-time, action-research focus that investigators will be able to identify the powerful but sometimes subtle role of executive leaders in developing, refining, and reinforcing the fit between the processes of character formation and strategy formation. These powerful subtleties involve the creation of decision-making settings, the framing of questions and symbols to guide and reinforce problem-solving activity, the selection of who will and will not be involved, the sequencing and timing of these events to optimize the potential of competing forces and uneven capabilities within the enterprise, and the development of knowledge and skills to manage the changing configuration of organizational character, strategy, and environment.

In addition, we know almost nothing about the advice given by external consultants to help executive leaders understand and capitalize on the relatively enduring features of their enterprises. Based on the diversification track record of the Big Six alone, it would appear that the advice executive leaders received from investment bankers and other external consultants did not include a sensitivity to many of the most important issues raised in this investigation. The costs of misread requirements of new acquisitions, misunderstood corporate capabilities, early divestitures, senior management turnover, and disappointing financial returns were simply too great for us to believe that the diagnosis and articulation of the character-formation and strategy-formation processes figured heavily in the roles played by these consultants.

However, from what we know in general about individuals experiencing difficulty in coping with performance situations, the processes of accurate self-appraisal and action planning are usually complicated by emotionality and defensiveness and, therefore, in many cases require the intervention and facilitation of a skilled clinician. These professionals are trained in the diagnosis of individual personalities and in the facilitation of self-assessment and action planning. Based on what we found to be important in the adaptive situations of the Big Six, the development of organization and management consulting skills analogous to the ones used by individual clinicians would appear to be of enormous benefit to complex organizations and their executive leaders. Indeed, the results of preliminary experimentation in complex organizations with the concepts and typologies developed in this study provide encouragement for the continued refinement of the diagnostic and intervention skills needed by consultants to help facilitate the long-term process of organizational development.

For several years, the senior author has used a preliminary version of the developmental perspective to help executive cadres in both public and private institutions examine themselves and their organizations. To say that some of these cadres have exhibited defensiveness and anxiety when exposed to self-analysis is perhaps an understatement. But such occasions have usually led to a deeper appreciation of the organization and its performance and have typically served as a catalyst to the development and refinement of the dynamic fit between organizational character and strategy. Thus, although it would be premature to attempt to prescribe an intervention methodology at this time, these consulting applications have revealed that even the preliminary concepts and typologies generated in this study can be of benefit to executive leaders struggling to appreciate the character and strategies of their enterprise and to develop an effective alignment between them under changing circumstances.

An important reminder in closing this chapter is that this study and the implications drawn from it have been concerned with the issues of *critical* decision making and *strategic* adaptation in complex organizations. These circumstances may be contrasted with the operating decisions and incremental refinements that make up the daily routines within organizations and that, instead of affecting the fundamental character and mission of an enterprise, are conducted within its established framework. Because the mainstream of research and theory building on organizations has focused primarily on these ongoing processes of operational adjustment within an established enterprise, it is little wonder that the factors identified as most important in this study have been rarely discussed in the contemporary literature on complex organizations. When the focus is shifted as in the present study, however, a different picture emerges. It is during times requiring critical decision making and fundamental adaptation that the basic processes of character formation, strategy formation, and executive leadership become visible and their central importance to organizational development and survival is confirmed.

But until now we have confined our assessments and implications to the relatively narrow perspective of the focal organizations and their industry. The remaining question concerns the potential side effects of successful organizational adaptation for the embedding society.

FOOTNOTES

[1] Perhaps Plato (*Laws*) expressed this perspective best when he said, "that God governs all things, and that chance and opportunity cooperate with Him in the government of human affairs. There is, however, a . . . less extreme view, that art should be there also; for I should say that in a storm there must surely be a great advantage in having the aid of a pilot's art. Would you agree?"

[2] Lorillard, the other industry Defender, which also was having trouble introducing innovative products, joined American Brands in the withdrawal from the Code.

[3] Aggressiveness in this instance refers to the degree of investment committed early in the formation of each company's overseas-expansion strategy. The purchase of overseas manufacturing facilities required the reallocation of far more resources than did the creation of licensing agreements or the reliance on exports from domestic production facilities.

[4] Recall from Chapter 5 that American Brands's late entry into the overseas market was in part

a product of the legacy of the 1911 trust bust, which gave British-American Tobacco Company the sole rights to AB's traditional cigarette brands abroad.

[5] Most of the contributions to the unfortunately small literature on organizational character and ideology (e.g., Clark, 1970; Rhenman, 1973; and Aldrich, 1979) tend to view the institutionalization of character as problematic for organizations exposed to environmental change. We wish to emphasize that our position is considerably less pessimistic given the broad range of strategic choices that we have found among our subject population of organizations. Most domains, we believe, are amenable to segmentation, and most organizations have at least some degree of domain choice flexibility which offers the opportunity to capitalize on their distinctive characters. The most important issue, therefore, is not that distinctive characters tend to emerge within complex organizations, but whether executive leaders appreciate these relatively enduring features of their enterprises and reflect this appreciation in the processes of strategic choice and strategy formation over which they preside.

[6] For an expanded discussion of the potential benefits and limitations of relying on biological metaphors to explain and predict organizational behaviors, refer to Kimberly, J.R., Miles, R.H., and associates, *The Organizational Life Cycle: Issues in the Creation, Transformation, and Decline of Organizations* (San Francisco: Jossey-Bass, 1980), especially pp. 6–14.

9

Implications
for Public
Policy Makers

Having covered most of the important aspects of this developmental history from the point of view of strategic managers, we will devote this closing chapter to the public-policy implications of the patterns of strategic organizational adaptation that we observed among the tobacco Big Six. First, we will review briefly some of the major public-policy initiatives of the smoking-and-health battle in the light of the behaviors of the target population of firms. In addition, our investigation has revealed, either explicitly or implicitly, that successful adaptation—the methods employed and the outcomes achieved by the Big Six—may generate some significant consequences for what has become an increasingly organized American society. Therefore, we want to conclude this book with a discussion of the potential economic and social side effects of the modes of strategic adaptation that were invented or adopted by the tobacco Big Six.

GOVERNMENT REGULATION: "ALL THUMBS, NO FINGERS"

The first set of implications for public-policy makers has to do with the degrees to which the intended goals of public policies developed by federal agencies—or "agency strategies"—were realized.

It is not easy to cast the public regulators of the U.S. tobacco industry, especially those in the FTC and FCC, in the script we have been reporting. In the face of overwhelming odds, these economists and attorneys shouldered the enormous responsibility of initiating the antismoking trade regulations against this firmly entrenched industry. In doing so, they had to move swiftly, and often without precedent, under the uncertain auspices of administrative authority. As Lee Fritschler, author of *Smoking and Politics,* has commented. ''The initiation and continuation of the cigarette controversy were possible because of both the political power and delegated authority possessed by bureaucratic agencies. Had the decision on cigarettes and health been left to Congress alone, it is safe to assume that the manufacturers would have triumphed and no health warning of any kind would have been required.''

But Yale political scientist Charles Lindblom, author of *Politics and Markets,* has observed that government authority is very "clumsy" when compared to the market mechanism. According to him, government agencies are characterized by "strong thumbs, no fingers," an observation that retrospective analysis reveals to be an accurate, if only partial, description of the well-intentioned initiatives of U.S. federal agencies during the smoking-and-health controversy. In addition, there is evidence that the same well-intentioned efforts of federal regulators were characterized by a certain degree of naiveté on the part of those who designed and implemented them. In discussing the failures of the antismoking movement, one economist has noted, "The regulation of advertising for cigarettes was, in large part, undertaken simply to make smokers better people in the sense that they might become more careful about the state of their own health. This regulation was blithely based on the expectation that because its intention was to discourage smoking, it would actually do so" (Riker, 1979:xiii).

History so far has revealed that several of the major federal-agency initiatives generated consequences that apparently were not fully appreciated at the time they were implemented by administrative bureaucrats. Indeed, in several instances, it is possible that cigarette consumption was actually maintained or even increased by the agencies' antismoking policies. These public-policy paradoxes may be identified for both of the major antismoking initiatives taken by federal administrative agencies: the enforcement of the health-warning labels and the broadcast ban of cigarette advertising.

The Health-Warning Paradox.   Health-warning labels were proposed by the Federal Trade Commission in hopes that consumers would be reminded constantly of the negative health consequences of their cigarette habit and would, therefore, be more inclined to reduce or quit smoking. It is doubtful, however, that the full effects anticipated from this policy have been realized.

In part, perhaps, this shortfall is due to the watering down by Congress of the strong health-warning message proposed initially by the FTC. In part also, its diminished and somewhat transitory effects may be attributed to the format of the label itself, which has remained constant for over a decade. Consumers simply do not see the label, or if they do, they do not seem to pay it any attention. The fact that an earlier Scandinavian system, employing multiple health-warning messages and formats, has been more successful seems to have escaped the scope of health-warning policy formation in the United States.

But far more serious than these health-warning shortfalls in terms of actual consumer behavior is the legal fact that such labels effectively put the consumer on notice about the health risks he or she accepts when lighting up. In a 1980 article titled, "The Cigarette Industry's Escape from Liability," law professor Donald Garner observed, "To date, the cigarette industry has never paid out one cent in compensation for tobacco-induced injuries,'' and that "tobacco law is a defendant's dream come true.'' "The paradox of the congressionally mandated warning,'' Garner explained, "is that when the danger of cigarette smoking was not known to the manufacturer, he was not liable under negligence principles. Now that the danger is known by the smoker, the manufacturer isn't liable under principles of strict liability. While the warning may have done very little to cut down cigarette consumption, it has worked miracles in relieving any legal anxiety felt by cigarette defense counsel.'' Thus, a far more effective way than labeling to curb the propensity toward expansion of the smoking habit might have been to organize a broad-based, class-action suit asserting the neglected responsibility of the tobacco companies for the American smoking "epidemic.'' But the weaker marketing initiative of the FTC preempted the stronger legal option. In essence, health-warning labels proposed by the FTC and approved by Congress provided a new defense for the Big Six as they attempted to fight off subsequent personal-injury cases brought by cigarette smokers (Drew, 1965).

The Broadcast-Ban Paradox. It is by now well recognized that the broadcast-advertising ban was associated with an increase—not a decrease—in U.S. total and per capita consumption of cigarettes. This apparent paradox, however, appears to have been fully appreciated in advance by the Big Six, which voluntarily withdrew their advertising from the broadcast media months before the ban became law. Not only was the ban followed immediately by increased sales of cigarettes, but the prohibition enormously strengthened the financial resources of the Big Six, who were no longer locked into an oligopolistic stalemate, involving huge advertising outlays but generating few tangible returns in terms of market-share improvement (Riker, 1979). In addition, the ban reversed the strongly negative impact of the "Fairness Doctrine" on both cigarette consumption and industry legitimacy.

A host of econometric studies have demonstrated consistently that the antismoking commercials had a far greater impact on cigarette consumption than the industry's prosmoking ads (e.g., Hamilton, 1972; Warner, 1977, 1978; Doron, 1979). All these econometricians, therefore, have concluded that the television and radio ad ban, beginning in 1971, was bad public policy—at least in the short term. James Hamilton, the first economist to systematically assess the impacts of the antismoking commercials and the subsequent ban, concluded that the elimination of prosmoking ads reduced broadcasters' contributions of free time to antismoking groups, required by the Federal Communications Commission's Fairness Doctrine. Another economist later confirmed Hamilton's conclusion. Gideon Doron (1979:17) found that during the 1969−70 pre-ban period under the Fairness Doctrine, the three television networks aired an average of 635 antismoking commercials annually, compared to an average of only 122 antismoking messages in each of the two years (1971−72) immediately following the ban. Indeed, during the "equal-time" years, it has been estimated (Fritschler, 1975:16) that health groups received $225 million worth of free broadcast time.

These consequences should not be surprising. Kenneth Warner (1977:648), an associate professor of health planning and administration at the University of Michigan, estimated, ''The antismoking TV and radio ads reduced consumption an average of better than 4 percent each of the three years they were aired under the Fairness Doctrine.'' Reflecting back on the implications of the ad-ban policy, Warner (1978:8) concluded later that ''the adopted policy rated high in principle but low, even negatively, in its effect. . . . The first three years of the ad ban saw the largest upward trend in smoking since the Surgeon General's [1964] Report, with per capita consumption rising 4.5 percent.'' Nevertheless, the consequences did not seem to be appreciated by the federal regulators who pressed the new policy on the industry.

What makes the apparent myopia of U.S. public-policy makers so difficult to understand is that others anticipated these effects when they did not. Certainly the senior managers in the Big Six anticipated the victory the ban would create for them. As an *Advertising Age* article reported the year after the ban, ''Tobacco men are smiling and counting their blessings as they end their first year of enforced abstinence from broadcast advertising'' (January 3, 1972:45). Scholars, in an all too rare moment of foresight, also seemed to understand. In May 1969, economics professor John Mueller of the University of Rochester wrote a letter, which unfortunately was not published, to the editor of the *New York Times Magazine* in which he argued:

> . . . *if the FCC is successful in banning cigarette commercials in this country, television stations apparently would no longer be required to present the antismoking messages as they are now under the "fairness" doctrine.*
>
> *The net effect of the ban, therefore, might be to maintain cigarette consumption at a higher level than would prevail without the ban.*
>
> With enemies like the FCC, the tobacco industry hardly needs friends. [*Doron, 1979:18*]

Finally, U.S. public-policy makers apparently either did not know about or chose to ignore the evidence generated by an earlier ban of cigarette broadcast advertising in the United Kingdom. The facts at the time indicated that the 1965 British ban did *not* reduce the level of cigarette consumption (Anderson and Skegg, 1973; Doron, 1979:18).

It was not until almost seven years after the enactment of the broadcast ban in the United States that this policy was questioned officially. In 1977, a Department of Health, Education and Welfare task force was convened by the soon-to-be-dismissed Joseph Califano to examine new antismoking strategies. The task force recommended that the broadcast ban be rescinded, at least with respect to low-tar-and-nicotine cigarettes, in order to reinstate the need for the ''equal-time'' antismoking messages (Russell, 1977). Since then, other proposals have been made that would alter the 1970 ad-ban policy. They include persuading broadcasters to devote more of their public-service time to the antismoking cause and raising the taxes on cigarette sales to enable the government to purchase broadcast time for a renewed antismoking campaign. But none of these proposals has been palatable to enough of the constituencies linked by the smoking-and-health controversy to alter in any way the 1970 policy on broadcast advertising.

The "Overseas Oversight"? But if errors of commission have been a problem for antismoking public-policy makers, an important error of *omission* must be considered in their assessment as well. In their efforts to modify the behavior of the traditional tobacco industry and the patterns of cigarette consumption at home, antismoking regulators in the United States apparently failed to consider the possibility that among the adaptive strategies chosen by the Big Six would be expansion of their domestic cigarette market into the global arena. To make matters worse, prosmoking agencies of the federal government have actually encouraged this industry development. One consequence is that the efforts to constrain the growth of the U.S. cigarette market have resulted in what one representative (Ross, 1980) of the American Cancer Society has described as the exportation of America's "smoking epidemic" to other parts of the world, especially to developing nations in the Third World. An excerpt from a recent *New York Times* article paints a shocking picture of the world situation that has emerged and the part the United States has wittingly or unwittingly played in its development:

"FILTER FUN FOR THIRD-WORLDERS"

"Try Winston, the great taste of America"—this advertising slogan exemplifies the marketing effort that transnational tobacco conglomerates have made to create an appetite for cigarettes among the hungry of the Third World.

Our Government, using tax dollars, has helped by making tobacco products and technology a major American export.

As a result, at a time when they are striving for political and economic independence, the developing nations are entering into a new form of life-threatening bondage—addiction to cigarette smoking.

Faced with the prospect of diminishing sales in North America and Europe, the tobacco industry identified the third world as a vast untapped market. An aggressive advertising campaign was developed to create the new demand. The effort, in most cases unhindered by regulations or health education programs, has been tragically effective.

While per capita cigarette consumption between 1970 and 1980 rose less than 4 percent in the United States, it increased an alarming 33 percent in Africa and 24 percent in Latin America.

While selling their products to consumers, the tobacco interests have also been appealing to Third-World governments, stressing the economic benefits of cigarette taxes.

That the product will increase health-care costs and substitute for food among the poor is somehow overlooked.

The dramatic rise in United States tobacco exports reflects the success of this sales program. Between 1971 and 1974, the average value of the tobacco products and leaf sent beyond our borders each year was $650 million. By 1979, the figure was $2.15 billion.

In three specific ways, our tax money has helped these frightening consumption and export figures grow.

First, the Agriculture Department encourages and supports domestic tobacco production. In 1979 alone, more than $337 million of public funds went for that purpose. The largest chunk was spent on the Commodity Credit Corporation's loans and price-support system: Net expenditures for tobacco loans last year were $157 million. While officials expect that some of these losses will be recovered this year, net expenditures for 1981 are now forecast at $231 million. These figures are defended as the cost of assuring farmers an adequate income. Unfortunately, they also insure the consistent harvest of more tobacco than we can sell.

Second, after subsidizing the growth of tobacco, the Government uses our tax dollars to buy some of the surplus. Since 1955, it has purchased more than 330 metric tons of domestic tobacco and shipped it to less-developed countries as part of the Food for Peace program. Although the quantities have been decreasing during the last few years, as recently as 1977 the United States sent abroad 13.53 million metric tons with an estimated value over $55 million. Senator Jesse Helms of North Carolina, justifying the presence of tobacco in the food-aid-program in 1977, explained that this supplied an outlet for the commodity, and said that "historically these sales have developed new markets for American tobacco."

Third, in addition to underwriting exports, our tax money has been used to encourage tobacco production overseas. Motivated by the belief that it represents a cash crop for farmers and a potential export good to generate foreign exchange, the World Bank and the United Nations Development Program have supported projects to expand tobacco cultivation. Both receive substantial annual financial contributions from the United States Government.

These trends in tobacco exports, consumption and production clearly indicate that the stage is being set for a new epidemic of smoking-related diseases in the less-developed nations. The epidemic may be prevented if we take action now to eliminate the programs funded by our tax dollars that accelerate the introduction of cigarettes abroad.

We cannot allow the health of the Third World to be sacrificed for the health of the tobacco industry. The price, in terms of life and resources, is just too high.*

---

*Margaret J. Sheridan, "Filter Fun for Third-Worlders," The New York Times, April 13, 1980, p. E19. Reprinted by permission.

The U.S. government's double standard regarding a smoking-and-health policy has required domestic tobacco companies to print warning labels on cigarettes sold in this country and to our armed forces overseas, but not on domestic brands sold internationally on airplanes or ships or in foreign countries. In addition, cigarettes manufactured abroad or licensed by the Big Six, according to Walter Ross (1980:144—145) of the American Cancer Society, "are frequently much more lethal than their look-alikes bought here. In a recent test, Marlboro, Kent, Kool and Chesterfield averaged 17.5 mg. tar within our borders but 31.75 mg. tar in the Philippines." As a result in large measure of the U.S. government's double health standard regarding tobacco, in 1979 the World Health Organization reported, "In some developing countries the epidemic of smoking-related disease is already of such magnitude as to rival even infectious disease or malnutrition as a public health problem" (Ross, 1980:145).

In the light of the historical evidence accumulated so far, it appears that the promises and achievements of the antismoking initiatives taken by U.S. federal agencies have fallen far short of what hindsight, at least, would label satisfactory. The implications of these shortfalls, reached almost a decade ago by James Hamilton, appears to be even more relevant for U.S. public policy makers today:

> *Policy makers must evaluate policy models carefully. Action based on wishful thinking seldom is as effective as that based on carefully specified models accurately depicting the forces influencing the policy objectives and the connections between forces and proposed policy actions.* [1972:409]

It is to be hoped that awareness of the public-policy pitfalls of the smoking-and-health controversy in the United States and of the range of strategic adaptive behaviors employed by the tobacco Big Six will contribute to more effective and lasting public-policy initiatives in the future. As economist Robert Leone has observed, "The indirect and unintended competitive consequences of regulation are an important and poorly understood part of the regulatory process" (1979:37). In particular, both current and future public-policy makers are well advised by this study to extend the boundaries around their normal training in traditional economic and political theory to embrace the new economics of multibusiness, global enterprises and the strategy mixes they employ to ensure uninterrupted growth and prosperity.

SIDE EFFECTS OF STRATEGIC ORGANIZATIONAL ADAPTATION

So far, we have discussed the relative effectiveness of the antismoking initiatives taken by public-policy makers in terms of their impact on the Big Six. We also have examined the extent to which different strategies were effective from the point of view of the threatened firms. We have not, however, examined either the potential side effects of organizationally successful strategies on society as a whole or the ability of U.S. public policy to protect society from these potential side effects. The most important of the side effects of successful organizational adaptation appear to be associated with the phenomena of corporate diversification and globalization.

The Cross-Subsidization Issue. First, a diversified company may be able to affect the competitive structure of an industry in which one of its businesses operates in a way that a single-business company operating exclusively in that industry cannot. "The large, diversified tenant of a market," according to economist Richard Caves (1977:41−42), "can potentially use the profits it earns elsewhere to discipline or even destroy its rivals in the market at hand. For example, it can lower its price, financing its own losses out of profits from other markets, and force losses on a rival until he quits." Thus, a potentially serious threat to the structure of competition in a particular industry is the possibility of cross-subsidization in a conglomerate operating a business in that industry.

Related to the issue of cross-subsidization is the fact that diversified companies can conceal, within the conventional consolidated income statement required of U.S. corporations, their profits and losses from one or several of their many businesses. Not only does the consolidated financial reporting requirement deny competitors and potential market entrants knowledge about the true state of market conditions; it also enables the managers of diversified corporations to hide their mistakes from stockholders long after bad investments should have been admitted and terminated (Caves, 1977:42).

In addition, diversified conglomerates, simply because of their presence in many markets, may be better able than single-business companies to support their competitive struggle in a particular market through reciprocity dealings across other businesses included in their portfolios (Markham, 1973:23). As economist Corwin Edwards has explained:

> A concern that produces many products and operates across many markets . . . may possess power in a particular market not only by virtue of its place in the organization of that market but also by virtue of the scope and character of its activities elsewhere. It may be able to exploit, extend, or defend its power by tactics other than those that are traditionally associated with the idea of monopoly. [1955:332]

It is this "discretionary power" (Williamson, 1964; Markham, 1973), which accrues potentially to management in diversified companies, that should be of concern to those who safeguard the marketplaces of competitive commerce. But until recently, there has been no way to examine either the prevalence or the consequences of conglomerate cross-subsidization and related issues.[1] However, after a series of court battles, the Federal Trade Commission won in November 1978 the right to collect financial information from major corporations on individual lines of business.[2] Litigation brought by affected corporations ceased when the U.S. Supreme Court refused to hear a challenge to the FTC's program for line-of-business reporting by more than two hundred companies. But it is too soon to be able to use these data to answer definitively some of the important questions raised by the cross-subsidization issue. Within the next half decade, perhaps scholars and public-policy analysts will make this new information the subject of serious investigation and debate.

The Aggregate-Concentration Issue.   Potentially far more serious than the cross-subsidization question is the issue of aggregate economic and political concentration associated with the proliferation of diversified corporations. Although most industry analysts agree that market concentration in the United States has not increased significantly with diversification, many are worried about the rising level of aggregate concentration in the overall economy. Current antitrust laws are responsible for the absence of concentration increases in particular markets because they enjoin horizontal merger; but these laws, according to the late economist Samuel Richardson Reid (1968:5), "have not been designed to cope with the variety of diversification-type mergers which are the major force in the current wave." As we have noted, because traditional economic models assume that firms are captives of a single product market and ignore almost completely the phenomenon of the diversified corporation, the antitrust laws that economists have helped to develop reflect their preoccupation with the structure of markets to the neglect of the structure of the national and world economies (Turner, 1965:313).

In order to appreciate the magnitude and potential implications of rising aggregate concentration brought about by unabated conglomerate diversification, one need only be reminded of some rather sobering statistics on this movement. Between 1955 and 1980, members of the current *Fortune* 500 list of America's largest corporations acquired almost 4,500 other companies. Moreover, 166 of the 1955 list of the largest U.S. corporations are now owned by other *Fortune* 500 companies. Most of the ten fastest-growing companies owe a large part of their sales growth to mergers and acquisitions. This group, which includes Philip Morris, made an average of twenty acquisitions apiece, many of which already generated very large sales volumes on their own (Hayes, 1980:88–96).

This high intensity of corporate acquisition activity is matched by the aggregate concentration that now exists in the U.S. economy. By the mid-1970s, Reid described the "new industrial order" that had emerged in America as follows:

> *Less than 1 percent of American manufacturers control 88 percent of the industrial assets and receive over 90 percent of the net profits of industrial firms in the American economy. About 100 firms receive a greater share of the net profits than the remaining 370,000 corporations, proprietorships, and partnerships engaged in manufacturing. The sales of* Fortune's *500*

> *Largest Industrials are almost ten times greater than the "second" 500*
> *largest firms (those ranked 501–1000). The assets of this second group are*
> *also less than one-tenth of the 500 largest industrials. Combined, the 1,000*
> *largest industrials, a fraction of a percent of American business firms,*
> *employ about 80 percent of the workers in manufacturing and mining.*
> *[1976:11–12]*

This high degree of overall economic concentration potentially carries with it some rather unsettling implications for society. On the economic front, the advantages to a conglomerate of "bigness" include potential economies of large scale in purchasing and financing as well as synergies in distributing a portfolio of products to the marketplace. These advantages may be combined to provide enough clout to push smaller firms, which are more responsive to particular markets or market segments or geographic regions, from existing markets and to forestall market entry of new, innovative companies. But the advantages of corporate "bigness" are not limited to the economic arena.

Huge, multi-industry conglomerates are also favored when it comes to politics. Elected officials, for example, are less likely to vote for measures that might adversely affect in a large way the employment and economic activity generated by huge conglomerates operating in their home districts. Indeed, Phillip Blumberg, dean of the University of Connecticut School of Law, has referred to these "megacorporations" as "private governments." According to Blumberg:

> *In addition to its primary economic role in providing goods, services, and*
> *employment, the megacorporation has developed into a social and political*
> *organization of profound significance. In fact, it has become a basic social*
> *institution and a center of power resembling government structures. It has*
> *been transformed into a politicized institution in which public concerns and*
> *values occupy increasing importance in the corporate decision-making*
> *structure. [1975:1]*

Blumberg draws attention to the fact that because the megacorporation's discretion transcends simple economics, corporate governance in no way reflects the interests of all the constituencies that may potentially be affected by its exercise. He argues, therefore, that the anachronistic legal and ideological foundations of corporate behavior in the United States require fundamental revision.

Corporate "bigness" has also been associated with harmful social effects. For example, FTC Chairman Michael Pertschuk recently protested that megacorporations give "remote hierarchies" the power to "profoundly affect such important matters as the quality of the food we eat, the books we read and the design of our cities and landscapes" (Taylor and Schorr, 1980:33). For all these reasons, the movement toward diversification, especially of the external-acquisition variety, deserves far more serious attention than it has received during the first three decades of the current merger wave.

The Globalization Issue. But diversification is only one of two primary strategies of domain creation that characterized the adaptive response of the tobacco Big Six. If diversification tends to increase the economic and political hegemony in the United States of a small number of large, multibusiness corporations, overseas expansion is simply a way of extending this hegemony globally. Thus, corporate globalization tends to magnify all the potential side effects that we have associated with domestic diversification; and our understanding of corporate globalization is hampered, as in the case of domestic diversification, by the absence of public disclosure about how multinational corporations operate.

Richard Barnet, founder and codirector of the Institute for Policy Studies in Washington, D.C., and Ronald Muller, a professor of economics at American University, have discussed these consequences in detail in their book, *Global Reach: The Power of the Multinational Corporations:*

> The global corporation is the first institution in human history dedicated to centralized planning on a world scale. Because its primary purpose is to organize and to integrate economic activity around the world in such a way as to maximize global profit, the global corporation is an organic structure in which each part is expected to serve the whole. Thus in the end it measures its successes and its failures not by the balance sheet of an individual subsidiary, or the suitability of particular products, or its social impact in a particular country, but by the growth in global profits and global market shares. . . . The managers of the global corporations are seeking to put into practice a theory of human organizations that will profoundly alter the nation-state system around which society has been organized for over 400 years. What they are demanding in essence is the right to transcend the nation-state, and in the process, to transform it. [1974:14−16]

As a first step, therefore, in understanding and controlling the multinational corporation, Barnet and Muller argue forcefully for laws requiring public disclosure of the decisions, behaviors, and outcomes of these large corporations. Second, they seek to have attention focused on the issue of corporate governance of the multinational, which is still treated as a private organization despite its increasingly public role. "Because the managers of global corporations are making major social-planning decisions for the society and many of these decisions are filled with risks, the responsibility of these individuals to the public," Barnet and Muller (1974:375) argue, "must be defined by law."

Other industry observers, however, have viewed the trend toward corporate diversification and globalization more positively. In the absence of uniform international laws regarding these phenomena, it would be imprudent, they argue, for U.S. policy makers to curb either trend; to do so would restrict the ability of U.S. corporations to compete against foreign-based diversified multinationals. Bruce Scott (1973), a professor of business policy at the Harvard Business School, who supports this view, believes that large diversified companies, constantly searching for and experimenting in the world's marketplaces for new opportunities, are less susceptible to becoming ossified in stagnating domains of irrelevant or illegitimate enterprise. Rather than interfere with these trends, Scott believes, U.S. public and economic policy should encourage geographical and even acquisitive diversification.

Although this investigation was able to raise these important public-policy issues, it remains the task of future research and debate to examine the tradeoffs they imply. The fact that domestic diversification and overseas expansion were selected as primary modes of adaptations by the tobacco Big Six suggests that they may serve also as primary strategic alternatives for other corporations that wish either to preserve or enhance their growth or to minimize their exposure to economic and political risk. On this basis alone, future investigations into the economic, political, and social side effects of these elements of successful organizational adaptation which may be successful from the narrow point of view of a particular industry or its population of firms are warranted and should be supported vigorously by public authorities.

CONCLUSION

The purpose of our investigation was to raise the consciousness of a variety of publics about the methods of strategic adaptation employed by large corporations for coping with external threats. From the perspective of strategic management, we have demonstrated that a broad range of alternatives for strategic adaptation exists, and we have attempted to identify some important situational and managerial factors that may inhibit or facilitate the adaptation process. From the perspective of the public-policy-making process, we have discussed the limits to public authority in controlling corporate behavior, limits inherent in the current legal and ideological framework surrounding corporate behavior that constrain the role of administrative authority, and limits to the appreciation of public-policy makers of the full range of economic consequences of their well-intentioned regulations.

Our guiding purpose is satisfied, therefore, if this book helps citizens, executives, regulators, and students of management and public policy develop a richer appreciation of the political economy of the complex organization in American society, and the role of executive leadership in complex organizations. But this investigation has also raised a number of issues associated with successful strategic organizational adaptation that are beyond its original intentions and scope. Three such issues deserve serious attention if a more complete understanding of the relationship between corporate strategy and public policy is to be achieved.

First, there is a need to know more about the day-to-day, month-to-month tactics executive leaders use to manage the internal political economy of their organizations in order to maintain satisfactory performance while adapting to changing conditions. This study has been able to provide only a glimpse into the internal politics of organizational adaptation and the role strategic managers play in that process. What is required for progress in understanding how executive leaders function under conditions requiring adaptation is action research in which skilled observers are involved directly in the process of organizational change and development.

Second, there is a need to evaluate the potential social and political, as well as economic, side effects of strategic organizational adaptation. In particular, we know that the strategies of diversification and globalization facilitated the process of strategic adaptation among our tobacco corporations. But based on the evidence available, we can only speculate about the cost and benefits of such strategies for society as a whole. We hope the accumulating information on line-of-business performance will stimulate others to pursue this critical line of inquiry.

Third, there is a need to understand the process of moral reasoning which becomes institutionalized within complex organizations. What rationale do executive leaders rely on to defend the production and aggressive distribution of products that have been determined to be harmful to consumers? How do they continue to recruit and socialize new members from the sensitized environment in which they conduct business? Are the individuals who join such organizations and rise to executive leadership in them different from their counterparts in organizations whose legitimacy is not in question?

An intensive examination of these important questions was beyond the scope of this investigation. But we were able to reveal that a number of institutional props, including the prevailing laws concerning product liability, economic values concerning employment and balance of payments, and vested political and economic interests, help to explain the persistence of the U.S. tobacco industry despite the harmful effects of its major product. Less explicit in the debates and testimony regarding the legitimacy of this business are the scenarios that one could imagine if the business were terminated and replaced by an underground market. For all of these reasons, the future study of the ethical dimension of corporate character and the quality of moral reasoning among executive leaders must include a consideration of both the individual and contextual elements of the situation.

Overarching all these issues, however, is our belief that progress toward understanding the role of the complex organization in a complex society demands a broader range of curiosity than any of the competing disciplines of knowledge has allowed in the past. Indeed a substantial portion of the past five years in the life of this investigation was devoted to understanding the contributions of disciplines beyond our own. But we are under no illusions that the fruits of these labors reveal more than a few fathoms below our giant corporate icebergs.

With the illusion of comprehensiveness rested, however, we would remind the reader that those responsible for the sinking of the unsinkable Titanic did not see even the exposed tip of the iceberg before it had begun to serve their calamity. Indeed, even the captains of nearby vessels dismissed as apparent jokes the distress signals they received. They *knew* the Titanic couldn't sink!

FOOTNOTES

[1] As one economist has noted, "Data problems . . . plague the researcher, the government official, and other interested individuals and groups concerned with the merger problem" (Reid, 1968:21).

[2] "FTC Wins Rights to Collect Data from Companies," *The Wall Street Journal*, November 7, 1978, p. 4.

Bibliography

Action on Smoking and Health, *Smoking and Health, History of the Battle: 1964—1975*. Washington, D.C., 1976.

Adelman, M.A., "The Measurement of Industrial Concentration," *Review of Economics and Statistics,* Vol. 33 (1951), 269—96.

Advertising Age, August 23, 1976, pp. 27—28, 126—27.

Alchain, A.A., "Uncertainty, Evolution, and Economic Theory," *Journal of Political Economy,* Vol. 58 (1959), 211—21.

Aldrich, H.E., *Organizations and Environments.* Englewood Cliffs, N.J.: Prentice-Hall, 1979.

"Along the Highways and Byways of Finance," *The New York Times,* June 7, 1953, Sec. 3, p. 3.

American Brands, Inc., *Annual Reports,* 1950—1979.

American Cancer Society, Inc., *Task Force on Smoking and Health, Target 5.* New York, 1976.

———, *Task Force on Tobacco and Cancer, Report to the Board of Directors.* New York, 1976.

Anderson, A.B., and J.K. Skegg, "Anti-smoking Publicity and the Demand for Tobacco in the U.K.," *Manchester School of Economics and Social Studies,* Vol. 41 (1973), 265—82.

Andrews, K.R., *The Concept of Corporate Strategy.* Homewood, Ill.: Richard D. Irwin, 1971, 1980.

"Annual Report on American Industry," *Forbes,* 1970, 1975, 1980.

"An Antismoking Pitch Gets a Cool Reception," *Business Week,* January 30, 1978, p. 24.

Argyris, C., and D.A. Schön, *Organizational Learning: A Theory of Action Perspective.* Reading, Mass.: Addison-Wesley, 1978.

Barnard, C.I., *The Functions of the Executive.* Cambridge, Mass.: Harvard University Press, 1938.

Barnet, R.J., and R.E. Muller, *Global Reach: The Power of the Multinational Corporation.* New York: Simon & Schuster, 1974.

Barney, J., "The Electronic Revolution in the Watch Industry: A Decade of Environmental Changes and Corporate Strategies," working paper. New Haven, Conn.: Yale School of Organization and Management, 1977.

Bates, F.L., "The Political-Economy Approach in Perspective," in M.N. Zald, ed., *Power in Organizations,* pp. 262—69. Nashville, Tenn.: Vanderbilt University Press, 1970.

277

Baumol, W.J., *Business Behavior, Value and Growth*. New York: Macmillan, 1959.

Bennis, W.G., "The Concept of Organizational Health," in W.G. Bennis, ed., *Changing Organizations*. New York: McGraw-Hill, 1966.

Biggadike, E.R., *Corporate Diversification: Entry, Strategy, and Performance*. Boston: Division of Research, Graduate School of Business Administration, Harvard University, 1976.

———, "The Risky Business of Diversification," *Harvard Business Review*, May—June 1979, pp. 103–11.

Blumberg, P.I., *The Megacorporation in American Society: The Scope of Corporate Power*. New York: McGraw-Hill, 1975.

Boulding, K.E., *A Reconstruction of Economics*. New York: John Wiley, 1950.

Bower, J.L., *Managing the Resource Allocation Process*. Homewood, Ill.: Richard D. Irwin, 1972.

———, and Y. Doz, "Strategy Formulation: A Social and Political Process," in D.E. Schendel and C.W. Hofer, eds., *Strategic Management: A New View of Business Policy and Planning*, pp. 152–60, 180–88. Boston: Little, Brown, 1979.

Brittain, J.W., and J.H. Freeman, "Organizational Proliferation and Density Dependent Selection," in J.R. Kimberly, R.H. Miles, and associates, *The Organizational Life Cycle: Issues in the Creation, Transformation, and Decline of Organizations*, pp. 291–338. San Francisco: Jossey-Bass, 1980.

Brown and Williamson Industries, Inc., *Annual Reports*, 1950–1979.

Burns, T., "Micropolitics: Mechanism of Institutional Change," *Administrative Science Quarterly*, Vol. 6 (1961), 257–81.

———, and G.M. Stalker, *The Management of Innovation*. London: Tavistock, 1961.

Campbell, D., "Variation and Selective Retention in Socio-Cultural Evolution," *General Systems*, Vol. 14 (1969), 69–85.

Campbell, D.T., and J.C. Stanley, *Experimental and Quasi-Experimental Designs for Reseach*. Chicago: Rand McNally, 1963.

Capon, N., "The Product Life Cycle," (ICCH: 9-579-072). Boston: Intercollegiate Case Clearing House, Harvard Business School, 1978.

Caves, R.E., *American Industry: Structure, Conduct, Performance*, 4th ed. Englewood Cliffs, N.J.: Prentice-Hall, 1977.

———, "Industrial Organization, Corporate Strategy and Structure," *Journal of Economic Literature*, Vol. 18 (1980), 64–92.

Chamberlain, N.W., *Enterprise and Environment: The Firm in Time and Place*. New York: McGraw-Hill, 1968.

Chandler, A.D., Jr., *Strategy and Structure: Chapters in the History of the American Industrial Enterprise*. Cambridge, Mass.: M.I.T. Press, 1962.

———, *The Visible Hand: The Managerial Revolution in American Business*. Cambridge, Mass.: Harvard University Press, 1977.

"Chemical, Tobacco Industries are Rated as 'Winners' by U.S.," *The Wall Street Journal*, November 7, 1980, p. 5.

Child, J., "Organizational Structures, Environment and Performance—The Role of Strategic Choice," *Sociology*, Vol. 6 (1972), 1–22.

Christensen, C.R., K.R. Andrews, and J.L. Bower, *Business Policy: Text and Cases*. Homewood, Ill.: Richard D. Irwin, 1973.

"Cigarette Makers Go All Out for Low-Tar Brands," *Business Week*, October 31, 1977, pp. 82, 86.

"Cigarette Sales Keep Rising," *Business Week*, December 15, 1980, pp. 52, 57

"Cigarette Study the Industry Likes," *Business Week*, August 28, 1978, p. 36.

Clark, B.R., *The Distinctive College*. Chicago: Aldine, 1970.

Clausewitz, K. von, *Principles of War*. Harrisburg, Pa.: Military Service Publishing Company, 1832.

"Companies Put Up the 'No-Smoking' Sign," *Business Week,* May 29, 1978, p. 68.

Cyert, R.J., and J.G. March, *A Behavioral Theory of the Firm*. Englewood Cliffs, N.J.: Prentice-Hall, 1963.

———, "Organizational Factors in the Theory of Oligopoly," *Quarterly Journal of Economics,* Vol. 70 (February 1956), 44−64.

———, "Organizational Structure and Pricing Behavior in an Oligopolistic Market," *The American Economic Review,* Vol. 45 (1955), 129−39.

Darran, D.C., R.E. Miles, and C.C. Snow, "Organizational Adjustment to the Environment," paper presented at the Annual Meeting of the American Institute for Decision Sciences, 1975.

Didrichesen, J., "The Development of Diversified and Conglomerate Firms in the United States, 1929−1970," *Business History Review,* Vol. 46 (1972), 202−19.

Dill, W.R., "Environment as an Influence on Managerial Autonomy," *Administrative Science Quarterly, Vol. 2 (1958), 409−43.*

Doron, G., *The Smoking Paradox: Public Regulation in the Cigarette Industry,* Cambridge, Mass.: Abt Books, 1979.

Dowling, J., and J. Pfeffer, "Organizational Legitimacy: Social Values and Organizational Behavior," *Pacific Sociological Review, Vol. 18(1) (1975), 122−36.*

Downs, A., *Inside Bureaucracy,* Boston: Little, Brown, 1967.

Drew, E., "The Quiet Victory of the Cigarette Lobby," *Atlantic Monthly,* September 1965, p. 77.

Drinan, R.F., "Dime Cigarette Tax Would Raise $3 Billion," *Washington Report,* May 1980, pp. 1, 4.

Duncan, R.B., "Modifications in Decision Structures in Adapting to the Environment: Some Implications for Organizational Learning," *Decision Sciences,* Vol. 5 (1974), 705−25.

Economic Research Service, U.S. Department of Agriculture, *Tobacco Situation,* TS-117, September 1966; TS-155, March 1976.

Edwards, C., "Conglomerate Bigness as a Source of Power," in *Business Concentration and Price Policy.* Princeton, N.J.: Princeton University Press, 1955.

Eleazer, T., "Planning Diversification at RJR," in *The Bottom Line.* Chapel Hill, N.C.: Graduate School of Business Administration, University of North Carolina, December 1977, pp. 1, 3.

Emery, F.E., and E.L. Trist, "The Causal Texture of Organizational Environments," *Human Relations,* Vol. 18 (1965), 21−32.

Enke, S., "On Maximizing Profits: A Distinction between Chamberlain and Robinson," *American Economic Review,* Vol. 41 (1951), 566−78.

Etzioni, A. *A Comparative Analysis of Complex Organizations.* New York: Free Press, 1975.

———, *Modern Organizations.* Englewood Cliffs, N.J.: Prentice-Hall, 1964.

Federal Trade Commission, *Federal Trade Commission Report to Congress: Pursuant to the Federal Cigarette Labeling and Advertising Act.* Washington, D.C., 1973.

———, *Federal Trade Commission Report to Congress: Pursuant to the Federal Cigarette Labeling and Advertising Act,* Washington, D.C., December 31, 1974.

———, *Report to Congress: Pursuant to the Public Health Cigarette Smoking Act,* Washington, D.C., December 24, 1979.

———, *Federal Trade Commission Report to Congress: Pursuant to the Public Health Cigarette Smoking Act,* Washington, D.C., 1969.

———, *Federal Trade Commission Report to Congress: Pursuant to the Public Health*

Cigarette Smoking Act, Washington, D.C., 1976.

———, news release, Washington, D.C., January 11, 1964.

———, Bureau of Economics, *Economic Papers 1966–69,* "Summary of Economic Report of Corporate Mergers," presented in *Hearings before the Subcommittee on Antitrust and Monopoly,* 1969.

Fienning, C.E., "Philip Morris Incorporated." Boston: Intercollegiate Clearing House, Graduate School of Business Administration, Harvard University, 1971.

Firth, M., "Takeovers, Shareholder Returns, and the Theory of the Firm," *Quarterly Journal of Economics,* March 1980, pp. 235–60.

Fishbein, M., *Consumer Beliefs and Behavior with Respect to Cigarette Smoking: A Critical Analysis of the Public Literature,* A Report Prepared for the Staff of the Federal Trade Commission. Washington, D.C., May 1977.

"For Trade Associations, Politics Is the New Focus," *Business Week,* April 17, 1978, pp. 107, 110, 115.

Friedman, K.M., "Tobacco Agriculture and Health: Towards a Positive Approach," paper read at the American Agricultural Economics Association, Blacksburg, Va., August 7, 1978.

Fritschler, A.L., *Smoking and Politics: Policymaking and the Federal Bureaucracy,* 2nd ed. Englewood Cliffs, N.J.: Prentice-Hall, 1975.

"FTC Wins Right to Collect Data from Companies," *The Wall Street Journal,* November 7, 1978, p. 4.

Gable, R.W., "NAM: Influential Lobby or Kiss of Death?" *Journal of Politics,* Vol. 15 (1953), 254–73.

Galbraith, J.R., *Designing Complex Organizations.* Reading, Mass.: Addison-Wesley, 1973.

Galbraith, J.K., *The New Industrial State,* 3rd ed. Boston: Houghton Mifflin, 1979.

Garner, D.W., "The Cigarette Industry's Escape From Liability," *Business and Society Review,* No. 33 (1980), 22–25.

Gort, M., *Diversification and Integration in American Industry.* Princeton, N.J.: Princeton University Press, 1962.

Hall, R., "Long Term Trends in Tobacco Consumption and Production," paper presented at the National Agricultural Outlook Conference, Washington, D.C., November 20, 1975.

Hamilton, J.L., "The Demand for Cigarettes: Advertising, the Health Scare, and the Cigarette Advertising Ban," *Review of Economics and Statistics,* Vol. 54 (1972), 401–11.

Hannan, M.T., and J. Freeman, "The Population Ecology of Organizations," *American Journal of Sociology,* Vol. 82 (1977), 929–64.

Harden, B., "The Feudal World of King Tobacco," *The Boston Globe,* May 5, 1980, p. 3.

Hawley, A.H., "Human Ecology," in D.L. Sills, ed., *Inernational Encyclopedia of the Social Sciences,* pp. 328–37. New York: Macmillan, 1968.

———, *Human Ecology: A Theory of Community Structure.* New York: Ronald Press, 1950.

Hayes, L.S., "Twenty-five Years of Change in the *Fortune* 500," *Fortune,* May 5, 1980, pp. 80–96.

Hirsch, P.M., "Organizational Analysis and Industrial Sociology: An Instance of Cultural Lag," *The American Sociologist,* Vol. 10 (1975), 3–12.

Hirschman, A.O., and C.E. Lindblom, "Economic Development, Research and Development, Policy Making: Some Converging Views," *Behavioral Science,* Vol. 8 (1962), 211–22.

Howard Chase Enterprises, Inc., *Corporate Public Issues*. Greenwich, Conn., Vol. 1, No. 13 (October 15, 1976).

Kasper, D., "Note on Managing in a Regulated Environment," (ICCH: 1-379-032). Boston: Intercollegiate Case Clearing House, Harvard Business School, 1978.

Kaufman, H., *Are Government Organizations Immortal?* Washington, D.C.: The Brookings Institution, 1976.

———, *The Limits of Organizational Change*. University, Ala.: University of Alabama Press, 1975.

Kefauver, E., *In a Few Hands: Monopoly Power in America*. Baltimore: Penguin Books, 1965.

Kellner, I.L., "The American Cigarette Industry: A Re-Examination," Unpublished doctoral dissertation, The New School for Social Research, New York, 1973.

Keynes, J.M., *General Theory of Employment, Interest and Money*. New York: Harcourt, Brace & World, 1936.

Kimberly, J.R., "Environmental Constraints and Organizational Structure: A Comparative Analysis of Rehabilitation Organizations," *Administrative Science Quarterly*, Vol. 20 (1975), 1–9.

———, R.H. Miles, and associates, *The Organizational Life Cycle: Issues in the Creation, Transformation, and Decline of Organizations*. San Francisco: Jossey-Bass, 1980.

Koten, J., "Liggett Agrees to Sell Assets of Cigarette Unit," *The Wall Street Journal*, January 29, 1979, p. 18.

Lawrence, P.R., and J.W. Lorsch, *Organization and Environment*. Homewood, Ill.: Richard D. Irwin, 1969.

Learned, E.P., R.C. Christensen, D.R. Andrews, and W.D. Guth, *Business Policy: Text and Cases*. Homewood, Ill.: Richard D. Irwin, 1969.

Leone, R.A., "Competition and the Regulatory Boom," in D.M. Tella, ed., *Government Regulation of Business: Its Growth, Impact, and Future*, pp. 27–39. Council on Trends and Perspectives, Chamber of Commerce of the United States, 1979.

Leontiades, M., *Strategies for Diversification and Change*. Boston: Little, Brown, 1980.

Levine, S., and P.E. White, "Exchange as a Conceptual Framework for the Study of Interorganizational Relationships," *Administrative Science Quarterly*, Vol. 5 (1961), 583–601.

Liggett Group, Inc., *Annual Reports*, 1950–1979.

Lilley, W., and J.C. Miller, "The New 'Social' Regulation," *The Public Interest*, Vol. 47 (1977), 49–61.

Lindblom, C.E., *Politics and Markets: The World's Political-Economic Systems*. New York: Basic Books, 1977.

———, "The Science of 'Muddling Through.' " *Public Administration Review*, Spring 1959, 79–88.

Lorillard, Inc., *Annual Reports*, 1950–1969.

Lorsch, J.W., and J.J. Morse, *Organizations and Their Members: A Contingency Approach*. New York: Harper & Row, 1974.

Loews, Inc., *Annual Reports*, 1969–1979.

Luce, B.R., and S.O. Schweitzer, "Smoking and Alcohol Abuse: A Comparison of their Economic Consequences," *The New England Journal of Medicine*, Vol. 2, 298 (10) (1978), 569–71.

McKenny, J.L., "A Field Research Study of Organizational Learning," working paper No. 78–23. Boston: Graduate School of Business Administration, Harvard University, 1978.

March, J.G., and H.A. Simon, *Organizations*. New York: John Wiley, 1958.

Marcial, G.G., "Analysts Favor Philip Morris, R.J. Reynolds as Firms Dominate Low-Tar Cigaret Market," *The Wall Street Journal*, June 27, 1977, p. 27.

Markham, J.W., *Conglomerate Enterprise and Public Policy*. Boston: Division of Research, Graduate School of Business Administration, Harvard University, 1973.

Marris, R., *The Economic Theory of Managerial Capitalism*. Glencoe, Ill.: Free Press, 1964.

Maurer, J.G., *Readings in Organization Theory: Open-System Approaches*. New York: Random House, 1971.

Maxwell, J., "Historical Trends in the Tobacco Industry." Richmond, Va.: Maxwell Associates, 1975.

Mayo, E., *The Human Problems of an Industrial Civilization*. New York: Macmillan, 1933.

Meyer, J., "Strategies for Further Research: Varieties of Environmental Variation" in M.W. Meyer and associates, *Environments and Organizations*, pp. 352–68. San Francisco: Jossey-Bass, 1978.

Miles, R.E., and C.C. Snow, *Organizational Strategy, Structure, and Process*. New York: McGraw-Hill, 1978.

Miles, R.H., "Findings and Implications of Organizational Life Cycle Research: A Commencement," in J.R. Kimberly, R.H. Miles, and associates, *The Organizational Life Cycle: Issues in the Creation, Transformation, and Decline of Organizations*, pp. 430–50. San Francisco: Jossey-Bass, 1980a.

———, "The Jim Heavner Story," (A), (B) (ICCH: 9-479-037, -038). Boston: Intercollegiate Case Clearing House, Graduate School of Business Administration, Harvard University, 1979.

———, "Learning from Diversifying," (ICCH: 9-481-060). Boston: Intercollegiate Case Clearing House, Graduate School of Business Administration, Harvard University, 1980b.

———, *Macro Organization Behavior*. Santa Monica, Calif.: Goodyear, 1980c.

———, and A. Bhambri, "Aetna and the Press of Public Issues, (A), (B), (B-1), (C)" (ICCH: 9-480-030, -031, -068, -032). Boston: Intercollegiate Case Clearing House, Graduate School of Business Administration, Harvard University, 1980.

———, and K. S. Cameron, "Coffin Nails and Corporate Strategies: A Quarter-Century View of Organizational Adaptation to Environment in the U.S. Tobacco Industry," working paper No. 3, Business-Government Relations Series (c). New Haven, Conn.: Yale School of Organization and Management, 1977.

———, and W.A. Randolph, "Influence of Organizational Learning Styles on Early Development," in J.R. Kimberly, R.H. Miles, and associates, *The Organizational Life Cycle: Issues in the Creation, Transformation, and Decline of Organizations*, pp. 44–82. San Francisco: Jossey-Bass, 1980.

Miller, L.M., and J.J. Monahan, "The Facts behind the Cigarette Controversy," *The Reader's Digest*, July 1954, pp. 1–6.

Miller, R.H., "Changing Trends in the World Tobacco Economy," paper presented at the Atlantic Economic Conference, Washington, D.C., September 12, 1975.

———, "The Domestic Tobacco Market: A Look Ahead through the 1980's," paper delivered to the Midwinter Board of Governors Meeting, Tobacco Association of the United States, Hilton Head Island, S.C., March 15, 1980.

———, "Factors Affecting Cigarette Consumption," paper presented at the National Tobacco Tax Association Annual Meeting, Kiamesha, N.Y., September 10, 1974a.

———, "Government Action Relating to Smoking and Health, 1964–1974," *Tobacco Situation*, June 1974b, pp. 33–38.

————, Commodity Economics Division, U.S. Department of Agriculture, personal correspondence. Washington, D.C.: January 5, 1978.

————, "Tobacco and Tobacco Products Consumption for 1980," paper presented at the National Tobacco Workers Conference, Economics Section, Chattanooga, Tenn., January 20, 1972.

————, "Tobacco and Tobacco Products Consumption for 1985," paper presented at the 25th National Tobacco Workers Conference, Hamilton, Ont., Canada, August 9, 1973.

————, "Tobacco Consumption Trends and the Antismoking Campaign," paper read at the 52nd Annual Meeting, National Tobacco Tax Association, Columbus, O., September 11, 1979.

Mintz, M., and J.S. Cohen, *America, Inc.: Who Owns and Operates the United States*. New York: Dial Press, 1971.

Mintzberg, H., "Patterns in Strategy Formulation," *Management Science*, Vol. 24 (1978), 934–48.

The Monopolies Commission, *Cigarette Filter Rods*. London: Her Majesty's Stationery Office, July 1969.

Moody's Industrial Manual, 1950–1980.

Mueller, D.C., "A Theory of Conglomerate Mergers," *Quarterly Journal of Economics*, Vol. 83 (1969), 643–59.

Mullally, D.P., "The Fairness Doctrine: Benefits and Costs," *Public Opinion Quarterly*, Vol. 33 (1969–70), 577–82.

Mulligan, R.J., "Liggett Group Inc.: Statement of Acquisition Policy and Criteria." Montvale, N.J.: The Liggett Group, Spring 1979.

Neuberger, M.B. *Smoke Screen: Tobacco and the Public Welfare*. Englewood Cliffs, N.J.: Prentice-Hall, 1963.

Nicholls, W.H., *Price Policies in the Cigarette Industry*. Nashville, Tenn.: Vanderbilt University Press, 1951.

Normann, R., *Management for Growth*. New York: Wiley-Interscience, 1977.

O'Keefe, M.T., "The Antismoking Commercials: A Study of Television's Impact on Behavior," *Public Opinion Quarterly*, Vol. 35 (1971), 242–48.

Parker, R., Jr., "Cigarettes Have Friends in Labeling Battle," *Raleigh* (N.C.) *News and Observer*, March 25, 1965.

Parsons, T., *Structure and Process in Modern Societies*. New York: Free Press, 1960.

Penrose, E.T., "Biological Analogies in the Theory of the Firm," *American Economic Review*, Vol. 42 (1952), 804–19.

————, *The Theory of the Growth of the Firm*. Oxford: Basil Blackwell, 1959, 1980.

Perrow, C., *Complex Organizations: A Critical Essay*, 2nd ed. Glenview, Ill.: Scott, Foresman, 1979.

————, *Organizational Analysis: A Sociological View*. Belmont, Calif.: Wadsworth, 1967.

Pettigrew, A.M., *The Politics of Organizational Decision-Making*. London: Tavistock, 1973.

Pfeffer, J., "Power and Resource Allocation in Organizations," in B.M. Staw and G. R. Salancik, eds., *New Directions in Organizational Behavior*, pp. 235–66. Chicago: St. Clair Press, 1977.

————, and G. R. Salancik, *The External Control of Organizations: A Resource Dependence Perspective*. New York: Harper & Row, 1978.

Philip Morris, Inc., *Annual Reports*, 1950–1979.

————, *Call News*, May 1980.

Phillips, A., "A Theory of Interfirm Organization," *Quarterly Journal of Economics*, Vol. 74 (1960), 602–13.

Pitts, R.A., "Diversification Strategies and Organizational Policies of Large Diversified Firms," *Journal of Economics and Business,* Vol. 28, Spring–Summer 1979, 181–88.

Poole, J.W., Jr., Acting Chief, General Litigation Section, Antitrust Division, U.S. Department of Justice, personal correspondence. Washington, D.C.: October 23, 1978.

Porter, M.E., *Competitive Strategy: Techniques for Analyzing Industries and Competitors.* New York: Free Press, 1980.

————, and M.S. Salter. "Diversification as a Strategy," working paper. Boston: Graduate School of Business Administration, Harvard University, Nov. 20, 1979.

Public Health Service, *The Health Consequences of Smoking: A Report of the Surgeon General, 1972.* Washington, D.C. U.S. Department of Health, Education and Welfare, Health Services and Mental Health Administration, 1972.

————, *Smoking and Health: A Report of the Surgeon General.* Washington, D.C.: U.S. Department of Health, Education and Welfare, 1978.

————, *Smoking and Health: Report of the Advisory Committee to the Surgeon General of the Public Health Service.* Washington, D.C.: U.S. Department of Health, Education and Welfare, 1964.

Ramirez, A., "Popularity of Cigaret Smoking Declines, Resulting in More Competition, Products," *The Wall Street Journal,* Jan. 2, 1980a, p. 7.

————, "Reynolds is Snuffing 5 Cigaret Brands, Including Real, but Will Unveil New One," *Wall Street Journal,* June 24, 1980b, p. 42.

Reid, S.R., *Mergers, Managers and the Economy.* New York: McGraw-Hill, 1968.

————, *The New Industrial Order: Concentration, Regulation and Public Policy.* New York: McGraw-Hill, 1976.

Reynolds Industries, Inc., *Analysts Meeting,* Winston-Salem, N.C., September 19–21, 1976.

————, *Annual Reports,* 1950–1979.

Rhenman, E., *Organization Theory for Long-Range Planning,* London: Wiley, 1973.

Riker, W.H., "Foreword," in G. Doron, *The Smoking Paradox: Public Regulation in the Cigarette Industry,* pp. xiii–xiv. Cambridge, Mass.: Abt Books, 1979.

————, *The Theory of Political Coalition,* New Haven, Conn.: Yale University Press, 1962.

Rogers, C., *On Becoming a Person.* Boston: Houghton Mifflin, 1961.

Roper Organization, Inc., "Study of Public Attitudes toward Cigarette Smoking and the Tobacco Industry in 1978," prepared for the Tobacco Institute, Inc., and included in Federal Trade Commission, *Report to Congress, Pursuant to the Public Health Smoking Act, for the Year 1978, (Appendix B.) Washington, D.C.: December 24, 1979.*

Ross, W.S., "Let's Stop Exploring the Smoking Epidemic," *Reader's Digest,* May 1980, pp. 143–47.

Rudnitsky, H., "Cigarettes with an Oil Chaser," *Forbes,* May 26, 1980, p. 67.

Rumelt, R.P., *Strategy, Structure and Economic Performance.* Boston: Division of Research, Graduate School of Business Administration, Harvard University, 1974.

Russell, C., "HEW Plots Tactics for Antismoking Campaign," *The Washington Star,* October 17, 1977. p. A3.

Salter, M.S., and W.A. Weinhold, *Diversification through Acquisition: Strategies for Creating Economic Value.* New York: Free Press, 1979.

Scott, B.R., "The Industrial State: Old Myths and New Realities," *Harvard Business Review,* March–April 1973, pp. 133–48.

Sease, D.R., "Cigarette Firms Eye Low-Tar Market," *Boston Evening Globe,* August 21, 1978a.

———, "Tobacco Tussle: Cigaret Companies Vie for Low-Tar Smokers, a Fast Growing Breed," The *Wall Street Journal,* March 21, 1978b, p. 1.

Selznick, P., *Leadership in Administration: A Sociological Interpretation.* New York: Harper & Row, 1957.

———, *TVA and the Grass Roots.* Berkeley: University of California Press, 1949.

Sheridan M.J., "Filter Fun for Third-Worlders," *The New York Times,* April 13, 1980, p. E19.

Sills, D.L., *The Volunteers.* Glencoe, Ill.: Free Press, 1957.

Simon, H.A., *Administrative Behavior: A Study of Decision-Making Processes in Administrative Organization.* New York: Free Press, 1945.

Skinner, B.F., *Beyond Freedom and Dignity.* New York: Random House, 1971.

Sloan, A.P., Jr., *My Years with General Motors.* New York: Doubleday Anchor, 1972.

Smith, Adam, *The Wealth of Nations.* London, 1776 (edited by Cannan, 1904).

Smith, Barney and Company, *The Cigarette Industry,* Topical Research Comment No. 97–69. New York, December 1968.

Snow, C.C., and L.G. Hrebiniak, "Strategy, Distinctive Competence, and Organizational Performance," *Administrative Science Quarterly,* Vol. 25 (1980), 317–35.

Sonnenfeld, J., *Corporate Views of the Public Interest.* Boston: Auburn House, forthcoming 1981.

———, and P.R. Lawrence, "Why Do Companies Succumb to Price Fixing?" *Harvard Business Review,* Vol. 56, No. 4 (July-August, 1978), 145–57.

Starbuck, W.H., "Organizations and Their Environments," in M.D. Dunnette, ed, *Handbook of Industrial and Organizational Psychology,* pp. 1069–1124. Chicago: Rand McNally, 1976.

State Legislation on Smoking and Health 1976. Atlanta: U.S. Department of Health, Education and Welfare, Public Health Service, Center for Disease Control, 1976.

Staw, B.M., and E. Szwajkowski, "The Scarcity-Munificence Component of Organizational Environments and the Commission of Illegal Acts," *Administrative Science Quarterly,* Vol. 20 (1975), 345–54.

Stigler, G., "A Theory of Oligopoly," *Journal of Political Economy, Vol. 72 (1964), 44–61.*

Stinchcombe, A.L., "Social Structure and Organizations," in J.G. March, ed., *Handbook of Organizations,* pp. 142–93. Chicago: Rand-McNally, 1965.

Stopford, J.M., and L.T. Wells, Jr., *Managing the Multinational Enterprise: Organization of the Firm and Ownership of the Enterprise.* New York: Basic Books, 1972.

"Study Finds Nonsmokers' Lungs Are Hurt by Smoke from Others," *The Boston Globe,* March 27, 1980, p. 20.

Taylor, F.W., *The Principles of Scientific Management. New York: Harper, 1911.*

Taylor, R.E., and B. Schorr, *"Government May Abandon Fight to Stem Conglomerate Takeovers," The Wall Street Journal,* November 24, 1980, p. 33.

Telser, L.G., "Advertising and Cigarettes," *Journal of Political Economy,* Vol. 70 (1962), 476.

Terreberry, S. "The Evolution of Organizational Environments," *Administrative Science Quarterly,* Vol. 12 (1968), 590–613.

Terry, L.L., "Tobacco and Politics," *The Washington Star,* August 15, 1979.

Thompson, J.D., *Organizations in Action.* New York: McGraw-Hill, 1967.

Tobacco Institute, *Tobacco Industry Profile.* Washington, D.C., 1976.

———, *Tobacco Industry Profile.* Washington, D.C., 1979a.

———, "A Word to Nonsmokers (about Smokers)," advertisement appearing in *The Boston Globe,* February 25, 1979b.

Tobacco Reporter, 1976.

Tobacco Tax Council, Inc., *The Tax Burden on Tobacco: Historical Compilation,* Vol. 10. Richmond, Va. (undated).

Turner, D.F. "Conglomerate Mergers and Section 7 of the Clayton Act," *Harvard Law Review*, Vol. 78(7), 1965.

U.S. Department of Agriculture, *Annual Reports*. Washington, D.C., 1955–1976.

U.S. Department of Health, Education and Welfare, *Use of Tobacco—1975*. Washington, D.C., June 1976.

"U.S. Opens Health Study of Low-Tar Cigarettes," *The Washington Post*, June 10, 1980, p. 20.

Vaccara, B.N., and P.H. MacAuley, "Evaluating the Economic Performance of U.S. Manufacturing Industries," *Industrial Economics Review*, Summer 1980, pp. 6–19.

Van de Ven, A.H., "Book Review of Howard E. Aldrich, *Organizations and Environments*," *Administrative Science Quarterly*, Vol. 24 (1979), 320–26.

Von Neumann, J., and O. Morgenstern, *Theory of Games and Economic Behavior*, 2nd ed. Princeton. N.J.: Princeton University Press, 1947.

Wamsley, G., and M.N. Zald, *The Political Economy of Public Organizations*. Lexington, Mass.: Heath, 1973.

Warner, K.E., "Clearing the Airwaves: The Cigarette Ad Ban Revisited," unpublished memeograph. Ann Arbor: School of Public Health, University of Michigan, October 1978.

———, "The Effects of the Anti-Smoking Campaign on Cigarette Consumption," *American Journal of Public Health*, Vol. 67 (1977), 645–50.

Weick, K.E., *The Social Psychology of Organizing*. Reading, Mass.: Addison-Wesley, 1969. (2nd ed., 1979.)

Weihl, P., "William D. Ruckelshaus and the Environmental Protection Agency," (C16-74-027). Cambridge, Mass.: The John F. Kennedy School of Government, Harvard University, 1974.

Weiss, L.W., "Average Concentration Ratios and Industrial Performance," *Journal of Industrial Economics*, Vol. 11 (1963), 237–54.

Wells, N., "The 50 Leading Exporters," *Fortune*, Vol. 102(6) (1980), 114–15.

Wharton Applied Research Center, "A Study of the Tobacco Industry's Economic Contribution to the Nation, Its Fifty States, and the District of Columbia: Report Summary." Philadelphia: University of Pennsylvania, April 1979.

"When Marketing Takes Over at R.J. Reynolds," *Business Week*, November 13, 1978, pp. 82–85, 89, 91, 93.

"Why a White Knight Likes Liggett," *Business Week*, May 19, 1980, p. 37.

"Why Tobacco Fears the California Voter," *Business Week*, September 11, 1978, p. 54.

Williamson, O.E., *The Economics of Discretionary Behavior: Managerial Objectives in a Theory of the Firm*. Englewood Cliffs, N.J.: Prentice-Hall, 1964.

Winter, S.G., "Economic 'Natural Selection' and the Theory of the Firm," *Yale Economic Essays*, Vol. 4 (1964), 225–72.

Wrigley, L., "Division Autonomy and Diversification," unpublished doctoral dissertation. Boston: Graduate School of Business Administration, Harvard University, 1970.

Yuchtman, E., and S. Seashore, "A System Resource Approach to Organizational Effectiveness," *American Sociological Review*, Vol. 32 (1967), 891–903.

Zald, M.N., *Organization Change: The Political Economy of the YMCA*. Chicago: University of Chicago Press, 1970a.

———, "Political Economy: A Framework for Comparative Analysis," in M.N. Zald, ed., *Power in Organizations*. Nashville, Tenn.: Vanderbilt University Press, 1970b.

Organizational Learning:

protocol
for the interview study

INTERVIEW PROTOCOL:
STUDY OF LEARNING FROM DIVERSIFYING

I. History

What were the factors that precipitated the initial decision to begin a program of diversification?

a. At what time did this occur?

b. Who were the major proponents? opponents? By what process was the decision reached?

c. Did you decide to start with internal development or external acquisition? Why?

d. What were the driving assumptions/premises underlying the decision to diversify?

e. How did this initial decision evolve into a corporate strategy?

II. Selection among Opportunities

How was the selection among alternative opportunities made?

a. What were your guiding principles for diversification? Did they precede your initial attempts or evolve later?

b. What balance have you struck between "related" versus "unrelated" modes of diversification? Why?

c. Why did you rely primarily on external acquisition rather than internal development to implement your diversification strategy?

d. Do you consider overseas expansion part of the diversification program?

III. Managing Diversification

How has your management system evolved to accommodate the shift from a single-business to multibusiness corporation?

   a. Please trace the development of organization structure. When did important reorganizations occur? Why?

   b. Has diversification created the need for managers who differ from those required in a single-business operation? If so, what has your company had to do to acquire or develop managers?

   c. What type of corporate-divisional relationship has emerged with diversification?

   d. How does the corporate planning and review function relate to the diversification program?

IV. Diversification Outcomes

What have been the primary outcomes of the diversification program?

Has profitability increased? Has risk exposure decreased? Have management career opportunities increased? Has additional "synergy" improved? Has the company been able to capitalize on its "distinctive competences" in nontraditional product markets? Have economies of scale been achieved?

V. What Has Been Learned?

Based on twenty years of experience, what has your company learned about diversification?

   a. What would your company have done differently given the hindsight that its management possesses?

   b. Are there any principles that could be distilled from your experience that might be helpful to other companies contemplating a move toward diversification?

   c. What was learned from early divestitures (if there were any)?

   d. Who learned what? That is, is there consensus among the beliefs about diversification within your company, or do these beliefs differ among management groups within the company?

VI. The Future

What are your company's plans for the future regarding diversification?

Name Index

Subject Index